S0-BSQ-218

History of the
CHICHIMECA NATION

History of the
CHICHIMECA NATION

Don Fernando de Alva Ixtlilxochitl's
Seventeenth-Century Chronicle
of Ancient Mexico

EDITED AND TRANSLATED BY

Amber Brian

Bradley Benton

Peter B. Villella

Pablo García Loaeza

Not my hill.
Brad

Long live Alva Ixtlilxochitl!
Amber

Peter V.

UNIVERSITY OF OKLAHOMA PRESS : NORMAN

Publication of this book is made possible through
the generosity of Edith Kinney Gaylord.

Library of Congress Cataloging-in-Publication Data

Names: Alva Ixtlilxochitl, Fernando de, 1578–1650, author. | Brian, Amber, 1970– editor,
    translator. | Benton, Bradley, 1980– editor, translator. | Villella, Peter B., 1978– editor,
    translator. | Loaeza, Pablo García, 1972– editor, translator.
Title: History of the Chichimeca nation : Don Fernando de Alva Ixtlilxochitl's seventeenth-
    century chronicle of ancient Mexico / edited and translated by Amber Brian, Bradley
    Benton, Peter B. Villella, and Pablo García Loaeza.
Other titles: Historia chichimeca. English
Description: Norman : University of Oklahoma Press, [2019] | Includes bibliographical
    references and index.
Identifiers: LCCN 2019010535 | ISBN 978-0-8061-6398-7 (hardcover : alk. paper) |
    ISBN 978-0-8061-6399-4 (pbk. : alk. paper)
Subjects: LCSH: Aztecs—History. | Nahuas—History. | Chichimecs—History. | Indians of
    Mexico—History. | Mexico—History—To 1519. | Mexico—History—Conquest, 1519–1540.
Classification: LCC F1219.73 .A4713 2019 | DDC 972—dc23
LC record available at https://lccn.loc.gov/2019010535

The paper in this book meets the guidelines for permanence and durability of the Committee
on Production Guidelines for Book Longevity of the Council on Library Resources, Inc. ∞

Copyright © 2019 by the University of Oklahoma Press, Norman, Publishing Division of the
University. Manufactured in the U.S.A.

All rights reserved. No part of this publication may be reproduced, stored in a retrieval
system, or transmitted, in any form or by any means, electronic, mechanical, photocopying,
recording, or otherwise—except as permitted under Section 107 or 108 of the United States
Copyright Act—without the prior written permission of the University of Oklahoma Press. To
request permission to reproduce selections from this book, write to Permissions, University of
Oklahoma Press, 2800 Venture Drive, Norman, OK 73069, or email rights.oupress@ou.edu.

For Susan Schroeder

CONTENTS

List of Illustrations   ix

Acknowledgments   xi

Introduction   3

Notes on the Translation   25

History of the Chichimeca Nation   29

Works Cited   315

Index   323

 ILLUSTRATIONS

Maps

1. Basin of Mexico   4

2. Anahuac   39

Figures

1. Códice Chimalpahin, vol. 2, folio 2r   6

2. Codex Xolotl, plate 7   11

3. Xolotl and Nopaltzin   43

4. Xolotl and his vassals   48

5. Chichimecas and Toltecas   55

6. Çoacuecuenotzin's death   77

7. Ixtlilxochitl Ometochtli's death   79

8. Nezahualcoyotl and the pulque seller   82

9. Teçoçomoc's dream   85

10. Teçoçomoc's funeral   88

11. Nezahualcoyotl pleads with Maxtla   92

12. Chimalpopoca's imprisonment   94

13. Nezahualcoyotl's escape   102

14. Nezahualcoyotl's palace   133

15. The Temple of Tetzcoco   138

16. Punishments   141

17. Adulterers' punishments   142

18. Coat of arms of the City of Tetzcoco   156

19. Nezahualcoyotl   178

20. Torquemada, *Monarchía indiana*, vol. 2, 1615,
    frontispiece   179

21. Nezahualpilli   185

22. López de Gómara, *Historia de las Indias y
    conquista de México*, 1552, frontispiece   238

23. Herrera, *Historia general de los hechos de
    los castellanos*, vol. 2, 1601, frontispiece   239

24. Códice Chimalpahin, vol. 2, folio 144v   313

✿ ACKNOWLEDGMENTS

This translation is the result of an extraordinary collaboration that began nearly a decade ago. Around 2010, Amber Brian and Bradley Benton, having noted in the course of their own research the need for an English translation of don Fernando de Alva Ixtlilxochitl's *Historia de la nación chichimeca*, both separately mentioned their desire to translate the work to Susan Schroeder. Soon after, Susan put Amber and Brad in touch and they each, in turn, contacted Pablo García Loaeza and Peter B. Villella about joining the collaboration. Peter and Pablo, it turned out, had just recently met one another at the Lilly Library at Indiana University when they each recognized by chance that the other was perusing rare books from colonial Mexico. Through both strategic introductions and fortuitous meetings, then, this project began. And thus it is to Susan that we owe the most gratitude, not only for her role as academic matchmaker, but for her tireless support, guidance, and friendship. Thank you, Susan.

In 2011, the four of us met in Pasadena at the annual conference of the American Society for Ethnohistory to present our work and explore the possibilities of collaboration. There, buoyed by Persian cuisine and the helpful insights of David Tavárez, we decided that this project was worthwhile and timely. With the encouragement of Kris Lane, editor of the *Colonial Latin American Review*, we assembled a special issue dedicated to Alva Ixtlilxochitl. That issue, edited by Camilla Townsend, was published in 2014 with the four of us and Leisa Kauffmann as contributors. This volume, therefore, also reflects the scholarship and professional support of David, Kris, Camilla, and Leisa, all of whom we deeply and sincerely thank.

In 2014 we received a Scholarly Editions and Translations Grant from the National Endowment for the Humanities (NEH), for which we are extremely grateful. We wish to thank Lydia Medici at the NEH in particular for her support during the proposal process and during the period of our award. The grant enabled us to work together virtually during the summer of 2015—thanks also to Skype—and face-to-face during July of 2016 and 2017 at the University of Iowa in Iowa City. Amber deserves praise for her energetic preparations that ensured we could be settled and comfortable during our stay in her town and also for her delicious Independence Day pies. We are grateful to the University of Iowa staff, including Ann Knudson in the College of Liberal Arts and Sciences for help with our grant proposal budget and the grant submission, Catherine Fountain in the Business Manager's Office for temporary housing assistance, and librarian Lisa Gardinier for assuring access to the university's resources during the team's stays in Iowa City. We are grateful to Rebecca Tritten, in the Division of World Languages, Literatures and Cultures, for arranging office space and administrative support while we worked and Director Russ Ganim for financial support. Amber is especially grateful to Beth Mellinger, accountant in the division, who was her bedrock of support in managing all financial aspects of the grant. Amber is also grateful to Mercedes Niño-Murcia, who as chair of the Department of Spanish & Portuguese, was an enthusiastic supporter of this project.

Our graduate student research assistants during these summers also deserve special thanks. Christian Supiot Pérez, John Kennedy, and Sarah Griebel all provided much-needed help. Christian lent us his skills with paleography and checked our transcription against the original manuscript. John lent us his research acumen and aided us with bibliographic research. Sarah, a skilled literary translator herself, lent those talents to our project and proofread our entire translation. This volume is stronger because of their assistance, though we, of course, take responsibility for any shortcomings.

Brad thanks North Dakota State University's former dean, Kent Sandstrom, of the College of Arts, Humanities, and Social Sciences for his financial support of this project and Marie Slanger in Sponsored Programs Administration for her help with complicated budget questions. Pablo wishes to thank West Virginia University's Katie Stores, associate dean for external research development, and Stephen Ballant, former administrative associate, for their assistance in preparing a budget and everyone at the business office of the Eberly College of Arts and Sciences for their help with grant management. Finally, Peter would like to thank his colleagues at the University of North Carolina at Greensboro who assisted with this project at various stages: Derek Krueger for helping refine the original NEH proposal, Rebecca Crews for arranging the budget, the staff at the UNCG

Office of Contracts and Grants, and Chuck Bolton and James Anderson, former chairs of the Department of History, for their unwavering support for this work.

We extend gratitude to the University of Oklahoma Press's Alessandra Tamulevich for her early and enthusiastic support of the project, the editorial committee and faculty advisory board for appreciating its value, and the anonymous reviewers for their helpful recommendations. We would also like to thank Scott Johnson for the care he took in copyediting our manuscript. The manuscript on which this translation is based was until recently housed in the British and Foreign Bible Society collection at the Cambridge University Library, which provided us with the high-quality digital copies from which we worked. In 2014, the manuscript was repatriated to Mexico, where it is preserved at the Instituto Nacional de Antropología e Historia. We are grateful to the Biblioteca Nacional de Antropología e Historia, in particular to its director, Dr. Baltazar Brito Guadarrama, for supporting our work on their newly acquired treasure and Enriqueta Loaeza for helping us secure permission to use images from the Codex Chimalpahin.

Our families deserve special thanks. Amber is grateful to Brian, Mira, and Silas for their steadfast support throughout the project and for helping to host Brad, Peter, Pablo, and their delightful families. Neely, Thomas, John William, and Mac forewent the joys of two Minnesota summers to keep Brad company in Iowa City; the Amish doughnuts of eastern Iowa would not have tasted nearly as delicious without them there to share them with. The Villellas also enjoyed Iowa City: Judy appreciated the beautiful parks and public spaces, Selma experienced a tornado warning, and Ruth first learned to walk (sort of). Amber, Tristan, and Lucas gracefully let Pablo get away during the whole month of July for two consecutive summers. Finally, each of us would like to acknowledge the insight, effort, and patience of the other three. This has been a most rewarding and enriching exercise in collaboration. Despite, or perhaps because of, our impassioned discussions of semicolons, chiles, blankets, and jerkins, we have become friends.

And we are grateful.

HISTORY of the
CHICHIMECA NATION

 INTRODUCTION

The *History of the Chichimeca Nation* [*Historia de la nación chichimeca*] was written in the first half of the seventeenth century by don Fernando de Alva Ixtlilxochitl (ca. 1578–1650).[1] It is an epic account of the origins of the indigenous peoples of central Mexico commonly referred to today as the Aztecs, but more properly called the Nahuas.[2] Alva Ixtlilxochitl's family lineage consisted of both indigenous Nahua royalty and Spanish settlers. As a child in the Spanish capital of Mexico City he absorbed the proud identity and memories of his grandmother, a noblewoman descended from the rulers of the nearby ethnic state, or *altepetl*, of Tetzcoco.[3] As an official in the colonial bureaucracy and a Nahuatl interpreter in the courts, Alva Ixtlilxochitl was thoroughly bicultural and bilingual, moving easily between the native and Spanish cultural spheres. Accordingly, as a historian he applied the historiographical conventions of early modern Western Europe to Mexico's pre-Columbian past, channeling his love of Mexican antiquity into a life-long project to compile and translate into Spanish the oral traditions and pictorial histories of central Mexico's native peoples. The result was a unique corpus that introduced the legendary cultural heroes of indigenous Mexico to Spanish readers. For centuries his writings—including his four historical accounts along with the culmination of his research, the *History of the Chichimeca Nation*—have served as some of the most important sources for Mexican indigenous history.

Like the author himself, the *History of the Chichimeca Nation* was a cultural bridge that asserted continuity between Hispano-Catholic, colonial-era Mexico and its pre-Hispanic past. Writing during a time of transition and upheaval, as colonization and depopulation devastated indigenous communities and their rulers, Alva Ixtlilxochitl represented Mesoamerican culture as a vital foundation to the viceroyalty of New Spain, which was centered in Mexico City.[4] In

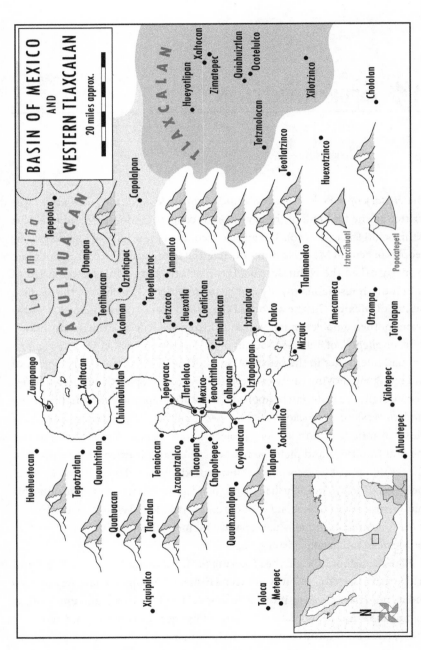

MAP 1. Basin of Mexico and Western Tlaxcalan.

contrast to contemporary European historians, he emphasized continuity over rupture in the history of the New World, thereby assigning a position of ongoing prominence, prestige, and relevance to its native heritage. Today, the *History of the Chichimeca Nation* continues to link Mexico's ancient past to modern readers. This English translation, in addition to bringing the text to an English-reading audience for the first time, presents its readers with the first published edition of the text based on Alva Ixtlilxochitl's original manuscript. Several Spanish editions exist, but they are all based on posthumous, eighteenth-century transcriptions. In contrast, our edition and translation is the first to be derived entirely from the original holograph manuscript, written in Alva Ixtlilxochitl's own hand, which was presumed lost during the early nineteenth century. In the 1980s, the original manuscripts of Alva Ixtlilxochitl's five historical texts were rediscovered by Wayne Ruwet in the archival holdings of the British and Foreign Bible Society. The manuscript was bound with other materials pertaining to native Mexican history in three volumes now known collectively as the Códice Chimalpahin (fig. 1).[5]

Don Fernando de Alva Ixtlilxochitl was born around 1578, more than a half-century after the Spanish conquest of central Mexico. While his father was a Spanish settler in Mexico City, his mother was a *cacica*, or indigenous noblewoman, who traced her lineage to the renowned ruling family of pre-Hispanic Tetzcoco, one of the three capital cities of the so-called Aztec Empire.[6] As cacica, his mother possessed the entailed estate, or *cacicazgo*, of San Juan Teotihuacan—a province in the old realm of Tetzcoco—that had belonged for generations to her family.[7] His mother's wealth and status allowed her to maintain a townhome in Mexico City in addition to her ancestral estate. In his youth, Alva Ixtlilxochitl likely split his time between the Spanish capital and the native city. Nonetheless, as an author Alva Ixtlilxochitl represented himself not as a Spaniard nor a *mestizo* (of mixed ancestry), but as a descendant of the royal line of Tetzcoco and its advocate before a Spanish audience. This was a highly significant choice, as it asserted the survival and relevance of pre-Hispanic identities in Mexico during a time of precipitous native population decline and Hispanic ascendancy. These efforts also signaled that the Spanish conquest did not represent a complete break in native history but rather was a milestone in an ongoing and ever-evolving set of traditions with ancient origins.

To those ends, Alva Ixtlilxochitl sought to rescue the reputation of native Mesoamerican civilization from European historians who scorned it as barbarous and primitive. His case revolved around explicit analogies with Europe's own

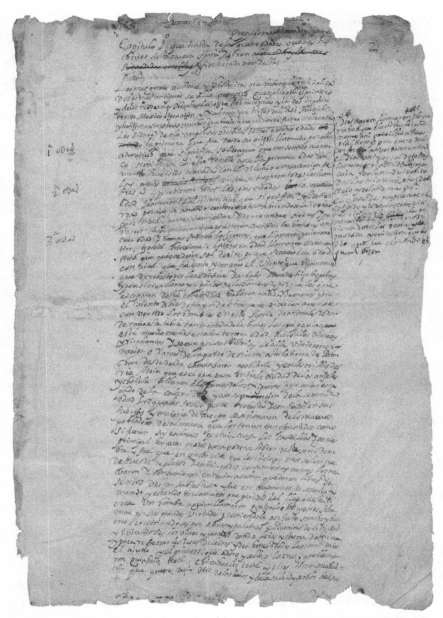

FIGURE 1. Códice Chimalpahin, vol. 2, fol. 2r. *Photo courtesy of the Instituto Nacional de Antropología e Historia.*

Greco-Roman antiquity. As he writes in the opening lines of the dedication that precedes the *History of the Chichimeca Nation*:

> Since adolescence, I have always greatly desired to know about the historical events in this new world, which were no less important than those of the Romans, Greeks, Medes, and other great pagan republics of universal renown. However, with the passage of time and the fall of the kingdoms and states of my ancestors, their histories were buried. For this reason, with much effort, searching, and utmost diligence, I have achieved my desire to bring together the painted histories and annals and the songs with which they preserved them.

This passage demonstrates Alva Ixtlilxochitl's deep familiarity with the contemporary European tradition of humanistic studies. Renaissance scholars had long been redefining their own cultures by studying ancient Greece and Rome, which served as steady referents in humanist literary, artistic, and historical endeavors. In early colonial Mexico, Renaissance humanism extended to native communities through their leaders, whom Franciscan friars educated in the history and culture of ancient Europe. The most famous of the Fransicans' efforts was the Imperial College of Santa Cruz de Tlatelolco, a school founded in Mexico City in 1536 to educate the sons of native nobles in Latin, rhetoric, and logic.[8] The school, however, had ceased to be a center of humanistic learning by the 1580s, and Alva Ixtlilxochitl, who was born in 1578, was not educated there. Nonetheless, his work bears the mark of the Franciscan scholarly and educational mission in New Spain. In fact, Alva Ixtlilxochitl collaborated closely with the Franciscan fray Juan de Torquemada, one of the most important scholars of Nahua history and culture of his time.

For this reason, Alva Ixtlilxochitl's project on ancient Mexico must be understood within the intellectual currents of the early modern world. It echoes the emphasis on exegesis and interpretation of ancient languages that was one hallmark of Renaissance humanism. In addition to Alva Ixtlilxochitl, there were other indigenous and mestizo intellectuals in New Spain at the turn of the seventeenth century producing new histories of the pre-Hispanic period, such as don Fernando de Alvarado Tezozomoc, don Domingo de San Antón Muñón Chimalpahin Quauhtlehuanitzin, and Diego Muñoz Camargo.[9] Moreover, Alva Ixtlilxochitl is often compared to renowned Andean mestizo historian El Inca Garcilaso de la Vega.[10] All of these authors, including Alva Ixtlilxochitl, were well versed in the Greco-Roman and Judeo-Christian traditions, but they turned their scholarly attention not to the ancient Mediterranean but to the deeds of their native forebears in the New World.

In the prologue to the *History of the Chichimeca Nation* Alva Ixtlilxochitl declares that his translation of native sources is "the result of hard work and effort spent understanding the substance of the paintings and glyphs that were [the native peoples'] letters and translating the songs to reveal their true meaning." Here he adapts the humanist model to his own colonial context so as to question and supplant earlier histories written by Europeans. For example, the most widely read Spanish chroniclers of the Indies, Gonzalo Fernández de Oviedo and Francisco López de Gómara, had relied on the bewildered and unreliable accounts of Spanish settlers and conquistadors, thereby portraying the ancient Nahuas as ignorant barbarians and devil worshippers.[11] Alva Ixtlilxochitl directly challenges such canonical versions of events by highlighting their authors' ignorance of native-language sources; lacking such knowledge, he argued, European historians had arrived at an erroneous understanding of ancient Mexico. In contrast, he utilized a broad array of native sources, including pictorial and alphabetic texts as well as oral traditions such as songs and stories. Thus, even as he appropriated the norms of Renaissance humanism to make ancient Mexico more comprehensible to European readers, he also produced a Nahua-centric counter-narrative to the dominant Spanish account of New World history. Far from the caricatures of Oviedo and López de Gómara, according to Alva Ixtlilxochitl the ancient Nahuas had politics, writing, and history, and the best among them had intuited the one true God long before the arrival of the conquistadors.

Beyond the broader polemic over New World history, Alva Ixtlilxochitl's writings were also deeply personal, as they revolved around a patriotic memory of his beloved Tetzcoco. In his account, fifteenth-century Tetzcoco was a thriving land of order and virtue guided by the sagely wisdom of his great-grandfather's great-grandfather, the revered philosopher-king Nezahualcoyotl, described as "the most powerful, courageous, wise, and fortunate prince and captain there has ever been in this new world" (chapter 49). According to Alva Ixtlilxochitl, under Nezahualcoyotl, Tetzcoco achieved the summit of human civilization, as prosperity, peace, and good government ensured its legacy as a center of learning, science, and enlightenment. Nezahualcoyotl is represented as a model of aristocratic virtue and heroism; a vision that simultaneously promoted the prestige of Alva Ixtlilxochitl's own family while yet again challenging Spanish and European contemporaries who continued to deny or ignore the value of indigenous history. This process, however, was fraught with ambiguity, for in seeking to align his forebears with the models of European humanism, Alva Ixtlilxochitl unavoidably transformed them. The *History of the Chichimeca Nation* has been and continues to be an extraordinarily valuable and illuminating resource for native history, yet it is important to remember that this is a colonial text and as such represents pre-Hispanic history within the norms of Hispanic religious and political culture and language. Weaving together European and New World perspectives in intricate and often surprising ways, Alva Ixtlilxochitl's *History of the Chichimeca Nation* therefore represents an opportunity to witness how indigenous groups living under colonial rule are defined (and redefined) through the writing (and rewriting) of history.

Alva Ixtlilxochitl's body of historical writings comprises five separate texts. In addition to the *History of the Chichimeca Nation,* he composed four accounts of varying length and completeness. They are:

"Summary Account of All the Things that Have Happened in New Spain, and of the Many Things that the Tolteca Achieved and Learned from the Creation of the World, until Their Destruction and the Arrival of the Third Settler Chichimeca, until the Arrival of the Spaniards, Taken from the Original History of this New Spain";

"Succinct Account in the Form of a Petition of the History of New Spain and Its Lordships until the Arrival of the Spaniards";

"Historical Compendium of the Kingdom of Tetzcoco"; and

"Summary Account of the General History of this New Spain from the Origin of the World until the Present Era, Collected and Taken from the Histories, Paintings, and Characters of Its Natives, and from the Ancient Songs with which they Observed It."

The subject matter of all four works overlaps considerably, as they all hail the native nobility of Tetzcoco and glorify their homeland. Yet despite their similarities, the works differ considerably in their detail and the quality of their prose. In many ways, these four can be considered preliminary texts that would eventually lead to the longer, more complete, and more thoroughly developed *History of the Chichimeca Nation.* According to the best scholarly estimates, they were written much earlier in his life, and a number of structural and textual parallels suggest that Alva Ixtlilxochitl used the "Summary Account of the General History" as an early draft of the *History of the Chichimeca Nation.*

The *History of the Chichimeca Nation* consists of ninety-five brief chapters that cover the history of Tetzcoco and central Mexico from the mythic creation of the world to the arrival of the Spaniards and their final assault on Mexico-Tenochtitlan in 1521.[12] Thematically, we can divide the text into five major sections:

Cosmology and myth-history (chapters 1–13): These initial chapters recount pre-Columbian creation stories and the lives and reigns of the earliest rulers. This section concludes with the founding of the city of Tetzcoco in the thirteenth century.

Tepaneca Wars (chapters 14–31): These chapters describe the struggle between rival ethnic groups for control of the Basin of Mexico in the fourteenth and fifteenth centuries. Alva Ixtlilxochitl's Tetzcoca ancestors forge an alliance that eventually emerges victorious in this struggle.

Reign of Nezahualcoyotl (chapters 32–49): These chapters chronicle the reign of the Tetzcoca ruler Nezahualcoyotl, one of the victors of the Tepaneca Wars and ancestor of Alva Ixtlilxochitl. He rules from 1431 to 1472.

Reign of Nezahualpilli (chapters 50–76): These chapters deal with the reign of Nezahualpilli, son and successor of Nezahualcoyotl. He rules from 1472 to 1515.

Spanish Arrival and Conquest (chapters 77–95): These final chapters record the Spanish conquest, which begins in 1519. The account ends abruptly, however, breaking off in midsentence as the final battle for Tenochtitlan is being fought in 1521.

Alva Ixtlilxochitl drew from an array of sources in his historical narrative.[13] The early sections rely heavily on pictorial texts, such as the Codex Xolotl and the Quinatzin Map.[14] In our edition we have included line drawings of these sources to accompany some passages where there is clear indication that the author was consulting them. For instance, Alva Ixtlilxochitl's description of the 1418 death of the Tetzcoca ruler Ixtlilxochitl Ometochtli (chapter 19) precisely follows the scene as depicted in the Codex Xolotl, plate 7 (fig.2).

In the latter part of the *History of the Chichimeca Nation*, there are indications that Alva Ixtlilxochitl consulted a range of Spanish historians. He cited some of these authors, such as fray Juan de Torquemada, whom he named explicitly in chapters 49, 73, and 90. In the final section of the text, which deals with the Spanish conquest, Alva Ixtlilxochitl relied on some of the sources that he also disparaged. In chapter 90, for example, he mentions four sources for a history of the conquest when he announces:

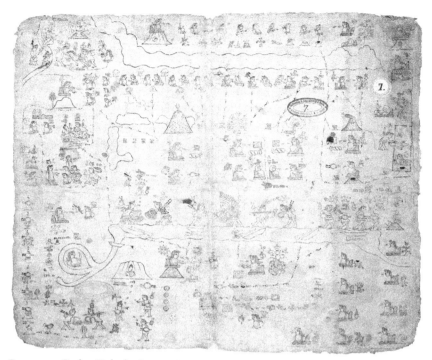

FIGURE 2. Codex Xolotl, plate 7. *Photo courtesy of the Bibliothèque nationale de France.*

Matters related to our Spaniards and the most noteworthy events of those times are all described in great detail by Francisco López de Gómara in his *Historia de las Indias,* by Antonio de Herrera in his chronicle, by the Reverend Father friar Juan de Torquemada in his *Monarquía indiana,* and by an eyewitness, the invincible don Hernando Cortés, Marquis of the Valley, in the letters and accounts that he sent to His Majesty.

Yet, he prefaces these remarks by distancing his own narrative from that of the Spanish historians: "The great majority of what I have written and shall continue to write is based on the accounts and paintings that were written by the native lords of this land just after its conquest, who were present for the events that occurred in those times." While Alva Ixtlilxochitl did rely on pictorials and oral accounts from the native community, he also drew liberally from the very same Spanish historians whose authority he challenged.

Fernando de Alva Ixtlilxochitl died in relative obscurity in 1650, his *History of the Chichimeca Nation* remaining incomplete and unpublished. Yet the explicit premise of his work—that he might effectively capture and transmit the accumulated historical knowledge of central Mexico's original peoples—made him an indispensable authority to later generations interested in Nahua and Mesoamerican history, in particular an influential cohort of educated creoles (American-born Spaniards) in the seventeenth and eighteenth centuries who regarded pre-Hispanic civilizations as the origins of their own patrimonial heritage. Following Mexican independence in 1821, Alva Ixtlilxochitl's heroic portrayal of ancient Tetzcoco inspired early nationalists, who viewed it as a rebuke to their former colonial masters. In the twentieth century, the *History of the Chichimeca Nation* remained an essential reference and guide for generations of anthropologists and cultural historians. Even today, Nezahualcoyotl's noble visage is the emblem of the 100-peso note, and Mexican schoolchildren continue to recite his poetry and learn of his deeds, perhaps unaware of the role of his far less famous descendant in preserving and disseminating such ideas. Beyond Mexico, writers continue to locate Tetzcoco and Nezahualcoyotl at the heart of elite Mesoamerican culture and learning. A leading undergraduate history textbook in the US, for example, describes Tetzcoco as "the Athens" of Mexican antiquity, while a recent *New York Times* bestseller describes Nezahualcoyotl as a New World analog to Locke, Voltaire, and the other heralds of Europe's Enlightenment.[15] Alva Ixtlilxochitl's quiet historiographical ubiquity is a paradoxical testament to his success as a historian: while his name is relatively unfamiliar outside academic circles, his historical vision has deeply influenced popular understandings of the Aztec world for centuries.

Alva Ixtlilxochitl's legacy originates in the decades after his death. In what is certainly one of the most momentous events in Mexican intellectual and cultural history, toward 1680 Alva Ixtlilxochitl's son gave his father's entire library—his chronicles as well as his vast collection of Nahua pictorial manuscripts—to the influential creole polymath don Carlos de Sigüenza y Góngora. Sigüenza, in turn, adapted Alva Ixtlilxochitl's view of Mesoamerican history and introduced it to his erudite creole peers, who devoured its tales of courtly intrigue, heroic princes, and imperial politics in the Aztec world. It was also by way of Sigüenza that contemporary European readers learned of Alva Ixtlilxochitl.[16] In 1697, Sigüenza showed the collection to the Italian traveler Giovanni Francesco Gemelli Careri during his stay in Mexico. Gemelli Careri subsequently referenced Alva Ixtlilxochitl in his hugely popular and widely translated travel memoir, *Giro del mondo*, describing him (not entirely accurately) as the direct heir to the ancient kings of Tetzcoco and his collection as comprised of the only Mesoamerican antiquities to escape the idolatry extirpation fires of the overzealous Spanish evangelizers.[17]

Upon his death in 1700, Sigüenza willed the bulk of his collection, which included Alva Ixtlilxochitl's writings, to the Jesuits of Mexico City, who maintained them in their school library. There his writings were seen and studied by many of the best and most influential minds of eighteenth-century Mexico, both Hispanic and indigenous.[18] As a result, eighteenth-century accounts of preconquest Mexico almost invariably regard Tetzcoco under Nezahualcoyotl and Nezahualpilli as the "Mexican Athens," Mesoamerica's premier center of learning, virtue, and high culture.[19] In the 1730s, the Italian Aztecophile Lorenzo Boturini Benaduci viewed and copied much of the Alva Ixtlilxochitl-Sigüenza library, including the *History of the Chichimeca Nation*, which he incorporated into his famous "Indian Museum," an extensive collection of alphabetic and pictorial texts of Nahua origin.[20] Boturini and many of his followers, such as the creole lawyer Mariano Fernández de Echeverría y Veytia and the Spanish priest José Joaquín Granados y Gálvez, regarded Alva Ixtlilxochitl's account of pre-Hispanic Mexico to be among the best and most authoritative.[21]

But perhaps the most influential eighteenth-century reading of the *History of the Chichimeca Nation* was that of the creole Jesuit Francisco Xavier Clavijero. Prior to the Jesuits' expulsion from Spanish-controlled lands in 1767, Clavijero taught for years at the Jesuit schools in Mexico City, where he encountered the Alva Ixtlilxochitl–Sigüenza collection. Later, while in exile in Bologna, he published *Ancient History of Mexico* (1780), based in part on the knowledge he had acquired from the collection. Alva Ixtlilxochitl's stately portrayal of Nezahualcoyotl's Tetzcoco was especially important, as Clavijero's work directly challenged a series of contemporary European histories that portrayed preconquest Mexico as barbaric and uncivilized.[22] Clavijero's work was widely read throughout the Americas on the eve of independence and has been recognized by scholars as critical to the development of a patriotic sensibility based on the notion of a prestigious Mexican antiquity, one that was great before—and even despite—Spanish conquest and rule.[23]

The *History of the Chichimeca Nation* first began to be published in the nineteenth century, two hundred years after its author's death. However, most early editions were incomplete, poorly contextualized, and inflected by contemporary political agendas and ideologies.[24] For example, the first of Alva Ixtlilxochitl's texts to be published was the thirteenth and final section of his

Historical Compendium in 1829. Originally titled "Thirteenth Relation: On the Arrival of the Spaniards and the Beginning of the Law of the Gospel," this text recounts the deeds of the author's great-grandfather, the Tetzcoca nobleman don Fernando Cortés Ixtlilxochitl, who allied with the Spaniards during the conquest of Tenochtitlan. However, the editor, Carlos María de Bustamante—a fiercely nationalistic lawyer, liberal statesman, and historian—published the account under the new title *Horrible Cruelties of the Conquerors of Mexico*, thus reframing a plea for royal recognition by the descendant of a Nahua who collaborated with the conquistadors as a nationalistic exposé of Spanish crimes.[25] This misrepresentation of Alva Ixtlilxochitl's work was reproduced in subsequent generations who knew of it only through Bustamante's edition.

Meanwhile, Continental, British, and Anglo-American scholars and antiquarians were also discovering Alva Ixtlilxochitl's works. In 1803–4, the German traveler and polymath Alexander von Humboldt passed through Mexico, met the learned elite of Mexico City, and became impressed with not only the great Mesoamerican pictorial texts, but also the rich trove of creole historiography founded, in part, upon the works of Alva Ixtlilxochitl. Humboldt's major work on Mexico appeared in the 1810s and liberally cited creole followers of Alva Ixtlilxochitl such as Sigüenza and Clavijero.[26] His portrayal of native Mesoamerica as an essentially "Asiatic" civilization—pagan and despotic, yet civilized and honorable—fueled new interest in Mesoamerican history. Foreign antiquarians soon flooded into Mexico following the War of Independence to seek out Mesoamerican artifacts, both to fill curiosity cabinets while also accumulating evidence for their particular theories about human history and development. As someone of noble Nahua descent who claimed to have translated the ancient knowledge of his ancestors into Spanish, Alva Ixtlilxochitl served as a crucial intermediary, just as he had among earlier generations of creoles.

As Alva Ixtlilxochitl's manuscripts had disappeared by the late 1820s, the path by which he came to the attention of an international cohort of scholars and antiquarians was circuitous. In the late eighteenth century, a Spanish military officer in Mexico named Diego García Panes copied various items from the Boturini library, including the *History of the Chichimeca Nation*.[27] Panes sent his copies to Spain as part of the grand historiographical project of Juan Bautista Muñoz, who had been commissioned by King Charles III to produce a new apologetic history of the Spanish empire.[28] The Panes-Muñoz copy, held at the Royal Academy of History in Madrid, would serve as the primary avenue by which French- and English-speaking historians would encounter Alva Ixtlilxochitl.

The first publication of the complete works of Alva Ixtlilxochitl, including the *History of the Chichimeca Nation*, appeared in volume 9 of the massive *Antiquities of Mexico*, printed in London between 1830 and 1848 by the Irish nobleman and antiquarian, Edward King, Viscount Kingsborough.[29] The Kingsborough edition was based on the Muñoz copy in Madrid. His enormous efforts to compile, preserve, and disseminate the pictorial records, codices, and alphabetic accounts of Nahua and Mesoamerican history and culture are recognized as a major landmark in the development of Mesoamerican studies. However, his antiquarian endeavors (and bankruptcy) were largely inspired by a lifelong quest to substantiate his belief that the native peoples of America descended from the biblical Lost Tribes of Israel, a theory with roots in the sixteenth century that remained popular in the nineteenth.[30] *Antiquities of Mexico*, therefore, does little to contextualize or historicize its materials and simply presents Alva Ixtlilxochitl's works as expressions of an arcane and ancient Mexican wisdom.

Due to close political, cultural, and commercial ties between Mexico and France after 1821, a French tradition of Mesoamerican studies also arose in the nineteenth century. Henri Ternaux-Compans was a French diplomat and bibliographer who traveled through the newly independent Spanish America copying manuscripts and collecting rare books; after returning to Paris, he published French translations of dozens of original texts comprising twenty volumes, including the *History of the Chichimeca Nation*, which he had likewise seen at the Royal Academy of History in Madrid.[31] Meanwhile, Joseph Marius Alexis Aubin was a French antiquarian who resided in Mexico in the 1830s, where he purchased many of the materials that remained of the old Boturini collection. Among these were copies of several items attributed to Alva Ixtlilxochitl, including the *History of the Chichimeca Nation*. Upon his departure from Mexico in 1840, Aubin illegally secreted away many of these priceless texts and sold them late in life to the collector Eugène Goupil, who in turn donated them to the Bibliothèque nacionale de France in Paris, where it forms the core of the invaluable Fonds Mexicain.[32] There, in keeping with Humboldt's original assessment, it was conceived as the material and textual record of an advanced but non-Western civilization, and incorporated into the museum's "Oriental" wing alongside artifacts and manuscripts from the Near, Middle, and Far East. Like Kingsborough's *Antiquities of Mexico*, the Aubin-Goupil collection thereby exoticized the works of Alva Ixtlilxochitl and other colonial-era indigenous and mestizo authors.

Alva Ixtlilxochitl and his *History of the Chichimeca Nation* also played a key role in the way that nineteenth- and twentieth-century Anglo-Americans learned of Mexican history. The Anglo-American historiography begins with William Hickling Prescott of Boston, a Harvard-trained scholar and one of the most influential early US historians. Although Prescott's epic account of the Spanish defeat of Tenochtitlan, *History of the Conquest of Mexico* (1843), mostly adopts the Spaniards' perspective, with Hernando Cortés as a larger-than-life hero, it also draws heavily from Alva Ixtlilxochitl to supply the details regarding Nahua mores, customs, and history. Indeed, Prescott—who received reproductions of the Panes-Muñoz copies from the Royal Academy of History in Madrid—dubbed Alva Ixtlilxochitl "the Livy of Anahuac" and accepted him as a premier authority on Mesoamerican history. The entire first volume of Prescott's account deals with "the ancient Mexicans" and closely follows the *History of the Chichimeca Nation*, echoing its chronology of the Tolteca and Chichimeca settlers, its portrayal of Tetzcoco as the center of elite culture, and its vivid and detailed account of Nezahualcoyotl's exile, victory, and reign.[33] With its captivating Romantic-period prose and the heightened interest in Mexico owing to the Mexican-American War of 1846–48, Prescott's account quickly went through multiple printings and can be considered the foundation of an entire tradition of professional and amateur Hispanism in the US.[34]

Following Prescott's lead, subsequent generations of scholars in the US continued to turn to Alva Ixtlilxochitl for information on Nahua and central Mexican ethnography and history. However, by the end of the nineteenth century, a new array of systematized approaches to anthropology and ethnology encouraged researchers to apply more skepticism toward the chronicler. Hubert Howe Bancroft's major account of the indigenous peoples of the Americas, *The Native Races* (1883), cites and quotes Alva Ixtlilxochitl liberally in its descriptions of Nahua ways.[35] Yet Bancroft also cautioned his readers against an uncritical reading of Alva Ixtlilxochitl, noting that "due allowance must be made" for his overzealous patriotism.[36] Similarly, the archeologist Adolph Bandelier noted that Alva Ixtlilxochitl's works, while useful for details, should be regarded as "representative of one tribe only."[37] Nonetheless, neither Bancroft nor Bandelier were interested in exploring the contours of Alva Ixtlilxochitl's particular perspective and the complex and transcultural political and literary world in which it arose. Rather, they treated his works as useful, if imperfect, guides in their quest to locate Mesoamerica within preconceived civilizational classification and ranking schemes.

In Mexico, Alva Ixtlilxochitl only became broadly known after 1891, when his complete works, drawn from Kingsborough, were published in two volumes by Alfredo Chavero.[38] Chavero was an official with the government of President

Porfirio Díaz (1876–1910) tasked with recovering and reproducing a proud and progressive vision of Mexico's past with which to face the world.[39] Although he reproduced the *History of the Chichimeca Nation* whole, Chavero's edition is often confusing and poorly edited, as it reorganizes various fragments of Alva Ixtlilxochitl's texts in an attempt to produce a linear chronology of preconquest Mexico. Yet despite the nationalistic and ideological purpose of the edition—it was commissioned to commemorate the quadricentennial of the voyages of Christopher Columbus—we should recognize that the Chavero volumes made the works of Alva Ixtlilxochitl reasonably available to Mexican readers for the first time, almost three centuries after they had been written. Alva Ixtlilxochitl's vision was surely essential to nurturing the generation of scholars who matured in the immediate wake of the Revolution of 1910 and who advocated new notions of the link between indigenous history and the modern nation-state.

Chavero's 1891 edition of Alva Ixtlilxochitl continued to serve as an important source for pre-Hispanic and colonial Mexico to scholars in the twentieth century. Academics in both Mexico and the United States from a variety of disciplines—history, anthropology, art history, and literature—have all relied heavily on Alva Ixtlilxochitl's work, which often served, as one anthropologist noted, as "the principal source on the kingdom of Tetzcoco."[40]

Early work in the interdisciplinary field that we might call Nahua studies began in earnest in Mexico in the decades following the Revolution of 1910. The most influential of these early scholars was Ángel María Garibay K., who published extensively on Nahuatl-language literature and translated many Nahuatl texts into Spanish, basing his translations and analysis on colonial-era historians like Alva Ixtlilxochitl.[41] One of Garibay's students, Miguel León-Portilla, perhaps the most well-known scholar of Nahua culture, continued in his advisor's footsteps, using colonial authors like Alva Ixtlilxochitl to inform his studies of Nahua philosophy, history, and literature.[42]

León-Portilla's contemporaries in the United States and Europe also drew upon Alva Ixtlilxochitl's work, as Nahua studies blossomed into an international endeavor in the mid-twentieth century. Anthropologists such as George C. Vaillant, H. B. Nicholson, and Charles E. Dibble made ample use of Alva Ixtlilxochitl in their studies of pre-Hispanic culture and society.[43] Likewise, historians such as Charles Gibson relied on the *History of the Chichimeca Nation* for a wide range of information pertaining to Nahua social and political organization.[44] And pioneering Mesoamerican art historian Donald Robertson based his interpretation of Tetzcoco-area pictorial manuscripts, in part, on Alva Ixtlilxochitl.[45]

As subsequent generations of scholars have worked to deepen our understanding of the Nahua past, the use of Alva Ixtlilxochitl's *History of the Chichimeca Nation* has only become more widespread. Citations of Alva Ixtlilxochitl's work appear especially frequently in anthropological works, where he is generally valued, as Michael E. Smith states, for his "non-Mexica point of view of the [Aztec] empire's history to balance the better-known Mexica versions."[46] The topics of many of these works are closely related to the topics included in Alva Ixtlilxochitl's chronicle. Burr Cartwright Brundage and Frances F. Berdan, for instance, draw on Alva Ixtlilxochitl in their overviews of pre-Hispanic Aztec history.[47] Pedro Carrasco cites him liberally as he describes the structure of the Triple Alliance.[48] And Jerome Offner and Frederic Hicks rely heavily on Alva Ixtlilxochitl for their studies of pre-Hispanic Tetzcoca politics and law.[49] But Alva Ixtlilxochitl is also cited in articles and books on a surprisingly wide range of issues. Anthony Aveni, for instance, in his 1983 book on the archaeoastronomy of Mesoamerica, turns occasionally to Alva Ixtlilxochitl, as does Mary Hrones Parsons's 1975 article on late Postclassic spindle whorls. The anthropological scholarship that cites Alva Ixtlilxochitl as an authority on pre-Columbian Mesoamerica is impressively broad in scope.[50]

Art historians, too, have continued to rely on Alva Ixtlilxochitl's *History of the Chichimeca Nation* for a wide range of information as they work to make sense of the often-esoteric iconography of Mesoamerica. Work on pre-Hispanic art, especially, has often relied on Alva Ixtlilxochitl to offer explanations, confirm hypotheses, or provide context for pictorial depictions. Cecelia Klein, Emily Umberger, and Luz María Mohar Betancourt, among many others, all draw something from Alva Ixtlilxochitl.[51] But art historians of the colonial world such as Xavier Noguez and Barbara Mundy have also looked to Alva Ixtlilxochitl for what he may be able to clarify about sixteenth-century visual culture.[52]

A different approach to Alva Ixtlilxochitl and his work emerged in Mexico in the 1970s, when the prolific Mexican scholar Edmundo O'Gorman published a new edition of the complete works of Alva Ixtlilxochitl in two volumes.[53] O'Gorman did not have access to the autograph manuscripts and instead relied on eighteenth-century copies, and with those he produced an edition of the texts that far exceeded the quality of Chavero's. In addition to the works themselves, he included a thoroughly researched introduction to the author and his texts. Moreover, O'Gorman—a specialist in postconquest history and literature, not preconquest Mesoamerica—and his team of scholars dove into the Archivo General de la Nación in Mexico City to find relevant archival material and included it in the appendix to the second volume, which aided in placing Alva Ixtlilxochitl in his historical context. O'Gorman's work thus represented a new way of understanding the Alva Ixtlilxochitl corpus, as his team was one of the first to consider it as the product of a specific cultural and historical moment, and not only as a source for knowledge of pre-Hispanic Mexico.

In the same vein as O'Gorman, scholars of the Nahua past from across the disciplines have begun to take a more critical approach to the work of Alva Ixtlilxochitl. Some literary scholars challenged our ability to learn about indigenous history from his works at all. Emphasizing his overtly Christian outlook, his adoption of the European chronicle style, and the fact that he wrote in Spanish, they regarded Alva Ixtlilxochitl as representing a "disindigenized" point of view that, in purporting to relay native history, actually alienated it into the hands of the colonizers.[54] Rolena Adorno, however, beginning in the 1980s, explored these same complexities within the author and his works, and demonstrated how they reflect the complex social and political environment of the colonial world.[55] This emphasis on colonial-era context and complexity has been echoed in subsequent literary criticism, particularly in the work of Salvador Velazco, Pablo García Loaeza, Jongsoo Lee, and Amber Brian.[56] Historians have also continued to view Alva Ixtlilxochitl's works as illustrative of his own time. D. A. Brading recognized his work as written "so as to procure . . . privileges" in the colonial period.[57] And Patrick Lesbre, Peter B. Villella, and Bradley Benton, for instance, have continued to insist on the value of his works for information on the colonial world.[58]

Alva Ixtlilxochitl's position among art historians has also begun to shift. As scholars such as Elizabeth Hill Boone have begun to argue for the restoration of the colonial-era pictorial documents to the colonial-era historiography, there is increased attention to the ways in which both pictorial sources and alphabetic sources such as Alva Ixtlilxochitl's are products of the early colonial setting.[59] Susan Spitler, Lori Boornazian Diel, and Eduardo de J. Douglas, for instance, have all been careful to recognize that the principal Acolhua pictorial manuscripts—the Codex Xolotl, Quinatzin Map, Tlotzin Map, and Tira de Tepechpan, among others—along with Alva Ixtlilxochitl's *History of the Chichimeca Nation* reveal as much or more about the period after the Spaniards arrived than about the pre-Hispanic era.[60]

We can clearly perceive coexisting, yet dissonant ways that modern readers have represented and utilized Alva Ixtlilxochitl's works: as essentially a direct translation of pre-Columbian knowledge or as a colonial-era writer with an agenda shaped by contemporary circumstances. The indispensable bridge between these two perspectives, the approach necessary for delineating precisely how Alva Ixtlilxochitl's works are meaningful, is a critical analysis of the chronicler himself as a writer and historian, one that accounts for the political, cultural, and intellectual currents within which he moved and the contemporary republic of letters in which he wrote. Yet for all its influence through the centuries, the *History of the Chichimeca Nation* has not been translated into English until now. In fact, the only one of his works to be translated into English was the "Thirteenth Relation" of the "Historical Compendium of the Kingdom of Tetzcoco."[61] But the *History of the Chichimeca Nation* is Alva Ixtlilxochitl's magnum opus, his most ambitious and influential work. An English translation has been long overdue.

Notes

1. Although the original manuscript carries the much more prosaic heading *Sumaria relación*, or "Summary Account," we shall refer to the text as the *Historia de la nación chichimeca*, or *History of the Chichimeca Nation*, which, since the eighteenth century, has been its most widely recognized title. In Alva Ixtlilxochitl's account, the Chichimecas were the tribal peoples who migrated from the northern deserts to central Mexico, where they founded the urbanized civilization he chronicles.

2. Nahua is a term that refers to all Nahuatl-language speakers regardless of ethnic identity. As Barlow (1945) noted, the term Aztec was not used by the Nahuas themselves. Rather, it was employed by scholars in the eighteenth century and popularized in the English-speaking world through the works of the nineteenth-century historian William H. Prescott (1843).

3. Tetzcoco was the leading altepetl of the Acolhua ethnic group, which dominated the eastern Valley of Mexico. At the time of the Spanish arrival, it was the second most powerful altepetl in central Mexico after Tenochtitlan, the capital of the Mexica people, upon which the Spaniards built Mexico City.

4. Spain's political control of its territories in the New World was, through the beginning of the eighteenth century, exercised through two *virreinatos*, or viceroyalties—the Viceroyalty of New Spain, founded in 1535 with its capital at Mexico City, and the Viceroyalty of Peru, founded in 1542 with its capital at Lima. The Viceroyalty of New Spain included the lands that now comprise Mexico, Central America, the US Southwest, California, Florida, islands in the Caribbean, and islands in the Pacific including the Philippine Archipelago.

5. In 1827, a Mexican priest, Father José María Luis Mora, presented the three volumes as a gift to James Thomsen, the representative for the Bible Society in Mexico. Though Mora was a Catholic priest and Thomsen a Protestant Bible merchant, they shared a passion for educational reform and collaborated on ways to distribute Bibles as part of the educational mission of newly independent Mexico (Schroeder 1994). In 2014, these three volumes were repatriated to Mexico and are now housed in the Instituto Nacional de Antropología e Historia (INAH). See Brian (2014; 2016).

6. The "Aztec Empire" was in reality a confederation of autonomous ethnic states and is more properly called the Triple Alliance of Tenochtitlan, Tetzcoco, and Tlacopan.

7. Though Alva Ixtlilxochitl's connections to Teotihuacan were very significant to his and his family's social status, he does not emphasize these connections in the *History of the Chichimeca Nation*, where the focus of the narrative is Tetzcoco. For more on Alva Ixtlilxochitl and Teotihuacan, see Munch (1976), Benton (2014), and Brian (2016).

8. See Cortés (2008) and Laird (2014).

9. For studies of native-identified authors from New Spain, see, for instance, Schroeder (1991; 2010), Adorno (1994), Velazco (2003), Schwaller (2014), Townsend (2017), and Brian (2017). For a broad study of colonial-era indigenous intellectuals in Mexico and the Andes, see Ramos and Yannakakis (2014).

10. Inca Garcilaso's two-part *Comentarios reales de los Incas* (1609; 1617) offers a history of Inca society, before and after Spanish colonization, based on native sources. Significant as much for their differences as similarities, Inca Garcilaso's texts were written and published in Europe, unlike Alva Ixtlilxochitl whose works were written in New Spain and not published until the nineteenth century. For comparisons of the two historians see Brading (1991) and García Loaeza (2006). For recent scholarship on Inca Garcilaso, see Fernández and Castro-Klarén (2016).

11. Gonzalo Fernández de Oviedo's *Historia general y natural de las Indias* was initially published in various forms at different moments beginning with the *Sumario* (1526), but the complete text remained unpublished until the mid-nineteenth century when José Amador de los Ríos published an edition for the Spanish Academy of History (1851–55). The various iterations of the work that were published prior to Ríos's edition, however, circulated widely. In 1552, Francisco López de Gómara published *Historia de las Indias*. Though the book was censored by royal decree the following year, it did in fact circulate and came to influence numerous historians.

12. The imperial city of Mexico-Tenochtitlan, located on an island in the middle of Lake Tetzcoco, was the largest and most powerful polity in central Mexico when the Spaniards arrived. Cortés and his forces first entered the city peacefully in 1519, but hostilities began and it fell in August of 1521.

13. For a comprehensive list of the sources and authors cited by Alva Ixtlilxochitl, see O'Gorman (1975, 47–85).

14. For the Codex Xolotl, see Dibble (1951). For the Quinatzin Map, see Mohar Betancourt (2004).

15. Mann 2006, 133–36; Meyer, Sherman, and Deeds 2011, 48.

16. See Sigüenza y Góngora (1680). See also García Loaeza (2009), More (2013), and Brian (2016).

17. Gemelli Careri 1700, 72–73.

18. The Jesuit College of San Pedro and San Pablo served Spanish students preparing for careers in the Church and viceregal government; the adjoining College of San Gregorio was dedicated to educating the sons of the indigenous nobility, who were to become the governors in their native towns. See Schmidt Díaz de León (2012) and Villella (2016, 198–204, 226–300).

19. Brading 1991, 450–64.

20. See Boturini Benaduci (2015, 201–74) and Glass (1978).

21. See Boturini Benaduci (2015, 155), Echeverría y Veytia (1836, 35–36), and Granados y Gálvez (1987, 228).
22. Clavijero 1844, 113–14.
23. Brading 1991, 450–62.
24. Torales Pacheco 1998, 168.
25. Alva Ixtlilxochitl 1829.
26. See Humboldt (1811–14), especially vol. 2.
27. Panes married into a wealthy creole family and befriended some of the most influential Mexican antiquarians of the age, including Mariano Fernández de Echeverría y Veytia, Antonio de León y Gama, and the indigenous aristocracy of Tlaxcala. Panes's own heavily illustrated, yet unpublished "Teatro de Nueva España" owes much to Alva Ixtlilxochitl's vision of pre-Hispanic central Mexico. Panes's original manuscripts are in the Biblioteca Nacional de México. See Panes (1976) and Gibson (1952, 49–50, 60, 241–43).
28. Cañizares-Esguerra 2002, 190–203.
29. Kingsborough 1829–48.
30. Gordon 1892.
31. Published in 1840 as *Histoire des Chichimèques ou des anciens rois de Tezcuco par don Fernando d'Alva Ixtlilxochitl, traduite sur le manuscrit espagnol* in vols. 12 and 13 of Ternaux-Compans (1837–41).
32. For an account of the Fonds Mexicain, its origins, its contents, and its contemporary value, see Galarza and Bejarano Almada (n.d.).
33. Prescott 1843, vol. 1.
34. For example, Edward E. Ayer (1841–1927) was a wealthy bibliophile whose acquisitions, which included Boturini's own copy of the *History of the Chichimeca Nation* and others of Alva Ixtlilxochitl's writings, formed the core of the important Mesoamerican collection at the Newberry Library in Chicago, IL. Famously, the book that sparked Ayer's interest in history—and the history of America's indigenous peoples in particular—was Prescott's *History of the Conquest of New Spain*, which he encountered by chance in the company library of a silver mine where he was working as a teenager. See Ayer (1950).
35. Bancroft 1883, passim.
36. Bancroft 1883, 134n2.
37. Bandelier 1881, 26.
38. Alva Ixtlilxochitl 1891.
39. See Tenorio Trillo (1996, 30–32).
40. Carrasco 1999, 11.
41. See, for instance, Garibay K. (1953–54; 1964–68).
42. See, for instance, León-Portilla (1956; 1959; 1961).
43. Vaillant 1953; Nicholson 1957 (published as Nicholson [2001]); Dibble 1951.
44. Gibson 1952; 1964.
45. Robertson 1959.
46. Smith 2012, 16. Alva Ixtlilxochitl also continues to be an important source for historians. See, for instance, Cline (1966) and Karttunen (1997).
47. Brundage 1972; Berdan 1982.
48. Carrasco 1996.
49. Offner 1980; Hicks 1982; 1994.

50. Aveni 1983; Parsons 1975. See also Ortiz de Montellano (1978); Townsend (1982); and Charlton, Nichols, and Charlton (1991).

51. Klein 1993; 2001; Umberger 1996; Mohar Betancourt 1994.

52. Noguez 1978; Mundy 2015.

53. Alva Ixtlilxochitl 1975–77.

54. Florescano 1985. On the "colonization of memory" via the spread of alphabetic history-keeping, see Mignolo (1995, 127–43). Similarly, historian James Lockhart flatly rejected Alva Ixtlilxochitl as a "Nahua writer," acknowledging that "though he functioned as an 'Indian' . . . [he] wrote in Spanish using Spanish genres" (Lockhart 1992, 587n6).

55. Adorno 1989; 1994.

56. Velazco 2003; Lee 2008; García Loaeza 2009; 2017; Brian 2016; 2017.

57. Brading 1991, 275.

58. Lesbre 1996; 1997; Villella 2014; Benton 2014; 2017.

59. Boone 2000, 6.

60. Spitler 1998; Diel 2008; Douglas 2010.

61. Alva Ixtlilxochitl 1969. The Ballentine edition, based on imperfect nineteenth century copies, is out of print and difficult to find today. In 2015, Amber Brian, Bradley Benton, and Pablo García Loaeza translated the "Thirteenth Relation" from the original Códice Chimalpahin. See Alva Ixtlilxochitl (2015).

◊ NOTES ON THE TRANSLATION

Our objectives with this translation have been readability and fidelity to the original, two goals that are inevitably in tension with each other. This tension between accessibility and accuracy has led us to make many difficult choices throughout the translation process. Should we use a semicolon or a period? One English word or another? Singular or plural? The final choices at each step have been the product of a—sometimes lengthy—discussion between the four collaborators, and we hope that this process has rendered the best possible English translation. Our edition is deeply informed by this collaborative method, from decisions about the punctuation and spelling to the translation of concepts and phrases that do not have a ready equivalent in English.

While Alva Ixtlilxochitl wrote in Spanish, he occasionally included Nahuatl-language terms and phrases. In these instances, he generally provided his own interpretation of these terms, fully aware that his intended audience would not necessarily have been familiar with Nahuatl. Our English translation strives to maintain this same text-reader relationship by preserving Alva Ixtlilxochitl's self-ascribed role as authority on Nahua culture and interpreter of the Nahuatl language. We have, therefore, retained Nahuatl words and phrases where they appear and not supplemented Alva Ixtlilxochitl's explanations except in instances where none was supplied, as is the case with most of the calendar dates.

We have sought to minimize explanatory notes and rather make evident within the text itself the context necessary for understanding the narrative. Significant emendations and marginal notes in the original text are indicated in footnotes. There is very little punctuation in the original manuscript, thus we have added punctuation and paragraphs to aid in reading the narrative. As part of this process, lengthy sentences have been separated into briefer sentences, with referents added for clarity. We have retained features of the original text including all of Alva Ixtlilxochitl's parentheses, his use of the ç, and his use of -*tzin*. The Nahuatl suffix -*tzin* is a reverential regularly affixed to the names of high-born nobles and leaders to signify respect and prestige. Alva Ixtlilxochitl does not apply the suffix universally and consistently; for example, at certain points in the text he uses "Chimalpopoca" and at other points he uses "Chimalpopocatzin." Though we have respected Alva Ixtlilxochitl's selectivity in the use of -*tzin* in our translation, we have chosen to regularize names that appear with varying spellings. For example, in the early chapters of the text the author uses each of the following versions of the name of Topiltzin's father: "Iztaccaltzin," "Iztacquauhtzin," and "Iztaccauhtzin." We have regularized this name to Iztaccaltzin, which is the most prevalent, in order to avoid any potential confusion; we have done the same with other names, dates, and numbers in Nahuatl that are written in multiple variants in the original. We use ellipses within brackets to signal rips and tears in the manuscript and we use bracketed words or phrases to indicate our best assessment of the text that is missing because of an omission on the part of the author or, and this is particularly relevant toward the end of the text, a rip or tear in the manuscript.

Here we offer several illustrative examples of choices that we made in the translation of specific terms, from seemingly minor adjustments to more intentionally interpretative renditions. Alva Ixtlilxochitl throughout *History of the Chichimeca Nation* uses *palacios* in the plural, but with the meaning of a "palace compound" that comprises many buildings. To avoid confusion in English, we use "palace" in the singular, understanding that this can connote a multitude of discrete buildings within a single compound. A second, and perhaps more involved, example is that of *señoría*, which we have translated as "confederation." In Alva Ixtlilxochitl's original, señoría is used exclusively with Tlaxcala as a way of distinguishing its political organization from that of other cities. We discussed various options including "republic," "alliance," and "confederacy," though we found each lacking or potentially misleading. We then consulted classic studies of Tlaxcala, like Charles Gibson's *Tlaxcala in the Sixteenth Century* (1952), and more recent scholarship, like that of our own Peter Villella (2016). After weighing options and carefully considering the denotation and connotation of each, we opted for translating señoría as "confederation," concluding that this term offered the best equivalent to señoría in its reference to the unique quadripartite political organization of Tlaxcala that Alva Ixtlilxochitl describes. A final example of a translation choice we made is rendering the name the author uses for the inhabitants of the altepetl Mexico-Tenochtitlan, *mexicanos*, as "Mexicas."

We have done this to avoid any potential confusion with the inhabitants of the present-day country of Mexico and because Mexica is the Nahuatl term for people from the altepetl of Mexico-Tenochtitlan. We have, in parallel fashion, normalized Alva Ixtlilxochitl's Hispanicized use of *tezcucanos*, to Tezcucas. Finally, in the translation, as part of our effort to hew as closely to the original as possible, we have chosen to follow Alva Ixtlilxochitl's spelling of the city of his ancestors, Tezcuco, though most contemporary scholars represent the name of this centerpiece of the author's narrative as Tetzcoco to reflect the early colonial Nahua orthography, and in present-day Mexico the city is called Texcoco.

 MOST ILLUSTRIOUS LORD[1]

Since adolescence, I have always greatly desired to know about the historical events in this new world, which were no less important than those of the Romans, Greeks, Medes, and other great pagan republics of universal renown. However, with the passage of time and the fall of the kingdoms and states of my ancestors, their histories were buried. For this reason, with much effort, searching, and utmost diligence, I have achieved my desire to bring together the painted histories and annals and the songs with which they preserved them.[2] Above all, in order to understand these paintings, I brought together many elders of New Spain who were renowned for their knowledge and understanding of those stories to which I have referred. Among all of these authorities I found only two with a thorough understanding and knowledge of the paintings and glyphs that provided true meaning to the songs. Since these are composed with allegorical meaning and adorned with metaphors and similes they are very difficult to understand. With the help of these elders, I was then able to understand easily all of the paintings and histories and to translate the true meaning of the songs. In this way I was able to satisfy my desire to always adhere to the truth. This is why I did not want to use the histories that deal with these matters.[3] The authors who write about them

---

1. The person to whom this is dedicated remains unclear. According to Edmundo O'Gorman, the salutation suggests that the author is addressing a prelate, possibly Bishop Juan Pérez de la Serna (1613–25).
2. Here he is referring to Nahua pictorial sources. They include such documents as the Codex Xolotl, the Quinatzin Map, and the Tlotzin Map, all of which contain historical information related to Tetzcoco.
3. Histories written by Spaniards. Elsewhere, Alva Ixtlilxochitl cites published works, such as Francisco López de Gómara's *Historia general de las Indias* [General History of the Indies] (1552) and the *Historia general de los hechos de los castellanos en las Islas y Tierra*

were given flawed accounts and conflicting interpretations, and, as a result, there is variation and confusion among them. All that I lack is the favor and patronage of a great prince such as Your Most Illustrious Lordship, under whom my work will come to light and to whom I want to offer and dedicate this brief account of the history of New Spain, as it is rightfully yours. That, and the particular concern that my elders and I have always had for Your Most Illustrious Lordship's affairs, emboldened me to dedicate this to you. I humbly beg you to receive it and grant it favor in accordance with the good will with which it is offered. May our Lord grant you long life and prosperity, as we your servants need and desire.

Firme del Mar Océano [General History of the Deeds of the Castillians in the Islands and Mainland of the Ocean Sea] (1601–15) by Antonio de Herrera y Tordesillas, as well as texts that were unpublished at the time, such as the "Historia de los Indios de la Nueva España" [History of the Indians of New Spain] by fray Toribio de Benavente (1858), who was known as "Motolinía."

PROLOGUE FOR THE READER

Given the variety and conflicting opinions of the authors who have written the histories of this New Spain, I have not wanted to follow any of them. Therefore, I relied on the paintings and glyphs by which their histories are written and memorized, since they were painted at the time when the events happened, along with the songs by which serious authors, knowledgeable in their discipline, preserved the histories. These were the kings themselves and the noblest and most educated people; they always acquired and adhered to the truth with as much precision as any of the most serious and trustworthy authors and historians in the world. They had specific writers for each genre. There were some who wrote annals and ordered the things that happened in each year even to the day, month, and hour. Others maintained the genealogies of the kings, nobles, and people of esteemed lineage, carefully recording those who were born and, with the same care, striking out those who died. Some authors were in charge of the paintings of the borders, limits, and boundary markers of the cities, provinces, towns, and villages and of the land plots and allotments and to whom they belonged. Others kept the books of laws, rites, and ceremonies that, during pagan times, the priests used in the temples of their idolatry, which included their idolatrous doctrine, the festivals to their false gods, and calendars. Finally, the philosophers and learned people among [fol. 1v] them were in charge of painting all the knowledge that they had acquired and understood and of teaching from memory all the songs with which they preserved their knowledge and histories.

Time changed all of this. With the fall of the kings and lords mentioned above, the travails and persecutions of their descendants, and the calamity suffered by their subjects and vassals, not only did they abandon what was good and not contrary to our Catholic faith, but the majority of their histories were recklessly and heedlessly burned by order of the first friars.[4] This was one of the greatest losses suffered in this New Spain. All of the aforementioned books, texts, and materials were kept in the royal archives in the city of Tezcuco,[5] as it was the center of all their knowledge, traditions, and mores, because its kings prided themselves on this, and they were the lawmakers of this new world. The materials that escaped the fires and calamities and that my ancestors kept safe came to me. And from them I have taken and translated the history that I intend to write, here presented as a brief and summary account. It is the result of hard work and effort spent understanding the substance of the paintings and glyphs that were their letters and translating the songs to reveal their true meaning. It will be succinct and simple, unadorned and without edifying examples. Nor will I include the fables and fictions that appear in some of their histories, because they are superfluous. I beseech the discriminating reader to ignore the many defects that may be found in my way of narrating. He may be assured that the history is very accurate and truthful and endorsed as such by all the noble and distinguished people of this New Spain.

---

4. The first friars in New Spain belonged to the Franciscan order; they began arriving in 1523 and officially established the *Provincia del Santo Evangelio*, or "Province of the Holy Gospel," in 1524.

5. Tetzcoco was spelled in various ways in during the colonial period. Modern scholars tend to favor "Tetzcoco," as it conforms to colonial Nahuatl-language spellings. Alva Ixtlilxochitl, however, consistently uses "Tezcuco." The present-day municipality spells its name "Texcoco."

SUMMARY ACCOUNT[6]

CHAPTER 1

Which deals with the creation of the world, its four ages, and the
end of each of them, according to the historians of this New Spain

Of the most serious authors and historians of pre-Christian times, one finds that
Quetzalcoatl was foremost among the ancients, and among the moderns were
Nezahualcoyotzin, king of Tezcuco, and the two princes of Mexico, Itzcoatzin
and Xiuhcozcatzin, sons of King Huitzilihuitzin, along with many others (whom I
will cite where necessary).[7] They declare in their histories that the god whom they
called *teotl tloque nahuaque tlachihualeipalnemoani ilhuicahua tlalticpaq*—which
in truth means "the universal God and creator of all things by whose will all
creatures live, lord of heaven and earth," etc.—after having created all things
seen and unseen, created the forefathers of men, from whom all others came.
And the dwelling and habitation he gave them was the world, which they say
has four ages.

They called the first age after the world began *atonatiuh*, which means "sun
of water." They said this in an allegorical sense to mean that this first age of the
world had been destroyed by deluge and floodwaters that drowned all men and

---

6. This is the only title that appears in the manuscript. The name *Historia de la nación
   Chichimeca* was likely given to the text by the historian Mariano Fernández de Echeverría
   y Veytia, who as a creole scholar born in New Spain was very interested in its ancient history. Echeverría y Veytia was among the scholars who made copies of Alva Ixtlilxochitl's
   works.

7. All parentheses are original to the manuscript.

killed all creatures. They called the second age *tlalchitonatiuh*, which means "sun of earth," for it was destroyed by earthquakes that tore apart the earth in many places, swallowing and toppling mountains and peaks such that almost all men were killed. This was the age and time of the giants, which were called *quinametin tzocuil hicxime*.

They called the third age *ecatonatiuh*, which means "sun of wind," because this age ended with wind. There was so much and such fierce wind at that time that all the buildings and trees were toppled; even the mountain peaks were destroyed, and the majority of mankind perished. And when those that escaped this calamity encountered a number of monkeys that the wind must have brought from other places, they said the monkeys were men who had been changed into this species of animal. This is the origin of the well-known fable of the monkeys. Those that inhabited this new world in the third age were the Ulmecas and Xicalancas, and according to their histories, they came to Potonchan in ships or boats from the east. From there they went out to settle the land, and on the banks of the river Atoiac—which flows between the city of Los Ángeles[8] and Cholula—they found some of the giants who had escaped from the disaster and destruction of the second age. These giants, being sturdy people and confident in their strength and large size, subjugated and oppressed the new settlers such that they were like slaves. The leaders and nobles therefore sought to liberate themselves from this servitude. So they held a grand feast for the giants, and once they were sated and drunk, the men killed and destroyed them with the giants' own weapons. With this deed, the Ulmecas and Xicalancas were liberated and released from this subjugation, and their dominion and power began to grow.

And when they were at the height of their prosperity, a man arrived in this land whom some called Quetzalcoatl and others Huemac. And he, for his great virtues, was considered just, holy, and good. He taught them by word and deed the way of virtue and to avoid vice and sin, giving them laws and good doctrine. And to restrain them from their pleasures and immodesty, he established the practice of fasting. He was the first to worship and erect the cross, which they called *quiahuiz teotl chicahualiz teotl* and others *tonacaquahuitl*, which is to say "god of rain and health" and "tree of [fol. 2v] sustenance or life." After preaching the aforementioned things in most of the cities of the Ulmecas and Xicalancas— and especially in Cholula, where he spent most of his time—and seeing that his

---

8. Puebla de los Ángeles, founded in 1531.

teaching bore such little fruit, he returned to the place from which he had come, which was to the east, disappearing off the coast of Coatzacualco. As he bade farewell to these peoples, he told them that in the future, in a year that would be called *çe acatl*,[9] he would return, and then his teaching would be received and his children would be lords and rule the land, and that they and their descendants would suffer many calamities and persecutions, and many other prophecies that later very clearly were fulfilled. Quetzalcoatl, in its literal sense, means "serpent of precious feathers," but in the allegorical sense, "wisest of men." And some say they gave him the name Huemac because he left his hand prints in a rock as if it were very soft wax as a testament that all he had said would come to pass. Others said that it meant "he of the large or powerful hand."

A few days after he had gone, the aforementioned destruction and devastation of the third age of the world took place. At that time, the striking and ostentatious tower of the city of Cholula, which was like a second Tower of Babel that these peoples had built with nearly the same design, was destroyed, knocked down by the wind. Later, those who escaped the devastation of the third age built a temple to Quetzalcoatl on top of its ruins and proclaimed him the god of wind, since the cause of its destruction was the wind; they believed that this calamity [. . .][10] by his hand. They also called him Çe Acatl, which was the name of the year of his arrival. According to the aforementioned histories and annals, all of this happened some years after the incarnation of Christ our Lord. Hereupon began the fourth age; they called it *tletonatiuh*, which means "sun of fire," because they said that this fourth and last age of the world would be destroyed by fire. According to the histories, Quetzalcoatl was a well-built man of stern countenance, white and bearded, and he wore a long tunic.

---

9. One Reed. For Nahua calendrics, see Hassig (2001) and Schroeder, et al. (2010).

10. Ellipses within brackets denote missing text, usually due to a tear or hole in the manuscript.

CHAPTER 2

*Which deals with the origin and arrival of the Tolteca nation,
the kings and leaders they had, their settlement, and events
that occurred in their time*

In this fourth age, the Tolteca nation arrived in this land of Anahuac, which at present is called New Spain. According to their histories, they were exiled from their homeland and, after having sailed along the coasts of various lands down to the South Sea[11] coast of what is now California, they came to a sea they named Huitlapalan—which is now known as the Sea of Cortés—so called because it appeared reddish, in the year they call *çe tecpatl*,[12] which was the year 387 of the incarnation of Christ our Lord. And having sailed along the coast of the land of Xalixco and all the southern coast, they landed at the port of Huatulco. After wandering through various lands, they reached the province of Tochtepec, which lies along the coast of the North Sea.[13] And having explored and surveyed the land, they finally came to the province of Tolantzinco. Along the way, they left behind some of their people to settle in the best places. This Tolteca nation was the third to settle this New Spain, counting the giants as the first and the Ulmecas and Xicalancas as the second.

Once they reached the site at Tolantzinco, they reckoned 104 years had passed since leaving their homeland. They brought with them seven leaders, and during this time they always elected from among these seven the one who would govern them. The first of these was called Tlacomihua, [fol. 3r] although [. . .] called him Acatl. The second was called Chalchiuhmatzin; the third, Heecatl; the fourth, Coatzon; the fifth, Tziuhcoatl; the sixth, Tlapalhuitz; and the seventh and last, Huitz. They eventually settled the city of Tolan, which was the seat of their monarchy and empire because it seemed to be a suitable place and a river passed through it. Seven years after its founding they elected a king and supreme lord, which was the first that they ever had. He was called Chalchiuhtlanetzin or Chalchiuhtlatonac. This occurred in the year that they call *chicome acatl*,[14]

---

11. The Pacific Ocean.
12. One Flint.
13. The Atlantic Ocean, including the Gulf of Mexico.
14. Seven Reed.

which was the year 510 of the incarnation. This king governed fifty-two years, in which time this nation grew and built relationships and friendships with the natives who inhabited the land at the time, and they took them under their rule and authority. He was succeeded by Tlilquechahuac Tlachinoltzin, who began his reign in the year likewise called *chicome acatl*, which was the year 562. He reigned for the same number of years and died in the year 613 of the incarnation, which they call *chiquaçen tochtli*.[15] Huetzin inherited the empire and reigned another fifty-two years, because it was customary among them to reign for periods of fifty-two years; if a king died before completing them, the republic[16] governed. This king Huetzin died in the year 664, likewise called *chiquaçen tochtli*. Totepeuh succeeded him; he reigned the same number of years and died in the year called *macuili calli*,[17] which was the year 716 of the incarnation. At his death he was succeeded by Nacazxoch, who reigned another fifty-two years and died in the year 768, which is also called *macuili calli*, whereupon Tlacomihua inherited the empire. Tlacomihua greatly enhanced and expanded his empire; he built very large and ostentatious buildings, including the Temple of the Frog, which he established as the goddess of water. He reigned fifty-nine years, surpassing and exceeding the custom of his ancestors, and died in the year 826, which they call *matlactli once acatl*.[18] At his death, Queen Xiuhquentzin succeeded him; she reigned four years and died in the year *ome acatl*,[19] which was the year 830. She was succeeded as ruler by Iztaccaltzin, father of Topiltzin, in whose time this nation was destroyed.

---

15. Six Rabbit.

16. In the ancient Roman sense of *res publica*, meaning the state as a whole.

17. Five House.

18. Eleven Reed.

19. Two Reed.

🌿   CHAPTER 3

Which deals with the life and deeds of Iztaccaltzin and Topiltzin,
last monarchs of the Toltecas, in whose time their empire ended

Iztaccaltzin assumed control of the empire and reigned for fifty-two years, which was the time ordained by his forebears. During this period, he had a love affair with Quetzalxochitzin, wife of a gentleman named Papantzin, scion of the royal house. With this noblewoman, the king had Topiltzin. Although born of adultery, he succeeded to the empire in the year 882 of the incarnation of Christ our Lord, which is also called *ome acatl*.[20] For this reason, some of his vassal kings and lords rose up against him, some aspiring to the empire themselves—believing themselves to be more legitimate and worthy than he—and others out of revenge for the adultery. The most notable of these were Coanacotzi, Huetzin, and Mixoiotzin, kings and lords of the provinces that lie on the coast of the North Sea. And so it happened that, having reigned the aforementioned fifty-two years, King Iztaccaltzin had his son Topiltzin acknowledged as emperor. Among the kings and lords that attended the ceremony were several of his allies, such as Iztacquauhtzin and Maxtlatzin.

After Topiltzin [fol. 3v] ascended to power, there were great [. . .] its destruction, and certain predictions and prophecies foretold by his elders came to pass. Among others, one held that when a king whose hair stood up from the front of his head to the nape of his neck like a crest of feathers ruled, then the Tolteca monarchy would end; also the rabbits in this period would grow horns like deer, and the *huitzitzilin* bird[21] would grow a spur like a turkey cock. All of this happened, for indeed King Topiltzin's hair was as described, and the aforementioned changes to the rabbits and *huitzitziles* were seen during his reign. Other wonders occurred that caused great fright and agitation in the king, and he gathered the priests and diviners to interpret these signs for him. According to the histories, after they told him that they signaled his destruction, he summoned his stewards and gave them his treasures, the greatest of the age, to safeguard them in the province of Quiahuiztlan, because he was wary of the kings that opposed him. After the wonders and omens, the land became barren and hunger set in; the majority

---

20. Two Reed.
21. Hummingbird.

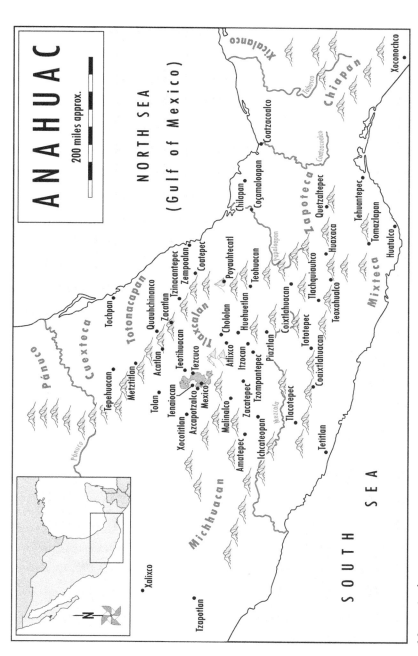

MAP 2. Anahuac.

of the people died, the provisions in their granaries were eaten by weevils and worms; and many other calamities and miseries came down from the heavens, as if it were raining fire. The drought was so terrible that it lasted twenty-six years, causing the rivers and springs to run dry.

Seeing Topiltzin's lack of troops and support, the kings that opposed him marched against him with a powerful army. They managed to capture many cities in a short time, ultimately taking Tolan, capital of the empire. Although King Topiltzin fled Tolan with all of his people, within a few days his enemies caught up to them and began killing them. The first to die was his father, old King Iztaccaltzin, and with him Lady Quetzalxochitl, both of whom, according to the histories, were nearly 150 years old. In the province of Totolapan, they caught the two kings Iztacquauhtzin and Maxtla (confederates of Topiltzin), where they suffered a miserable death, despite struggling to defend themselves. King Topiltzin was lost and never heard from again. Of his two sons, only one, Prince Pochotl, escaped. He was saved by his nursemaid, named Tochcueie, who raised him in the deserts of Nonoalco. The few Toltecas that remained took refuge in the rugged mountain ranges and among the reeds of Lake Colhuacan. This was the end of the Tolteca Empire, which lasted 572 years. Seeing it in such ruin, the kings that had come to subjugate it went back to their provinces, for, though victorious, they were exhausted and had lost the majority of their armies to starvation. And the same calamity ravaged their territories, because there was widespread drought and barren land. It would seem that God allowed this nation to be punished in every way, since hardly any survived on either side.

These Toltecas were highly skilled in all the mechanical arts; they built great and noteworthy cities, including Tolan, Teotihuacan, Chololan, Tolantzinco, and many others, as their grand ruins attest. They wore long tunics in the style of the robes that the Japanese use, they wore sandals as footwear, and some wore a style of hat made of straw or palm leaf. They were not great warriors, but they were very dedicated to good public governance. They were great idolaters, specifically worshiping the gods of the sun and the moon. According [fol. 4r] to the aforementioned histories, they came from the west, sailing along the coast of the South Sea. Their complete and utter destruction occurred in the year 959 of the incarnation of Christ our Lord, which is called *çe tecpatl*,[22] when the Roman John XII was pontiff of the Church of God; Otto, first of this name, was emperor of Germany; and don García was king of Castile.

---

22. One Flint.

🌿 CHAPTER 4

*Which deals with the arrival of the Great Chichimeca Xolotl
and how he settled the lands of the Toltecas*

Five years had passed since the Toltecas had been destroyed, and the land was
uninhabited, when the Great Chichimeca Xolotl arrived to settle it, having learned
from his scouts of its destruction. This was in the year 963 of the incarnation
of Christ our Lord, called *macuili tecpatl*.[23] He set out from the north, from the
region and province that they call Chicomoztoc. He crossed the borders into
the lands of the Toltecas until he came to the city of Tolan, seat of their empire.
There he found very large ruins, uninhabited and without people, and so chose
not to stay in Tolan. Instead he moved on with his people, always sending scouts
ahead to see if they could find anyone who might have escaped the destruction
and ruin of this nation and to locate the best sites and places to settle and live. He
reached a place called Tenaiocan Oztopolco, a place of many caves and caverns
(which were this nation's most common dwellings), temperate, with good air and
water, facing east, close to the great lake that now is called the Lake of Mexico.
He and the highest-ranking captains of his army agreed to establish his court
and principal residence there. Having peacefully taken possession of all the
land contained within the boundaries of the Tolteca Empire for himself and
for his captains—the most important of whom were six lords called Acatomatl,
Quauhatlapatl, Cozcaquauh, Mitliztac, Tecpatl, and Iztacquauhtli—he settled it
with the people of his army. None of the most powerful princes in this new world
before or since ever had an army as large as his, for according to the histories,
excluding women and children, it numbered more than a million. This great
army first settled the area that lies within the ring formed by the mountain towns
of Xocotitlan, Chiuhnauhtecatl, Malinalocan, Itzocan, Atlixcahuacan, Temalacatitlan, Poiauhtlan, Xiuhtecuhtitlan, Zacatlan, Tenamitec, Quauhchinanco,
Tototepec, Metztitlan, Quachquetzaloian, Atotonilco, Quahuacan, and back again
to Xocotitlan. In all, it is more than two hundred leagues[24] in circumference. He

---

23. Five Flint.
24. Although the league was commonly used to talk about distance, the value assigned to it
varied widely. The official Spanish league, which was also used in New Spain, was equivalent
to 4.2 km or 2.6 mi (Garza Martínez, 2012). Assuming this equivalency, Xolotl's domain
had a circumference of 838 km or 521 mi and, therefore, an area of 55,883 km² or 21,576 mi².

allowed the few Toltecas who had escaped destruction to remain in the places where they had settled and reestablished themselves, each with his clan. This was in Chapoltepec, Tlatzalan, Tepexoxoma, Totolapan, Quauhquecholan, and up to the North Sea coast in Toçapan, Tochpan, Tzicuhcoac, and Xicotepec, and also in Chololan, although some of them [fol. 4v] did not stop until they reached Nicarahua[25] and other remote lands where the drought and catastrophe were not as extreme, and there they settled.

This Great Chichimecatl brought Queen Tomiauh as his wife. They had a son, Prince Nopaltzin, who was already a young man when he came to these parts and one of the highest-ranking captains in his army. They also had two daughters, the Princesses Cuetlaxxochitzin and Tzihuacxochitzin, who were born in Tenaiocan where Xolotl had his court. He came from the very ancient lineage of kings called the Teochichimecas, whose empire and domain lay to the north. Among these kings were Nequametl, Namacuix, and many others, as named in the history of the Chichimeca kings and the song composed by the princes of Mexico, Xiuhcozcatzin and Itzcoatzin, which is titled "Song of the History of the Chichimeca Kings." (They have been called Chichimeca from the beginning. This name is derived from their own language, and it means "eagles," rather than what it sounds like in the Mexican language. It should also not be read as "sucklers," which is a crude interpretation of the paintings and glyphs, but rather as "children of the Chichimecas born of Tolteca women."[26] The historians used the lip glyph, which makes the *te* sound, in order to render *tepilhuan* [the children].)[27]

This great pioneer had been establishing settlements for a little more than twenty years when another six captains from his nation began arriving with many people. Following Xolotl, each captain arrived one after the other in successive years. The first of them was called Xiyotecua; the second, Xiiotzoncua; the third, Zacatitechcochi; the fourth, Huihuaxtin; the fifth, Tepotzotecua; and the sixth and last, Itzcuintecua. He received them and sent them to settle the lands around Tepetlaoztoc. The Toltecas who had escaped destruction and calamity had reestablished themselves and made Nauhyotzin their principal leader. He resided in Colhuacan and later became Prince Pochotl's father-in-law. The Great

---

25. Nicaragua.

26. The Nahuatl verb *chichi* means "to suckle." However, the etymology of "Chichimeca" remains uncertain.

27. The Nahuatl word for "lip" is *tentli*.

FIGURE 3. Xolotl and Nopaltzin (based on the Codex Xolotl, plate 1).

Chichimeca Xolotl decided to demand of them a certain amount of tribute and that they recognize him as supreme and universal lord of this land of Anahuac. Nauhyotzin, on behalf of his nation, responded that the land had belonged to his elders, and they had never recognized nor paid tribute to any foreign lord. And although few and diminished, they intended to preserve their liberty and not bow to anyone, with the sole exception being the sun and the rest of their gods. Seeing their determination not to submit peacefully, Xolotl turned to arms. He dispatched Prince Nopaltzin, his son, with a modest army (fig. 3). Only a small force was necessary, because his opponents, although they gathered as many people as they could, were not as accomplished in warfare as the Chichimecas. The battle took place on the lake and in the marshes of Colhuacan, and although the Culhuas[28] had a strategic advantage because they fought in canoes, they were

---

28. Colhuacan means "place of the Culhuas." In Nahuatl, there is no phonemic distinction between *o* and *u*.

quickly defeated and destroyed by Prince Nopaltzin. After he conquered them, he reinstated Achitometl as ruler of the Culhuas—which is what those of the Tolteca lineage were called at the time—provided that they pay a certain amount of tribute each year to the Great Chichimeca Xolotl, his father. All this occurred in the year 984 of the incarnation of Christ our Lord, which they call 13 *calli*.[29]

---

29. House.

🌿 CHAPTER 5

*Which deals with the arrival of the Aculhuas, Tepanecas, and
Otomies; how Xolotl received them and gave them lordships
and lands on which to settle, marrying the two leaders to his
two daughters, and the children that they had; and likewise
the marriage of Prince Nopaltzin and the children that he had*

Xolotl had been establishing settlements in this land of Anahuac for forty-seven
years—fifty-two years since the final destruction of the Toltecas—when the
Aculhua people arrived, in the year 1011 of the incarnation of Christ our Lord.
They had departed from the outermost lands of the province of Michhuacan
and were of the same nation as the Chichimecas Michhuaque, although they
came divided in three groups, each of which had a different language and its own
leader and lord. Those who were called Tepanecas had Acolhua, who was the
most important of the three, as their leader. The second was called Chiconquautli,
leader and lord of the Otomies, who were the most foreign of the three with a
very strange and different language, and according to their histories appear to
have come from the other side of that inland sea that is known as the Vermilion
Sea,[30] whwich is where the Californias now lie. The third was called Tzontecomatl,
leader and lord of the Aculhuas proper. They appeared before Xolotl in order
that he should admit them into his domain and give them lands on which to
settle. Thoroughly satisfied that these leaders were of very ancient lineage, he was
immensely pleased. Not only did he admit them, but he also gave them lands for
their vassals to settle. And he married two of them to his two daughters, giving
[fol. 5r] them also towns and dominions. He married Princess Cuextlaxxochi to
Acolhua, and with her, Xolotl gave him the city of Azcapotzalco to be the seat
of his domain. He married the other princess, Tzihuacxochi, to Chiconquautli,
and he gave him Xaltocan to be the seat of the Otomi nation, as it was for many
years. To Tzontecomatl, captain of the Aculhuas, he gave Coatlichan to be the

---

30. The Gulf of California, also known as the Sea of Cortés.

seat of his domain and married him to Quatetzin, daughter of Chalchiuhtlatonac, lord of the Tolteca nation and one of the first lords of the province of Chalco.

Acolhua, first lord of Azcapotzalco and the Tepanecas, had three sons with Princess Cuetlaxxochitzin. The first was called Teçoçomoc, who, at the end of his father's days, inherited the lordship. The second was called Hepcoatzin, who later became the first lord of the Tlatelolcas; and the youngest, Acamapichtli, first lord of the Tenochcas—which is the Mexica nation—who were the last to arrive and settle. Chiconquautli, lord of Xaltocan and of the Otomi nation, had three children with Princess Tzihuacxochitzin. The first, a daughter, was named Tzipacxochitzin and married Chalchiuhtotomotzin, first lord of Chalco Atenco; the second, a son, Macuilcoatl Ohopantecuhtli; the third, a daughter, was named Quetzalmapantzin and married Tzonpantecuhtli, and they became the first lords of the province of Metztitlan. Tzontecomatl Tecuhtli had only one son, who was named Tlacoxin and who married a daughter of Cozcaquauh, one of the first lords and settlers of the province of Chalco. At around the same time, Prince Nopaltzin married Azcalxochitzin, legitimate[31] daughter of Prince Pochotl and granddaughter of Topiltzin, the last king of the Toltecas. This union and marriage ushered in perpetual peace and accord, and they began to intermarry among one another. He had three sons with this noblewoman. The first was Prince Tlotzin Pochotl; the second, Huixaquen Tochintecuhtli; and the third and last, Coxanatzin Atencatl. Before these, he also had an illegitimate son named Tenancacalitzin.

---

31. The Nahua did not distinguish between legitimate and illegitimate offspring. Alva Ixtlilxochitl dubs "legitimate" the children born to the highest-ranking wife.

CHAPTER 6

*Of how the Great Chichimeca gave settlements and domains
to other lords*

Before the arrival of the Aculhuas, none of the captains and lords whom the Great
Chichimeca brought with him had their own particular domains, because he
kept them occupied moving between provinces settling the land. But after the
Great Chichimeca had made large and splendid grants to the Aculhua lords, who
were foreigners, it was finally time to reward his own lords. Hence he decided,
that same year, to allocate domains and estates to all of them in accordance
with their status and merits. Three of the six lords that he brought with him,
who were Acatomatl, Quauhatlapatl, and Cozcaquauh, were to be—together
with Chalchiuhtlatonac, a Tolteca nobleman—lords of the province of Chalco,
a most fertile land, full of all the necessities for human life. To the fourth, Mitliztac, he allocated the province of Tepeyacac. He made the other two, Tecpatl
and Quauhtliztac,[32] lords of the province of Maçahuacan. And he sent his two
grandsons Huixaquen and Coxanatzin, sons of Prince Nopaltzin who were
outside of the line of succession, to Zacatlan and Tenamitec to be lords of all
the lands beyond the aforementioned ring, extending from the boundaries of
the lands of the Cuexteca[33] up to those of the Mixteca, a domain appropriate to
their status, because it included many and very large provinces (fig. 4). [fol. 5v]
Moreover, they owed no vassalage or tributes to the empire, with the exception
of paying homage, attending court when summoned, and sending people to
support the empire in times of war. All the other aforementioned lords were
obliged to offer tribute and fealty. The daughters and sons-in-law of the Great
Chichimeca enjoyed the same privileges and favors.

In the same year, Xolotl fenced off a large forest in the mountains of Tezcuco,
which he stocked with many deer, rabbits, and hares. And in the middle of it,
he built a *cu*, which was like a temple, in which he or Prince Nopaltzin or his
grandson Prince Pochotl offered the first prize of the morning hunt as victim
and sacrifice to the sun, whom they called father, and to mother earth; this was
their form of idolatry, and they did not recognize any other idol as god. Here

---

32. In chapter 4, this lord's name appears as Iztacquauhtli.
33. The Huasteca.

FIGURE 4. Xolotl and his vassals (based on the Codex Xolotl, plate 1).

they also obtained sustenance and skins for their garments. This enclosure was maintained by four provinces, which were Tepepolco, Cempoalan, Tolantzinco, and Tolquauhiocan.

He gave Prince Tlotzin, his grandson, the imperial rents paid by the provinces of Chalco, Tlalnahuac, and Tlalhuic. He also gave him all the lands from the snow-capped volcano to the end of the Tezcuco mountain range, which run from the valleys of La Campiña[34] in the north down to the lands of the Mixteca in the south, including all of its plains and lakes. He established his seat and court in a place called Tlatzalantlalanoztoc. He married Pachxochitzin, daughter of Quauhatlapatl, one of the aforementioned lords of the province of Chalco, with whom he had six children. The first two were daughters; the third—and first son—was Prince Quinatzin Tlaltecatzin; the second son was Nopaltzin Cuetlachihui; the third son, Tochintecuhtli, who came to be the first lord of the city and province of Huexotzinco; and the fourth and last son was Xiuhquetzaletecuhtli, first lord of the city and province of Tlaxcalan.

---

34. The region around Otumba, Teotihuacan, and northern Aculhuacan.

🌿 CHAPTER 7

Of other things that happened in the time of this great monarch
Xolotl until his death

Tlacoxin, son of Tzontecomatl, lord of Coatlichan and of the Aculhuas, married Malinalxochitzin, eldest of the two daughters of Prince Tlotzin Pochotl. With her he had two children: the first, a son, Huetzin and the second, a daughter, Chichimecazihuatzin. Seeing that he was related to the imperial house and his obligations were very great and his estate and domain very small, he decided to visit the Great Chichimeca Xolotl and request some favors for Xolotl's great-great-grandson Huetzin. He presented his request while Xolotl was at his retreat near the lake. The Great Chichimeca granted Huetzin, a youth of few years at the time, many favors, including the province of Tepetlaoztoc, which had been settled by those six leaders who came soon after Xolotl arrived in this land, had been paying tribute and vassalage for eighty-one years, and were members of Xolotl's private council. In this way he enlarged his domains. The Chichimecas paid tribute in the form of rabbits, hares, deer, wild animal hides, and henequen cloth.[35] Prince Nopaltzin, who was there with his father at this time, ordered that his great-grandson Huetzin marry Atototzin—the eldest of the two princesses, daughters of Achitometzin, first king and lord of the Culhuas—and that the younger, who was called Ilancueitl, marry his nephew Acamapichtli, son of Acolhua, first lord of Azcapotzalco and king of the Tepanecas. Both of the princesses were nieces of Princess Azcalxochitl, his wife. These orders were carried out right away. This happened in the year 1050 of the incarnation of Christ our Lord, which is called *çe acatl*.[36]

The people of the province of Tepetlaoztoc felt oppressed [fol. 6r] under the lordship of the young Huetzin, and although they still rendered the tribute that they were obliged to give, it felt like a heavy burden, especially to Yacanex, who was their principal leader. Yacanex grew so shameless that he committed two very insolent acts. First, upon learning of the marriage of his Lord Huetzin with Princess Atototzin, he objected and demanded her for himself with violence and

---

35. We have translated *mantas* as "cloth" throughout the text unless there is a clear, more specific application for the cloth, such as tapestry, canopy, or cloak.
36. One Reed.

threats against her father, King Achitometzin, which infuriated the king and his entire court. The king responded that he could not break his promise to Prince Nopaltzin. And while they argued back and forth, the princess was sent to her husband, Huetzin, for fear that this tyrant Yacanex would seize her by force of arms, because he had men and weapons at the ready. Second, he completely refused obeisance to Huetzin, his lord, by inciting an uprising among most of the Chichimecas of the province of Tepetlaoztoc. In order to quell the disturbances and unrest and avoid war, the Great Chichimeca Xolotl, in the year 1062—which is called 13 *acatl*[37]—was forced to summon Tochintecuhtli, son of Quetzalmaçatl, lord of Quahuacan, a brave and very skilled warrior, along with many Chichimeca clans. As soon as Tochintecuhtli arrived, Xolotl ordered him to go to Xaltocan, promising to reward him if he followed his instructions exactly. Along the way, Tochintecuhtli was to marry Xolotl's great-granddaughter Tomiauh, daughter of Opantecuhtli, who had recently been installed as the lord of Xaltocan and king of the Otomies. Next, Tochintecuhtli was to go to Huexotla and deploy his army in the defense and protection of Huetzin; Tochintecuhtli would henceforth be lord of all those lands and of Teotihuacan and other places. He was also to attempt to capture and kill Yacanex and his allies, without bloodshed if possible, and if not, to help Huetzin and kill them by force of arms. Tochintecuhtli did all these things and took control of Huexotla in the following year, 1064, which is called *çe tecpatl*.[38]

Prince Quinatzin moved his court and residence to Oztoticpac, which is in Tezcuco, and began to settle this city, leaving his father behind in Tlatzalan. He did this, first, because it seemed to him to be the best place, and second, to protect his nephew Huetzin. This was necessary because, two years earlier, the prince had built three large enclosures, including one below Huexotla near the lake and another in the city of Tezcuco. These two had been set up for planting maize and other seeds that the Culhuas and Toltecas used. The third enclosure, in the town of Tepetlaoztoc, was for deer, rabbits, and hares. He had placed two Chichimeca captains in charge of them, one called Ocotoch and the other Coacuech. And though they had been happy to tend the third enclosure, the first two were for farming, which they were not accustomed to doing and found to be a very heavy burden. Therefore, they had allied themselves with the tyrant Yacanex and other rebels, compelling Prince Quinatzin and his nephew Huetzin to join forces with

---

37. Reed.
38. One Flint.

Tochintecuhtli, first lord of Huexotla, and attack the enemy in two places. First, Huetzin set upon Yacanex where he was holed up, which is where the town of Chiauhtla is now, and they fought a very fierce battle in which many people on both sides died, until the rebels were vanquished. And their leader Yacanex fled to Panuco without stopping, because he intended to take refuge in the mountains where they enjoyed some support. At the same time, Prince Quinatzin routed and killed many of the rebels with his fighters, although their leader Ocotoch, one of the two aforementioned, escaped and followed Yacanex. After that, the land was peaceful, and in the remote provinces everyone was busy settling and increasing the population.

In this same year, Acolhua, lord of Azcapotzalco, fought with Cozcaquauh, one of the rebel Chichimecas who had incited the province of Tepotzotlan, [fol. 6v] which was part of Acolhua's domains. After Cozcaquauh was defeated, he escaped, fleeing in the same direction as the others. These battles took place 104 years after the final destruction of the Toltecas—they were the first wars the Chichimecas fought among themselves—in the year 1075 of the incarnation of Christ our Lord, which they call *matlactli omei tecpatl*.[39] Xolotl, great monarch and patriarch, died in his city and court of Tenaiocan, in the 112th year of his reign, 117 years since the final destruction of the Toltecas, leaving this new world in the greatest prosperity, peace, and harmony that it had ever seen. They performed very grand funeral rites in his honor, and his body was buried in one of the caves of his residence. The majority of the princes and lords of his empire were in attendance.

---

39. Thirteen Flint.

🌿 CHAPTER 8

Of how Prince Nopaltzin succeeded to the empire and the things
that happened in his time

After the funeral rites of the Great Xolotl, all the princes and lords pledged
themselves to Prince Nopaltzin as their supreme and universal lord, as the one
who rightfully ascended to the imperial throne. And he governed it so well that in
the thirty-two years in which he reigned, no lord dared disobey him. Rather, he
ruled them with a firm hand, and the empire gained much in wealth, stature, and
dominion; for at this time, almost all the lands of the Chichimecas, Cuextecas,
and Michhuaques and the entire coasts of the South and North Seas were settled.
During this time, Calcozametzin became king of the Culhuas. He was the third
to ascend, installed and confirmed by Nopaltzin. In addition to keeping the laws
of his forebears, Nopaltzin decreed the following: First, that, under penalty of
death, no one should clear land with fire in the fields or mountains without his
permission and only in necessary cases. Second, that no one should take any
game caught in another's net or ever hunt without permission, under penalty of
forfeiting one's bow and arrows. Third, that no one take the game shot by another,
even if found dead in the field. Fourth, that, under penalty of death, where the
boundaries of hunting grounds have been marked, no one should remove the
markers. Fifth, that adulterers should have their throats shot through with arrows
until dead, men as well as women. And besides these, he decreed and established
other laws that were suitable for the good government of the empire at the time.

His grandson, Prince Quinatzin Tlaltocatzin, who had his seat and court [fol.
7r] in the city of Tezcuco, married Quauhcihuatzin, daughter of Tochintecuhtli,
first lord of Huexotla. Quinatzin had five sons with her: the first was called
Chicomacatzin; the second, Memexoltzin or, according to others, Memeloctzin;
the third, Matzicoltzin; the fourth, Tochpilli; the fifth and youngest of all was
Prince Techotlalatzin, who inherited the empire for reasons which are explained
below. Huetzin, who married Princess Atototzin, as mentioned above, had seven
children with her. The first, a son, was Acolmiztli, who succeeded him in the
lordship; the second, a daughter, was called Coaxochitzin; the third, a daughter,
Coaçanac; the fourth, a son, Quecholtecpantzin Quauhtlachtli; the fifth, a son,
Tlatonal Tetliopeuhqui; the sixth, a son, Memexoltzin Itztlolinqui; and the
seventh and last, a son, Chicomacatzin Matzicol, who went with Tlacatlanex to

Huexotzinco; Memexol went to Tlaxcalan. Tochintecuhtli, first lord of Huexotla, had five children with Tomiauhtzin. The first, a son, was called Matzicoltzin; the second, a daughter, Quauhcihuatzin, who was queen of Tezcuco; the third, a son, Quiauhtzin; the fourth, a daughter, Nenetzin, who married Acolmiztli, lord of Coatlichan; and the fifth and last, a son, was called Iaotl. And the second son of Acolhua, called Hepcoatzin, married Chichimecazoatzin—sister of Huetzin, lord of Coatlichan—with whom he had two children; the first, a son, was Quaquauh-pitzahuac, who became the second lord of the Tlatelolcas; and the second and last, a daughter, married Chalchiuhtlatonac, her first cousin, who became the first lord of Colhuacan. Acamapichtli, youngest of the children of Acolhua, had three sons with Princess Ilancueitl; the first was called Huitzilihuitzin, second lord of the Tenochcas and king of the Culhuas; the second was Chalchiuhtlatonac, who was the first lord of Coyohuacan, as mentioned; and the third and last was Xiuhtlatonac, who was killed by Huepantecatl. All of these lineages originated in the time that Nopaltzin reigned; it is worth mentioning these lineages because from them came the most illustrious people of New Spain.

At the end of Nopaltzin's reign, most of them resided in the forest of Tezcuco, which was by this time known as Xoloteopan, which means temple of Xolotl, where he gave his son Prince Tlotzin many helpful documents about how he was to reign and govern the empire—which was strong and counted many powerful kings and lords as its subjects—reminding him of the greatness of his grandfather Xolotl and the rest of his forebears. And every time that he did this, he was overcome with emotion and tears filled his eyes. Nopaltzin died in the city of Tenaiocan in the year 1107 of the incarnation of Christ our Lord, which they call *macuili acatl*.[40] His body was entombed alongside his father's. The empire was filled with much sorrow and grief, and many lords attended his funeral rites and obsequies.

---

40. Five Reed.

[fol. 7v]

🌿 CHAPTER 9

Which deals with the life of Tlotzin and the things that happened
during the years of his reign

After Tlotzin was acknowledged as ruler by the empire, one of his foremost
concerns was farming the land. During his grandfather Xolotl's lifetime, he lived
mostly in the province of Chalco, where he realized how necessary maize and
other seeds and vegetables were to sustain human life, due to the contact he had
there with the Culhuas and Toltecas, since his mother was their natural ruler.
Specifically, his tutor and teacher had been Tecpoio Achcauhtli, who resided with
his clan on the hill of Xico and from whom, among other things, he learned how
to farm. As a person accustomed to this, he ordered all the land to be tilled and
sowed. And although many of the Chichimecas thought this was a good idea
and set to work, others, who still followed the coarse ways of their ancestors, left
for the mountains of Metztitlan and Tototepec and other remote areas, without
daring to take up arms as Yacanex and his allies had done. And from this time
on, all the land was farmed; they sowed and harvested maize and other seeds
and vegetables as well as cotton for their clothing in the warmer regions.

Their way of pledging fealty to and crowning the Chichimeca emperors was
to crown them with a mossy plant they call *pachxochitl*, which grows in the hills,
and to adorn them with bundles of golden eagle feathers set into little hoops
made of gold and jewels, which were called *coçoiahualol*, together with another
two bundles of green feathers, which were called *tecpilotl*; all of them were tied
to the head with red straps made of deer hide. And after adorning their heads in
this manner—which was done by the elders and oldest lords of the empire—they
went out to certain fields where many wild animals of all types were corralled,
and they fought them, displaying countless skills as befitted noblemen. And
once they had killed and butchered the wild animals, run and jumped around,
shot arrows at each other, and done other things to entertain themselves after
their fashion, they went to their palaces, which were large caves, where they
ate all manner of game roasted over a grill, and not, as some believe, dried in
the sun, because the Chichimecas had always used fire. And their law dictated
that when they took possession of a piece of land, they were to light fires on the

FIGURE 5. Chichimecas and Toltecas (Quinatzin Map, top panel). *Photo courtesy of the Bibliothèque nationale de France.*

highest peaks and mountains. According to the histories, Xolotl did this at the time when he took possession of this Anahuac. The fires in the mountains and high peaks also served to signal with smoke when they were at war.

They lived in clans, and those that did not dwell in caves, which was their most common type of residence, made their huts out of straw. Each group ate together the game that they hunted, but the hides belonged to the hunter (fig. 5). They made their clothing with these hides, which they softened and cured for this purpose, wearing them with the fur turned in during periods of cold and, during the rainy season when it was warm, with the fur facing out. The kings and lords, however, [fol. 8r] usually wore beneath their hides certain undergarments made of a fine henequen fiber or cotton for those who had the means. They married only one wife, and she was not to be a relative in any degree, although afterwards, their descendants married their first cousins and aunts, a custom they borrowed from the Toltecas. Finally, they were the most bellicose nation that this new world has ever had, for which reason they lorded over all the rest.

Tlotzin Pochotl, having reigned thirty-six years, died in the year 1141 of the incarnation, in the one they call *yei tochtli*,[41] and his body was entombed in the same place as his father and grandfather; princes and lords attended his burial and funeral rites. For burial, immediately after death they would place the body in a sitting position with the knees to the chest, dress it in the royal vestments and insignia, and bring it to the throne room to be seated. The deceased's children and relatives would then enter, and after having spoken to the body with tears and sorrow, they would remain with it until the time came to take it to the burial cave. There a round hole would have been dug more than a fathom deep into which they would place the body and cover it with earth. This prince was the last to have his court at Tenaiocan. His son Quinatzin chose not to live there, because by this time he had constructed many buildings and dwellings in the city of Tezcuco, where he resided and had his court. Instead, he left Tenaiocan to his uncle Tenancacalitzin, making him its lord.

---

41. Three Rabbit.

🌿 CHAPTER 10

Of the ascension of Quinatzin to the lordship of the empire,
the arrival of the Mexicas, and the children of Acolmiztli, lord
of Coatlichan

The city of Tezcuco was originally settled in the time of the Toltecas, and it was called Catemhaco, but it was destroyed and ruined with the rest of the Tolteca cities. Afterward, the Chichimeca kings went about rebuilding it, especially Quinatzin, who greatly improved it and remained there, making it the capital and court of the empire. After the arrival of the Chichimecas, they named it Tetzicoco,[42] which means "stopping place," as indeed it was, for nearly all the nations of New Spain settled there. Having buried his father in Tenaiocan, Quinatzin Tlaltecatzin came to Tezcuco with all of the lords who attended the funeral rites. Along with other lords that came later, they received him and pledged themselves to him as supreme lord. He remained in Tezcuco from that time forward.

In the same year that Tlotzin died, the Mexicas arrived in the place where the city of Mexico is now located, which was within the territory of Acolhua, lord of Azcapotzalco. They had wandered many years through diverse lands and provinces and spent time in Aztlan, which is in the furthest reaches of Xalixco, from where they came. According to the paintings and glyphs of the ancient history, they were of Tolteca descent and of the line of Hezitin, a nobleman who fled with his people and their families during the time of the destruction of the Toltecas from Chapoltepec, which was later destroyed. He passed through the kingdom of Michhuacan, until he got to the province of Aztlan, as mentioned. There he died, and his son Oçelopan took his place. And he fathered Aztatl, and this Aztatl fathered Oçelopan, second of this name, who remembered the land of his ancestors and decided to return to it, taking with him those of his nation, who by this time were called the Mexitin. He led them jointly with [fol. 8v] Izcahui, Cuexpalatl, Iopi, and, according to others, Aztatl and Acatl. A sister

---

42. The etymology of Tetzcoco is uncertain. According to mestizo historian Juan Bautista de Pomar, whose writings were among Alva Ixtlilxochitl's sources, the word *tetzcotl* was of Chichimeca origin and its true meaning had been lost (Pomar 1975, 4). The elements commonly used in pictorial documents to represent the altepetl's name, a stone (*tetl*) and a pot (*comitl*), appear to have had phonetic, rather than etymological, value.

of his, a manly woman called Matlalatl, also went with them. They reached their destination, after various and sundry things happened to them on their journey, which the histories recount. Huitzilopochtli, whom they carried as their specific idol, ruled them through his priests.

To avoid the reoccurrence of their past calamities and to obtain the protection of the king of Azcapotzalco, in whose lands they began to settle, they asked him to give them someone to govern them in his name. He gave them two of his sons, because they were already divided into two groups, one called Tenochcas and the other Tlatelolcas. The groups took their names from the places in which they settled, because the Tenochcas found an eagle eating a snake on top of a nopal that had grown up between some rocks, from which they took the etymology of their name.[43] The Tlatelolcas found an island with a mound of sand in the middle of it;[44] Acolhua gave them Hepcoatzin as their lord and leader. And to the Tenochcas he gave Acamapichtli. Both of them were his sons, and they were the first lords of the Mexicas, and through them the Mexicas were ennobled and their power grew. Finding themselves in this position, they were stirred to take revenge on those who had offended them, such as the Culhuas, who although they were of the same nation, had been very antagonistic toward them. And so they attacked the city of Colhuacan before dawn and sacked it; the residents were unable to defend it. The second year after their founding, they went to war with Tenancacalitzin, lord of Tenaiocan, though they were unable to defeat him. Seeing that his own nephews—which the Mexica lords were—had defied him, he decided to leave for the northern lands of his ancestors. From this time on, relatives began to usurp one another's kingdoms; the kings of Azcapotzalco and those of their house and clan were the first tyrants. The Mexicas expanded their domains around those of the Tepanecas up to the province of Atotonilco. Acolmiztli, lord of Coatlichan, had four children with his wife Nenetzin. The first, a son, was called Coxcox, who inherited the kingdom of the Culhuas; the second, a son, Huitzilihuitzin; the third, a son, Moçocomatzin, who inherited the lordship of Coatlichan; the fourth and last, a daughter, was Tozquentzin, who married Techotlalatzin, who was later Chichimeca emperor.

---

43. The glyph usually associated with Tenochtitlan is a prickly-pear cactus (*nochtli*) on top of a stone (*tetl*) and, while there is some debate about whether the glyph elements have phonetic or etymological value, the name is commonly taken to mean "at the place near rock-cactus fruit."

44. Tlatelolco literally means "mound-shaped place," from *tlatelolli*, "something made in the shape of a mound," and the locative particle -*co*.

❧ CHAPTER 11

Of the civil wars among the Chichimecas and others that
occurred during the reign of Quinatzin

If Tlotzin took particular care to farm the land, Quinatzin's efforts during his reign yielded greater results, as he compelled the Chichimecas not only to farm, but also to settle and build cities in the manner and style of the Toltecas, bringing them out of their rustic and wild way of life. This infuriated many of the Chichimecas. Seeing that the four eldest of the king's five children—whose names are mentioned above—along with other noblemen and high-ranking people, were of the same opinion, they revolted. And the first to commit this act of insolence were those who lived in Poiauhtlan. They burned many fields and then allied themselves with the tyrant Yacanex (mentioned above), who had been hiding with other rebels in the northern lands. They incited those of the provinces of Metztitlan, Tototepec, Tepepolco, and other places of less importance to rebel as well. Quinatzin was unable to prevent them from amassing a large army, with which they marched on the city of Tezcuco and besieged it from four sides, which were Chiuhnauhtlan and Zoltepec and the mountains of Tezcuco.

As quickly as he could, Quinatzin gathered his people and divided them into four squadrons, appointing captains to lead them. He sent Tochintecuhtli against Yacanex, who made his [fol. 9r] camp in Chiuhnauhtlan. He gave another squadron to his brother Nopaltzin Cuetlachihuitzin, who was to go to Zoltepec, where Ocotoch, the other tyrant, was encamped with some of the people from the provinces of Metztitlan and Tototepec. And Huetzin, lord of Coatlichan, was to go with another squadron to Patlachiuhcan, where the majority of the troops from the provinces of Tototepec and Metztitlan were encamped. And Quinatzin led another squadron himself and went to a place in the mountains called Quauhximalco, where some people from the province of Metztitlan and some from Tototepec were encamped; he was accompanied by people from Tepepolco, led by their governor Zacatitechcochi. Everyone began fighting at the same time. And although the tyrants did everything possible to achieve their aim, they were vanquished and destroyed. Quinatzin and those of his army killed most of them, and the rest fled, retreating until Quinatzin reached a mountain region called Teapazco on the far side of the province of Tepepolco. Huetzin, Nopaltzin, and Tochintecuhtli enjoyed similar victories. Tochintecuhtli himself killed the old tyrant Yacanex, and Nopaltzin killed Ocotoch, although he was unlucky in this battle because, as he was chasing his enemies, drunk with victory, troops from the province of Tolantzinco lay in wait and ambushed him. They seized him and killed him, while his men were powerless to defend him.

Gathering all of the squadrons, Quinatzin sent them to punish the aforementioned rebellious provinces, which surrendered and placed themselves at the mercy of the emperor. The Chichimecas who escaped from the hands of Quinatzin went to the northern mountains, where they became bandits, recognizing neither king nor lord, as they remain to this day. And all those who were captured, most prominently the sons of Quinatzin, other noblemen, and those from Poiauhtlan, were exiled to the provinces of Tlaxcalan and Huexotzinco so they would be ruled by Quinatzin's brothers, who were the lords there. Although exiled as punishment, they were very well received by their uncles and became lords of those provinces, as did their descendants after them.

In this same period, Coxcox succeeded to the kingdom of the Culhuas due to the death of Calcozametzin, who had been king, as mentioned. He fought wars with the Mexicas over past grievances and over the boundaries between their lands. He came to the aid of the high priest of the city of Chololan, named Iztacima, whom he was obliged to protect, because those of Quecholan, Chalchiuhapan, and other Chichimecas who were settled nearby had been fighting him. Coxcox came to Iztacima's aid with all the men he could muster and with those provided by Quinatzin, expelling from those lands the Chichimecas who had opposed the high priest and the Chololtecas.

[fol. 9v]

 CHAPTER 12

*Of the arrival of the Tlailotlaques and Chimalpanecas, whom
Quinatzin settled in the city of Tezcuco and elsewhere because
they were great artisans, and of some wars that occurred up
until his death*

When Quinatzin was newly installed in his empire, two nations arrived from
the provinces of the Mixteca that were called Tlailotlaque and Chimalpaneca,
who were likewise of Tolteca lineage. The Tlailotlaques brought as their leaders
Aztatl and Texcan or, according to the general history,[45] Coatlitepan; they were
highly skilled in the art of painting histories, more than in the other arts; they
brought Tezcatlpopoca as their principal idol. The Chimalpanecas brought
as their captains and leaders two noblemen who were called Xilocuetzin and
Tlacateotzin. They were of Quinatzin's house and lineage, and so he married
them to his granddaughters. He married Xilocuetzin to Coaxochitzin, daughter
of his son Chicomeacatl; and Tlacateotzin to Tetzcocazihuatzin, daughter of
Memexoltzin. He selected the best and most highly skilled people among them
and settled them within the city of Tezcuco. The rest he distributed to other cities
and towns, settling them in their own neighborhoods. Today, their descendants
remain in the neighborhoods of Tlailotlacan and Chimalpan, which were named
after them, though these two nations had previously spent a long time in the
province of Chalco.

Toward the end of Quinatzin's reign, the people of the provinces that were at
the time named Cuitlahuac, Huehuetlan, Totolapan, Huaxtepec, and Çaiolan
rebelled. To punish and defeat them, he ordered the lords whose territories
surrounded them to attack. He ordered the Mexica lords Hepcoatzin and
Acamapichtli to march on those from Cuitlahuac. This was the first war in
which the Mexicas fought on the side of the empire. Amintzin, who was at
that time lord of Chalco Atenco, marched on those from Mizquic and Acatlan;
Huetzin, lord of Coatlichan, against those from Huehuetlan; Acacitzin, lord
of Tlalpican in the province of Chalco, against those from Huaxtepec; and

---

45. Alva Ixtlilxochitl refers to the Codex Xolotl, the main pictorial source for chapters 4–29
of the *Historia de la nación Chichimeca*, as "the general history."

Tlacatepoz Nonoalcatl, likewise lord of the province of Chalco, against those from Çaiolan; and Quinatzin personally marched against those from Totolapan and easily defeated and punished them, so that they remained subjects of the empire.

In the more remote territory, there was no war of any kind, for there were few people and settlement progressed slowly. During this period, the wars that occurred took place within the ring of mountains that bounded the aforementioned original settlements. Many lords and high-ranking people incited these uprisings, although after these wars, none of them dared rise up or secede from the empire again during Quinatzin's lifetime. He [fol. 10r] died in the year 1253 of the incarnation of Christ our Lord, having reigned nearly 112 years. He died in the year called *chicuei calli*[46] in the woods of Tetzcotzinco and was buried in the same way as his forebears.

---

46. Eight House.

‎🔥‎ CHAPTER 13

Of the reign of Techotlalatzin

Despite being the youngest of Quinatzin's sons, Techotlalatzin inherited the empire owing to his virtues and for having always conformed to the will of his father. His nursemaid was a Tolteca noblewoman named Papaloxochitl, native of the city called Colhuacan, so he was the first to speak the Nahua tongue, which is now called the Mexican language. His ancestors never spoke it. He ordered all those of the Chichimeca nation to speak it, especially those who held public offices and posts, for the Nahua tongue was used for the names of all the places and the words necessary for the good order of public life and civic matters, such as the reading of paintings.[47] This was easy for them, because they were already very intermixed with the Toltecas by this time.

Four Tolteca communities had settled on the slopes of the mountain Huexachtecatl, where they constructed temples and likenesses of their idols and false gods; they were therefore regarded as very devout in their religious rites and ceremonies. But because they had very intense debates and disagreements over which of their gods should receive their greatest devotion, Coxcox, king of the Culhuas at the time, cast them out. They scattered to different places, and the highest-ranking of them ended up in the city of Tezcuco, where they asked Techotlalatzin to give them lands on which to settle. He ordered them to settle in the city of Tezcuco since they were civilized people and suitable for his plan for the orderly administration of civic life. And so they settled within the city in four districts, one for each of these Tolteca clans, who were called Culhuas at this time. In one district, those of the Mexitin clan settled; their leader was called Aioquan. Techotlalatzin gave the second district to the Culhuaque;[48] Nauhyotl was their leader. The third he gave to the Huitznahuaque,[49] whose leader was called Tlacomihua. He gave the fourth to the Tepanecas, whose leader was called Achitometl. He likewise sent others to settle in other cities and towns. The settlement of these four districts took place in the year 1301. These people

---

47. Pictorial records often included phonetic graphic elements that correspond to Nahuatl words.
48. Nahuatl plural of Culhua.
49. Nahuatl plural of Huitznahua.

were all very civilized, and they brought many idols that they worshiped, among which were Huitzilopochtli and Tlaloc. Techotlalatzin's love for the Tolteca nation was so great that he not only [fol. 10v] allowed them to live and settle among the Chichimecas but also gave them permission to make public sacrifices to their idols and dedicate temples to them, which his father Quinatzin had not permitted. And from this time on, Tolteca rites and ceremonies began to prevail.

Emperor Techotlalatzin married Tozquentzin, daughter of Acolmiztli, lord of Coatlichan, with whom he had five children. The first was Prince Ixtlilxochitl Ometochtli, first of this name. The second, a daughter, was called Chochxochitzin; the third, a son, Tenancacalitzin; the fourth, a son, Acatlotzin; the fifth, a son, Tenannahuacatzin. To Prince Ixtlilxochitl, who was born at the woodland retreat of Tzinacanoztoc, he gave as nursemaid a noblewoman named Zacaquimiltzin from the province of Tepepolco, and he assigned the following towns to provide for the prince's upbringing: Tepetlaoztoc, Teotihuacan, Teçoiocan, Tepechpan, Chiuhnauhtlan, Cuextecatlichocaian, Tepepolco, Tlalanapan, Tiçaiocan, Ahuatepec, Axapochco, and Quauhtlatzinco. At this time, Acolhua, king of Azcapotzalco, died after many years of rule, and his son Teçoçomoc succeeded him, because according to the histories, these Chichimeca and Aculhua lords lived between two hundred fifty and three hundred years. This ceased to be true for their descendants once they began to indulge in sumptuous foods and pleasures and relations with many women. Previously, as mentioned above, they did not have more than one wife, and they did not have intercourse with her during pregnancy or after childbirth until their children were grown.

🌿 **CHAPTER 14**

Of some wars that Teçoçomoc, king of Azcapotzalco, and the
Mexica lords fought that expanded his domain; the succession of
Acamapichtli in the kingdom of the Culhuas through Ilancueitl,
his wife; and other things that happened until the death of
Techotlalatzin

As soon as Teçoçomoc assumed control of the kingdom, he called on his two
brothers Hepcoatzin and Acamapichtli, lords of Mexico, to wage war against
Tzonpantecuhtli, reigning king of the Otomies, who had his court at Xaltocan,
and against those of the provinces of Maçahuacan, Quauhtitlan, and Tepotzotlan.
And so they joined forces and marched on them. They fought so ably that they
took over the kingdom of the Otomies, and Tzonpantecuhtli their lord fled to
the province of Metztitlan, where he was also lord. Techotlalatzin, seeing these
disturbances, gathered his forces and went with them to Chiuhnauhtlan in order
to ascertain from there the intentions of the Tepanecas and Mexicas. On the night
that the Tepanecas and Mexicas battled against Tzonpantecuhtli and won the city
of Xaltocan, a squadron of fleeing Otomies passed close to Techotlalatzin's army
with many helpless women, children, and elderly at its center. And believing that
they were some of the enemy trying to enter the lands of the kingdom of Tezcuco,
Techotlalatzin pursued them up to Teçontepec, where he realized that they were
refugees. He learned of [fol. 11r] their calamity and travails and that they were not
fighters; he told the Otomies to turn back and he gave them lands and places to
settle in the province henceforth known as Otompan. This was how Teçoçomoc
usurped the kingdom of the Otomies, the province of Maçahuacan, and those of
Quauhtitlan and Tepotzotlan, allocating some towns and places to the Mexica
lords. Other Otomies from the kingdom of the Tepanecas and the province of
Quahuacan also arrived to seek Techotlalatzin's protection and receive lands to
settle, because their lord Teçoçomoc oppressed them by continuously demanding
excessive tributes from them. Techotlalatzin admitted them and sent them to
settle in Yahualiuhcan and Maçaapan, where they remained.

By this time, Acamapichtli, lord of the Tenochcas, was powerful and enjoyed
the support of King Teçoçomoc and Hepcoatzin, his brothers. So he sought to
take over the kingdom of the Culhuas, asserting his right through Ilancueitl his
wife, who was the daughter, although the younger one, of Achitometzin, first king

of the Culhuas. In so doing, he would deny the throne to the lords of Coatlichan, who were the rightful heirs through Princess Atototzin, Achitometzin's eldest daughter. He did this easily, because, at that time, Coxcoxtzin, king of the Culhuas, was weak for lack of warriors and territory, having abandoned the rulership of Coatlichan to his brother Moçocomatzin in order to acquire the kingdom of the Culhuas, which he later attained. Moreover, the Culhuas themselves were riven by factions and discord over their idolatries and the antiquity of their gods. And so Acamapichtli took control of the kingdom without any conflict whatsoever. Coxcoxtzin left for Coatlichan with some of the defeated Culhuas and settled there, while some others went to Tezcuco, as mentioned above. Acamapichtli did not want to remain in Colhuacan, capital of that kingdom, so he appointed as governor his grandson Quetzalia, son of Chalchiuhtlatonac, lord of Coyohuacan.

Both Acamapichtli and his brother Hepcoatzin, lord of Tlatelolco, died at almost the same time, each having reigned fifty-one years, according to the general history, which is the one I follow. Huitzilihuitzin succeeded to the kingdom [of the Tenochcas]. He married Tetzihuactzin, daughter of Acolnahuacatzin, lord of Tlacopan, and of Tzihuacxochitzin; they had eight children. The first, a son, was Chimalpopocatzin, who succeeded him in the lordship; the second, a daughter, Matlalcihuatzin, married Ixtlilxochitl, king of Tezcuco; the third, a son, Omipoztectzin; the fourth, a son, Tlatopilia; the fifth, a son, Zacahuehuetzin; the sixth, a son, Itzcoatzin, also became king of Mexico; the seventh, a son, Temilotzin; and the eighth and last, a son, Temictzin. Hepcoatzin was succeeded in the lordship of Tlatelolco by Quaquauhpitzahuac. He married Coaxochitzin, noblewoman of the house of Coatlichan, and had three children, the first of whom was a son, Amantzin; the second, a son, Tlacateotzin, third lord of Tlatelolco; and the last and third, a daughter, Matlalatzin.

King Teçoçomoc married Chalchiuhcozcatzin, with whom he had eleven children. The first, a son, was Maxtla, who later inherited the kingdom of Azcapotzalco; the second, a son, Tecuhicpaltzin; the third, a son, Taiatzin; the fourth, a daughter, Cuetlachcihuatzin, married Tlacateotzin, lord of Tlatelolco; the fifth, a daughter, Cuetlaxxochitzin, married Xilomantzin, son of Quetzalia of Colhuacan; the sixth, a daughter, Tzihuacxochitzin, married Acolnahuacatzin, lord of Tlacopan; the seventh, a daughter, Chalchiuhcihuatzin, married [fol. 12v] Tlatocatlatzacuilotzin, lord of Acolman; the eighth, a daughter, Tecpaxochitzin, was married to Tecpatl, lord of Atotonilco, but he then repudiated her, and her father later attempted to give her as legitimate wife to Ixtlilxochitzin, king of Tezcuco, who would have her only as a concubine, which was one of the excuses Teçoçomoc used to usurp the empire; the ninth, a daughter, was named Papaloxochitzin, who married Opantecuhtli, lord of Coatlichan; and the other younger ones were daughters.

Near the end of the reign of Techotlalatzin, Quaquauhpitzahuac, lord of Tlatelolco, died, and his son Tlacateotzin took his place. He had three children with Cuetlachcihuatzin, daughter of Teçoçomoc. The two sons had shared a womb; they were called Tzontemoctzin and Quauhtlatoatzin. Huitzilihuitzin also died, and Chimalpopocatzin succeeded to the throne of Tenochtitlan and kingdom of the Culhuas. He married Matlalatzin, daughter of Quaquauhpitzahuac, lord of Tlatelolco, with whom he had seven children; the last two were Quatlecoatzin and Motecuhçomatzin Ilhuicamina, first of this name, who became king of Mexico, the youngest of all his siblings. After all of these things had happened, Emperor Techotlalatzin died at his Oztoticpac palace within the city of Tezcuco, having ruled 104 years, which caused everyone in the empire great sorrow. At this time in this New Spain there were sixty-seven kings and lords, according to the general history, and most of them attended his funeral rites and burial, which took place in the year 1357 of the incarnation of Christ our Lord, which they call 8 *chicuei calli*.[50]

---

50. Eight House. Alva Ixtlilxochitl usually spells out dates in Nahuatl or, less commonly, gives them in Arabic numerals. Here, however, he has included both the Arabic numeral and the word *chicuei*, "eight."

🌿 CHAPTER 15

*Of how Emperor Ixtlilxochitl Ometochtli succeeded to the
empire and Teçoçomoc and the Mexica lords refused to pledge
themselves to him, vexing the empire*

After the obsequies and burial of Techotlalatzin, the lords who had been present
swore allegiance to Ixtlilxochitl as their universal lord. But Teçoçomoc, as soon
as he received news of Techotlalatzin's death from his grandson, Teiolcocoatzin,
who was lord of Acolman at the time, summoned the Mexica lords. And among
other things he said to them, he told them that he was offended by Ixtlilxochitl's
excessive arrogance and conceit, believing himself without equal in his authority
and lordship. Teçoçomoc felt he had more right to inherit the empire, for he was
a grandson of Xolotl, its first settler; moreover, Ixtlilxochitl was a youth with too
little experience to be able to manage such a large domain. And so Teçoçomoc
would by no means [fol. 12r] be present at the oath-swearing, nor would he
recognize him as supreme lord. Instead, he would subjugate Ixtlilxochitl to his
authority and lordship, for he had numerous and high-ranking kin, such as
themselves and the lords of Acolman and Coatlichan and all the lords of his house
and clan, whom he would easily rally to his cause. The Mexica lords replied that
they agreed with what he intended to do, but that it should not be done without
support, because Ixtlilxochitl, although young, was a brave warrior and loved
by his vassals. To that, Teçoçomoc agreed.

Ixtlilxochitl, after he succeeded to the empire, married Matlalcihuatzin,
noblewoman of Mexico Tenochtitlan and sister of King Chimalpopoca, with
whom he had two children. The first was Prince Acolmiztli Nezahualcoyotzin;
the second, Princess Atototzin. With Tecpaxochitzin he had Iancuiltzin, and he
had other children with other concubines. Prince Nezahualcoyotzin was born
in the year 1402 of the incarnation of Christ our Lord, the twenty-eighth day
of the month of April, in the year that they call *çe tochtli*,[51] under the day-sign
that they call *çe maçatl*[52] and on the last day of the month of *toçoztzintli*.[53] The
astrologers and diviners of that time recognized that his birth was significant; it

---

51. One Rabbit.
52. One Deer.
53. Short Vigil.

happened in the morning at sunrise, which very much pleased his father. Upon his birth, Ixtlilxochitl assigned towns and villages to provide for his upbringing and appointed tutors capable of giving him a proper education, among them Huitzilihuitzin, who was considered a very great philosopher of that era.

Seeing the agitation and pretensions of the king of Azcapotzalco, the lords who were not at court increasingly neglected their duties, so that the empire began to decline. And Ixtlilxochitl did not dare venture out to punish them because he had (as they say) the enemy inside his house, who might easily take it over. With Teçoçomoc whispering to them, Ixtlilxochitl left it for another time. He tried to win over the tyrant Teçoçomoc and his allies through peaceful means, but in no way could he appease them, so he resorted to violence. He mustered his forces, and sixteen provinces joined his side, including Tolantzinco and Tepepolco, and the lords of Huexotla, Coatlichan, Acolman, and another ten or twelve, some of which did it out of duty, such as those of Acolman and Coatlichan. And with the forces that he mustered from the aforementioned provinces he began to punish the towns and villages within his domains that secretly favored and sided with the Tepanecas, such as those from Xaltepec, Otompan, Axapochco, Temazcalapan, and Tolquauhiocan.

✳ CHAPTER 16

Of the fealty-swearing to Prince Nezahualcoyotzin as heir to the empire in the courts that were established at Huexotla, where the wars that took place between Ixtlilxochitl and Teçoçomoc over the empire were decided

The following year, 1414 of the incarnation of Christ our Lord, which they call *matlactli omei tochtli*,[54] Ixtlilxochitl convened an assembly and meeting of the lords and captains [fol. 12v] who supported him to discuss how to proceed in order to subjugate the king of Azcapotzalco and all of his allies, who were trying to usurp the empire. They agreed that, before anything else, they should swear fealty to Nezahualcoyotl as crown prince of the empire and blockade the cities of Azcapotzalco and Mexico from the lake. They also agreed that the army, punishing and subjugating the towns of the kingdom of Tezcuco, should continue advancing through the lands of the Tepanecas until it reached the city of Azcapotzalco. All of this was carried out, and they swore fealty to Nezahualcoyotzin, who was twelve years of age. And among the highest-ranking captains who were selected for this war were Çihuacnahuacatzin, who was in charge of the assault from the lake, and Çoacuecuenotzin, captain and general in charge of the incursion by land into enemy territory. The enemy was at this time very well supplied with troops and everything necessary to defend their kingdom and do battle with Ixtlilxochitl. Tlacateotzin, lord of Tlatelolco and general of the Tepaneca army, went out to engage Çihuacnahuacatzin on the lake before he had come halfway across it and forced him to retreat toward Tezcuco and await the enemy near the shore. There they fought a very fierce battle without either side gaining an advantage, although the enemy did prevent Çihuacnahuacatzin from reaching the other side of the lake to blockade the cities of Mexico and Azcapotzalco.

The following year, which they call *çe acatl*,[55] the sixth day of the second month on the day they call *matlactli omei tecpatl*,[56] the Tepanecas invaded through Aztahuacan. They took every town up to Itztapalocan, which belonged to the kingdom

---

54. Thirteen Rabbit.
55. One Reed.
56. Thirteen Flint.

of Tezcuco. Although the residents of those towns defended themselves, many were killed and taken captive, and among those who died was Quauhxilotzin, the king's steward in Itztapalocan. They burned and sacked most of the houses, and this was the first of the Tepaneca victories. Çoacuecuenotzin and his army set out from Xilotepec and passed through Çitlaltepec and Tepotzotlan, razing the towns and villages that resisted, until he reached Quauhtitlan, where the Tepanecas met him with a powerful army and fought against him. He roundly defeated them and continued on through Cuetlachtepec until he reached the foot of the mountain that they call Temocpalco. From there he blockaded the city of Azcapotzalco and did not allow any reinforcements or supplies to enter from that side; he remained there for almost four years. In his view, most of the work necessary to end the war, ravage the city of Azcapotzalco, and restore the empire had been accomplished.

[fol. 13r]

🌿 CHAPTER 17

How Teçoçomoc, seeing that Emperor Ixtlilxochitl had his city
surrounded and blockaded, proposed a truce under the pretense
that he wanted to pledge fealty and sue for peace

Seeing that the wars against the Chichimecas had lasted four years and that he had been unable to subdue them and had lost many of his troops and that with only a little more effort they would enter his city where he, his kin, and his allies would be at risk, Teçoçomoc decided to shift tactics. He sent his ambassadors to Ixtlilxochitl to ask for a truce for a period of time, promising to pledge fealty to Ixtlilxochitl and to negotiate peace and accord, which he claimed he wanted for the empire. Being extraordinarily honorable and heedless of the danger that might result, Ixtlilxochitl ordered the blockade of Azcapotzalco lifted, and he sent his troops back to their towns to rest, leaving himself alone and unsuspecting in the city of Tezcuco. Teçoçomoc, aware of Ixtlilxochitl's vulnerability and realizing that his plans were coming together, pretended to hold celebrations in Ixtlilxochitl's honor at the foot of the mountain called Chiuhnauhtecatl to seal the peace that he falsely said he wanted. For appearances, he took with him many dancers and other delightful and entertaining attractions that these lords enjoyed, but he also took a sizable army with him, so that at the right moment they could attack the Tezcucas and kill Ixtlilxochitl and everyone with him. And party to this treason and pact of tyranny were those of the house and lineage of Teçoçomoc, including the Mexica lords and the others mentioned above. Teçoçomoc took all of them to a nearby woodland retreat called Temamatlac. There he waited for Ixtlilxochitl.

Ixtlilxochitl realized that the false festivities that Teçoçomoc wanted to hold in his honor were meant to enable the crafty old man's tyranny and treason. What most distressed King Ixtlilxochitl was that it was nearly too late to fortify himself in his city and send for help; most of the lords had already sided with the tyrant, and even some of the noblemen of his court whom he greatly trusted were party to this conspiracy. So Ixtlilxochitl played along; he pretended to be indisposed and sent his regrets, saying that they should postpone the festivities. He called his brother, Prince Tocuiltecatl Acatlotli, and asked him to take this message. The prince knew that the undertaking with which he had been entrusted was very risky and that he would not escape with his life. He told the king, his brother, to look after his children and protect them and grant them the two villages of

Quauhiocan and Tequizquinahuac, which the king had recently granted him, but of which the prince had not yet taken possession. [fol. 13v] The king consoled him and told him that he himself faced the same risk, since he found himself so bereft of support and troops, while the tyrant had the upper hand, using Ixtlilxochitl's own arms and the men of his own house against him. And after offering further explanations, Ixtlilxochitl ordered the prince to dress in certain clothes that the king usually wore and to adorn himself with gold and jewels. Then the king summoned certain of his servants to accompany Prince Tocuiltecatl, who went to the forest of Temamatlac, which, as mentioned, was in Chiuhnauhtlan. When he arrived, he saw that they were all in conversation, and among the tyrant's allies were many of the distinguished and high-ranking people from the kingdom of Tezcuco, some from Huexotla and others from Coatlichan and Chimalhuacan, Coatepec, Itztapalocan, and those from Acolman, with all of their retainers. Tocuiltecatl greeted the tyrant and everyone else and delivered his message; they responded that they had not summoned him, but rather Ixtlilxochitl. They immediately killed him, flayed him alive, and displayed his skin on some nearby rocks; they killed everyone who was with him in the same manner.

King Ixtlilxochitl was informed of this, and by this time he was ready and waiting for the enemy. Seeing that they had failed to capture him, the tyrant and his confederates marched with great haste in order to catch Ixtlilxochitl unawares and sack the city. And although they hurried, Teçoçomoc was unable to execute his evil scheme, because Ixtlilxochitl put up a fight and defended the city for more than fifty days, during which time many different things occurred. Among them, a nobleman called Tochpilli, one of Ixtlilxochitl's closest companions, and the Chimalpanecas from the district within Tezcuco, switched to the tyrants' side. Together they killed the advisors and men of the king's chamber, including Iztactecpoyotl and Huitzilihuitl. They entered their homes with their *macanas*[57] and hacked them to pieces. They also stoned Tequixquinahuacatl Xicaltzin to death in his house and dragged him outside into the streets; they looted the house, for he was a very rich person. Ixtlilxochitl was in a very difficult position. He saw that even those in his house and court and in whom he had placed great trust had all rebelled against him and joined the Tepaneca faction. Most of the residents and other noblemen who had defended him and his city were dead. The people, wretched and defenseless, were retreating to the mountains, and he was forced [. . .]

---

57. The term refers to the pre-Hispanic *macuahuitl*, a wooden club edged with sharpened obsidian blades.

🌿   CHAPTER 18

Of how Emperor Ixtlilxochitl retreated to the mountain, from where he sent a request for help to those of the province of Otompan, where his captain general was killed, and everything else that occurred at this time

So great was the confusion, not only within the city of Tezcuco, but also in all the rest of the cities, towns, and villages of the kingdom, that some declared themselves for Ixtlilxochitl and others for the tyrant. Parents defended one faction and children the other, and even among brothers and kin there was this confusion and division, which allowed the tyrant and his confederates to ravage the kingdom with ease. The common people did not stop until they crossed to the other side of the mountains, most of them settling [fol. 14r] in the provinces of Tlaxcalan and Huexotzinco. Ixtlilxochitl, having abandoned the city, fortified himself in one of his forest retreats, called Quauhiacac, with his captain general, Çoacuecuenotzin; Prince Nezahualcoyotzin; and all of their retainers. From there they fought against the enemy, who were so strong that they forced them to retreat further into the mountains to another forest called Tzinacanoztoc. There they received news of how Ixtlilxochitl's supporters Itlacauhtzin, lord of Huexotla; Tlalnahuacatl, lord of Coatlichan; and Totomihua of Coatepec had likewise fled and retreated to the mountains, and they and their vassals faced the same peril. Ixtlilxochitl decided to send an envoy to the province of Otompan to ask for help from Quetzalcuixtli, captain and general whom he had put in charge of the warriors of that province.

For this, he sent his nephew and captain general of his army, Çoacuecuenotzin, saying to him:

> My nephew, great are the travails and persecutions that my vassals the Aculhua Chichimecas suffer, for they have abandoned their homes and now live in the mountains. Go and tell my fathers, those of the province of Otompan, that I wish them to know of the great persecution that my people suffer. I ask for their help, because the Tepanecas and Mexicas greatly oppress us, and with their next attack, they will overrun the empire and put to flight the poor Aculhua Tezcuca people, who have already begun to cross over to the provinces of Tlaxcalan and Huexotinzco.

To these words Çoacuecuenotzin responded:

> Very high and powerful lord, I greatly appreciate the favor Your Highness
> shows me in choosing me for this journey. I shall do it willingly, but I
> warn Your Highness that I shall not return, because as you know, in that
> province they already proclaim the name of the tyrant Teçoçomoc. I only
> ask you not to abandon your servants Tzontecomatl and Acolmizton. God
> saw fit to give you the prince, my lord Nezahualcoyotzin, who will be able
> to use them in his service.

The emotion and tears that these words provoked were so great that for a while
neither could speak to the other, until, regaining his composure, the king said,
"My very beloved nephew, may God watch over you and favor you. And be
reassured that you leave me in the same peril to which you go. In your absence,
the tyrants may take my life."

Çoacuecuenotzin left on his mission and was recognized in the town of
Ahuatepec. He had gone that way to visit certain of his farms and fields in order
to gather as many supplies as he could for the army. Those from Quauhtlatzinco
imprisoned him and took him to Otompan. And there, in the middle of the
plaza, where everyone from the province had gathered and convened, he was
asked his reasons for coming, and he told them why he had been sent. Captain
Quetzalcuixtli, after having heard the message, shouted to everyone present,
"You have heard Ixtlilxochitl's desire that we aid him. Under no circumstances
shall we do it, for we are all to place ourselves under the protection of the great
lord, Teçoçomoc, who is our father." Then Yacatzone, governor of that province,
spoke, saying, "Why should we go to Ixtlilxochitl? Since he claims to be such a
great lord and he boasts of his exalted lineage, let him defend himself alone. And
since his captain general came to ask for help, tear him to pieces here, come what
may," commanding those present to tear him to pieces (fig. 6). The first to grab
Çoacuecuenotzin was a soldier named [fol. 14v] Xochipoio, native of Ahuatepec.
And although Çoacuecuenotzin wanted to defend himself, others arrived and tore
him to pieces, and all shouted, "Long live the great lord, Teçoçomoc, our emperor."
Then Yacatzone approached and asked for Çoacuecuenotzin's fingernails, and
once he got them, he strung them together and wore them as a necklace in a
mocking and insulting way, saying, "Since these fingernails come from such a
great nobleman, they must be made of precious and invaluable stones, and so I
want to adorn myself with them." And the common people began to throw the
pieces of Çoacuecuenotzin's body at each other. Likewise they killed another four

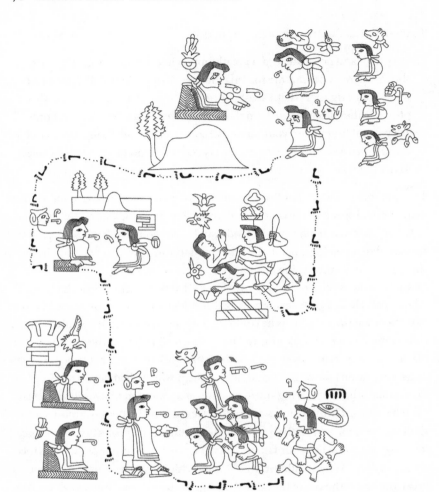

FIGURE 6. Çoacuecuenotzin's death (based on the Codex Xolotl, plate 7).

of his servants who had accompanied him. This unfortunate death occurred on the eighteenth day of their eighth month, called *micailhuitzintli*,[58] on the day *macuili coatl*,[59] which was August 24 of the year 1418 of the incarnation of Christ our Lord.

Itzcuintlatlacça, a nobleman from Ahuatepec who was present at all of the aforementioned events, went with great haste to see King Ixtlilxochitl and give

---

58. Small Feast of the Dead.

59. Five Snake.

him an account of the unhappy affair. Ixtlilxochitl, having heard it, summoned Çoacuecuenotzin's wife to console her, and said:

> Dear niece, my beloved nephew and captain general of the empire did what a loyal vassal should; he sacrificed his life to protect and defend mine. I beg you now to have courage in the face of the adversities that fortune sets before us and console yourself among my children and grandchildren here with you; what matters is that we help them escape this persecution.

And he spoke many other words to her, shedding many tears, and then left this place and went to another called Chicoquauhiocan, where he remained for thirty days.

CHAPTER 19

Of the unfortunate and unhappy death of Emperor Ixtlilxochitl

Seeing himself abandoned by his own people, Ixtlilxochitl left all those of his house and family in the forest of Chicoquauhiocan, taking with him only two captains—one called Totocahuan from Papalotlan and the other named Coçamatl—and his son Prince Nezahualcoyotzin. He went to a deep ravine called Cuetlachac, beside which was a large fallen tree, under whose roots he spent the night. When the sun rose the next day—which was called *matlactli cozcaquauhtli*,[60] the ninth day of their tenth month, called *ochpanaliztli*,[61] which was September 24 of the aforementioned year—a soldier called Tezcacoacatl, one of the spies he had posted, rushed up to [tell] him that he had seen a great number of armed men in those hills coming at great speed. Realizing that death was upon him and that he had no choice but to fight his enemies, Ixtlilxochitl told the few soldiers that were there with him to try to escape with their lives, for he would surely be killed and torn to pieces at the hands of his enemies. Then he called for the prince, [fol. 15r] and he said to him with heartfelt and tender words:

> My very beloved son, Lion-Arm[62] Nezahualcoyotl, where might I take you to find some kinsman or relative to shelter you? My misfortune ends today; I am forced to leave this life. I beseech you not to abandon your subjects and vassals, nor forget that you are Chichimeca. You must train in the use of bow and arrows, recover your empire, which Teçoçomoc so unjustly usurps, and avenge the death of your poor father. For now, you must hide yourself in these trees, so that the ancient empire of your ancestors does not end with your innocent death.

The tears streamed from the eyes of son and father such that they could speak no more to each other. And having embraced each other tenderly, the prince pulled away and went to a very leafy tree and hid among its branches. From there he witnessed his father's unfortunate end (fig. 7).

---

60. Ten Vulture.
61. Sweeping.
62. Alva Ixtlilxochitl translates Acolmiztli, one of Nezahualcoyotl's personal names, as "Brazo de León."

FIGURE 7. Ixtlilxochitl Ometochtli's death (based on the Codex Xolotl, plate 7).

Ixtlilxochitl went out to meet the enemy. The majority of those who came with the Tepaneca tyrants were from the provinces of Otompan and Chalco, to whom Ixtlilxochitl had just granted many favors. Ixtlilxochitl charged. He fought for a long time, killing some of them before he fell to the ground dead, his body pierced in many places by the spears they wielded. Seeing a large contingent of Ixtlilxochitl's soldiers descending to aid him, his enemies were content to leave him dead and hastily withdrew by the road to Otompan. And Totocahuan, one of his captains, was the first to reach his king and lord. He took him in his arms and began to lament, addressing his lifeless body, saying:

> O Ometochtli Ixtlilxochitl, now comes the end of your misfortune and the beginning of your rest. Let now the whole of the empire weep and embrace its orphanhood and *orbatio*,[63] for it has lost its light and father. Now my sole concern is where my young prince and lord Acolmiztli Nezahualcoyotl will go, together with your loyal and unhappy vassals.

---

63. Latin in the original; state of bereavement.

Having delivered this apostrophe and speech to the body of his king and lord, he wrapped it in a shroud. Others began to arrive, among them a nobleman called Chichiquiltzin from Tlailotlacan, and there beside the river Cuetlachac, in the most appropriate place they could find, they built a dais and royal throne as well as they could, and they placed the body of the great Ixtlilxochitl upon it. That night they sat with him, and they burned his body at dawn, on the day they call *matlactli once olin*.[64] They saved his ashes until such time as they could find a burial place suited to his rank and status.

These final wars with the Tepanecas lasted 3 years and 273 days, Prince Nezahualcoyotl being 15 years and 200 days old, and he was sworn to and received as successor to the Chichimeca Empire. Ixtlilxochitl was the first Chichimeca emperor [fol. 15v] to be buried in this manner, which corresponds to the rites and ceremonies of the Toltecas.

---

64. Eleven Movement

🌿 CHAPTER 20

Of how the tyrant Teçoçomoc had himself proclaimed Chichimeca emperor, how he caused the death of many children from the kingdom of Tezcuco, and the declaration he gave on the plains of Tolteca Teopan, where everyone from Tezcuco and from some of the other kingdoms that belonged to the empire gathered

After the death of Ixtlilxochitl, sixth Chichimeca emperor, the killers took the news to the tyrant Teçoçomoc, who granted them great favors. Teçoçomoc had himself proclaimed emperor, granting many favors to his allies and confederates, such as the Mexica lords Tlacateotzin of Tlatelolco and Chimalpopoca of Tenochtitlan; Teiolcocoatzin, lord of Acolman; and others who were present at the festivities and ceremony. However, most of the lords of the remote provinces were increasingly rebellious due to these latest upheavals and recognized neither faction; the tyrant later attempted to subjugate them but failed because he had little time and had to fight other wars. His first act against the loyal vassals of Ixtlilxochitl was to have their children—those who knew how to talk up to age seven—questioned about whom they recognized as their king and natural lord; those who responded Ixtlilxochitl or Nezahualcoyotzin would be killed, and those who named him would be rewarded, along with their parents. He used these cruel means so that they would detest Ixtlilxochitl and Nezahualcoyotzin, their natural lords, forever more. This was done. And since these innocent children had always heard their parents and elders say they were vassals of Ixtlilxochitl and Nezahualcoyotzin, they responded with this truth, for which they perished at the hands of the cruel executioners, who killed many thousands of them. This was one of the greatest cruelties and injustices committed by any prince in this new world.

His second act was to summon everyone, both the high-ranking and plebeian people of all nations, cities, towns, and villages that were part of the empire, to the plain between the city of Tezcuco and the town of Tepetlaoztoc. A captain climbed to the top of a *cu* or "temple" (that was in the middle of the aforementioned plain) and loudly announced in both languages, Chichimeca and Tolteca—which was at the time generally spoken throughout the empire—that from that day forward they would recognize Teçoçomoc, [fol. 16r] king of the Tepanecas, as their emperor and supreme lord. They were to pay him all rents

FIGURE 8. Nezahualcoyotl and the pulque seller
(based on the Codex Xolotl, plate 8).

and tributes owed to the empire and not to anyone else, under penalty of death.
Moreover, if they were to find Prince Nezahualcoyotl, they should seize him and
deliver him dead or alive to Teçoçomoc their lord, who would reward them for
this service. Prince Nezahualcoyotl was present for all of this, listening from
a rugged hillside nearby called Quauhiacac, and from that time on he strove
to live with caution and vigilance, abandoning his homeland. This happened
during the last days of the year 1418.

After having spent time hiding in the province of Tlaxcalan with its lords—his
uncles—to escape the tyrant's snares, early the next year Prince Nezahualcoyotzin
left for the province of Chalco to be closer to his homeland and ascertain the plans
of the tyrant and his other enemies. He entered the province secretly, disguised
as a soldier, and joined a company of the Chalca army, which was fighting over

boundaries with certain nearby towns. He was able to hide and remain disguised for a few days, until one day he killed a noblewoman named Zilamiauh, in whose house he was lodged, because she was selling *pulque* (which is their wine), on which many people got drunk; he believed this to be unbecoming of her status and against the law (fig. 8). He was then recognized and imprisoned by the Chalcas and taken before the supreme lord. Toteoçitecuhtli, which is what they called their ruler in that province, had Nezahualcoyotzin put in a cage inside a jail guarded by Toteoçitecuhtli's brother Quetzalmaçatzin and many men. No one was to give him any food or drink for the next eight days, because Toteoçitecuhtli wanted to serve the tyrant Teçoçomoc and avenge the death of that noblewoman with this cruel death sentence. Quetzalmaçatzin pretended to comply with his brother's orders but secretly, with some deception, gave the prince food and drink, which sustained him through these aforementioned days, because he pitied Nezahualcoyotzin and how unjustly he had been treated merely to please a tyrant. At the end of the eight days, Toteoçitecuhtli asked Quetzalmaçatzin if the prisoner had died. He told him no. Toteoçitecuhtli was greatly angered and ordered them to tear him to pieces the next day at the province's general fair. Quetzalmaçatzin, who pitied Nezahualcoyotzin, came to the prince in secret later that night, telling him what had happened and about the cruel sentence issued against him, believing it unjust that it should be carried out upon the successor to the empire. Rather, out of love, Quetzalmaçatzin would suffer this death in his place. He instructed him to swap clothes in order to slip past the guards, then quickly get to safety, leaving that night for Huexotzinco, [fol. 16v] or another foreign province, where he could not be caught. As a reward for this service, Quetzalmaçatzin only asked that Nezahualcoyotzin remember his wife and children and protect them should the gods favor him and he recover his empire. Grateful for a boon as great as the one that this nobleman gave him, the prince thanked him and promised to do all that he asked, which he deserved for his loyalty. Nezahualcoyotzin escaped without being recognized by the guards, and he walked quickly all night toward Tlaxcalan, leaving Quetzalmaçatzin in his place inside the cage. Upon learning what happened, Toteoçitecuhtli ordered the death sentence he had handed down to Nezahualcoyotzin carried out on his brother.

🌿   CHAPTER 21

How the tyrant Teçoçomoc distributed the lands that belonged
to the empire of the Chichimecas, and other things he did, and
of the dream he had

The following year, 1420 of the incarnation of Christ our Lord, called *chiquaçen tecpatl,*[65] two years and some days after the death of the unfortunate Ixtlilxochitl, when the inhabitants of the city of Tezcuco and everyone in its province who had fled to various other places had finally returned to their homes and were living somewhat peacefully—although robbed of their possessions and personal property and ruled by cruel tyrants—the tyrant Teçoçomoc decided to divide the kingdom of Tezcuco in the following manner: He took for himself the town of Coatlichan with all of its attendant lands, which at that time comprised many Aculhua towns and villages and ran from the boundaries of the province of Chalco to those of Tolantzinco, where the provinces of Otompan, Tepepolco, and Cempoalan began. Huexotla—which was the other capital and likewise comprised many towns interspersed among those of the city of Tezcuco and those of Coatlichan—he gave to Tlacateotzin, lord of Tlatelolco. And the city of Tezcuco, with the rest of its attendant towns, he gave to Chimalpopoca, king of Mexico. He also elevated his grandson Teiolcocoatzin, lord of Acolman, and Quetzalmaquiztli, lord of Coatlichan, to the rank of king, giving them a number of towns and provinces from among the aforementioned: to the lord of Coatlichan, he gave those that fell to the south and to Teiolcocoatzin of Acolman, those to the north, dividing between the [two of them] the government of the entire empire of Tezcuco. He granted other favors to other noblemen and lesser lords. And having done this, he began to wage wars and advance with his captains against those of the remote provinces, acting with severity. Many of the lords there yielded to him, thereby preserving their subjects from the calamities and persecution caused by wars. This occupied him for the six years that remained of his life.

Nezahualcoyotzin was [fol. 17r] in the province of Tlaxcalan with his uncles, the lords there, with whom he discussed his plans, and they told him what he needed to do in order to recover his empire and domains. In the meantime, the Mexica noblewomen, who were his aunts and very close kin, pitying him,

----

65. Six Flint.

Figure 9. Teçoçomoc's dream (based on the Codex Xolotl, plate 8).

begged the tyrant to have mercy on their nephew's life. Teçoçomoc granted it on the condition that Nezahualcoyotzin live within the city of Mexico, and with this decision they sent for him. Once there, he stayed some days in the city of Mexico without leaving, until the same noblewomen approached the tyrant a second time to ask if Nezahualcoyotzin could go to the city of Tezcuco, where Teçoçomoc restored to him the palaces and houses of his fathers and grandfathers and some villages to serve him. With that, he achieved still more freedom to undertake the restoration of the empire.

In the year 1400 [sic 1426] of the incarnation, which is called *matlactli omome tochtli*,[66] with the empire in the aforementioned state, the tyrant Teçoçomoc dreamed early one morning, when the morning star rose from the horizon, that Prince Nezahualcoyotzin took the shape of a golden eagle that ripped apart and ate pieces of his heart; then he transformed into a tiger, and with his claws and teeth he tore apart his feet; then he entered the waters and the mountains,

66. Twelve Rabbit.

becoming their heart (fig. 9). Teçoçomoc awoke terrified and worried and summoned his diviners to interpret this dream. They responded that the golden
eagle that ripped and ate his heart signified that Prince Nezahualcoyotzin would
destroy his house and lineage, and the tiger signified that he would raze and
ravage the city of Azcapotzalco and all of his kingdom, and the transformation
into the heart of the waters and mountains signified that he would recover
the empire that Teçoçomoc usurped and become its lord. Having heard the
interpretation of his dream, Teçoçomoc asked for their advice so that he could
prevent these things before they came to pass. The fortune-tellers responded that
they knew of no other way but to kill Nezahualcoyotzin and catch him unawares,
because it would be impossible to kill him any other way. After Teçoçomoc sent
the fortune-tellers away, he summoned before him his three sons—Maxtla,
Taiatzin, and Tlatoca Hicpaltzin—and among the things he said was [fol. 17v]
that if they wanted to be lords of the empire, they must kill Nezahualcoyotzin
when he came to the city of Azcapotzalco to attend the funeral rites after his
death. This would be very soon, because the end of his days was nigh, for as they
knew, he had governed 188 years. Taiatzin, whom he named as his successor,
would take his place.

🌿 CHAPTER 22

Of the death of the tyrant, Emperor Teçoçomoc; how Maxtla,
second tyrant, succeeded to the empire; how he killed his brother
Taiatzin; and other things that came to pass

On the fourth day of the year called *matlactli omei acatl*,[67] the fourth day of their
first month called *tlacaxipehualiztli*,[68] on the day *yei cozcaquauhtli*,[69] which was
the year 1427 of the incarnation of Christ our Lord, on March 24, Teçoçomoc died
a natural death in the city of Azcapotzalco, having lived hundreds of years. The
Mexica lords and all the rest of his kin and friends were notified of his death so
that all might attend his funeral rites and obsequies. As the morning star arose
early the next day, called *nauholin*,[70] Nezahualcoyotzin arrived with his nephew
Tzontecochatzin, along with the other lords, and he offered his condolences for
Teçoçomoc's death to his three sons and to the Mexica lords and the other nobles
of that lineage (fig. 10). He sat among them, observing the funeral obsequies and
other rites and ceremonies, which the priests of their idols performed, until they
burned the body. Taiatzin, who had not forgotten their father's instructions to kill
Nezahualcoyotzin, privately reminded his brother Maxtla. Maxtla told him to
set the matter aside for the time being and stay calm, for the opportunity would
arise to do it later; this moment should be dedicated to their father's funeral rites
and obsequies to which so many lords and high-ranking people had come, and
it would be unseemly, since they were all [fol. 18r] sad and grief-stricken over the
death of their father, to kill another lord now without proper planning. Therefore,
Teçoçomoc's orders were not carried out. Having been warned of their scheming
against him by his cousin Motecuhçoma, Nezahualcoyotzin returned to the city
of Tezcuco as soon as the body of Teçoçomoc was burned and his ashes placed
in the main temple of the city of Azcapotzalco, as was the Mexicas' custom.

Maxtla, who at the time was lord of Coyohuacan, was a bellicose man with
an arrogant disposition and yearned to have the empire for himself, regardless
of his father's decision. He believed himself more deserving of it because he was

---

67. Thirteen Reed.
68. Flaying of Men.
69. Three Vulture.
70. Four movement.

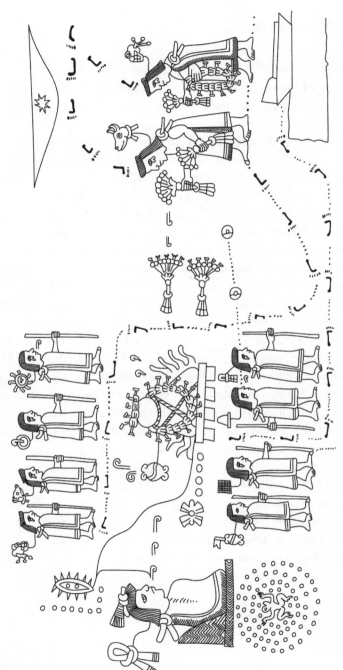

FIGURE 10. Teçoçomoc's funeral (based on the Codex Xolotl, plate 8).

older and possessed the skills necessary to govern an empire such as the one his father bequeathed. And four days after his father's rites, he made himself ruler, and everyone made obeisance to him. One night, five months and five days after the rites (which, following the count of the natives, is 105 days), Taiatzin spoke with King Chimalpopoca, as he often did after he had been denied the throne that his father had left him. They were discussing that very topic, and Chimalpopoca said, "I am amazed, my lord, that you have been dispossessed of the title and lordship that your father, Emperor Teçoçomoc, left to you, and that your brother Maxtla has taken them for himself. They do not belong to him, for he is nothing more than the lord of Coyohuacan." Taiatzin responded, "My lord, it is a difficult thing to recover lost lordships once powerful tyrants possess them." Chimalpopoca replied, "Take my advice; it is very straightforward. Build a palace, invite him to its inauguration, and kill him through some deception. I will show you how to do it." And then they pursued other topics.

Taiatzin had brought a page with him, a dwarf named Tetontli, who had heard the discussion they were having from behind a pillar in the room. After they left for Azcapotzalco, the dwarf secretly informed King Maxtla, who told him to keep it to himself, promising to grant him many great favors. [fol. 18v] Maxtla was outraged at his brother over this. He summoned the palace builders and ordered them to build some houses in a certain part of the city for his brother Taiatzin to live in, for although he gave him the lordship of Coyohuacan, he wanted to have him always at court. They did as he commanded, and after the houses were built, he sent for Taiatzin, inviting him to their inauguration under the pretense that they would be his. There Maxtla took Taiatzin's life by the very same means that had been suggested by King Chimalpopoca, whom the tyrant had also invited with the same intent. But Chimalpopoca sent his regrets, saying that he was occupied with a very important sacrifice that he was making to his gods.

 CHAPTER 23

*Of how the tyrant Maxtla had Chimalpopocatzin, king of
Mexico, imprisoned and later released and the dangers in which
Prince Nezahualcoyotzin found himself*

Chimalpopoca, learning how Taiatzin died, deduced that the tyrant Maxtla had
surely been told about the conversation he had with Taiatzin about how Maxtla
had taken and usurped the empire for himself. He was convinced that Maxtla's
plan had been to trap Tlacateotzin and him, had they been at the inaugural
festivities, together with Taiatzin and to kill all three of them, as he had his
brother. And he was sure that, although they had escaped this time, Maxtla was
going to kill them as soon as he found a way. He was unnerved, trying to find the
best way to escape Maxtla's grasp. Tecuhtlehuacatzin, one of the highest-ranking
noblemen of his court and his kinsman, suggested that the two of them arm
themselves as if for war and with the symbols of men to be offered as sacrifices
to the gods. Dressed in this manner they should go to the courtyard of the
main temple and make a show of wanting to sacrifice themselves to their gods.
In this way, they would be able to ascertain the loyalties of their vassals. If their
vassals truly cared for them, once they understood why their lords planned to
sacrifice themselves, they would not allow it to happen but would immediately
take up arms to defend them. But if their vassals hesitated, the two of them
should follow through with their plan and sacrifice themselves to their gods,
for it would be more glorious to die in sacrifice than to fall into the hands of the
tyrant. All of this was done. And they were performing the acts and ceremonies
that they typically performed for similar sacrifices, when his son Motecuhçoma,
who was at this point captain general of the kingdom, arrived at their sides,
wanting to stop them from carrying out their plan, but he could not. He sent
a messenger [fol. 19r] to tell Maxtla, who was supreme lord, about this, so that
he might prevent it. As soon as he found out, Maxtla sent some noblemen with
many troops to take King Chimalpopoca prisoner and put him in a strong cage
inside his own city with a substantial number of guards and limit his food;
only Tecuhtlehuacatzin would be sacrificed. This was immediately carried out,
so that Chimalpopocatzin and his advisor Tecuhtlehuacatzin failed to execute
their plan, because the Mexicas lacked the forces necessary to resist the fury and
anger of a tyrant as powerful as Maxtla.

Nezahualcoyotzin learned of this from his brother Yancuiltzin. And since his uncle King Chimalpopoca was imprisoned and upset and they hardly gave him anything to eat, he decided to go see the tyrant and entreat him to release his uncle and pardon him if he had in some way offended him. He set out to do it, taking with him Tzontecochatzin. If nothing else came of it, at least they would see his uncle again. He arrived in the city of Azcapotzalco after dark and went straight to the house of a nobleman named Chacha, chamberlain of Emperor Maxtla; Nezahualcoyotzin told him he had come to kiss the hand of the great lord. Chacha welcomed him, and said that in the morning he would take him and arrange for him to be seen. As soon as Nezahualcoyotzin awoke, Chacha took him to the palace and escorted him inside to the rooms where Maxtla was. This chamberlain asked Maxtla to give Nezahualcoyotzin an audience, for he had come to see him. And being summoned before Maxtla, Nezahualcoyotzin greeted him and, among other things, said:

> Very high and powerful lord, I well understand that the great weight of governing Your Highness's empire is heavy upon you. I come to ask and beg you on behalf of my uncle King Chimalpopoca, who is like a precious feather that you have plucked out of your imperial headdress, who is like a string of gold and jewels that you have removed from your royal neck and instead clutch in your hands. I beseech you as a compassionate king to forget vengeance and punishment and cast your eyes upon the unfortunate old man, for his body is weakened and his natural strength and vigor have abandoned him.

Having heard these words, Maxtla said to his chamberlain Chacha, "What do you think of this? Nezahualcoyotzin my son is a true friend, for he asks me to forget my vengeance. You Tepanecas, when will you do the same?" And to Nezahualcoyotzin he said, "Prince, do not despair, for your uncle King Chimalpopoca is not dead. Go see him. I imprisoned him for the commotion he was causing, for the bad example he set for the commoners, and because he brought shame to the Mexicas. And you, Chacha, go with him so that the guards will allow Nezahualcoyotzin to see him." Nezahualcoyotzin took these steps to see if he could free his uncle Chimalpopocatzin from the prison where he was held (fig. 11). Taking his leave of Maxtla, Nezahualcoyotzin went with the chamberlain to the city of Mexico Tenochtitlan to see his uncle.

Maxtla, as soon as he had left, [fol. 19v] sent another of his chamberlains named Huecan Mecatl to go see Tlailotlac Tecuhtzintli, a nobleman of his council.

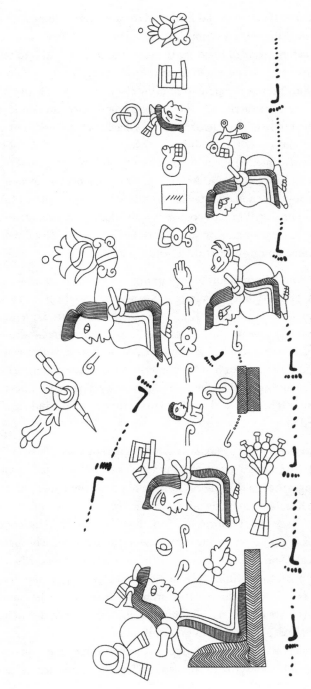

FIGURE 11. Nezahualcoyotl pleads with Maxtla (based on the Codex Xolotl, plate 8).

He was to inform him at length of everything that had happened regarding Nezahualcoyotl's request to free his uncle Chimalpopoca and that he was on his way to see him. Huecan Mecatl was also to have Tlailotlac Tecuhtzintli send his advice about whether it would be permissible to kill Chimalpopoca and Tlacateotzin first and wait to kill Nezahualcoyotzin, given that his father, the emperor, had emphatically instructed him to kill the latter, and he had been negligent, putting it off. The advisor sent his reply, saying that His Highness need not worry, that he held all the power, and that he could carry out his justice when and wherever he saw fit; even if he killed Nezahualcoyotl later, no one would dare stay his hand. If it was his wish that Chimalpopoca and Tlacateotl die first, then let it be so; Nezahualcoyotl would not escape, for neither the trees nor the rocks could conceal him. Having heard the arguments of his advisor, Maxtla decided not to kill Nezahualcoyotzin at that time.

Nezahualcoyotzin with his nephew Tzontecochatzin, having been allowed entry by the guards, visited with his uncle, and among other things, he said:

> Powerful lord, these are the sorts of trials that princes and lords are bound to suffer in the course of their reigns. You must accept the struggles that ruling among tyrants entails. You can console yourself with one thing, which is that within the court and capital of the kingdom that your father and grandfather, Acamapichtli and Huitzilihuitl, left to you, your subjects and vassals have great sympathy for your hardship. The Mexicas and Tenochcas will continue to agonize until they know how Your Highness's imprisonment and privation will end and what it is that Maxtla intends to do. I have already been to see him.

Chimalpopoca responded:

> My prince, how daring and audacious you are to have come all this way to see me at such risk to yourself. You could have avoided such risk, for nothing can preserve me from the cruelty that Maxtla wishes to inflict upon me. I entreat you to join with your uncle Itzcoatzin and your cousin Motecuhçoma and discuss what should be done. You will be the strength and shield of the Mexicas and Aculhuas; do not neglect your subjects and vassals, because they will be miserable if you abandon them. Be sure always to have an escape tunnel behind your throne, in case the tyrant Maxtla pronounces a death sentence. Be always alert and cautious (fig. 12).

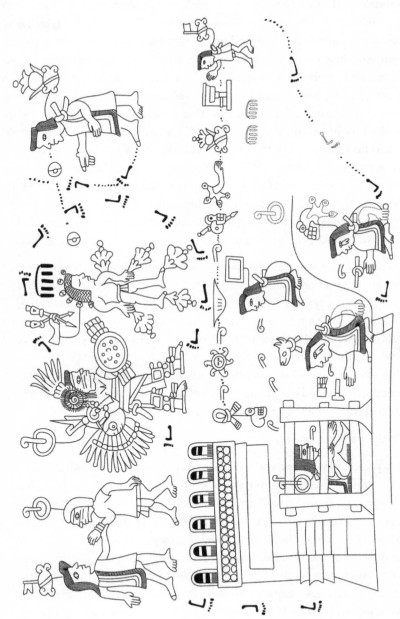

FIGURE 12. Chimalpopoca's imprisonment (based on the Codex Xolotl, plate 8).

Having said these and many other things, he took off the pieces of gold and precious jewels with which he had adorned his head, face, and neck and gave them to his nephew Nezahualcoyotzin. To Tzontecochatzin he gave some ear and lip plugs made of carnelian, and he said goodbye. After they left, an order from Maxtla arrived to release King Chimalpopoca from the prison, which was immediately done, and the guards were dismissed.

🌿 CHAPTER 24

Of how Nezahualcoyotzin twice escaped from the hands of the tyrant, and the deaths of King Chimalpopoca and Tlacateotzin, lord of Tlatelolco

The words of his uncle Chimalpopocatzin were etched deeply in Nezahual-coyotzin's soul. He remembered and followed the advice he had been given in metaphorical and allegorical terms, but he also implemented it in its literal sense. For as soon as he reached the city of Tezcuco, he ordered the walls behind his seat and dais to be tunneled through in secret, which later allowed him to escape alive (as will be seen below). When this task was done, he returned to the city of Azcapotzalco to see the tyrant and thank him for the mercy he had shown by releasing his uncle. Nezahualcoyotl arrived at dawn and went immediately to the palace where, in the main courtyard, he saw many armed men and numerous shields and spears lining the walls, because King Maxtla had just ordered them to go to the city of Tezcuco to kill him. When one of the captains saw him, he came forward to greet him and said, "Welcome, lord. At this moment, the king sends us to your city and court to search for Pancol, who has run away." Then he took him to a hall to await Maxtla's orders. As he passed among the soldiers, Nezahualcoyotzin greeted them all and told them that he wanted to see the great lord. One of the palace servants quickly informed the king that Nezahualcoyotl wanted to see him and was waiting in a hall. Maxtla summoned him.

When Nezahualcoyotl appeared before him, Maxtla turned away and refused to speak to him. Nezahualcoyotl saw that two concubines of his uncle King Chimalpopoca accompanied Maxtla on his dais; one was named Quetzalmalin and the other Pochtlampa. Nezahualcoyotl presented the king with bouquets of flowers, but Maxtla would not accept them, so he placed them at his feet. And when Nezahualcoyotl spoke to him, Maxtla did not respond. Seeing this, Nezahualcoyotzin left, and Chacha the chamberlain told him in private how his lord the king had ordered his death, how the armed soldiers he had seen in the courtyard had just been sent to kill him, and that he should try to leave and escape with his life if possible. [fol. 20v] So Nezahualcoyotzin left by a side door that led to some gardens within the king's palace and entered a large hall that had a straw roof. He ordered Xiconocatzin, who had come with him from the city of Tezcuco, to stand watch at the door while he escaped, and if anyone should come looking for him, to say that he had gone outside to attend to his necessities; if he managed to escape, he would wait for him near Tlatelolco. And so he broke through the roof of the hall where he found it easiest, escaped through the hole, and made for the agreed-upon place.

Nezahualcoyotzin had barely escaped when some captains rushed up to Xiconocatzin. When they questioned him, he answered as he had been instructed. They told him to go get Nezahualcoyotzin immediately because the king was looking for him. Xiconocatzin did not wait for further explanations; he left the palace as quickly as he could, making himself inconspicuous until he could rejoin Nezahualcoyotzin. By now, all the soldiers and king's guard were frantically searching for Nezahualcoyotzin all over the city, and though some of his pursuers nearly caught him, he was so fleet of foot that he evaded their grasp. And as he ran, he shouted that he would soon destroy them in blood and fire. Having survived these dangers and perils, Nezahualcoyotzin and Xiconocatzin met near Tlatelolco. They were weak from hunger, so they were forced to buy food in the first houses they came to outside the city. Then they boarded a canoe and crossed over to their city of Tezcuco.

Seeing that Nezahualcoyotzin had escaped and the soldiers had not been able to kill him, the tyrant Maxtla took his cruelty and fury out on them and killed them all. Then he sent others to Mexico with specific orders to kill Chimalpopocatzin and Tlacateotzin. And going straight to Tenochtitlan, they found the king in a temple chamber where some sculptors were carving an idol named [fol. 21r] Tecuhxilotl. When they saw the king, the soldiers led him away from those craftsmen to another chamber, called *huitzcali*, as if they wanted to discuss serious matters with him. When they were alone with him in that chamber, they bludgeoned him to death with a cudgel. And as they left the hall, they told the Mexicas that they should go in to see their lord, who was sleeping, and they hurried off to Tlatelolco. Finding their king dead, the Mexicas chased after them. When they caught up with them, there was a fight, which allowed Tlacateotzin to escape. Getting into a large canoe laden with gold, jewels, and riches, he fled across the lake toward Tezcuco. The Tepanecas set off in pursuit. They caught up with him in the middle of the lake where they speared him to death. This was the end of these two Mexica lords.

After they died, their Mexica vassals took them and performed their customary funeral rites. They yearned to avenge this affront, but they left it for another time because they did not have enough troops and finding successors to rule and govern them was a more pressing matter. So the Tenochcas swore allegiance and fealty to Itzcoatzin, Chimalpopocatzin's younger brother, who possessed all the necessary qualities of a king, especially one who was to rule during such dire and difficult circumstances. The Tlatelolcas chose Quauhtlatoatzin, who was no less brave than King Itzcoatzin, as their lord.

🌿 CHAPTER 25

How Nezahualcoyotzin twice more eluded the grasp of his enemies

Once the Mexica lords were dead, the only thing the tyrant Maxtla needed to do to gain uncontested control over the empire was to take the life of Prince Nezahualcoyotzin. Despite his best efforts, he had been unsuccessful the last time. He thus proceeded with his scheme in another way, which was to order his nephew Yancuiltzin, the bastard brother of Prince Nezahualcoyotzin, to host a banquet and, in the safety of his own home, kill the prince. But Nezahualcoyotzin's tutor Huitzilihuitzin, a nobleman of the city of Tezcuco [fol. 21v] skilled in astrology, learned of this betrayal and through his divinations sensed that Nezahualcoyotzin would be in great danger were he to attend the banquet. To prevent this, he summoned a young commoner from Coatepec, in the province of Otumba, who was close to the prince in age and appearance. Time was short, but in just a few days they secretly instructed him in courtly manners and conventions, while Nezahualcoyotzin postponed the banquet that his brother was to hold in his honor.

It was customary for everyone to participate in a dance on the first night of such banquets and feasts. Unaware of the danger he was in, the young man arrived adorned in royal vestments. Once he was seated on the royal throne accompanied by the servants, tutors, and confidants of Nezahualcoyotzin, Yancuiltzin arrived to escort him with great fanfare into the festivities that were being held at his house. He led the young man through great halls, corridors, and patios, alight with braziers and torches. After paying his compliments, Yancuiltzin brought him into his house, and the dance began as soon as he entered. He had danced around the hall three times when a captain approached from behind and struck him on the head with a cudgel. He fell to the ground stunned, and they immediately cut off his head and sent it quickly to King Maxtla, certain that it was Nezahualcoyotzin's.

Nezahualcoyotzin was ready, and as soon as he learned of the death of the man serving as his decoy, he embarked for Mexico to congratulate his uncle Itzcoatzin for his recent election as ruler. He arrived at the palace at dawn and went in to visit with Itzcoatzin. They had been chatting a short while when some messengers arrived from King Maxtla bearing the head of the young

man and informing Itzcoatzin that Prince Nezahualcoyotzin was dead. The
messengers, seeing him alive there with his uncle, were dumbstruck with fear
and awe. Aware of what they were thinking, Nezahualcoyotzin told them not
to waste their energy trying [fol. 22r] to kill him, because the great and mighty
God had made him immortal.

The messengers took this news to King Maxtla at once. Upon hearing it, he
became so angry and indignant that he immediately gathered his forces and
sent an army of considerable size to the city of Tezcuco, knowing that Nezahualcoyotzin would have returned there. He ordered the four captains that
led the army[71] to enter the city of Tezcuco quickly and spread their soldiers
throughout it; once all the city's streets, entrances, and exits were secured, they
were to go with as many people as necessary to find and kill Nezahualcoyotzin.
The captains marched their army to Tezcuco. Tomihua, the lord of Coatepec,
warned Nezahualcoyotzin, who convened his council to decide a course of
action. The lords who were on Nezahualcoyotl's side met in his palace called
Çilan. They included his older brother Quauhtlehuanitzin, who was his father's
illegitimate son, Tzontecochatzin, and others. Nezahualcoyotzin told them that
his enemies would arrive the next day to kill him and that he was determined
to wait for them, welcome them, and not hide from them. Quauhtlehuanitzin
answered by saying:

> My lord and brother, strengthen your heart so that you may withstand
> the blows of fortune. These difficulties and dangers were bequeathed to
> you by your father, King Ometochtli Ixtlilxochitl. You are well aware of
> the toils and persecutions that he suffered until he died while defending
> his kingdom. His body was left as the foundation and bulwark of the
> Chichimeca Empire and Aculhua Kingdom. And now you have seen what
> happened with the Mexicas: the tyrant Maxtla went so far as to kill his
> uncle King Chimalpopoca. What greater threat and calamity could there
> be than what the world is now facing?

Then Tzontechochatzin told Nezahualcoyotl:

> Powerful lord, great are the toils and burdens that afflict Your Highness;
> they were left to you by my lord, King Ixtlilxochitl, and by his captain
> general, Çoacuecuentzin, my father, when the tyrant Teçoçomoc cruelly

---

71. A blank line in the manuscript was reserved for the names of the captains.

killed them. I can find nothing appropriate to say to Your Highness, nor offer any counsel beyond that given by the lord Quauhtlehuanitzin, your brother.

After Tzontecochatzin had [fol. 22v] spoken, Quauhtlehuanitzin spoke again, telling Nezahualcoyotl, "Lord, it is clear from what you have said that Your Highness's soul is troubled. But what else could the tyrant Maxtla, possibly want?" To these words, Nezahualcoyotl replied, "It will be well to have a ballgame[72] tomorrow, which will distract us until the arrival of our enemies, the Tepanecas; Coiohua will go out to greet them and will lodge them in my house, where they will be entertained." Then they discussed several things related to this plan, such as mustering soldiers to help Nezahualcoyotl and defend him from his enemies if necessary.

That night, Nezahualcoyotl sent one of his servants, whose name was Tehuitzil, to go meet his tutor Huitzilihuitzin, whose advice Nezahualcoyotl always followed. He was to tell him that he had decided to welcome his enemies and that the time had come to carry out the plan Huitzilihuitzin had suggested for recovering the kingdom of the Aculhuas and empire of the Chichimecas, because he knew for certain that they were coming tomorrow to kill him. Having heard what the messenger had to say on behalf of his student, Huitzilihuitzin started to cry and told the messenger,

Tehuitzil, go tell my son, Prince Acolmiztli Nezahualcoyotl, to take heart and have courage and to undertake what he must, for I have already told him how and when and which places will come to his aid, such as the provinces of Huexotzinco, Tlaxcalan, Zacatlan, and Tototepec; he knows that they are men of courage and most of them are Chichimecas and others are Otomies, and they will not abandon him, rather they will give their lives for him.

Then Huitzilihuitzin sent the messenger away. Having heard the message from his tutor and teacher, that very night Nezahualcoyotl began sending dispatches to the lords who supported him. He sent one of his servants, whose name was Coztotolomi Tocuiltecatl, to the city of Huexotzinco to inform Xaiacamachan,

---

72. The ballgame, or *ollamaliztli* in Nahuatl, pitted two individuals or teams against one another who tried to win by passing a solid-rubber ball through a vertical ring set into the side of the court, using only the hips, buttocks, or knees. It was widely played throughout Mesoamerica.

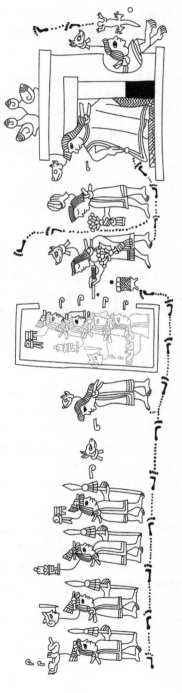

FIGURE 13. Nezahualcoyotl's escape (based on the Codex Xolotl, plate 9).

who was lord at the time, about the peril he faced. The servant was to tell Xaia-camachan that the time had come to help Nezahualcoyotzin avenge the death of King Ixtlilxochitl, his father and lord; recover the empire; and punish the rebels. For it would not be right that the tyrant should kill Nezahualcoyotl before his mission was complete. Then Nezahualcoyotl dispatched the messenger.

The next day, while they waited for their enemies, Nezahualcoyotl and all his men organized a ballgame at the court near the palace gates. Following King Maxtla's commands, the four captains came to Nezahualcoyotl's palace accompanied by some of their forces. [fol. 23r] And when Nezahualcoyotl and his men saw that they were approaching, Coiohua, who was tasked with receiving them, welcomed them (fig. 13).They asked him where Nezahualcoyotzin was. He told them to come in and rest a while and that very shortly Nezahualcoyotzin would come out to meet with them. Once they had entered one of the rooms of the palace that faced the royal hall, Nezahualcoyotzin came out, and giving them bouquets of flowers and sticks of liquidambar, he bade them welcome and invited them to rest and make themselves at home. They told him that they had come to play ball with him. He replied that they should have something to eat first and that there would be time for everything later. He then ordered the tables to be very splendidly laid. While this was being done and they were eating, he went to the aforementioned hall, where he sat on his seat and throne in such a way that his enemies had him always in their sight. They were eating very contentedly when it seemed to Coiohua that it was a good time for Nezahualcoyotzin to leave through the tunnel that had been dug out behind his seat and chair (as explained above). Coiohua, his servant, gave him the signal to leave, which was to shake out his mantle and remove some specks from it while exiting through the door of the hall. With that, Nezahualcoyotzin escaped through the aforementioned hole and tunnel, which led to another tunnel formed by a water duct that entered the palace. In this way, he was able to escape, having made good use of his uncle Chimalpopoca's advice.

When they had finished eating, the four captains went to the hall in which they expected to find Nezahualcoyotzin. Finding him gone, they seized Coiohua and wanted to kill him. He told them that it would be of little use to kill him, for he was a poor old man. It would be better for them to escape, because he did not think they would leave the palace alive, given the number of warriors whom Nezahualcoyotzin had gathered together to defend himself from them. When the captains heard this information, though it was untrue, it caused them much terror and fright. And they left in a great hurry, fleeing the palace and calling on their soldiers to steel themselves to fight against those whom they believed were there to defend Nezahualcoyotzin. With that, Coiohua was left free, and he escaped from their hands, having outwitted them. They stayed awake all that night; some of them kept watch, while others went around looking for Nezahualcoyotzin, who [. . .][73]

---

73. In the manuscript, this chapter was left unfinished; the last sentence is incomplete: *Nezahualcoyotzin, el que . . .*

[fol. 23v]

 CHAPTER 26

Of Nezahualcoyotzin's life and journey through the mountains and deserts to the place where Quacoz, an Otomi nobleman, lived

A few hours later, the tyrant Maxtla was informed that Nezahualcoyotzin had escaped. Maxtla sent orders to the lords throughout the land to seize him wherever they found him and send him back, dead or alive. He promised great rewards and favors to the one who succeeded in doing this. He also had it proclaimed in all the kingdom's cities, towns, and villages that the man who found him, if he were young, would be given a beautiful noblewoman for a wife along with lands and many vassals, even if he had been born a peasant; and if he were already married, instead of a wife, he would receive many male and female slaves, along with everything else. All of this was done. The Tepanecas were like rabid dogs hunting for Nezahualcoyotzin throughout the land. And within an area more than one hundred leagues in circumference, there was not a town or village where gangs did not roam looking for him. The day that Nezahualcoyotzin escaped through the tunnel and hole he had made was called *çe cuetzpalin*,[74] the twelfth day of their seventh month, called *huey tecuhilhuitl*,[75] which by our count is July 20 (of the aforementioned year).

Having escaped that danger, Nezahualcoyotl went to a house near the city called Coatlan that belonged to a vassal of his named Tozoma, whom he told about the danger he was in and how he was fleeing from his enemies. As they were closing in on him, Tozoma hid him under a dais that he covered with a pile of henequen—which is the fiber made from the maguey plant. The soldiers entered and searched all over the house, and when they did not find him, they beat the entire household to make them deliver Nezahualcoyotl. But Tozoma and the people of the house were so steadfast that they would not betray him, even after two elderly people died from the blows they received. When the soldiers left, Nezahualcoyotl came out from his hiding place and, washing his head and face, thanked them and promised to reward their loyalty. Then he climbed up a

---

74. One Lizard.
75. Great Festival of the Lords.

hill, where he was spotted once again by the enemy. And approaching a woman who was harvesting chia, he told her to instruct her people to hide him under the stalks she was cutting before the enemy arrived. The woman quickly [fol. 24r] hid him under a pile of sheaves. When they arrived, the Tepanecas asked about Nezahualcoyotl. The woman told them with great cunning that he had run past a short time ago and that he seemed to be headed to Huexotla. The soldiers quickly took off in that direction, hoping to catch him, while Nezahualcoyotzin turned the other way, heading for the woods of Tetzcotzinco, where he slept that night. And he sent his messengers to different places. He sent Tecuhxolotl specifically to the province of Chalco to ask Totequiztzin and Quateotzin, lords of the town of Tlalmanalco, on his behalf to send people to help him. And on behalf of Huitzilihuitzin, Nezahualcoyotzin's tutor and mentor, Tecuhxolotl was to go request the same from Toteoçitecuhtli, Huitzilihuitzin's brother-in-law, who was supreme lord of the whole province at the time.

The next day, very early in the morning, Nezahualcoyotzin climbed up the mountain, and in order to travel more securely, he ordered two of his servants, one called Colicatl and another Calmimilolcatl, to walk ahead of and behind him and to remain watchful and vigilant in case his enemies should appear at some point. If they should see any, they were to signal by coughing. In this way, he was able to continue his journey safely without being seen by his enemies. Coming to a place called Metla, he was fed by a servant of his named Tecpan. And from there, after he had eaten, he passed through a place called Zacaxo- chitla on his way to the home of an Otomi nobleman named Quacoz, who had been page to his mother, the queen. There he spent the night, and his enemies would have caught him but for Quacoz's quick thinking. Having learned that the enemy was headed to his town, Quacoz quickly summoned all the Otomies who lived there, ordering them to come with their bows and arrows. He placed a large drum in the middle of his courtyard with Nezahualcoyotzin inside of it and started beating it, and everyone began singing as if going to war. When the Tepanecas arrived, the Otomies asked them what they were looking for. Prince Nezahualcoyotzin, they replied. Quacoz told them that princes, who lived at court, had no place there, and that they must be bandits, since they came armed and under such pretense. He called to his people and rushed at the Tepanecas, [fol. 24v] driving them out. The Tepanecas fled, most of them wounded, and dared not stop anywhere on that mountain.

On the following day, Quacoz took Nezahualcoyotzin to a very remote, rugged, and rocky place where he had a hut prepared for him. He told him to stay there, assuring him he would be safe. Meanwhile, Quacoz would ascertain whether the enemy had left those mountains and whether Nezahualcoyotzin might continue safely on his journey. The prince told Quacoz that his greatest concern was for his own house; he worried that the enemy had ransacked it and taken the women of the court prisoner. Quacoz told him he would go and find out and that he would bring the noblewomen to him and relieve him of that worry and woe. Nezahualcoyotzin thanked him, enjoining him to do it carefully and discreetly. Quacoz was so skillful that he managed to reach the palace a few hours later, where he found the women grief-stricken. He told them he had been ordered by their lord the prince to come for them and that they should exchange their clothes for the humble attire of commoners, that a servant he had brought with him would travel ahead with their bundles, and that they should follow his lead. Sometimes he would go in front and sometimes in back so that no one would realize that he was escorting them. He ordered the palace servants to look after the house and not to reveal where the women had gone if anyone asked about them. Walking with the women near a hill called Patlachiuhcan, at the place they call Olopan, he encountered the enemy looking for Prince Nezahualcoyotzin. They seized him and asked him where Nezahualcoyotzin was and about those women passing by, whom they thought must be women of his court. Quacoz replied that he did not know who Nezahualcoyotl was, that he belonged to the Chichimeca nation and that he had grown up in those hills and mountains. Recognizing his barbarous language and dress, they left him alone. Quacoz continued on his way with the women until they reached Prince Nezahualcoyotzin. By then, Quauhtlehuanitzin and his nephew Tzontecochatzin were already with him.

The next morning, Nezahualcoyotzin left that place. Quacoz bid him farewell, explaining that he would not accompany him. The enemy would surely come looking for him because of the way he had treated them two days earlier, [fol. 25r] and they would notice his absence if he were not there, thereby discovering Nezahualcoyotzin. Six Otomies called Nochcuani, Nolin, Coatl, Tlalolin, Toto, and Xochtonal would instead go with Nezahualcoyotzin and scout the land; they were rugged mountain men who knew their way around those hills. Nezahualcoyotl thanked Quacoz for his service and proceeded on his way. Some of the Otomies went ahead and others followed behind, and pretending to hunt, they reconnoitered the land and guarded Nezahualcoyotzin, who was traveling with Quauhtlehuanitzin and Tzontecochatzin.

🌿   CHAPTER 27

Which deals with how Nezahualcoyotzin continued on his
journey and wanderings until he reached Capolac and what
happened to him on the way

As Prince Nezahualcoyotzin neared a place called Tlecuilac, he was very sad and
pensive, reflecting on the calamities and travails that he suffered since the death
of his father. He looked behind him and saw the many people still following
him, including many of the citizens of Tezcuco, some noblemen, and most of his
tutors and servants. He addressed them with some passion and anger, saying:

> Where are you going? Why do you follow me as though I were a father who
> could protect and defend you? Can you not see how wretched and alone I
> am as I wander these mountains and deserts along the deer paths and rabbit
> trails? Can you not see that I do not know whether I will be welcomed where
> I go, or if my enemies will catch me and kill me? They killed my father, who
> was more powerful than I, and I am but an orphan, abandoned by all. Go
> back to your homes. Do not die with me or provoke the displeasure of the
> tyrant and forfeit your homes and property for my sake.

Quauhtlehuanitzin and Tzontecochatzin, along with everyone else, replied
that they wanted only to follow him and die wherever he should die. Hearing
this, Nezahualcoyotzin was greatly moved and wept, as did all the people in his
company. Regaining his composure, he thanked them profusely and begged them
to return to their houses, where they could serve him by ascertaining the plans
of the tyrant and his enemies. And he promised to be diligent in keeping them
informed of everything that happened on his journey and quest. So everyone
turned back, except those who were necessary to attend to his [fol. 25v] needs.
His brother Quauhtlehuanitzin and his nephew Tzontecochatzin also insisted
on going with him, saying that nothing could make them turn back, for if at
any point they should be seen, they faced the same risk as His Highness. They
therefore wanted to go on serving him wherever he went.

Proceeding on their journey, they traversed one mountain called Papalotepec
and reached the top of another called Huilotepec just before sunset, and from
there Nezahualcoyotzin surveyed his surroundings, looking toward the plains
of Huexotzinco, which were already darkened by the shadows of the mountains.

In the other direction, he saw the hills of the town of Tepepolco, where a few rays of sunlight still shone. From here, he sent another message to the lords of the province of Huexotzinco, telling them that he would wait in Capolapan for their decision about when they would arrive to help him. The men who took this message were called Coiohua and Teotzincatl.

After spending the night in these mountains, Nezahualcoyotzin continued his journey the next day before dawn. Descending through some hills, he found himself in farmland near some caves. On a nearby road, Nezahualcoyotzin and his companions saw approaching a group of enemy soldiers who had been searching for him in the provinces of Huexotzinco and Tlaxcalan, so they hid in some elderberry bushes near the road. When the soldiers drew near to their hiding place, they encountered a young man from a nearby village carrying chia. They asked him if he had seen Nezahualcoyotzin. The young man answered that he had never met him. Taking their leave, they told him to inform the Tepanecas if he did and that he would receive the promised rewards. When Nezahualcoyotzin saw that the enemy was far away, they proceeded on their way and caught up to the villager, who told them what had happened with the soldiers he had met. Nezahualcoyotzin asked him whether he would denounce the person they were looking for if he saw him. He said no. Nezahualcoyotl argued that it would be a shame for him to forego a beautiful wife and everything else that King Maxtla had promised. The young man chuckled, dismissive of all of those promises. [fol. 26r]

Nezahualcoyotzin continued on his way toward Yahualiuhcan, and halfway there, Mihua, one of his servants, brought him food. After eating, he reached Yahualiuhcan, where he spent the night. The next day he went to a different place called Quauhtepec, where he also spent the night. Messengers sent by the lords of the city and province of Huexotzinco arrived there to console him and tell him that on the appointed day they would do everything within their power to help him. They also brought a large gift of cloth and many provisions from the lords Xaiacamachan and Temaiahuatzin. The following day he went to a place called Calnapanolco, which belonged to the province of Tlaxcalan. Tlotlililcauhtzin, ambassador of the confederation of Tlaxcalan,[76] came out to greet him and

---

76. We have chosen to translate Alva Ixtlilxochitl's term *señoría* as "confederation." Señoría translates more literally as "lordship, sovereignty, seigniory, or lordly title." However, in this text, Alva Ixtlilxochitl uses it exclusively to refer collectively to the semiautonomous lordships of Tlaxcala, whose political organization was distinct from that of the Chichimeca Empire. Medieval and early modern Spanish writers often used the term

escorted him to Calnapanolco. On behalf of his lords, Tlotlililcauhtzin reassured Nezahualcoyotzin and promised aid in the form of men and supplies to recover his kingdom and the Chichimeca Empire. He also gave Nezahualcoyotzin great quantities of cloth and supplies sent by the confederation as a gift. Nezahual-coyotzin spent the night there, and the next morning, the ambassador told him that he would take him to a different place called Capolapan, where the confederation had readied many large huts for him to lodge his entire army, and they would march from there to Tezcuco. When he reached Capolapan, all the messengers he had sent to various places arrived with news that help that was on the way, specifically troops from Zacatlan, Tototepec, Tepepolco, Tlaxcalan, Cempoalan, and other places, who would gather there four days later. They also said that the troops from Huexotzinco, Chololan, and Chalco would join him within sight of Coatlichan. This brought him great reassurance and confidence that he would succeed.

---

señoría in a similar way to distinguish between the señoría of Venice and the *imperio* of Rome. While the señoría of Venice is often called a "republic" in English, the term "confederation" more accurately reflects the Tlaxcalteca arrangement.

🌿 CHAPTER 28

Of how Prince Nezahualcoyotzin marched with a powerful
army toward Tezcuco, how he recovered the kingdom of the
Aculhuas, and some noteworthy events that occurred

The message delivered by Tecuhxolotl to the province of Chalco is one of the most elaborately portrayed events in the general history of the Chichimeca Empire. Therefore, it would not be right to ignore it or what befell Huitzilihuitzin, Nezahual-coyotzin's tutor. [fol. 26v] So it went that after Huitzilihuitzin left Nezahualcoyotzin the night he slept in the woods of Tetzcotzinco, he went home with Tecuhxolotl. From there, Huitzilihuitzin dispatched Tecuhxolotl to the province of Chalco, and no sooner had he sent him off than the enemy arrived, seized Huitzilihuitzin, and took him as a prisoner to Yancuiltzin, who had been made lord of the city of Tezcuco by order of his uncle Maxtla. Yancuiltzin had the old man tortured with cords[77] to force him to reveal the location of his student Nezahualcoyotzin. But Huitzilihuitzin would not confess, so they sent him to be sacrificed at a nearby temple of the idol Camaxtle. Once they had taken him to the top of the temple for this purpose, a great storm arose, and a strong wind began to uproot trees and tear the roofs off of houses. The wind eventually picked up the battered old man and carried him a great distance. His two sons, who were watching fearfully from afar to see how this would end, witnessed their father freed from his ordeal and took him to a hiding place, where they nursed him back to health.

Tecuhxolotl went to Chalco through the mountains to avoid being seen by the enemy and became lost in the most rugged part. There he ran into a very fierce lion. Tecuhxolotl wanted to run away, but the lion began to nuzzle him, as though coaxing him toward a path. The lion led him all the way out of the mountains, leaving him at the outskirts of the town of Tlalmanalco. Once there, Tecuhxolotl gave his message to Totequiztecuhtli and Quateotzin, who were greatly saddened by the persecution and toils of Prince Nezahualcoyotzin. They told Tecuhxolotl that they were very willing to provide the help he asked of them but Toteoçitecuhtli was the supreme lord [of Chalco] at that time, therefore, Tecuhxolotl should go see him first. And so Tecuhxolotl went to Toteoçitecuhtli's

---

77. The *tormento de cordeles* involved wrapping cords around the legs, arms, or fingers of the victim and progressively tightening them, sometimes by twisting a stick.

court. But before he did anything else, he spoke to Atototzin, Toteoçitecuhtli's wife and Huitzilihuitzin's sister. Anguished and brought to tears by the prince's travails, Atototzin promised to do everything she could to ensure that her husband, Toteoçitecuhtli, would grant the requested aid. Toteoçitecuhtli ordered all the lords and nobles to present themselves at court the following day and decide if they should provide the support Nezahualcoyotzin requested. Then, before dawn, he had Tecuhxolotl put on a stage in the plaza with his hands and feet tightly bound to a post in a way that seemed cruel. When the time came for the lords and nobles to assemble and the plaza was full of people, Toteoçitecuhtli ordered the messenger Tecuhxolotl unveiled and had a town crier announce the reason for his visit, so that those in the province could decide for themselves what should be done. If they wanted to provide aid, Toteoçitecuhtli would set him free and send him back and if not, he would have him killed. The announcement aroused great pity; everyone shouted for him to release the prisoner and that they wanted to provide aid and succor to Nezahualcoyotzin, for his claim was just. With that, Toteoçitecuhtli had Tecuhxolotl unbound and sent away with his mission accomplished. Tecuhxolotl went straight to Huitzilihuitzin. When Tecuhxolotl explained what had happened, Huitzilihuitzin comforted him and encouraged him to go on to Capolapan, where he would find Nezahualcoyotzin, which is what he did, [f. 27r] as described above.

Old Huitzilihuitzin also resolved to go meet Nezahualcoyotzin. When he reached the top of the mountain of Tepetlaoztoc, he was somewhat stiff with cold and sought shelter in a nearby hut, hoping to find fire. When he did not find any, he took some ashes and mixed them with a few leaves of a plant called *picietl*[78] in order to comfort his stomach, for this is a warming plant. Suddenly it ignited as if it were gunpowder, which he took as an auspicious sign of the success that his lord the prince would have. Meanwhile, Nezahualcoyotzin had left the town of Ahuatepec with his forces that same day and was on the march. He came out above Zoltepec, where to his great joy he encountered Huitzilihuitzin, and they comforted one another. That day he stopped and spent the night at old Huitzilihuitzin's house, where he was visited by all the lords and nobles who were on his side. And he saw fires and smoke on the highest peaks, which were the agreed-upon signals of the lords who would support and aid him; these people were already near because the battle was to take place on the next day. They had specifically agreed to attack Acolman and Coatlichan, where the entirety of the enemy's forces was located. The

---

78. The name for tobacco in Nahuatl.

Tlaxcaltecas and the Huexotzincas were tasked with Acolman, and the Chalcas would fight against Coatlichan. Nezahualcoyotzin took command of the rest of the army, including those from the provinces who were helping him as well as the natives of the kingdom of Tezcuco, firstly, to help either of the aforementioned forces as necessary and, secondly, to enter the city of Tezcuco, plunder the houses of his enemies, and kill the Tepanecas and anyone else who resisted.

The battle began on both fronts at dawn the next day. Nezahualcoyotzin charged so suddenly and with such a great number of troops that the Tepanecas and their allies were quickly defeated and killed, despite their best efforts to defend themselves. The houses in and around the cities of Coatlichan and Acolman were pillaged; the temples and lords' houses were burned. Temoyahuitzin, lord of the province of Huexotzinco, who fought alongside the Tlaxcalteca forces in the battle for the city of Acolman, personally killed Teiolcocoatzin, Teçoçomoc's grandson, whom the tyrant had appointed as one of the two leaders of the Aculhua Kingdom. The other leader, named Quetzalmaquiztli, lord of Coatlichan, met the same fate at the hands of the Chalcas; he was also a grandson of the tyrant Teçoçomoc. He and the most important captains of his kingdom had retreated to the city's main temple and barricaded themselves inside, where they were killed. Quetzalmaquiztli was thrown off of the temple and his body broken to pieces. When Nezahualcoyotzin, who had taken part in both battles, saw that his work there was done, he entered the city of Tezcuco and destroyed his enemies' houses. The [fol. 27v] whole city soon fell to him and surrendered.

Nezahualcoyotl went to Huexotla to thank the Chalca army, granting to them all the spoils they had won from the capital city of Coatlichan. He thanked their lords for the service they had rendered to him and he sent them off, telling them to prepare to recover the rest of the empire and that he would send word when the time came. From there he headed back to Acolman because he had learned that the armies of the Huexotzincas and Tlaxcaltecas wanted to go home. And so, in the town of Chiauhtla, he bid them farewell, granting them the same reward as the Chalcas and thanking them for the service they had rendered him. He asked them likewise to be ready so that when he sent word, they could send the help he needed to recover the whole of the empire. In the same manner, he dismissed those from Zacatlan, Tototepec, Chololan, and other places. The only ones who remained with him were the best soldiers, whose sole occupation was warfare. With them and the people of his kingdom who had remained loyal, he fortified the city of Tezcuco and established the borders with the Tepanecas and the Mexicas. With this he was finally triumphant and victorious in his city.

🌿 CHAPTER 29

Which deals with how the general history of the empire of the Chichimeca lords ends, the state in which it was left by the authors who painted it, and what the tyrant Maxtla did up to this point

When Maxtla learned that Nezahualcoyotzin had escaped and was trying to free himself from persecution and recover the empire, he quickly sent offers of very generous gifts and rewards not only to those in the city and kingdom of Tezcuco, who belonged to the house and lineage of Nezahualcoyotzin, but also to every lord of every province throughout the empire, asking them to capture and kill Nezahualcoyotzin, as described above. Some of Nezahualcoyotzin's relatives were eager to please the tyrant; those most opposed to Nezahualcoyotzin were his brother-in-law Nonoalcatzin, who was married to his sister Princess Tozquentzin, his brother Yancuiltzin, and Tochpilli. They did everything they could to kill Nezahualcoyotzin, but they were thwarted, as previously stated. The ones who did not die in the battle fled the city to avoid falling into Nezahualcoyotzin's hands and paying for their crimes.

Nezahualcoyotzin recovered the Aculhua Kingdom, capital [fol. 28r] and foundation of the Chichimeca Empire, so quickly that it seemed to Maxtla like a lightning bolt from the heavens. In only fourteen days, Nezahualcoyotzin had slipped through Maxtla's fingers, crossed the mountains, amassed a powerful army without being noticed, and recovered the kingdom of Tezcuco, as described. Amazed by this, Maxtla began making preparations, working intently to stop his progress. Additionally, he began to oppress the Mexicas greatly at this time, imposing excessive tributes that were impossible to pay, as a means of revenge.

The general history of the Çoacuecuenotzin Empire, authored by Çemilhuitzin and Quauhquechol, ends here, eleven years after the death of Emperor Ixtlilxochitl and his great captain general, Çoacuecuenotzin, when Nezahualcoyotl was preparing the army to attack the enemy. This was at the beginning of the year 1428 of the incarnation of Christ our Lord, which they called *çe tecpatl*.[79] All that follows hereafter is taken from other particular histories and from the

---

79. One Flint.

annals of this New Spain. This prince recovered his kingdom of Tezcuco on a day they call *çe olin*,[80] which falls on the fifth day of their eighth month called *micailhuiltzintli*,[81] on the eleventh day of the month of August in the year of our Lord 1427.

---

80. One Movement.
81. Little Festival of the Dead.

🌿 CHAPTER 30

Of how the Mexicas, finding themselves greatly oppressed by
the tyrant Maxtla, decided to send ambassadors to Prince
Nezahualcoyotzin so that he would help them, and the things
that happened to them during this time

The Mexicas, who had been the main allies of the tyrant Teçoçomoc, king of the Tepanecas, refused to obey Maxtla because he had killed their lords and committed other cruelties and offenses against them. He demanded as tribute items that were difficult to find or hard to deliver, asking them to bring produce and game birds across the lake. Most outrageously, he attempted to force himself on the queen, King Itzcoatl's legitimate wife, insulting and offending the Mexicas. Thus, afflicted by Maxtla on one the hand and threatened by Prince Nezahualcoyotzin on the other for having been accomplices in the betrayal and death of his father, the Mexicas gathered in council to figure out what to do. [f. 28v] They decided to seek the good will of Nezahualcoyotzin, whom fortune had begun to favor, in order to achieve peace and liberty. And although they were partly to blame for Teçoçomoc's tyranny, they nonetheless decided to send their ambassadors to Nezahualcoyotzin to beg forgiveness. They were also to ask him to send his forces to their aid as soon as possible because Maxtla greatly oppressed them and had them trapped within their city; it would not be long before they were consumed and destroyed. In return, they were to offer him their troops and assistance in recovering the empire. Finally, the ambassadors were also to remind Nezahualcoyotzin of his great obligation toward the Mexica nobility, from which he himself was descended.

The ambassadors chosen for this mission were Motecuhçomatzin Ilhuicamina, Nezahualcoyotzin's beloved first cousin, who was their captain general, and two other noblemen, one named Totopilatzin and the other Telpoch. As stealthily as possible, the ambassadors left the city of Mexico and headed for Tezcuco. At the Aculhuacan border they were seized by the soldiers of Nezahualcoyotzin stationed there. When the soldiers realized that the ambassadors were relatives of their lord, they did not kill them, but instead they escorted them under heavy guard as prisoners. Nezahualcoyotzin was pleased to see them when they were brought before him, but once they delivered their message and he learned of the Mexicas' hardships, he became very sad. In order to help them quickly, he sent his brother Quauhtlehuanitzin, his cousin Motecuhçoma, and Totopilatzin to the province of Chalco, the nearest place from which he could expect aid, to ask Toteoçitecuhtli to provide it as quickly as the situation demanded; the nobleman named Telpoch remained with him. Similarly, Nezahualcoyotzin sent his brother Xiconocatzin and three other high-ranking noblemen to summon his captain general, Itlacauhtzin, lord of Huexotla, who was gathering forces and preparing for the agreed-upon campaign against the tyrant. The messages that Nezahualcoyotzin sent were displeasing to the Chalcas and Itlacauhtzin, his captain general, because they utterly despised the Mexicas for the insults and cruelties they had committed against them when they were at the height of their power and in the good graces of the Tepaneca kings. So the captain general replied by tearing to pieces the prince's brother and the noblemen who were with him, preferring to betray his king rather than support the Mexicas.

Toteoçitecuhtli had those who went to Chalco seized and placed under heavy guard and put Quateotzin, one of the two lords of Tlalmanalco, in charge of them. That night, Quateotzin gave the order to release the prisoners and set them free. [fol. 29r] Toteoçitecuhtli had sent messengers to inform Maxtla that he had imprisoned the ambassadors. He had hoped to find favor with Maxtla, but the tyrant was so indignant about the help Toteoçitecuhtli had provided Nezahualcoyotzin in recovering his kingdom, that he responded by threatening to destroy him. Maxtla also told him to do whatever he wanted with the prisoners. When Toteoçitecuhtli learned that the prisoners had escaped the night before, he became angry with Quateotzin and had him killed. When the ambassadors returned to the city of Tezcuco, Nezahualcoyotzin comforted them and sent them to Mexico, telling them that he would soon follow with as many troops as he could muster. For he had received news from Tlaxcalan, Huexotzinco, and other provinces that they were already on their way to aid him.

🌿   CHAPTER 31

*Of how Nezahualcoyotzin went to Mexico with his army to
support the Mexicas*

Seeing the plight of his uncles and their vassals the Mexicas, Nezahualcoyotzin
quickly gathered as many men as were willing to follow him over land and water,
and they left for Mexico. But as they set off across the lake, he was attacked from
the rear by Itlacauhtzin, his captain general, who had betrayed him along with all
the other rebels who proclaimed support for the Tepanecas. Nezahualcoyotzin
advanced across the lake as best he could, ignoring his general's insubordination
and deferring punishment until a more appropriate time. When he reached
Mexico, he disembarked at Tlatelolco, where his uncle Itzcoatzin and Quauhtlatoatzin, together with the rest of the Mexica lords, came out to greet him. After
discussing the strategy for their liberation, they joined their forces and began
fighting the Tepanecas until they drove them out of the entire city. The battle
continued. They came out in two squadrons against Maxtla, whose camp was
behind some fortifications he had built, and fought him for three days. On the
morning of the fourth day, Nezahualcoyotzin and his troops attacked from one
side and the Mexicas from the other. They fought furiously, and many people
died on both sides. But in the end, Maxtla's army was vanquished and began to
retreat, until they were forced back beyond Mexico's borders.

At this time, the lords of the Huexotzincas and the Tlaxcaltecas, along with
other allies, arrived and joined Nezahualcoyotzin's forces. Then Nezahualcoyotzin, Itzcoatzin, and the rest of the lords agreed to divide the army into three
squadrons. One [fol. 29v] would be led by Nezahualcoyotzin; he would have
Xaiacamachan by his side and half of the Huexotzincas, as well as the general
from Tlaxcalan with his men, and they would advance by way of the hill of
Quauhtepetl. Another squadron would be commanded by Itzcoatzin and would
include the other half of the Huexotzincas led by their lord Temoyahuitzin and a
great many allies that had come to support Nezahualcoyotzin; they would position
themselves opposite. Motecuhçoma and Quauhtlatoatzin, lord of Tlatelolco,
would take the third squadron. Nezahualcoyotzin told them all to await his
signal and, when they saw it, to attack their enemies all at once. At daybreak,
the battle began. And although Nezahualcoyotzin and the Mexicas were able to

gain ground, it was only with much effort and death on both sides. The fighting lasted 115 days because King Maxtla defended himself valiantly and committed all of his remaining forces. But in the final days of the war, Nezahualcoyotzin and all of the Mexica lords assailed Maxtla's men relentlessly until they were broken and defeated. They were forced to flee, and many died as they were being pursued. Nezahualcoyotzin's forces entered the city and destroyed and razed it, tearing down the temples and the largest houses belonging to all the lords and high-ranking people and putting everyone to the sword. Maxtla had hidden in a pool in his gardens and was dragged out in shame. Nezahualcoyotzin took him to the city's main plaza and tore out his heart as if he were a sacrificial victim for their gods, saying that he did it as payment for the death of his father, Emperor Ixtlilxochitl. And to further disgrace Maxtla, he decreed that his city of Azcapotzalco would henceforth host slave markets. That was the end of that famous city, which was one of the largest that existed in this New Spain. It had been given the name Azcapotzalco, which means "anthill," due to its large population.

Even though the Tepanecas who escaped from the city regrouped, fortifying themselves within Coyohuacan and Tlacopan, Nezahualcoyotzin and Itzcoatzin followed them and subjugated them. The lord of Tlacopan quickly surrendered and said that he secretly supported Nezahualcoyotzin and the Mexica lords, who were his close kin. Nezahualcoyotzin and Itzcoatzin advanced with their army, razing with equal severity all the most important cities of the [fol. 30r] Tepaneca Kingdom, such as Tenaiocan, Tepanoaian, Toltitlan, Quauhtitlan, Xaltocan, Huitzilopochco, and Colhuacan. The kingdom's other cities, towns, and villages that are not mentioned here surrendered peacefully. All of this happened in the aforementioned year of 1428. They spent the next two years attacking the city and kingdom of Tezcuco, which was in a state of upheaval at the hands of Itlacauhtzin, lord of Huexotla, and other lords and noblemen of his faction. Though they attempted to defend themselves, they could not withstand Nezahualcoyotzin's fury. Finding themselves crushed and vanquished, they fled before him; some went to the province of Chalco and others to Tlaxcalan and Huexotzinco. Since almost every city, town, and village of the kingdom of Tezcuco participated in this uprising, Nezahualcoyotzin sacked them all, burning their main temples and the houses of some of their lords. Placing a garrison in the city of Tezcuco and in other places where he thought it was warranted, he returned to Mexico. There, he and his uncle King Itzcoatzin ordered the subjugation of the city and province of Xochimilco and then Cuitlahuac. Since these places were on the lake, they had been defiant and would not submit. Until the year 1430, Nezahualcoyotzin was occupied with this, along with fencing in the forest of Chapoltepec, building an aqueduct to bring water to the city of Mexico, building a palace there, and other public works. After all of this, most of the empire was subjugated.

🌿 CHAPTER 32

Of how fealty was sworn to Nezahualcoyotzin as king of Tezcuco
Aculhuacan and emperor of the Chichimeca Empire jointly
with his uncle Itzcoatzin, king of Mexico, and Totoquihuatzin
of Tlacopan, who was given the Tepaneca Kingdom of
Azcapotzalco

In the year 1431 of the incarnation of Christ our Lord, which they call *nahui acatl*,[82] nearly four years after Nezahualcoyotzin conquered the city of Azcapo-tzalco together with his uncle King Itzcoatzin and the other allied lords and almost three years after he sacked and punished his kingdom of Aculhuacan and accomplished all that is mentioned above, Nezahualcoyotl decided the time had come to be recognized as emperor with the appropriate ceremonies. He thought that the empire, which in the time of his ancestors had been ruled by [fol. 30v] a single leader, would be better off and more enduring if ruled by three leaders, the kings and lords of the three kingdoms of Mexico, Tezcuco, and Tlacopan. To accomplish this, he discussed it with his uncle King Itzcoatzin and presented him with strong arguments in favor of his plan. Itzcoatzin liked what he heard, though he differed on the matter of Tlacopan. For one, Totoquihuatzin was nothing more than a minor lord who had been subject to the lord of Azcapotzalco. Moreover, since he belonged to the Tepaneca clan, it would be unwise to include him, lest this ignite another fire bigger than the last. Nezahualcoyotzin replied that it would be a great injustice to completely annihilate the ancient kingdom of the Tepanecas, from where so many lords, nobles, and distinguished individuals had come. Besides, they would arrange things such that there would be no cause for disturbances and upheavals.

They argued back and forth about this matter, but Nezahualcoyotzin's will and opinion prevailed. And so, once all the Mexica lords and Nezahualcoyotzin's supporters had assembled, all three rulers were recognized as successors to the empire. Each one was also individually recognized as king and ruler of his own kingdom. The king of Tezcuco was called Aculhua Tecuhtli; he was also granted the title and prerogatives of his ancestors as Chichimecatl Tecuhtli, which was the title and sovereign power that the Chichimeca emperors had possessed. His

---

82. Four Reed.

uncle Itzcoatzin was given the title of Colhua Tecuhtli after the Culhua Tolteca nation. Totoquihuatzin was given the title of Tepanecatl Tecuhtli, which was the title of the kings of Azcapotzalco. Henceforth, their successors also bore these titles and designations, just as the Roman emperors were called caesars.

These three lords thus ruled together over the empire of this New Spain until the arrival of the holy Catholic faith. Yet it is a fact that while the kings of Mexico and Tezcuco were always equal in rank, authority, and income, the king of Tlacopan received a smaller portion of the income—about a fifth—and only after the other two had been paid. Further proof (even though it is common knowledge) that the three rulers of New Spain were the kings of Mexico, Tezcuco, and Tlacopan is to be found in the ancient song called *xopancuicatl*, which the natives sing at their feasts and gatherings in almost all the towns of this New Spain where the Mexican language is spoken. It says, "çan con icuilotehuaque on intlalticpac, conmahuiçotitihuia atlian tepetl Mexico nican Acolihuacan Neçahualcoiotzin Motecuhçomatzin Tlacopan on in Totoquihuatzin yeneli in [fol. 31r] aiconpiaco in ipetl icpal in teotl ipalnemoani, et cetera," which properly means "those who exalted the empire—in Mexico and here in Aculhuacan, the Kings Nezahualcoyotzin and Motecuhçomatzin, and in Tlacopan, Totoquihuatzin—left their mark on the universe; truly you shall be eternally remembered for how well you judged and ruled on the throne and tribunal of God, creator of all things, et cetera." It is therefore very clear that the aforementioned were the three rulers of this New Spain and the ones from Tezcuco and Mexico were equals and below them Tlacopan. Moreover, this is well known. After the swearing ceremony had been performed with all the rituals that the Mexicas used for the coronation of their kings, which will be described elsewhere, many grand and stately feasts took place.

🌿 CHAPTER 33

*Of how Nezahualcoyotzin gave the order for his court to depart
for Tezcuco and the disagreements over it*

Because of their betrayal, Itlacauhtzin, lord of Huexotla, who had been captain
general, and Motoliniatzin, lord of Coatlichan—the two most important lords
in the kingdom of Tezcuco, from whose lineage descended many of the noblest
houses of the empire—had stayed away since Nezahualcoyotzin sacked the city
and kingdom of Tezcuco. But seeing how he was now recognized as king of
Tezcuco and successor to the empire, they decided to send him a grand gift of
gold, jewels, featherwork, and fine cloth. They also sent gifts to Nezahualcoyotzin's
uncle King Itzcoatzin and other Mexica lords, who would serve as mediators
and beg Nezahualcoyotzin to forgive their past offenses and pardon their lives.
Nezahualcoyotzin forgave them and sent messengers to reassure them and tell
them not to stay away from their homeland; he gave them his solemn word
that he would not dishonor them or do them any harm. Once they received
Nezahualcoyotzin's pardon, they sent messengers a second time, humbly begging
him to return to his palace, for his subjects and vassals were like defenseless
orphans in his absence. [fol. 31v] For this purpose, they again used his uncle King
Itzcoatl as their mediator. Though Nezahualcoyotl had been gravely offended by
his subjects and vassals, he nonetheless agreed to go to the city of Tezcuco with
all his household and retinue, which he had maintained for nearly four years in
the city of Mexico, as seen above.

Before leaving, he divided the land between himself and his uncle King Itzcoatzin. He marked a border running north to south from a hill called Cuexomatl,
through the middle of the lake, laying very thick stones and setting markers and
pillars as far as the Acalhuacan River, and from there to a hill called Xoloc and
another called Techimali, all the way to the mountains of Tototepec; this was
everything that had been conquered in the north by this time. And everything on
the east side, Nezahualcoyotzin took for himself; and his uncle King Itzcoatzin
took what was on the west side, except for the part that was left for Totoquihuatzin,
king of Tlacopan. To further beautify the city of Tezcuco, he asked his uncle to
provide him with many craftsmen skilled in all the mechanical arts. He took
them to the city of Tezcuco, along with others from the city and kingdom of
Azcapotzalco, from the city of Xochimilco, and from elsewhere.

He crossed the lake to the city of Tezcuco and landed at some woods, which, because they were near the lake, were called Acaiacac. There he was welcomed by all the lords and distinguished people of the kingdom with much celebration and rejoicing. But he noted the absence of Itlacauhtzin, lord of Huexotla; Ochpancatl, the other lord of Coatlichan; Motoliniatzin; Totomihua of Coatepec; his brother-in-law, Nonoalcatl, Princess Tozquentzin's husband; and another named Tochpilli. He had indeed forgiven them, but considering the seriousness of their offenses, they did not dare remain there. When Nezahualcoyotzin found out they had left, he was greatly saddened. He sent a nobleman named Coiohua on his behalf to reassure them and bring them back. He was to ask them where were they going, abandoning their own houses and homeland to live unhappy and impoverished in the lands of others, and to say that he had not returned of his own will, but rather out of the [fol. 32r] great love he had for them. Coiohua was also to say that if they were worried about what had happened in the past, that they should know that he had already forgiven them and forgotten it, and they could return without worry.

The messenger caught up with them in the mountains, at a place called Chalchihuitetemi. Begging forgiveness, they replied that they would not appear in His Highness's presence under any circumstance; their crimes had been very grievous, and they knew they deserved a serious punishment. Nevertheless, Totomihua, lord of Coatepec, sent his two sons, one named Aioquantzin and the other Quetzaltecolotzin, telling them, "Go and serve your king and natural lord, for your innocence protects you." Those two young men were therefore the only ones who returned with Nezahualcoyotzin's messenger. All the rest continued their journey, some to Tlaxcalan and others to Huexotzinco and the province of Chalco, which greatly saddened Nezahualcoyotzin. Once Nezahualcoyotzin entered the city, he was welcomed and lavishly entertained. He went to live in his palace called Çilan.

✤ CHAPTER 34

Which deals with how Nezahualcoyotzin waged war against his uncle Itzcoatzin over certain disagreements and then reconciled with him once he entered the city of Mexico with his army, how he reinstated all the lords in their domains, and other things that happened during this time

Nezahualcoyotzin spent some time in the city of Tezcuco laying the groundwork for the good governance of the Aculhua Kingdom. This occupied him for most of the rest of the year in which he returned to the city of Tezcuco. Meanwhile, his uncle Itzcoatzin, among many other things, discussed with the Mexica lords how it had been a mistake to recognize his nephew as supreme lord of the empire and give him the title of Chichimecatl Tecuhtli, which was the one his Chichimeca ancestors once held. Itzcoatzin was old and, as Nezahualcoyotzin's uncle, was almost like a father to him, for Nezahualcoyotzin was the son of his younger sister, Queen Matlalçihuatzin. Itzcoatzin, therefore, felt he had a greater claim to this title and the supreme lordship and that it was sufficient for Nezahualcoyotzin to possess the title of king of the Aculhuas and joint ruler of the empire, like the lord of Tlacopan.

Itzcoatzin did not handle this business with enough discretion to prevent it from reaching [fol. 32v] Nezahualcoyotzin's ear. His uncle's arrogance seemed like ingratitude to Nezahualcoyotzin, considering the friendship and assistance he had extended by liberating Itzcoatzin from the captivity and servitude that he and all the Mexicas had suffered under the king of Azcapotzalco. Moreover, Itzcoatzin was nothing more than the lord of Tenochtitlan and heir merely to the Culhua Kingdom, which at the time was very small, had been largely usurped by the king of Azcapotzalco, and remained in the possession of other lords not yet subjected to the empire. Nonetheless, Nezahualcoyotzin had given to Itzcoatzin half of everything that was rightfully Nezahualcoyotzin's by virtue of the fact that it had belonged to the empire of his Chichimeca ancestors or because he had personally won it in battle. Itzcoatzin's kingdom had thus become greater than that of any of the previous Mexica lords, his ancestors, for Itzcoatzin and Nezahualcoyotzin were equal in rank and authority over the empire. Therefore, Nezahualcoyotzin resolved to gather his troops, march on the city of Mexico, and by force of arms make clear to his uncle and the Mexica lords that he was worthy of the power and title of Chichimecatl Tecuhtli.

So as not to give the impression that he wanted to catch them off guard, Nezahualcoyotzin first notified his uncle that, in a few days' time, he would descend upon the city of Mexico with his army and by force of arms make him understand that he was worthy of the title and authority of Chichimecatl Tecuhtli of the empire. Seeing his nephew's anger and determination, King Itzcoatzin conveyed his apologies as best he could. And to further appease his anger, he sent to Nezahualcoyotzin twenty-five maidens, the most beautiful he could find in his court and of the most illustrious lineage, since they were all from Mexico's royal house. He sent with them other gifts and offerings of gold, jewels, feathers, and fine cloth. Nezahualcoyotzin welcomed these noblewomen and entertained them, treating them with great honor and presenting them with many gifts of gold, cloth, and jewels. And when he saw that they were rested, he sent them back to his uncle the king and thanked him for the offering. He insisted, however, that the issue and disagreement between them could not be negotiated or resolved with women, but rather face to face and with weapons. Nezahualcoyotzin also reciprocated with other gifts, including a golden serpent made into a circle so that its mouth was inside its own sex, which had a certain meaning that they understood well among themselves. In this way, he left no doubt that he would march upon Mexico with his army on the appointed day.

Seeing his nephew's resolve, Itzcoatzin gathered his troops and fortified his city as best he could. At the appointed time, Nezahualcoyotzin marched upon the city of Mexico and attacked it from the place called Tepeyacac, which is now called Our Lady of Guadalupe. The city defended itself bravely. Nezahualcoyotzin spent seven days trying to force his way in but was unable to enter the city because a very famous Mexica captain named Ichtequachichitli valiantly held the entrance. On the [fol. 33r] seventh day, a young man named Teconaltecatl, a porter in Nezahualcoyotzin's army, charged the Mexica captain with great courage and abandon, engaged him, and with only a few blows killed him and broke the Mexica army. Nezahualcoyotzin's forces followed him, pillaged the city's most important houses, and burned the temples. Seeing this, King Itzcoatzin sent the elderly people of the city to tell his nephew that he had done enough and to bear in mind the white hair of his uncles and elders, the Mexicas.

This was what Nezahualcoyotzin had been waiting for, and he immediately ordered the army to withdraw. He and his uncle then met and, after expressing their feelings publicly, made peace. Nezahualcoyotzin ordered that henceforth he would receive tribute and recognition from all the cities, towns, and villages in and around the lake that belonged to the two kingdoms of Mexico and Tlacopan, including the city of Tenochtitlan, the district of Xoloco, the city of Tlacopan, and Azcapotzalco, Tenaiocan, Tepotzotlan, Quauhtitlan, Toltitlan, Hecatepec, Huexachtitlan, Coyohuacan, Xochimilco, and Cuexomatitlan. Each of these cities and towns would give him a yearly tribute of 100 loads of white cloth trimmed in rabbit fur of every color, each load being 20 pieces; 20 loads of royal cloaks, the sort kings wore at public events, with the same trimming; another 20 of the kind that were called cornered, in two colors and with the same trimming, which the kings wore during their festivals and dances; 2 shields of feather-work, with their designs made of yellow feathers; some headdresses called *tecpilotl*, which is what the kings of Tezcuco wore on their heads; and 2 pairs of feather tassels for tying their hair. Nezahualcoyotzin chose a man named Cuitol to oversee the collection of these tributes. His uncle King Itzcoatzin and Totoquihuatzin, the king of Tlacopan, along with all the other high-ranking people of all the cities and towns mentioned above pledged to give him each year the tribute he specified, because he deserved it, having won it by his valor.

   After being entertained in the city of Mexico and before leaving for the city of Tezcuco, Nezahualcoyotl told his uncle King Itzcoatzin that he had decided to restore all the lords to their domains, though not as they were before, but in such a way that, [f. 33v] as time went by, neither they nor their descendants would ever consider rising up and rebelling again. Itzcoatzin replied that this was altogether inadvisable for many reasons. First, by rebelling they had relinquished all rights to their titles; they had lost them. Besides, it would reduce their tribute and royal income. Rather, the lords should be content to live at the mercy and pleasure of the three rulers of the empire, rewarded only when their deeds and good service merited it. Nezahualcoyotzin countered that to do so would be as tyrannical as what the Tepaneca kings had done; it would be nothing more than usurping and stealing what was not theirs. Besides, they were obliged to bestow upon them respect, status, and privileges, for they were all descendants of the same house and lineage, and they would marry and honor each other's future sons and daughters. Moreover, it was a mark of greatness for kings and sovereign lords to have others below them.

   It was finally determined that the lords should be restored to their domains. And soon after, Itzcoatzin had all those who belonged to the royal house of Mexico restored; and those who belonged to the former royal house of Azcapotzalco were restored by Totoquihuatzin, king of Tlacopan. There were nine lords from

Mexico, seven from Tlacopan, and thirteen from the royal house of Tezcuco, plus one more whom he added, which made fourteen. The total came to thirty lords, grandees of the whole empire, who attended at the courts of the three rulers either in person or through their children. The only duty they owed was homage and attendance at court and to bring their vassals to serve their kings in times of war. They owed no other tribute or duty. All of this was done, and Nezahualcoyotzin came to live and hold court in the city of Tezcuco.

🌿 CHAPTER 35

Which deals with how Nezahualcoyotzin restored the lords of
the Aculhua Kingdom to their domains and distributed the
lands

[fol. 34r] Everyone praised Nezahualcoyotzin for restoring the lords, by which he demonstrated his nobility and great valor. Thus he would not be remembered as a tyrant, but rather he would ennoble the memory of his ancestors. At this point, the absent lords, who were fugitives in the provinces of Tlaxcalan, Huexotzinco, and Chalco, realized that the pardon Nezahualcoyotzin had granted them was not a trick and he was not summoning them under false pretenses only to punish them, as they had believed. Upon his return, Nezahualcoyotzin restored Tlaçoliaotzin as lord of Huexotla; he was the son of Itlacauhtzin, who had fled to Tlaxcalan because of his aforementioned rebellion and treason. In Coatlichan, he reinstated Motoliniatzin, who had previously held the title; he was brought back from the province of Huexotzinco, where he was living in the town of Tetzmolocan. He made Tezcapotzin lord of the town of Chimalhuacan. The towns of Coatepec, Iztapalocan, and others that lay in that direction he kept for himself. He made Cocopintzin lord of the town of Tepetlaoztoc and Motlatocaçomatzin, son of Teiolcocoatzin, lord of Acolman. He made Tencoiotzin lord of Tepechpan, Techotlalatzin lord of Teçoiocan, and Teçoçomoctzin lord of Chiuhnauhtlan. He gave Chiautla to his son named Quauhtlatzacuilotzin, who would be lord when he grew up, for at this time he was too young. With the towns of Xaltocan, Papalotlan, and others he did the same as he had done with Coatepec. He gave Quetzalmamalitzin the lordship of Teotihuacan, which had belonged to the late Huetzin, Quetzalmamalitzin's father; he gave Quetzalmamalitzin the title of captain general of the nobility, and any litigation and disputes among nobles of the towns in the provinces of La Campiña would be heard in his city. In Otompan, he made Quecholtecpantzin lord, giving him the same title of captain general but of the commoners, and he would likewise handle the disputes and conflicts among the common people of La Campiña provinces. As time went by, he restored and confirmed in their titles Tlalolintzin of Tolantzinco, Nauhecatzin of Quauhchinanco, and Quetzalpaintzin of Xicotepec.

All the other cities, towns, and villages of the kingdom and province belonging to the Aculhua, he divided into eight parts. In each one he placed a steward to collect tribute and rents in the following way: In the city of Tezcuco with its districts and villages, he named Matlalaca as steward. Besides being in charge of all the city's rents and tribute, it was his responsibility to maintain the king's house and court for [fol. 34v] seventy days. Each day, he provided 25 *tlacopintlis* of shelled maize for tamales. This was a unit of measure used at the time; each tlacopintli was equal to 1 bushel and 3 pecks. Therefore, in bushels, the amount was equal to 31 bushels and 3 pecks.[83] He also provided 3 tlacopintlis of beans; 400,000 tortillas; 4 *xiquipiles*[84] of cacao, which amounts to 32,000 cacao beans; 100 roosters; 20 salt cakes; and 20 large baskets of dried chile, another 20 of *chiltepin*,[85] 10 of tomatoes, and 10 of pumpkin seeds. This steward was obligated to provide all of this each day.

The second steward, named Tochtli, was in charge of all the rents owed by Atenco, which was the district near the lake, including its towns and villages, which totaled twelve. Besides collecting tribute, it was his duty to maintain and feed the household of the king for another seventy days with the same amount of food. The third steward, named Coxcoch, was in charge of the rents and tribute from Tepepolco, with all its subject towns and villages, which totaled thirteen. Likewise, he was obligated to maintain the king's household for another seventy days. The fourth steward, named Tlematl, was in charge of collecting the rents and tribute from Axapochco, with all its villages and hamlets, which also numbered thirteen; he was also in charge of maintaining the king's household for forty-five days. The fifth was named Yaotl; he was in charge of the tribute and rents from Quauhtlatzinco, which had twenty-seven villages and hamlets, and he was obligated to provide the aforementioned provisions for sixty-five days. The sixth was named Quauhtecolotl, the steward of Ahuatepec and the eight villages and hamlets subject to it. Besides collecting the tribute, he had the same duty of maintaining the king's household for forty-five days. The seventh, named Papalotl, was in charge of collecting the tribute from Tetitlan, which included the towns of Coatepec, Iztapalocan, Tlapechhuacan, and some villages. The eighth was named Quateçonhua; it was his duty to collect the tribute from

---

83. Alva Ixtlilxochitl uses the terms *fanega* (bushel) and *almud* (peck) which commonly served as measures for dry goods. However, the value of both units varied by region. Relative to the fanega, an almud could be as little as a twelfth part and as much as a half.
84. A quantity of eight thousand.
85. Small chiles.

Tecpilpan and its eight villages and hamlets. This was the king's estate, [fol. 35r] which belonged to Nezahualcoyotzin. Additionally, he gave and distributed 160 villages to his sons, relatives, and deserving individuals.

The lands of each town or city were divided in the following way: The large parcels, better situated than the others within any given city or town, were four hundred units in length and width, more or less; they were sometimes called *tlatocatlali* or *tlatocamili*—meaning "lands or fields of the lord"—and sometimes *itonal in tlacatl*, which means "lands that contribute to the joy or good fortune of the kings or lords." There was another kind of land called *tecpantlali*, which means "lands belonging to the palace and chamber of the kings or lords"; the natives who lived on them were called *tecpanpouhque*, which means "people who belong to the chamber and palace of such kings or lords." Another kind of land was called *calpollali* or *altepetlali*, which is like saying "lands belonging to the districts or to the town"; all the common people lived on a part of these lands, and the rest they sowed and harvested to pay their tributes and for their own sustenance. This was the main type of land and comprised the largest and most important parts of the towns and cities. None but the heirs of the kingdoms and lordships could inherit these lands. The *macehuales*, which is what the people who lived on them were called, could not give them to others, but the lands passed to their children and relatives on the same terms with which they had enjoyed them; if they left for another town, they were free to give them to others on the same terms. These three kinds of land and settlements belonged exclusively to the kings and lords and no one else.

There was another kind of land called *pilali*, which means they belonged to the nobles and descendants of the aforementioned kings and lords. Another kind was called *tecpilali*, which were very similar to those called *pilali*. These belonged to certain nobles who descended from the ancient lords and were also possessed by individuals of merit. This is how land was divided in towns and cities. However, in the cities and towns of conquered and subjugated lords there was another kind of land called *yaotlali*, which were lands that had been taken away in war. Most of these belonged to the three rulers of the empire; the rest were distributed among the lords and noblemen who, along with their vassals, had personally participated in the conquest of these towns. [fol. 35v] Most of the time, this amounted to one third of the conquered towns or provinces.

✷ CHAPTER 36

Of how Nezahualcoyotzin built a palace for his residence, which was the grandest in New Spain, and its description

Mexico and Tlacopan divided and distributed land in towns and villages in the same way as in the kingdom of Tezcuco, because the other two kings and rulers of the empire always ended up using its laws and style of governance, for it seemed to them to be the best they had ever had. And thus, the following account and description of the kingdom of Tezcuco should be understood to apply equally to Mexico and Tlacopan. Moreover, the paintings, histories, and songs that I follow always deal first with Tezcuco, and so does the painting of the rolls and royal tributes that existed in this New Spain in pagan times. I take my description of the dwellings of King Nezahualcoyotzin from a very ancient painting,[86] which depicts very clearly the grandeur of their buildings, halls, bedchambers and other private rooms, gardens, temples, patios, and all the rest contained in the residence, as may be clearly seen today from its ruins (fig. 14). Together, all three capitals of this New Spain—Tezcuco, Mexico, and Tlacopan—constructed these houses by drafting all of their available laborers; this work employed more than two hundred thousand people daily. The master builders of these houses were Xilomantzin, lord of Colhuacan, and Moquihuitzin of Tlaltelolco, although King Nezahualcoyotzin oversaw everything personally.

From east to west, the compound was 411½ units long, which converted to our measurements was 1,234½ yards,[87] and in width, from north to south, 326 units, which equal 978 yards. On the south and east sides this compound was enclosed by a very strong adobe wall, the foundations of which were of a very strong cement; they were two yards thick and three fathoms high. On the west side, which was toward the lake, and on the north, it was enclosed by a very strong wall [fol. 36r] that was five fathoms high. The bottom third of this wall narrowed incrementally as it ascended, in the style of a buttress, and the remaining two-thirds were plumb and square. The king's living quarters were within this compound, as well as the council chambers and the other apartments that will be described in turn.

---

86. Most likely, the Quinatzin Map.
87. We have translated *vara* as "yard." The length of vara varied by region.

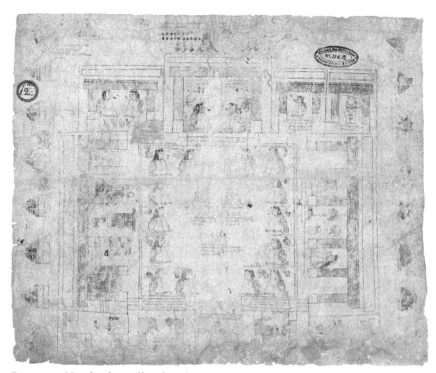

FIGURE 14. Nezahualcoyotl's palace (Quinatzin Map, central panel). *Photo courtesy of the Bibliothèque nationale de France.*

The king's quarters surrounded two main patios. The largest one served as a plaza and marketplace—as it still is for the city of Tezcuco today—and the other, interior one was where the council chambers were located. The hall of the royal council was on the eastern side, where the king had two tribunals, and in the middle was a large hearth where a fire was kept continuously burning. On the right side of the hearth was the supreme tribunal, called *teohicpalpan*, which is like saying the "seat and tribunal of God." Besides sitting higher and above the other, its seat and backrest were made of gold inlaid with turquoise and other precious stones. In front of it there was something like a pedestal, on top of which was a shield, macana, and bow with its quiver of arrows. Atop all of this was a skull, and atop that an emerald pyramid, on which was set a plume or ornament of feathers called tecpilotl, as described above; there were piles of jewels on the sides. The skins of tigers and lions and weavings made of golden-eagle feathers served as rugs, and there was an arrangement of many golden armbands and greaves. The walls were hung and decorated with tapestries made of rabbit fur of every color, which depicted various birds, animals, and flowers. Behind the chair there was a canopy of rich featherwork, and set in the middle were rays and glimmers made of gold and precious stones.

The other tribunal, called the king's tribunal, had a simpler seat. It also had a feather-work canopy with the insignia of the coat of arms used by the kings of Tezcuco. The kings regularly presided at this tribunal, where they issued their rulings and held public hearings. And [fol. 36v] when they weighed serious and important cases or they confirmed a death sentence, they would move over to the tribunal of God, placing their right hand on the skull and holding in their left the golden arrow that served as a scepter; and then they put on the diadem they wore, which was like a half miter. And there were also three of these diadems on the aforementioned pedestal: one of gold inlaid with jewels, one of featherwork, and a third woven from cotton and blue rabbit fur. On this tribunal sat the fourteen grandees of the kingdom according to their rank and seniority. There were three sections. The first was where the king sat. In the second, six of the grandees had their seats and daises; to the right the lord of Teotihuacan came first, the lord of Acolman second, and the lord of Tepetlaoztoc third; on the left side, the lord of Huexotla came first, the lord of Coatlichan second, and the lord of Chimalhuacan third. And in the third section—which was the farthest away—sat another eight lords according to their rank and seniority; on the right side, the lord of Otompan came first, the lord of Tolantzinco second, the lord of Quauhchinanco third, and the lord of Xicotepec fourth; on the left side, the lord of Tepechpan came first, the lord of Teçoiocan second, the lord of Chiuhnauhtlan third, and the lord of Chiauhtla fourth.

On the west side, there was another hall that matched this one and was likewise divided into two sections. In the first, which was the inner section, there were eight judges, who occupied the most important seats at the front of the room; four were noble gentlemen and the other four were from among the citizens. And seated behind them were another fifteen provincial judges, from all the cities and major towns of the kingdom of Tezcuco. They heard all the cases, civil as well as criminal, governed by the eighty laws established by Nezahualcoyotzin; even the most serious lasted no more than eighty days. In the [fol. 37r] other section of the hall, the outer one, there was a tribunal for the four supreme judges, who were the four supreme presidents of the councils; there was a side door through which they went in and out to speak with the king.

On the north side of this patio, there was another large hall, called the hall of science and music, where there were three supreme tribunals. In the first, which faced the patio, was the tribunal and seat of the king of Tezcuco; and on the right side was another tribunal, which belonged to the king of Mexico; and on the left side was the tribunal of the king of Tlacopan. Here were many insignia of rank, such as shields, tassels, headdresses, and other symbols of rich featherwork, many loads of expensive cloth, and many jewels of gold and precious stones. This was where the kings sat when they met together. There in the middle there was a musical instrument called *huehuetl*. The philosophers, historians, poets, and some of the most famous captains of the kingdom regularly gathered there, singing songs about their history, matters of morality, and maxims.

Behind this hall, one could ascend to another, built at the top of a strong wall, where there were many captains and brave soldiers, who were the king's guard. Then there was another hall, almost opposite the royal hall, where the ambassadors of the kings of Mexico and Tlacopan gathered. Then there was a corridor that connected this patio with the large one that was the plaza. And on the other side, there was another large hall for the war council; six captains, three nobles and three citizens native to the city of Tezcuco, sat in the front, and behind them sat another fifteen captains from the cities and major towns of the kingdom of Tezcuco. All the business of the war council was conducted here. On the south side, there were another two halls. One was for the council of the treasury, where an equal number of judges sat in the same aforementioned order. Behind this hall [fol. 37v] was another, where there were men of high standing who were like investigative judges that went outside the city to the provinces and cities to conduct inquiries and carry out the king's justice. Behind this hall was another that served as the armory.

Farther inside were the rooms for the queen and the noblewomen, kitchens, and rooms and private chambers where the king slept, with many patios and labyrinths whose walls had different pictures and decorations. Each of these chambers, which were nearly square, was fifty yards long and almost as wide, and others were more or less the same. South and east of the said chambers were the king's gardens and parks with many water fountains, ponds, and canals with many fish and many species of waterfowl; all of this was bounded by more than two thousand juniper trees, most of which are standing today. And in the gardens the king had baths where there were also many labyrinths in which the men who entered could not find their way out. The residence was adorned with many towers and spires. In the middle of the other patio, which was the largest and served as a plaza, there was the ball court. And toward the entrance of the second patio there was a great brazier on top of a pedestal that burned day and night without ever going out. This plaza was surrounded by arcades. And on the west side, it had another large hall with many rooms all around it; this was the university where all the kingdom's poets, historians, and philosophers gathered, divided by field and school according to each one's branch of knowledge. The royal archives were also here. To one side of these halls was one of the main entrances and gates to the palace, and then came other rooms with a patio, halls, and bedchambers where the kings of Mexico [f. 38r] stayed when they went to Tezcuco.

Then there were the rooms where the tribute from the province of Quauhna-huac was collected and kept and then others for that of the province of Chalco. Only these two provinces had their tribute storehouses inside the palace; the others had them outside in storehouses exclusively dedicated to this purpose. On the north side, next to where the king sat, were the temples (as will be described below). And outside the aforementioned wall were the houses where the kings of Tlacopan stayed when they came to this city. And further on, in front of the temples, was the aviary, where the king kept many different species of birds, animals, snakes, fish, and serpents brought from different parts of this New Spain. Likenesses of those that could not be captured were fashioned out of gold and precious jewels; it was the same with the fish—those that lived in the sea as well as in rivers and lakes. All the birds, fish, and animals found in this land were represented here, whether alive or meticulously fashioned from gold and precious jewels. And finally, counting all the large and medium-sized halls, bedchambers, and private rooms, the king's residence had more than three hundred rooms, everything built with great architectural skill. When they were raising the roofs of some of the halls, they wanted to cut the edge off the wooden beams and planks and remove the ropes they had used to drag them, which were incredibly large. The king ordered that they be left as they were because a time would come when others would be able use them without having to drill new holes and put in new ropes to drag them; it was done. I have seen these holes through openings in the pillars and doorframes upon which the beams and planks rested; his prophecy came true because they have torn down everything and made use of the wood.

🌿 CHAPTER 37

*Which continues the description of Nezahualcoyotzin's residence
and the temples within it*

[fol. 38v] The residence we have been describing had only three main doors and
entrances. One was on the side facing the lake to the west, another faced the
mountains to the east, and the other faced the south. These entrances were like
boulevards, eighteen yards wide. The residence had other entrances and gates that
faced the temples. These entrances had steps by which they entered and exited
the palace. West of the temples there were other rooms with a patio, halls, and
bedchambers, called *tlacateco*, where the king's sons were raised and educated by
their tutors and teachers, who taught them all the civilized practices of a virtuous
way of life; all the sciences and arts that they knew and mastered, including the
mechanical ones of goldsmithing, jewelry, featherwork, and the others, as well as
military training, all with such discipline that they were never allowed to be idle.
The king's daughters were raised and educated in separate rooms. It was required
by law that every eighty days the king, all his sons and relatives with their tutors
and teachers, all his daughters, even the very young, with their tutors and teachers,
and the kingdom's grandees gathered in a large hall in these tlacateco rooms.
They sat according to rank, the males on one side and the females on the other,
and everyone, even the king, wore rough henequen cloaks. A speaker got up on
a stage that was like a pulpit, and there he began to rebuke everyone, from the
king to the youngest one, for their vices and misdeeds, recalling the destructive
consequences that would follow; he praised the rewards and value of virtue. And
there he gave an account of the misdeeds committed in those eighty days. If the
king had done any wrongs, he related them to him, so there was nothing that was
not freely revealed and rebuked. And he reminded them of the eighty laws that
the king had instituted and how they must be kept and enforced. This speaker
delivered this [fol. 39r] speech abhorring all the vices and glorifying all the virtues
and their consequences with such eloquence that it caused tears of emotion. He
also spoke persuasively about many other good and very moral things.

There were over forty temples. The largest and most important one, which
was dedicated to Huitzilopochtli and Tlaloc, was square and solid; the outer
walls were made of concrete, and inside, the construction was of mortar and
stone (fig. 15). Each side measured 80 arm spans, and the rampart, or cu, was 27

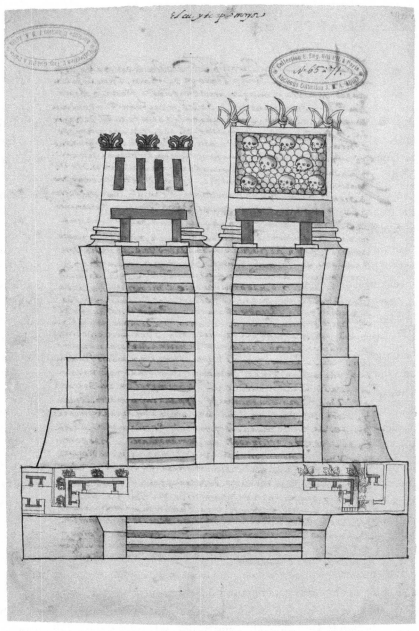

El au y ta po maga

FIGURE 15. The Temple of Tetzcoco (Codex Ixtlilxochitl, fol. 112v). *Photo courtesy of the Bibliothèque nationale de France.*

fathoms high; it was 160 steps high on the west side. The building was wide at the foundation and tapered as it rose, narrowing on all sides to form a pyramid with great inclines that also became smaller as they rose; the stair had landings at certain intervals. And two chapels were built on top of the temple, one bigger than the other. The larger one, which housed the idol Huitzilopochtli, was on the south side. The smaller one, which was on the north side, belonged to the idol Tlaloc. These chapels and their idols faced west. In front of this temple there was a rectangular patio running north to south in which five hundred men could fit easily. Between the doorways of the two chapels was a stone with a rounded top, called *techcatl*, where they sacrificed the war captives. Both of these chapels had three stories inside that could be reached by movable wooden ladders; each floor was full of all sorts of weapons, such as macanas, shields, bows, arrows, spears, sling stones, and all sorts of armor, gear, and adornments for war.

The rest of the temples were almost all of this same shape; some had two, three, or more chapels, and some had only one. Near the temples, there were more than four hundred halls and bedchambers that served as living quarters for the temples' priests and ministers and where [fol. 39v] the boys of the city were raised and educated. There was one temple where many women lived cloistered and in seclusion and also where some of the daughters of the lords and citizens were raised and educated. There was a round temple that belonged to Quetzalcoatl, god of wind, and also a pool of water, called *hezapam*, where all the sacrificial vessels were washed; those who made an offering of their own blood also went there to wash. There was also an enclosure called *teotlalpan*, which means the "land of God," with all sorts of thorny trees and bushes. This compound of buildings had over forty patios both large and small, not counting the gardens and labyrinths. And because many authors describe the design and ornament of the temples, the idols, and the different kinds of priests, they are not dealt with or specified here.

◣   CHAPTER 38

Which deals with the eighty laws established by Nezahualcoyotzin
and how he enforced them

Nezahualcoyotzin put the city of Tezcuco and all the other polities of his kingdom in perfect order and harmony; the description of Tezcuco is representative of the rest. He divided it into six districts: Mexicapan, Colhuacan, Tepanecapan, Huitznahuac, Chimalpan, and Tlailotlacan. He assigned the inhabitants to their neighborhoods by rank and trade. The gold and silversmiths were in one neighborhood, the featherworkers in another, and likewise all the other crafts-men, of which there were many sorts. He also built many houses and palaces for the lords and nobles who attended his court, according to the rank and merits of each one, which totaled more than four hundred houses for lords and nobles of renowned lineage. And for the good governance of his kingdom and also that of the whole empire, he established eighty laws that he viewed as necessary for the public good at that time. They were divided into four categories corresponding to the four supreme councils he had set up. These included the one that heard all civil and criminal cases and punished all manner of crimes [fol. 40r] and sins. One such crime was sodomy, which was punished with very great severity: the active one was tied to a post, and all the boys of the city covered him with ashes until he was buried alive; the passive one was disemboweled through his penis and also buried in ashes (fig. 16).

A traitor to the king or the state was dismembered at the joints, his house was ransacked and razed, his land was sown with salt, and his children and his household were enslaved through the fourth generation. If a subject lord were to rise against the three rulers and was not defeated and captured in battle, then his skull would be crushed with a club when he was seized. A lord or nobleman who wore the royal cloaks or emblems received the same punishment—though in Mexico they cut off a leg—even if it was the crown prince, because no one dared attire or adorn themselves in this way or build a residence, even if one had done something to deserve it, without the king's express command and permission. Otherwise they died for it.

As for adulterers: If the husband caught the wife in adultery with another man, both were stoned to death. If the evidence was circumstantial or the husband

FIGURE 16. Punishments (Quinatzin Map, bottom panel).
Photo courtesy of the Bibliothèque nationale de France.

only suspected it and the truth of the matter was discovered, both adulterers were killed by hanging and then dragged to a temple outside the city. This happened because of the infamy and the bad example it set for the neighborhood, even if the husband did not accuse them. The same punishment was inflicted on those who served as go-betweens. If the adulterers killed the cuckold, the man was roasted alive, and while he roasted he was sprayed with brine until he died; the woman was hanged (fig. 17). And if the adulterers were lords or nobles, they were garroted and their bodies burned, which was their customary funeral rite.

As for a thief: If the robbery took place inside a house in a populated area and the loot was of little value, he became the slave of the victim, as long as he had not broken through the wall of the house, in which case he was hanged. The thief who stole valuable things, large amounts, or in the market was also hanged. The thief who stole from the fields, even if it was no more than seven ears of maize, was killed with a blow to the head with a club. The children of nobles who squandered their parents' wealth or property were garroted.

As for the drunkard: If he was a commoner and it was his first offense, his head was publicly shaved in the market plaza and his house was ransacked and razed to the ground, because the law states that he who deprives himself of judgment is unworthy of having a house and should instead live like a beast in the wild. The punishment for the second offense was death. The first time a noble was caught committing this crime, he was immediately punished with death. [fol. 40v] This tribunal also enforced the laws about slaves and [handled] conflicts and disputes over property, lands, possessions, and status, as well as disputes among craftsmen.

The supreme council of music and science enforced the laws under its jurisdiction and punished superstition and the kinds of wizards and sorcerers that existed at that time with death. Only necromancy was allowed, because it harmed no one. The war council enforced other laws. For example, a soldier who failed to obey his captain's orders or somehow failed in his duties was beheaded; and anyone who stole another's captive or plunder was hanged; and the same was done to anyone who gave his captive away. A soldier who was of noble lineage received this same punishment if, after being captured, he escaped and returned home, whereas a commoner was rewarded. The captured noble was spared, however, if

FIGURE 17. Adulterers' punishments (Quinatzin Map, bottom panel, detail).

he managed to defeat or kill the four enemy soldiers who were designated to fight him just before he was to be sacrificed—this was the reason for taking captives. If he freed himself this way, he was welcomed and rewarded by the king. Death was also the punishment imposed on the soldiers and captains who, while guarding the king when he fought in war, allowed him to fall into enemy hands, because it was their duty to bring him back, dead or alive. And if this should happen to the crown prince or one of the king's sons, the soldiers and captains who had trained him in warfare received the same punishment.

When there was to be an attack or a war against one of the lords of the remote provinces, it had to be for good reasons—for example, when a lord killed merchants who had gone to trade and deal in his province, preventing trade and contact with those here. These three rulers justified their rule and dominion over all others because they claimed all the land that had belonged to the Tolteca, whose heirs and successors they were, and because of its acquisition and settlement by the Great Chichimeca Xolotl, their ancestor. To wage war, all three together held a war council with their captains and advisers to discuss the way in which it should be conducted. The first order of business was to dispatch certain Mexica messengers called *quaquahnochtin* to put the rebellious province on notice. They warned the elders in particular, assembling many old men and women. [fol. 41r] On behalf of the three rulers, the messengers advised the elders that they would suffer the calamities and hardships of war if their lord arrogantly persisted in refusing the friendship, protection, and security of the empire. Since the elders had much experience, they should stop him and convince him to correct his error and cease his insolence against the empire within a period of twenty days. And so that they could not say that they had been violently conquered and defeated, they gave them a certain number of shields and macanas. Then these messengers set up camp to await the decision of that province's government and elders, who either responded to the messengers themselves or attempted to sway their lord within the appointed time. Then, once he vowed never to oppose the empire again and to allow its merchants and people to move freely to trade and deal, and once he had sent some gifts of gold, jewels, feathers, and cloth, he was forgiven and accepted as a friend of the empire.

And if the lord did not comply within twenty days, other messengers arrived. They were called *achcacauhtin* and were Aculhuas, natives of Tezcuco, the investigative judges mentioned previously. They delivered their message to the lord of that province and to all the nobles and gentlemen of that house and lineage, advising them to surrender peacefully and return to the empire within a period of another twenty days. They warned them that if they did not yield by the deadline, the lord would be punished with death in accordance with the law, by having his head smashed with a club, assuming he did not die in battle or fall captive to be sacrificed to the gods. The other noblemen of his house and court would also be punished according to the will of the three rulers of the empire. If the lord and all the nobles of the province surrendered within twenty days after having received this warning, the people of his province would be obligated to pay a yearly, though moderate, tribute to the three rulers and the lord and all the nobles would be forgiven and granted the grace and friendship of the three rulers. And if he refused, these messengers immediately anointed his right arm and his [fol. 41v] head with a certain liquid they carried, which was meant to fortify him to resist the fury of the army of the empire's three rulers. They also placed a feather headdress called tecpilotl on his head, tied with a red strap, and they presented him with many shields, macanas, and other implements of war. And then they joined the first messengers to wait for the twenty-day term to end.

If they had not surrendered by then, a third group of messengers came. This time they were from the city of Tlacopan, of the Tepaneca nation, and they had the same office and duty as the others. The delivered their message on behalf of the empire's three rulers to all the captains, soldiers, and other men of war, giving them a final warning that, as those who would endure the blows and burdens of war, they should bow to the empire within twenty days and be pardoned and welcomed back into its good graces. But should the deadline pass, they would descend upon them and mercilessly raze the whole province; all the captives would be made slaves and everyone else tributaries and vassals of the empire. If the soldiers surrendered before the deadline, only the lord would be punished and the province would be forced to pay a larger tribute than the one stipulated in the second warning, to be taken from the lord's income. And if they did not comply within twenty days, these Tepaneca messengers would give the captains and warriors shields and macanas as presents and would join the other messengers. Then, together they would bid the lord, the republic, and the warriors farewell, warning them that in another twenty days the three rulers or their captains would be upon them, and they would carry out everything they had warned them about. Once this time had passed, the battle began immediately, for the army had already begun marching. After they were conquered and defeated, everything described above would be carried out. The tribute and the lands would be divided among the three rulers. The kings of Mexico and Tezcuco would receive equal shares, while the king of Tlacopan would get about a fifth.

Once the legitimate heir and successor of the conquered lord had assumed the lordship of that province, he was responsible for the aforementioned duties and tribute, however, they were careful to give him a sufficient amount of lands and vassals. [fol. 42r] And then the army of the three rulers would return home, leaving a garrison with as many soldiers as were needed for the security of that province. In this way they conquered all the land. The council and tribunal of war also enforced other laws of lesser importance.

The fourth and final council, the council of the treasury, enforced the laws related to the collection and distribution of tribute and the royal records. The collectors who collected more than the subjects and vassals owed received the death penalty. The judges of these tribunals could not accept any bribes or be partial to any of the litigants under penalty of death. All of them were provided for by the king; every eighty days he rewarded them with gifts of gold, cloth, featherwork, cacao, and maize according to their merits and the quality of their work. There was not a set amount—only the king's judgment of what was appropriate. And he did the same with the captains and persons who had demonstrated bravery in war and servants in his household and court.

🌿 CHAPTER 39

How King Nezahualcoyotzin extended the lands of the
confederation of Tlaxcalan and the treaties he made with it

The confederation of Tlaxcalan had always supported Nezahualcoyotzin in
the wars he fought both to recover the kingdom of Tezcuco and to subjugate
the Tepanecas. And so, to show them his gratitude, he often visited them and
sent them great gifts of gold, jewels, cloth, featherwork, and other things. On
one of his visits, he extended their territory on the side that bordered Tezcuco,
placing his boundary markers from the hill called Quauhtepetl to another called
Oçelotepetl and then to Huehue Ichocaian, as far as the hill called Coliuhcan.
And then, at the request of the confederation, they established a treaty, agreeing
from that [fol. 42v] time on to assist each other without attempting to seize each
other's domains through violence, war, or other means. They further agreed that
if a tyrant ever rose against the said Nezahualcoyotzin or his descendants, the
confederation would aid him with all its might and troops. Those of the kingdom
of Tezcuco would have the same obligation to support and defend the confederation's interests, providing aid and assistance against those who would attack it.
They would do the same in years of famine, helping each other with supplies.

Once this agreement was made, Nezahualcoyotl returned to the city of Tezcuco, where he began preparing his forces to wage war against the province
of Tolantzinco and the mountain province of Totonacapan. He began with
Tolantzinco, which belonged to the empire. Once he defeated it, he reinstated
Tlalolin as lord, as previously described, with certain obligations. Quauhchinanco surrendered peacefully, and he confirmed Nauhecatl as lord; he did
the same in Xicotepec, thereby winning all of Totonacapan, which occupies
more than eighty leagues. When he returned from this campaign to recover
his patrimony, he joined his forces with those of his uncle Itzcoatzin and with
those of Totoquihuatzin, king of Tlacopan, and they marched on the land of the
Tlalhuicas and won it. And dividing it according to the method described above,
Nezahualcoyotzin got nine towns, including the head town of Quauhnahuac;
he named Zaca as the steward, who collected as tribute 4,300 bundles of fine
cloaks, loincloths, and huipiles—which totaled 86,000 individual cloaks, huipiles,
underskirts, and loincloths—and a certain quantity of golden ornaments, jewels,
and featherwork each year in addition to maids and servants needed for service

in the king's household and the flowers that usually decorated the palace. The king of Mexico got Tepoztlan, Huaxtepec, and others, with the same amount of tribute, and the king of Tlacopan got his share. And then they continued their conquest and won the province of Chalco, though it later rebelled. Once this province was won, they went to the province of Itzocan and won it. And then, moving on, they won the provinces of Tepeyacac, Tecalco, Teohuacan, Coaixtlahuacan, Cuetlachtlan, Hualtepec, and Quauhtochco.

Having subjugated these provinces to the [fol. 43r] empire with the same conditions as the rest, Nezahualcoyotzin marched with his troops on the great province of Tochpan and the province of Tzicuhcoac. After conquering them, he appointed his stewards. In the province of Tzicuhcoac he appointed Yaotl, who collected 1,800 bundles of cloth—both plain cloth and fine multicolored tapestries that lined the king's halls and rooms—underskirts, and huipiles along with 100 bundles of *ilacatziuhqui*[88] cloth of triple-breadth, each piece of which was eight arm spans long, and another 100 bundles of more delicate and fancy pieces of cloth, four arm spans long, so that both kinds amounted to 40,000 pieces. He also collected 400 wicker hampers and 400 deerskins, 100 live deer, 100 loads of chiles, 100 loads of pumpkin seeds, 100 large parrots, 40 sacks of soft feathers used for weaving, and another 40 sacks of bird feathers of different colors. The tribute also included maids and servants necessary for service in the palace.

In the great province of Tochpan he appointed Huehuetli as his steward. Each year he collected 1,580 bundles of cloth of the aforementioned kind, plus 25 cloaks and huipiles; 400 bundles and 10 pieces of ilacatziuhqui cloth eight arm spans long; another set of bundles and pieces of fine ilacatziuhqui cloth four arm spans long; which all together totaled 47,645 cloaks, underskirts, huipiles, pieces of ilacatziuhqui cloth, and loincloths. They also provided maids and servants necessary for service in the palace. The great Tochpan was divided into seven provinces that all together comprised sixty-eight subject towns.

Once these provinces belonging to the patrimony of the kingdom of Tezcuco were conquered, Nezahualcoyotl with his army continued along the North Sea coast to another province called Tochtepec, which he also conquered and subjugated. Along with the garrisoned forces he left in each conquered province, he appointed [fol. 43v] Toiectzin steward and tribute collector. Each year he collected 40 bundles of fine cloth and 20 bundles of shirts finely embroidered with rich colors, which totals 120 pieces. Every year they also planted and harvested

---

88. "Something twisted," likely referring to spiral designs on the cloth.

for him a cacao orchard that was four hundred units long and two hundred wide and collected an additional 33 loads of cacao as tribute, along with 2,000 balls of rubber, 400 cakes of red dye, and many items of featherwork, such as shields, headdresses, and other adornments that the kings used when they waged war, made from fine feathers called *quetzalli*. This province had twelve subject towns, which also gave as tribute a certain number of maids and servants for service in the palace.

On his way back, Nezahualcoyotzin marched together with the kings of Mexico and Tlacopan on the provinces of Maçahuacan and Tlapacoyan. And having subjugated them using the same method described above, he marched on the province of Tlauhçoçauhtitlan, conquered it, and appointed Huitzilteuh as his steward. The yearly tribute he received from this province was 16 trays of color, 20 loads of copal, 168 fine drinking gourds and bowls, and 20 loads of *tlacuilolquahuitl* wood. This province and the others where he appointed his stewards and tribute collectors were assigned exclusively to the kingdom of Tezcuco; the other two kings received nothing. The provinces where he did not appoint stewards had their tributes divided among the three rulers of this New Spain following the aforementioned method. All this tribute was gathered and taken to the city of Mexico, where it was distributed to the stewards and agents of the three kings, who each received what belonged to their lord. The rents that belonged to King Nezahualcoyotzin were stored in the city of Mexico in his old palaces. He used them to reward all the lords of his kingdom, his sons and relatives, and other worthy individuals. And they were administered by the Mexica lords, so that each would fairly receive what his virtues merited. This was the main reason that his tribute—the portion he received after the division with the other two kings—was [fol. 44r] kept in the city of Mexico.

Nezahualcoyotzin was busy waging these wars, when, one night, those of the province of Tolantzinco, who remained restive, burned three forts where the king had garrisoned his men. They were located at Maçanacazco, Tlaiacac, and Chiquiuhtepec, and all the soldiers Nezahualcoyotzin maintained in these forts were killed. As it had been four years since he last subjugated the said province, he decided to gather a large army. He marched on them and punished them with the utmost severity. And, even though Nezahualcoyotzin allowed the local lord to keep his position and continue as one of the fourteen grandees of the kingdom, he was nonetheless obligated to pay a yearly tribute of 60 bundles of cloth and 400 measures of beans, which is 500 bushels; he was also charged with the task of planting groves in the gardens and woods. The steward for the collection of this tribute and service was Pachcalcatl. In this way they remained subdued and subjugated from that time on. Also, Nezahualcoyotzin established a town with people from the city of Tezcuco where the garrisons were. He named it Tzihuinquilocan, and it belonged to the patrimonial estate until the death of his grandson don Fernando Cortés Ixtlilxochitl.

🌾 CHAPTER 40

Of the death of King Itzcoatzin of Mexico; how Motecuhçomatzin
Ilhuicamina, first of this name, took his place; and some wars the
three rulers of the empire waged against the remote provinces

In the final days of the year 1440, which they call *matlactli omei tecpatl*,[89] the
most valiant King Itzcoatzin died. He was the first of the kings of Mexico who,
alongside the kings of Tezcuco and Tlacopan, ruled this land of Anahuac, called
New Spain; he reigned for almost fourteen years. Since one of the laws established among the three was that whenever one of them died the two remaining
would elect the successor, Nezahualcoyotzin decided to issue a general summons
throughout the empire. And meeting with King Totoquihuatzin of Tlacopan,
they agreed that the [fol. 44v] successor to the kingdom of Mexico and coruler
of the empire should be Motecuhçomatzin, also known as Ilhuicamina, who was
at the time captain general and high priest of Mexico's main temple, a very brave
soldier, and a man of great virtue and worth. He was, moreover, the first cousin of
King Nezahualcoyotzin, his beloved companion in arms. Motecuhçomatzin was
thus received as said successor in the city of Tezcuco and then acknowledged in
the city of Mexico according to the rituals and ceremonies of the Mexicas. Of the
three rulers, King Motecuhçoma is regarded as the second most famous in the
empire of this New Spain, behind Nezahualcoyotzin, who was the most famous,
as attested by the songs and histories. Motecuhçoma and Nezahualcoyotzin, along
with King Totoquihuatzin of Tlacopan, gathered their armies and marched on
the provinces of Cohuixco, Oztoman, Cueçaltepec, Ichcateopan, Teoxahualco,
Poctepec, Tamaçolapan, Chilapan, Quiauhteopan, Ohuapan, Tzonpahuacan,
and Coçamaloapan. They subjugated them to the empire along with many of
their subject towns, divided them up by the same method used with all the
rest, and returned to their lands. When they undertook these campaigns, all
three armies marched together as one, and once they reached the province to
be conquered, they divided up again. And though they engaged in battle at the
same time, each entered the fight against the enemy from a different side, so
that after a few maneuvers they routed and subdued them, each army striving
to distinguish itself.

---

89. Thirteen Flint.

After King Nezahualcoyotzin returned to his city, he gave the order to march on the provinces of the Cuexteca—today Panuco—which belonged to his patrimony. He therefore gathered the necessary army and sent his son Prince Xochiquetzaltzin as his captain general. Six days after this prince had departed from the city of Tezcuco, Nezahualcoyotzin dispatched another son of his named Prince Acapipioltzin with more forces to aid the first son because the people of this Cuexteca nation were very bellicose. Seeking to gain fame and glory, Prince Acapipioltzin, who by this time was a very good soldier, [fol. 45r] took a different route to avoid being seen by his brother. He led his support troops so skillfully that, despite leaving six days after Xochiquetzaltzin, he arrived with his forces three days before his brother did with the army. With a ferocious spirit and a much smaller army, Acapipioltzin attacked and defeated the Cuextecas near a great river, breaking their army; many drowned attempting to cross the river, and he crossed in pursuit. When his brother arrived with the army, Acapipioltzin had already nearly subdued the Cuextecas and won some of their territory, so Xochiquetzaltzin could do little more than support him. The most noteworthy provinces and towns won in this conquest were Tlahuitolan, Coxolitlan, Acatlan, Piaztlan, Tetlcoioian, Otlaquiquiztlan, and Xochipalco. After they conquered them, placed garrisons, and established boundaries with other Chichimeca lands in the province of Panuco, they returned home. There they entered triumphantly and were warmly welcomed by Nezahualcoyotzin, their father. Xicotencatl, one of the four rulers of the confederation of Tlaxcalan, participated in this campaign on Nezahualcoyotzin's side. He was a young man of great and invincible courage who was beginning to flourish; he returned home laden with plunder and riches won in this conquest.

❧ CHAPTER 41

*Which deals with the hunger and death suffered in this land,
and why Tlaxcalan, Huexotzinco, and Chololan began waging
wars against the empire*

The empire enjoyed great prosperity, with abundant supplies and a large population, so much so that even the rugged hills and mountains were used for planting
and other purposes. According to the records of the time, the smallest town
in those days had more people than the biggest city in present day New Spain.
But [fol. 45v] everything is always changing and calamities abound, such as
the ones that befell them. The first ones were in the year 1450, which they call
matlactli tochtli.[90] So much snow fell over all the land—it was a fathom and a
half deep in most places—that many houses were toppled and ruined, and all
the plants and trees were destroyed. It became so cold that there was a catarrhal
pestilence that killed many people, especially the elderly. And during the three
subsequent years, all the plantings and harvests were lost, so that most of the
people perished. Then, at the beginning of the year 1454, there was a great solar
eclipse, and the sickness quickly grew worse. So many people were dying that
it seemed not a single person would remain; such was the calamity that had
befallen this land. The hunger was so extreme that many sold their children for
maize in the provinces of Totonacapan, which did not suffer this calamity. Since
the people in those provinces were great idolaters, they sacrificed to their gods
all the slave children they bought, so as to gain their favor and thereby prevent
the same calamity from ravaging their land.

Nezahualcoyotzin, Motecuhçoma, and Totoquihuatzin did everything they
could to help their subjects and vassals in their respective kingdoms. Not only
did they suspend tribute collection for six years, which was how long these
calamities lasted, but they also gave out and distributed the entire stockpile of
maize tribute they had accumulated in their granaries over more than ten or
twelve years. And seeing that the calamity would not end, all three gathered
together with the confederation of Tlaxcalan to discuss the best remedy for this
problem. The priests and satraps of the temples of Mexico said the gods [fol.
46r] were angry with the empire and that they should sacrifice many men to

---

90. Ten Rabbit.

appease them and to do it regularly to remain in their favor. Nezahualcoyotzin was strongly opposed to this idea. He argued emphatically against it, saying that it would suffice to sacrifice war captives, who would die in battle anyway, and it would therefore be only a small loss. Moreover, it would be a great achievement for the soldiers to capture their enemies alive; they would be rewarded for this and serve the gods as well. The priests replied that the wars were so far away and infrequent that any captives intended for sacrifice to the gods would arrive only sporadically and greatly weakened; sacrifices should be frequent and the victims recently captured and fit for sacrifice to the gods, as was usually the case with their children and slaves. Xicotencatl, one of the four lords of Tlaxcalan, suggested that they should, from that time forward, stage regular wars between the confederation of Tlaxcalan and Tezcuco and their allies. They should designate a field where the battles would be fought, and those who were captured and taken prisoner would be sacrificed to their gods, who would be pleased, for their feast would be warm and freshly harvested from this field. Moreover, it would be a place where the lords' sons could practice and become famous captains. The wars should be resolved within the boundaries of the designated field and without the aim of winning lands or territory. It should also be with the condition that if either side faced some trouble or calamity, the said wars would cease and they would come to each other's aid, as was previously agreed to with the confederation of Tlaxcalan.

Everyone agreed with Xicotencatl, and since they were devout and very zealous in the service of their false gods, they endeavored to make it happen. Nezahual-coyotzin designated the field, which lay between [fol. 46v] Quauhtepec and Ocelotepec. And because there were three capitals in the empire, he designated three provinces as opponents: the aforementioned province of Tlaxcalan, along with the provinces of Huexotzinco and Chololan. They called these three the enemies at home. He also established the following conditions: that they fight with equal numbers, with the three capitals fighting together; that they fight battles on the first days of their months; and that Tlaxcalan would fight first, then a month later Huexotzinco would fight second in the designated field, Chololan would fight third in the field defended by those from Atlixco, and then the sequence would begin again with Tlaxcalan. Thus the priests of the temples of Tezcatlipoca, Huitzilopochtli, Tlaloc, and the rest of the Mexicas' idols would reap plentifully, as would the enemies' gods, Camaxtle, Matlalcueye, and Quetzalcoatl. This is how these wars and abominable sacrifices to the gods or, more precisely, demons began, until the invincible don Hernando Cortés, first

Marquis of the Valley,[91] came to plant the holy Catholic faith. It was also decreed that none of the people from the three aforementioned provinces could come to these parts, nor could those from here go there, under penalty of being sacrificed to the false gods. They sacrificed the men captured in the aforementioned wars when they celebrated the eighteen major feasts to the false gods, which took place on the first days of the eighteen months that made up their solar year, and on other movable feast days.

---

91. The Valley of Oaxaca. Cortés would only receive this title from Charles V in 1528.

🌿 CHAPTER 42

Of how Nezahualcoyotzin built retreats and planted woods and gardens, and the people he ordered to beautify and maintain them and the royal houses

[fol. 47r] King Nezahualcoyotzin built gardens, labyrinths, and retreats in addition to the ones that he had at his grand⁹² palace called Hueitecpan, those at his father's palace of Çilan, and those of his grandfather, Emperor Techotlalatzin. These included the famed woods of Tetzcotzinco, which are celebrated in the histories, and the retreats at Quauhiacactzin, Acanoztoc, Cozcaquauhco, Cuetlachatitlan, and Otlatlitec as well as those at the lake: Acatetelco and Tepetzinco. He also designated the best parts of the wilderness as hunting grounds, where he would go when he had leisure time. In these woods and gardens—adorned with grand lavishly wrought ornamental castles, fountains, canals, aqueducts, ponds, baths, and other splendid labyrinths—he planted a variety of flowers and all sorts of exotic trees brought from faraway places. In addition to all this, he designated five parcels of the most fertile land near the city, where they planted fields that he tended personally for his own pleasure and enjoyment, including one in Atenco, which is on the lake, and others in the town of Papalotlan, and in Calpolalpan, Maçaapan, and Yahualiuhcan.

The towns near the court took turns handling the adornment and maintenance of all the king's palaces, gardens, and woods. Of these towns, Huexotla, Coatlichan, Coatepec, Chimalhuacan, Itztapalocan, Tepetlaoztoc, Acolman, Tepechpan, Chiuhnauhtlan, Teçoiocan, Chiauhtla, Papalotlan, Xaltocan, and Chalco maintained, decorated, and cleaned the king's palaces for half the year. During the other half of the year, it was the duty of the towns of La Campiña, which were Otompan, Teotihuacan, Tepepolco, Cempoalan, Aztaquemecan, Ahuatepec, Axapochco, Oztoticpac, Tiçaiocan, Tlalanapan, Coioac, Quatlatlauhcan, and [fol. 47v] Quauhtlatzinco. And the towns of Calpolalpan, Maçaapan, Yahualiuhcan, Atenco, and Tzihuinquilocan were responsible for the king's quarters. The provinces of Tolantzinco, Quauhchinco, Xicotepec, Pahuatla,

---

92. The phrase "at his grand" appears crossed out earlier on the same folio. We believe Alva Ixtlilxochitl neglected to reinsert it in the appropriate place; we have reincorporated it and added the word "palace" in order to make sense of this passage.

Figure 18. Coat of arms of the City of Tetzcoco (after Peñafiel 1979, ii).

Iauhtepec, Tepechco, Ahuacaiocan, and Quauhnahuac, with their subject towns, were responsible for the woods and gardens; each went to tend them in turn, with each province or town in charge of a particular garden, forest, or field.

The most pleasant and wondrous of the gardens were the woods of Tetzcotzinco. In addition to very wide ramparts, it had steps, some made from cement and some carved into the rock itself, by which one could climb to the top and walk all around. To deliver water from its source to the fountains, cisterns, baths, and pipes that branched out to irrigate the flowers and groves in these forests, it was necessary to build strong and very tall cement walls of incredible size from one peak to another. On top of the wall, Nezahualcoyotzin had a channel built that went up to the highest part of the forest. On the back side of the peak, at the first pool of water, there was a rock upon which were carved in a circle the year signs since King Nezahualcoyotl's birth until that point in time. Encircling these year signs, paired with each one of them, his memorable deeds were also carved. Carved inside the circle was his coat of arms: a crumbling house engulfed in flames and another house embellished with many structures, and between the two, a deer's foot with a precious stone tied to it and a crest of precious feathers on top; also an arm holding a bow and arrows on top of a mountain; a morion helmet with ear pieces and a jerkin arranged as a man would wear them; [fol. 48] on the sides, two tigers with fire and water coming out of their mouths; and as a border, twelve heads of kings, lords, and other things (fig. 18). The first archbishop of Mexico, the friar don Juan de Zumárraga, ordered this destroyed, believing it to be idolatrous. But in fact, Nezahualcoyotzin's coat of arms symbolized everything recounted up to this point.

As it flowed out of the first pool, the water divided in two, with half going around the edge of the forest to the north and the other to the south. At the top of the woods, there were some towers, the tops of which resembled masonry pots with feather crests emerging from them; these represented the name of the Tetzcotzinco forest. Further below, a winged and feathered lion more than two arm spans long was carved from a rock. It was lying down and facing east; from its mouth emerged an exact likeness of the king's face. A canopy made of gold and feathers usually hung over the statue. A little farther below were three pools of water. At the edge of the middle pool, three frogs were carved from the rock itself; the pool represented the great lake, and the frogs represented the three rulers of the empire. To the north there was another pool, and the name and coat of arms of the city of Tolan, which was the capital of the Tolteca Empire, were carved into a rock. On the left, to the south, was the other pool, and the coat of arms and name of the city of Tenaiocan, which was the capital of the Chichimeca Empire, were carved into the rock. Water drained from this pool through a channel and, breaking over some rocks, showered a garden filled with fragrant flowers [fol. 48v] from coastal lands so that as the water fell and pounded on the rock it seemed to be raining. Behind this garden were baths carved into the mountain itself. And even though there were two baths, they were of a single piece of rock. Beyond this, one could descend a large outcrop by using steps cut in the rock itself that were so smooth and well carved they seemed like mirrors. Carved into the railing of these steps was the day, month, year, and hour when King Nezahualcoyotzin learned of the death of a lord of Huexotzinco he loved dearly, for this news reached him when these steps were being made.

Then, next to this, was the castle the king had in the forest. Among the many halls, bedchambers, and private rooms within was a very large hall opening out onto a patio, where he received the kings of Mexico and Tlacopan and other great lords when they came to be entertained. They held dances and performances for enjoyment and amusement in the patio. The castle was so masterfully and wondrously made, and with such a variety of stone, that it did not seem to be the work of man; the bedchamber where the king slept was round. Everything else in these forests, as I have said, was planted with an assortment of trees and fragrant flowers; in them were many different kinds of birds, not including the ones brought from faraway places that the king kept in cages. Their songs and chorus were such that people were unable to hear one another. Outside the forests, which were enclosed by a wall, the wilderness began, where there were many deer, rabbits, and hares. If everything here and in this king's other forests were described in detail, it would be necessary to write a separate history.

[fol. 49r]

 CHAPTER 43

Of how king Nezahualcoyotzin married Azcalxochitzin, daughter of his uncle Prince Temictzin, and the strange way this marriage came about

King Nezahualcoyotzin had fathered many children with the many concubines he kept in his palaces and gardens; some of these children had helped him in the wars and conquests described above and were already very famous captains. However, he had not married according to the custom of his ancestors and taken a legitimate wife who would bear the successor to the kingdom. Neither his uncle King Itzcoatzin nor King Motecuhçoma, who by this time was king of Mexico, had dared make any mention of marriage, because they remained chastened from when he refused the twenty-five maidens, and so he had yet to marry. Once he decided to marry, he ordered that maidens be brought to him who were legitimate daughters of the lords of Huexotla and Coatlichan, the kingdom's most noble and ancient houses, into which his ancestors, the Chichimeca emperors, had married. However, only one could be found, and she was from the house of Coatlichan. She was so young that he gave her to his brother Prince Quauhtlehuanitzin to raise and educate until she reached the appropriate age, whereupon he would bring her to the palace to be married. In the meantime, Prince Quauhtlehuanitzin, who was already very old, died. His son Ixhuetzcatocatzin, heir to the house and title, succeeded him. When he saw such a noble and beautiful maiden, he married her, not knowing for what purpose she was being raised. Thus, by the time the king thought it appropriate to celebrate the wedding, she was already his nephew's wife. Unaware of what had happened, Nezahualcoyotzin summoned Ixhuetzcatcatzin and told him to bring the lady who had been raised by his father; he wanted to marry her, for this was the reason he had entrusted her to his father. [fol. 49v] Ixhuetzcatocatzin told the king that she was already his wife, that he had married her unaware of the agreement between his father and His Highness, and that, with this knowledge, he should do as he pleased. Without saying a word, the king handed him over to the judges, who were to punish him if he had committed a crime. But they found him blameless and released him.

Accustomed to good fortune in all his endeavors, his failure to marry caused him great sadness and melancholy. Close to despair, he left the palace all alone and went to his woods near the lake. Failing to find solace there, he continued his journey until he reached the town of Tepechpan. When Quaquauhtzin, the local lord and one of the fourteen grandees of the kingdom, saw him, he came out to greet him and took him to his palace, where he served him food, for he had not yet eaten that day. And to show him greater hospitality, he had Azcalxochitzin serve him at the table; she was a Mexica noblewoman and Nezahualcoyotzin's first cousin, daughter of his uncle Prince Temictzin. Quaquauhtzin was raising her to marry and take as his legitimate wife. Heretofore, he had not enjoyed her because she was too young; she had been given to him as a small child by her parents in exchange for a large gift of gold, jewels, cloth, feathers, and slaves. This was the plunder from one of the conquests described above, in which Quaquauhtzin had participated as captain general. When the king saw this lady, his first cousin, so beautiful and endowed with nature's charms and graces, all the melancholy and sadness he felt melted away. She had stolen his heart.

Concealing his desire as best he could, Nezahualcoyotzin said goodbye to Quaquauhtzin and returned to his court. To win the object of this desire, the king orchestrated the death of Quaquauhtzin with the utmost secrecy, never revealing his intentions. It was done as follows. He dispatched the most trusted messenger of his household to the confederation of Tlaxcalan [fol. 50r] to say that it was in his kingdom's interest that Quaquauhtzin, one of its grandees, should die for some serious crimes he had committed. To give him an honorable death, he asked the confederation to order its captains to kill him in battle; he would send him on the appointed day for this purpose, and they should not let him return alive. Then the king called two captains he trusted greatly and told them that on a certain day he wanted to send Quaquauhtzin to the war that was regularly fought on the field that bordered Tlaxcalan, and that they should place him where the battle was fiercest, so the enemy would kill him and he would not escape alive. This was appropriate because Quaquauhtzin had committed a serious crime; Nezahualcoyotzin was only granting him this honorable death because of the goodwill he felt toward him. Then he summoned Quaquauhtzin and told him to prepare himself to serve as general in the upcoming war. Quaquauhtzin was surprised and amazed, for he was an old soldier and it did not befit his status to lead this campaign, but he obeyed his king's command. Anticipating his demise, he composed sorrowful songs, which he sang at the farewell gathering he held with all his friends and relatives. He left on this campaign and died, cut to pieces by the Tlaxcaltecas.

Having taken care of this matter, another remained, which was to ascertain the will of his cousin. So that no one would discover his intent, Nezahualcoyotzin went to visit his sister Princess Tozquentzin. He revealed his desire to her, telling her he wanted to marry but could not find anyone suitable in the kingdom except for Azcalxochitzin, the betrothed of Quaquauhtzin, lord of Tepechpan, who had been killed by the Tlaxcaltecas a few days earlier. Now he needed to know this lady's wishes, but since the death of her betrothed was so recent, it would not be proper to ask her openly. Tozquentzin should devise a way to speak to her secretly and inquire as to her preference. His sister the princess replied that she [fol. 50v] had in her household an old maidservant who regularly visited Azcalxochitzin to do her hair; His Highness could send word through her. Accordingly, the king ordered the maidservant to tell his cousin on his behalf that he was sorry for the death of her betrothed, and that he felt obligated, as her first cousin, to take her as his legitimate wife and make her queen and ruler of his house and domain, and to tell her this secretly without anyone else hearing it. The old woman was so adept that she was able to relay the message when the lady was alone and did so persuasively, for Azcalxochitzin replied that His Highness should do with her as he pleased, since, as his relative, he had a duty to honor and protect her.

As soon as the king knew the lady's will, he ordered a reinforced causeway built from Tepechpan to the forest of Tetepetzinco. Once it was finished, a boulder was to be brought from a retreat in Chiuhnauhtlan, where the skin of his brother Acatlotzin—who, as described earlier, was killed and flayed by the tyrant Teçoçomoc—had been displayed. He set a deadline for all of this to be done. Then he returned alone to the house of his sister, the princess, where he ordered the old woman to go see his cousin Azcalxochitl and tell her that on a certain day a boulder being brought from Chiuhnauhtlan to be placed in the forest of Tetepetzinco would pass by her town and that she should follow it and go see it placed in the woods with as many companions as possible. She was not to give any hint that she went at his command, but rather because she was curious to see that grand display. He would be on a balcony where he would see her and have her taken to the palace. There the wedding would be celebrated, and she would be received and acknowledged as queen and ruler of Tezcuco. All of this was done. On the appointed day, the lady, accompanied by all her attendants and servants and other noblewomen, arrived with all the noblemen of Tepechpan. The king, who was standing on a balcony with all his grandees, feigned amazement at seeing such a large number of people and so many women where there were seldom any and offhandedly asked his grandees who that lady was. They replied that she was his cousin Azcalxochitl, who had come to see [fol. 51r] where the boulder they had brought would be placed. Hearing this, the king said it was not right for his cousin, who was so young, to be in a place such as this, and that she should be taken to the palace, where she would be more comfortable.

After she had been there a few days, the king told his grandees that it would be well for him to marry her, for she was a maiden and of high birth. All the grandees wholeheartedly agreed. And so the wedding was celebrated with much ceremony, feasting, and rejoicing in the presence of Kings Motecuhçoma and Totoquihuatzin and many other lords. She was received and acknowledged as queen and ruler of the Aculhuas and Chichimecas through the ruse described above. Nezahualcoyotzin took this lady without it ever being known for certain if the death of Quaquauhtzin was intentional or a fortuitous accident. His son and grandsons, the authors who discovered this secret, condemn it as the worst thing he did in his life. But this is the only wicked and reprehensible action of his they could find, and even in this case he was blinded by love and desire.

🌿 CHAPTER 44

Of the children that King Nezahualcoyotzin fathered and other things that took place during this time, until the death of Prince Tetzauhpiltzintli

King Nezahualcoyotzin's wedding took place prior to the calamities, famines, and plagues described above, so it seems that God saw fit to punish him for the unjust death he gave Quaquauhtzin. Nezahualcoyotl had two sons with this noblewoman. They were not born one after the other, but rather many years passed after the birth of the first one, Prince Tetzauhpiltzintli, who was graced with all the gifts nature could give an enlightened prince. He was very handsome and, with little effort from his tutors and teachers, accomplished in all things. He was a refined philosopher and poet and an excellent soldier; he even excelled in most of the [fol. 51v] mechanical arts. Where he was most naturally inclined was warfare and building palaces, such as the one he built at Ahuehuetitlan, where he found a cypress tree and was inspired to build around it. He took the name for his palace from this tree.

While Tetzauhpiltzintli was engaged in these pursuits, Prince Huetzin, his father's illegitimate son, carved a precious stone in the shape of a bird so realistic that it seemed to be alive. And since this jewel was so lovely, he wished to offer it to his father the king. Nezahualcoyotzin was delighted when he saw it and decided to give it to his son Prince Tetzauhpiltzintli, because he loved and cherished him immensely. He sent Prince Ecahue, another of his illegitimate sons, to give it to Tetzauhpiltzintli. Ecahue told Tetzauhpiltzintli it had been carved by Prince Huetzin, his brother. Prince Tetzauhpiltzintli sent thanks to the king, his lord and father, for his kindness, saying he was delighted that his brother was such a good craftsman. But he added that he would be much more delighted were Huetzin inclined to warfare, which would garner him more esteem and better serve His Highness. When he went to deliver Prince Tetzauhpiltzintli's reply, Prince Ecahue altered the words on the advice of his mother. Ecahue's mother was one of the king's concubines and spent much time alone with Nezahualcoyotzin so as to prevent him from having a legitimate son with the queen. In this way she hoped that her sons would succeed to the kingdom at the end of the king's days, because, in her opinion, she was superior to the rest of the king's concubines in both status and favor. Accordingly, Prince Ecahue told the king he had gone to see

Prince Tetzauhpiltzintli, who had given an inappropriate response that suggested he wanted to take over the kingdom. He said that Prince Tetzauhpiltzintli had replied that he scorned the mechanical arts that occupied the prince who had carved the jewel, and valued only warfare, by which he intended to rise up and subjugate the world and, if possible, surpass his father in renown and dominion. And he said that when Prince Tetzauhpiltzintli spoke these things, he showed Prince Ecahue a storehouse full of weapons, which His Highness could confirm for himself. With this final claim, Prince Ecahue gave credence to the [fol. 52r] allegations that, following his mother's order and counsel, he made against his brother the prince. For Tetzauhpiltzintli was so fond of battle that his rooms were decorated with all sorts of weapons and insignia of war. When his father, the king, sent one of his chamberlains to ascertain if the prince had a stockpile of weapons, he came back and reported that the rooms and houses he was building were decorated with them.

Believing the accusations against Tetzauhpiltzintli were true, Nezahualcoyotzin decided to prevent him from acting and have him reprimanded and punished by King Motecuhçoma of Mexico and King Totoquihuatzin of Tlacopan, who had the proper judicial authority. To that end he invited them to the city of Tezcuco. When they arrived, Nezahualcoyotzin reported everything he had heard about his son the prince. He asked them to reprimand and punish him, because, as a youth of little wisdom and knowledge, he had grown vain. But he did not want to be present when the punishment was administered; rather he would go to the woods of Tetzcotzinco. Nezahualcoyotzin charged them above all to adhere to the law, for it would be unjust to disregard it for his benefit. After he had left for the woods, the Kings Motecuhçoma and Totoquihuatzin conducted the inquest with great discretion, gathering the information about the case from the people who made the allegations against Tetzauhpiltzintli and without hearing his side or notifying him of the charges. They went to his palace as if they were going to visit him and see the residence he was building. Some captains who accompanied them pretended to put a flower necklace around Tetzauhpiltzintli's neck and strangled him to death. Once he was dead and lying in state, shrouded with all the insignia usually worn by princes and kings, Motecuhçoma and Totoquihuatzin hastily embarked for their cities, taking their leave of those who were there. They told them to tell King Nezahualcoyotzin that they had done their duty and acted in accordance with the law.

The news reached Nezahualcoyotzin at the woods [fol. 52v]. When he learned about the death of the prince, whom he loved and cherished deeply, he wept bitterly for his loss. He lamented the two kings' lack of mercy and sorely regretted having entrusted them with the case. On the other hand, he felt they must have done what was right, for it must have been as difficult for them to pass judgment as it would have been for him, for they were his uncles. He spent many days in the woods sad and troubled, lamenting his sorrows, because he had no other legitimate son who could inherit the kingdom, although he had seventy sons and fifty-seven daughters with his concubines. Most of the sons turned out to be very famous captains who helped him greatly in the aforementioned campaigns and conquests and in the ones that came later. He married the daughters to lords of his court and kingdom as well as to those of Mexico and Tlacopan. And to both sons and daughters he gave plenty of lands, towns, and villages, which provided them income and service, and they were held in high regard.

❧ CHAPTER 45

Which deals with how the province of Chalco was won thanks
to Prince Axoquentzin and the birth of Prince Nezahualpilli

King Nezahualcoyotzin found himself forsaken by fortune. For one, he was without a successor to his kingdom, and second, the people of the province of Chalco, whom he had previously subjugated, were acting insolently and without shame. All the land was subjected to his will and rule, yet the audacity of these people at his very doorstep had reached such extremes that they had killed two of his sons and another two princes from the kingdom of Mexico, sons of Axayacatzin, who at the time was captain general and high priest of the [fol. 53r] temple of Mexico. Worst of all, the Chalcas used their dead bodies as candleholders in the hall where they held dances and gatherings in the evenings. And as a sign of his arrogance and vain presumption, their lord Toteoçitecuhtli adorned himself with their hearts, along with the hearts of other captains and distinguished people they had killed in the course of this war, set in gold as jewels in a necklace. What finally broke Nezahualcoyotzin's heart was that, one night, a woman from the city of Tezcuco who had been captured by the Chalcas and served at the palace, moved and hurt by this cruel spectacle, carried off the bodies of these princes, which they kept dried and mummified, and took them that very night to King Nezahualcoyotzin. Although they were dead, she freed them from the clutches of their enemies.

All the things described above moved the king to seek the appropriate remedy, which the hands of mere mortals could not provide. He gathered the most learned men in his kingdom; they told him that he should make grand and solemn sacrifices to their gods in order to appease their anger and secure victory against his enemies and an heir to his kingdom and title. Even though he had always been opposed to serving and appeasing the gods of the Mexica Culhuas in this manner, Nezahualcoyotzin felt obliged to offer them grand and solemn sacrifices and allow people to worship them and to build temples dedicated to them, which he had not permitted before this time. Therefore, they began building temples for the Mexica gods within his palace at this time, as described above. All the sacrifices, victims, and services that Nezahualcoyotzin offered to the false gods—speechless stones and sticks without any power whatsoever—were useless. Not only did he not get what he asked of them, but on the contrary, his affairs went from bad to worse. And so he realized he was not mistaken in his opinion and that those [fol. 53v] idols were demons, inimical to human life, since no amount of sacrificial victims satisfied them.

He left the city of Tezcuco and went to his woods at Tetzcotzinco. There he fasted for forty days, offering prayers to the unknown God, creator and origin of all things, and in whose honor he composed some sixty songs, which have been preserved to this day. They are full of moral teachings and maxims, with many sublime names and epithets suitable to God. He prayed four times each day: at sunrise, noon, sunset, and midnight, burning offerings of myrrh, copal, and other aromatic resins. One night at the end of the forty days, around midnight, one of his chamberlains, named Iztapalotzin, heard a voice calling his name outside. When he came out to see who it was, he saw a handsome young man, and the place where he stood was bright and shining. The young man told him not to be afraid and to go in and tell his lord, the king, that on the following day before noon his son, Prince Axoquentzin, would win the battle against the Chalcas. His wife, the queen, would also bear a son who would succeed him in the kingdom and be a very wise and capable ruler. Once this vision disappeared, Iztapalotzin entered the king's sleeping quarters and found him praying and burning incense and perfume, facing the coming dawn. Iztapalotzin told Nezahualcoyotzin what he had seen and heard and been told to tell him. The king called his guards and ordered them to put Iztapalotzin in a cage as punishment for what he thought were preposterous lies. The next morning before dawn, Axoquentzin, a young man no older than eighteen, went with his friends to the battlefield in Chalco, eager to see his brothers the Princes Ichantlatoatzin, Acapipioltzin, and Xochiquetzaltzin, who for a long [fol. 54r] time had been leading the army that the king had sent to the Chalca front. Axoquentzin arrived just as they were sitting down for lunch before going to battle against their enemies, who were doing the same thing at the time. All three were eating lunch around a large shield. Acapipioltzin, who was the first to recognize his brother, was very pleased to see him. Calling him over to sit next to him to eat together, he asked Axoquentzin why he was there. This annoyed Ichantlatoatzin, who said a young boy who had never fought in any war had no business being there, that he would be useless even as a porter, and that he would be better off at the skirts of the women and maids who had nursed him. He said other harsh words to him and shoved him out of the spot where his brother had placed him. Shamed and offended by the things his brother said to him, the young man went to a weapons tent he saw nearby, entered, and armed himself. He went to the enemy's camp on a rampage, preferring to be killed and cut to pieces by his enemies than to live disgraced and scorned by his brother. Axoquentzin moved with such dexterity and speed that in just two strides he was inside the tent of Toteoçitecuhtli, lord and leader of the Chalca army, who in spite of being very old and blind, valiantly commanded the field through his two famous captains called [. . .].[93] Axoquentzin charged at him, grabbed him by the hair with one hand and defended himself from his enemies with the other. So sudden was his attack, that by the time the Chalcas thought to defend themselves and free their lord, the Tezcucas had already defeated half the army, for the bravest captains present had followed Prince Axoquentzin in order to protect him. With their help he was able to safely capture Lord Toteoçitecuhtli while wounding and killing [fol. 54v] the opponents that confronted him. By the time his three brothers realized what had happened, the glory of their brother Axoquentzin's victory and triumph was already being sung. And joining the fray, they pressed on until all the Chalcas were defeated and conquered, and their province was subjugated.

After Axoquentzin accomplished this deed, they sent messengers to inform his father, the king, who was immensely pleased. And Iztapalotzin was freed from the cage where he had been imprisoned, and great feasts were celebrated. A few days later, the queen bore a son who was named Nezahualpiltzintli, which means the longed- and fasted-for prince. And in recompense for the great favors he had received from the unknown God, creator of all things, the king built him a sumptuous temple, opposite the main temple of Huitzilopochtli. Besides having four landings, the cu formed the base of a very tall tower built on top of it; it had nine levels, which symbolized the nine heavens. The tenth served as the pinnacle of the other nine levels; it was painted black with stars on the outside. The inside was full of gold, jewels, and feathers offered to the aforementioned God, yet unknown and unseen, without any statue or any other representation of him. The aforementioned pinnacle ended in a three-tiered spire. On the ninth level there was a musical instrument called a *chililitli*—from which this tower temple took its name—as well as others, such as horns, flutes, conchs, and a metal kettle, called a *tetzilacatl*, that served as a bell, which was rung with a metal mallet and produced almost the same sound as a bell. There was also a very large sort of drum, which is the instrument they use for their dances; this one, along with the others, and especially the one called chililitli, were played four times each day, at the aforementioned times when the king prayed.

---

93. A blank space was intentionally left in the manuscript to insert the captains' names at a later point.

[fol. 55r]

 CHAPTER 46

Which deals with the death of King Motecuhçoma of Mexico, the election of Axayacatzin, and some of King Nezahualcoyotzin's admirable words, deeds, and judgments

Prince Nezahualpiltzintli was born on the day they called *matlactli omome coatl,*[94] which was the eighth day of their fifteenth month, called *atemoztli,*[95] and of their year called *matlactli onçe tecpatl,*[96] which according to our calendar, was January 1 of the year 1465 of the incarnation of Christ our Lord. In this same year—but in the next according to the native calendar, called *matlactli omome calli*[97]—the Chalcas started building halls and rooms of incredible grandeur in the houses and palaces of the king, the lords and gentlemen of his kingdom, and the other two kings and rulers of the empire. This was the punishment for their obstinacy and rebellion. The Chalcas brought from their province the wood, stone, and other materials needed for the aforementioned buildings, which entailed such harsh and extraordinary labor that there could be none worse in the world. Since they had waged war for so many years, most of the Chalca men had died, and so even the women were compelled to perform this labor. King Nezahualcoyotzin took note of this situation and the tragic suffering of the Chalcas and that, worst of all, they were dying from hunger. Saddened and upset by this, he ordered the construction of some big straw houses, called *jacales,* and commanded his stewards to stock them with large quantities of food for the Chalcas who were working on the aforementioned buildings. Beyond providing great relief to these laborers, this also helped the Chalcas endure the famine that ravaged their province at the time, because hoards of them came willingly to work on the buildings, seeing that by doing so they alleviated their hunger. The Chalcas worked [fol. 55v] for almost four more years.

In the following year of 1469, near the end of the year they call *yei calli,*[98] the great Motecuhçoma Ilhuicamina died in his city of Mexico. And once the news reached Nezahualcoyotzin, he did as he had done the last time. In Motecuhçoma's place, they

94. Twelve Snake.
95. Falling Water.
96. Eleven Flint.
97. Twelve House.
98. Three House.

acknowledged and pledged fealty to Axayacatzin, son of Teçoçomoc, whose father was Itzcoatl, and Atotoztli,[99] legitimate daughter of the late Motecuhçomatzin, who had had no other legitimate children. Thus he succeeded his grandfather, having the necessary qualities, virtues, and rank. After he was acknowledged and the feasts of oath-swearing and coronation were over, Axayacatzin came to the city of Tezcuco, which he visited many times for as long as King Nezahualcoyotzin lived.

Among the deeds that made him worthy of fame and renown, Nezahualcoyotl allowed lumber for building and everyday firewood to be gathered deeper in the woods beyond the boundaries that he had previously set; exceeding those boundaries had been punishable by death. For on one occasion he was out walking with one of the grandees of his kingdom wearing hunting clothes, which he did very often, going out alone and disguised to avoid recognition and to learn about the wants and needs of the people so as to remedy them. And so, on this occasion, with the same purpose, he headed toward the woods. Near the aforesaid boundaries, he came across a boy, very poor and wretched, gathering sticks to take back home. The king asked him why he did not go deeper into the woods where there was so much dry firewood to be had. The boy answered, "I will do no such thing because the king would take my life." He asked him who the king was. The boy answered, "A miserable little man, since he takes away what God freely gives." The king replied that the boy could easily go beyond the boundaries set by the king, since no one would report having seen him do it. The boy got angry and began to scold him, calling him a traitor and an enemy [fol. 56r] of his parents for advising him to do something that could cost them their lives. Returning to his court, the king left an order with one of his servants who had been following them at a distance to seize that boy and his parents and take them to the palace, which he promptly did. They were taken, very troubled and afraid, without knowing why they were being brought before the king. When they arrived, the king ordered his stewards to give them many bundles of cloth and great quantities of maize, cacao, and other gifts. He said goodbye to them, thanking the boy for the scolding he had given him and for keeping the laws he had established. After this, he had the established boundaries removed so everyone could go into the woods and take the lumber and firewood that were there, provided they did not cut down any standing tree, under penalty of death.

---

99. In the manuscript, the names Teçoçomoc and Atotoztli appear in the margin. In the body of the text, Axayacatzin's father is identified as Techotlalatzin, lord of Itzapalapan, and his mother as Aihuitzin, but these names are struck through.

On another occasion, while he was standing on a balcony of the royal palace that overlooked the gates of the main courtyard, a wood peddler, weary from carrying his load of firewood, stopped to rest beneath the balcony with his wife. Leaning against his load for a moment, the peddler looked at the magnificence and greatness of the king's palace and said to his wife, "The owner of all this must be sated and full, while we are tired and starving." The woman told him to shut his mouth lest someone hear him and they be punished for his words. The king called one of his servants and ordered him to go get the wood peddler who was resting beneath the balcony and bring him to his council chamber. The servant left to do this, and the king went to await him in the chamber. Once the very frightened peddler and his wife stood before Nezahualcoyotzin, he asked the peddler what he had muttered about the king and to tell the truth. After he confessed, the king told him [fol. 56v] never again to grumble or speak ill of their natural lord because the walls have ears. Moreover, although it might seem to the peddler that the king was full and sated and all else he had said, he ought to consider the number of burdensome issues the king had to manage, and the responsibility of protecting, defending, and maintaining peace and justice in a kingdom as large as his. Then he summoned one of his stewards and ordered that the peddler be given many bundles of cloth, cacao, and other things. Once these items were brought before the king, he told the peddler that with this small amount he would have enough to live happily, whereas, though the king might seem to have plenty to satisfy him, he had nothing. With that, he sent him away.

Another episode occurred with a hunter. One day, this man, who lived on wild game, had wandered through mountains and ravines and returned home tired without having managed to kill anything. And to feed himself that day, he started hunting the tiny little birds found nearby in the trees. His neighbor, a young man, seeing how upset the hunter was and that he was unable to shoot the little birds, mocked and insulted him, inviting him to try and hit his manly member, for perhaps it would make for an easier target.[100] Because he was upset, the hunter nocked and aimed an arrow, shot it, and hit his mark. Finding himself wounded by the arrow, the young man began to scream and disturbed the whole neighborhood. The hunter was seized and taken before the judges in the palace along with his wounded victim. As they were passing through the main courtyard of the palace, the king, who was watching them, asked what the noise was about. Informed that it was a wounded man who had been struck by a hunter who was

---

100. "Bird" serves as a euphemism for penis in both Nahuatl (*tototl*) and Spanish (*pájaro*).

being brought as a prisoner, he had them brought before him. Once he learned the truth of the matter, he ordered the hunter [fol. 57r] to care for the wounded man; should he recover, the hunter would either be the young man's slave or pay him for his freedom. With that, the king let the hunter go.

Seeing how magnanimous the king had been toward him, the hunter sought ways to receive further favors. And so, one night he placed a turkey outside the door of his house where it could be taken by a coyote—which is an animal that looks like a jackal and is a type of wolf—and he stood where he could see the wolf take the prey. Before midnight, the wolf arrived, having followed the turkey cock's scent, and snatched it. The hunter pursued the wolf so that it could not eat the turkey until it entered its cave, which was deep in the woods. There the hunter struck and killed it with an arrow and carried it, along with the turkey, to the palace. He arrived as the king was getting dressed, for it was very early in the morning. The hunter told the chamberlains that he wanted to kiss the king's hands and ask for justice. The king ordered that he come before him. Once in his presence, the hunter said, "Powerful lord, I come to seek justice against Your Highness's namesake.[101] Last night, it stole this turkey, which I have also brought; it was all that I had. Let Your Highness remedy it." The king replied that if his namesake had wronged him by killing the turkey, it had already paid with its life, whereas if he had brought it alive, he would have punished it. He also warned the hunter not to let something like this happen again, because next time the joke would be on him. Then he ordered that the hunter be paid for his turkey what ten turkeys might be worth. He had the wolf skinned and its pelt placed among his weapons in the armory.

This king was very merciful toward the poor. He regularly stepped out onto a balcony that looked onto the square to see the pitiable people who peddled there, usually the salt, wood, and vegetables sellers who could barely feed themselves. And if he noticed that they were not selling anything, he refused to sit down and eat until his stewards went to buy everything the peddlers were selling for double its value. Then he gave these wares to other poor people, because he was very conscientious about feeding and clothing the elderly, the sick, those maimed in war, and the widows and orphans. He spent a large amount [fol. 57v] of his tributes on this and appointed certain lords and gentlemen to be in charge of it, for no one was allowed to beg in the streets or elsewhere under penalty of death.

---

101. The king's name is Nezahualcoyotl, or "Fasting Coyote."

🌿   **CHAPTER 47**

*Which deals with some of the prophecies and sayings of King
Nezahualcoyotzin*

Of the songs composed by King Nezahualcoyotzin, those in which he most clearly
made prophetic statements that have plainly come to pass and been seen in our
time were the songs called *xompancuicatl*—which means "song of spring"—that
were sung at [fol. 58r] the feasts and gatherings held for the opening of his grand
palace. One of them begins *Tlacxoconcaquican ha ni Nezahualcoyotzin* etc., which
translated according to its true and proper meaning into our vernacular Castilian is:

> Hear what King Nezahualcoyotzin says in his lamentations of the calamities
> and travails that his kingdoms and domains shall suffer. After you have
> departed this life for the next, O King Yoyontzin, a time will come when
> your vassals will be defeated and destroyed, leaving all that is yours in the
> darkness of oblivion. Truly, lordship and power will then no longer be in
> your hands, but in those of God.

And in another, he said:

> Then there will be suffering, misery, and persecutions, which your children
> and grandchildren will suffer. They will remember you tearfully, realizing
> that you left them orphans in the service of others, strangers in their own
> land of Aculhuacan. For this is what power, sovereignty, and lordship come
> to; they are but transitory and precarious. We only borrow the things of
> this life, for in an instant we shall leave them, as others have left them, just
> as you no longer see the lords Cihuapain, Acolnahuacatzin, and Quauh-
> tzontecoma, who had always accompanied you in these fleeting pleasures.

And in this way, he said many other noteworthy things.

And in the year 1467, which they call *çe acatl*,[102] the temple of the idol Huitzilopochtli in the city of Tezcuco was finished and dedicated. He said:

> In a future year called *çe acatl*,[103] this temple, which is now being dedicated,
> will be destroyed. Who will be present? Will it be my son or my grandson?

102. One Reed.
103. In the Nahua calendar, the names of years repeated every fifty-two years.

At that moment the land will begin to fail and the lords' rule will end. The maguey cactus, still small and undeveloped, will be harvested, the immature trees will bear fruit, and the soil will be depleted and continue to decline. Then malice, vice, and hedonism will reach their peak; men and women will indulge in them from a young age. People will steal one another's property. Prodigious things will happen; birds will speak. And in this time the light and the tree of health and life shall arrive. To free your children from these vices and calamities, have them commit themselves to virtue and good works beginning in childhood.

All this upheaval and the rise in immorality have come true exactly as foretold; things that were considered prodigious and supernatural in those times are now commonplace and conspicuous and cause no wonder. Because if someone had the misfortune to be drunk in public in those times, then, besides being insulted and punished on the spot, his house would be unroofed and ransacked, and he would be forbidden from living among people. Yet now drunkenness is so common that it is regarded as an everyday occurrence. And the maidens that were twenty-five and thirty years old would not have thought of leaving their parents' side, but now they are not even twelve and have already lost their innocence. Like the other examples, this clearly demonstrates the difference between then and now and the extent of the changes.

This very wise king ordered all the artisans to depict him, each in the medium of his own craft. For in time, his descendants, hearing tales of his actions and deeds, would want to see him and know his likeness, and this desire would be fulfilled upon seeing his image. Therefore, each rendered a likeness according to his abilities. The goldsmiths made a very realistic gold statue; jewelers made another of precious stones; featherworkers created a portrait on a canvas with a variety of feathers that was so realistic it seemed alive; painters painted another portrait using the best technique; sculptors created a statue in the same way; stone carvers went to the woods of Tetzcotzinco and made the lion described above, depicting only his face; and even the potters did the same. And one by one they [fol. 58v] presented him with the portraits they had made, except for the one carved into the rock, which he had to travel to see. After he saw that one, it was the only one that pleased him. He rejected all the rest, saying that the gold and precious stones would be lost to greed, portraits would deteriorate and fade with time, clay would break, and wood would be eaten through by worms. Only the one carved in rock would endure to be enjoyed by his grandchildren and descendants.

🌿 CHAPTER 48

Of the remarkable deeds of Acatentehuatzin

Acatentehuatzin was the son of Nonoalcatl and Princess Tozquentzin and the nephew of King Nezahualcoyotzin. Because of his noteworthy deeds and sayings, some considered him a fool and others a philosopher and sage, for all his sayings bore upon the true knowledge of the end of all things and love and goodwill toward his fellow man. To illustrate this, I say that one day a prince, his cousin, the son of King Nezahualcoyotzin, came to ask him what he thought about a palace he had just built and whether its construction was sturdy enough to last. Acatentehuatzin answered that it would last just as long as a beautiful woman given to sensual pleasures, who in a short time is ruined and dies of venereal pox. And when his cousin asked him why he had compared it to a woman, of all things, he answered that it was because it was built on a poorly chosen site where the saltpeter would eat away the walls.

One of the side walls in the main hall of Acatentehuatzin's house cracked. He called for masons and builders and asked them how the crack could be repaired. They replied that, because the crack was so large and located where the beams of the roof rested, it was necessary to remove the roof and build the wall anew. He answered that the repairs would take too long and time was short. And considering how long he had left to live, he would fix it more quickly. After sending the masons away, he called for drillers and had them make holes on either side of the crack in the wall, which was made of adobe bricks. Then he had it bound with thick rope, which made everyone laugh heartily. And for this he was rewarded by his uncles the kings.

Another time, while going to the city of Mexico to visit his uncle King Motecuhçoma, as[104]

---

104. One or more folios are missing. They were already missing when the foliation on the top right corner was done. A different foliation begins on the next folio (fol. 59r) with the Arabic numeral *1* on the bottom right corner. Chapter numbers also stop here.

[fol. 59r]

 # CHAPTER [49][105]

Which deals with the death of Nezahualcoyotzin

Nezahualcoyotzin was seventy-one years old and had governed for nearly forty-two years alongside the Mexica and Tepaneca kings when he was stricken with an illness that resulted from the many travails he had endured in recovering, pacifying, and building the empire into the greatest it had been or ever would be. He had seventy-one sons and fifty-seven daughters, although only two of his children were legitimate, as was previously described. Being near death, one morning he ordered Prince Nezahualpiltzintli, who was little more than seven years old, to be brought before him. Taking him into his arms, he hid him beneath the royal vestments that he was wearing and then summoned the ambassadors of the kings of Mexico and Tlacopan who attended his court and who had been waiting to greet him in a nearby chamber. And after they had bid him good morning and left, Nezahualcoyotzin uncovered the child, stood him up, and ordered him to relate what the ambassadors had said and how Nezahualcoyotzin had responded. And the child, without missing a word, delivered his account with great eloquence and grace.

After this, Nezahualcoyotzin spoke with Princes Ichantlatoatzin, Acapipi-oltzin, [fol. 59v] Xochiquetzaltzin, and Hecahuehuetzin, his oldest sons, who presided over the councils and were present along with the rest of their brothers and sisters. He began by reminding them of the toils and wanderings that he endured in his youth, of the death and persecution of his father, Ixtlilxochitl, and of how he finally recovered the empire and governed it wisely and diligently, as they were aware. He told them that in order to preserve the empire, they should cherish one another and love peace and harmony, and if anyone among them attempted to rise up or rebel—even if he were the oldest and most esteemed—he should be immediately punished with death. And then he said to them:

> You see before you your prince and natural lord who, although a child, is wise and prudent. He will maintain peace and justice among you, uphold-ing your privileges and domains, and you will obey him as his loyal vassals

---

105. From this point forward in the manuscript, Alva Ixtlilxochitl has continued to indicate chapter breaks with "Capt." or "Cap." and a title, but chapters are no longer numbered. We have inserted numbers in brackets.

without straying a whit from his commands and wishes. I find myself very near death. Once I am gone, you will sing joyful songs rather than sad laments, demonstrating the courage and strength of your spirit. Thus the nations we have subjugated and placed within our empire will find no weakness in your resolve as a result of my death, and they will realize that any one of you alone is sufficient to keep them subjugated.

And after he had told them many other things and instructed the child in how he was to govern and rule his subjects and vassals by upholding every law he had established without exception, he spoke with Prince Acapipioltzin. He said to him, "From now on you will assume my role as father to your lord the prince, whom you will teach so that he may always live as he should. He will govern the empire with your council, and you will assist with his duties until he is able to rule and govern on his own." The king gave Acapipioltzin this position and charged him with other duties required on such occasions because he was pleased with the prince's loyalty, prudence, and wise council.

With tears in his eyes, Nezahualcoyotzin bid farewell to all his children and the people close to him, ordered them to [fol. 60r] leave, and told the doormen to keep everyone out. A few hours later, his condition worsened and he died. This happened in the year they called *chiquaçen tecpatl*,[106] which was the year 1472. Thus ended the life of Nezahualcoyotzin, the most powerful, courageous, wise, and fortunate prince and captain there has ever been in this new world (fig. 19). When one recalls and considers well his excellent qualities, graces, and abilities—his indomitable spirit; his incomparable strength; the victories he won in battle, the nations he defeated and subjugated, and the prudence and cleverness he displayed in doing so; his magnanimity, clemency, and generosity; and his soaring ideas—it becomes eminently clear that there never was a captain, king, or emperor in this new world that could surpass him in these and other qualities, but rather in most of them he bested them all. He had fewer weaknesses and vices than any of his predecessors, took great care and diligence to punish such things, and always pursued the common good rather than personal gain. He was so merciful toward the poor that he never sat down to eat until he had helped them. In the plaza and marketplace he frequently purchased their meager wares for twice the amount they were worth and then distributed them to others, especially widows and orphans, the aged and infirm. [fol. 60v] And in years

---

106. Six Flint.

FIGURE 19. Nezahualcoyotl (Codex Ixtlilxochitl, fol. 106r).
Photo courtesy of the Bibliothèque nationale de France.

of famine he would open his storehouses, which he always kept full in order to give and distribute needed sustenance to his subjects and vassals. In such times he would also forgive the taxes and duties that his vassals were obligated to pay.

He regarded all the gods that people worshiped in this land as false, saying that they were nothing but statues of demons and enemies of humankind, for he was very wise in matters of morality. And more than anyone, he pondered and searched for the light by which to know the true God and creator of all things,

FIGURE 20. Torquemada, *Monarchía Indiana*, 1615 (vol. 2, frontispiece). *Courtesy of the John Carter Brown Library at Brown University.*

as has been seen in the story of his life. The songs that he composed attest to his pursuit. He proclaimed that there was only one God, who was the maker of heaven and earth; he sustained all that he had made and created; he resided without equal throughout the nine heavens; he had never been seen in human or in any other form; and after death the souls of the virtuous went to reside with him and those of evil people went to the nethermost reaches of the earth, a place of punishment and dreadful toil. And although there were many idols that represented different gods, he never mentioned them, neither collectively nor individually; rather, whenever he spoke of the divine, he would only say, *in tloque in nahuaque ipalnemoaloni*, the meaning of which was explained above. He said only that he recognized the sun as his father and the earth as his mother. Moreover, he would often secretly admonish his children [fol. 61r] not to worship the statues of the idols—that what they did in public should be only for the sake of appearances—because the devil was deceiving them with those statues. And although he was unable to eradicate entirely the Mexicas' rites of human sacrifice, he managed to persuade them to sacrifice only those obtained in war, slaves, and captives, rather than their own children and compatriots, as had once been their custom.

The sources for all of the aforementioned and everything else about his life and deeds are the Mexica princes Itzcoatzin and Xiuhcozcatzin, other poets and historians, and also the annals of the three capitals of this New Spain, especially the annals written by Prince Quauhtlatzacuilotzin, the first lord of the town of Chiauhtla, which run from the year of Nezahualcoyotzin's birth to the time of King Nezahualpiltzintli's reign. It is also found in the accounts written by the princes of the city of Tezcuco don Pablo and don Toribio; by don Hernando Pimentel and Juan de Pomar, children and grandchildren of Nezahualpiltzintli, king of Tezcuco; by Prince don Alonso Axayacatzin, lord of Itzapalapan, son of King Cuitlahua and nephew of King Motecuhçoma; and recently, in our own times, by the extremely diligent Reverend fray Juan de Torquemada, priest in this Province of the Holy Gospel,[107] who first deciphered the meaning of the paintings and songs and wrote about it in his *Historia y monarquía indiana* (fig. 20).[108]

---

107. The Franciscan order established the Province of the Holy Gospel in 1524 to manage its missionary efforts in New Spain. By the early seventeenth century, it comprised the Franciscan missions of central and eastern New Spain.

108. First published in Seville in 1615 with the title *Veinte i un libros rituales i monarchía indiana con el orígen y guerras, de los Indios Occidentales de sus Poblaciones, descubrimento, conquista, conversión y otras cosas maravillosas de la mesma tierra, distribuydos en tres tomos.*

🌿 CHAPTER [50]

Which deals with the fealty-pledging ceremony and coronation
of the very prudent and wise Nezahualpiltzintli Acamapichtli

[fol. 61v] After King Nezahualcoyotzin died, they celebrated his funeral rites and obsequies with great pomp and grandeur according to the rites of the Mexicas. And since modern authors describe these, no further details are offered here, except to say that he was the second Chichimeca king to receive such rites. In attendance were Kings Axayacatzin of Mexico and Chimalpopocatzin of Tlacopan; many other grandees and lords from various regions; and ambassadors from the rulers of Tlaxcalan, Huexotzinco, and Cholan as well as those from distant and hostile kings, such as those of Michhuacan, Panuco, and Tehuantepec. On such occasions they would all be notified and send their ambassadors without risk.

As these commemorations were taking place, the prince's older brothers—particularly the three named above who wielded power and authority—plotted secretly to depose Prince Nezahualpiltzintli and take control of the empire. Learning of this, the two kings, as absolute lords of the empire in charge of the election of and fealty-swearing to the king of Tezcuco, their ruling partner, decided to have the crown prince brought with them to the city of Mexico together with the three aforementioned scheming princes. Acapipioltzin, the prince's counselor, was the only other brother who was to accompany them. All the grandees and lords of the realm were also to go in order to discuss what should be done. Everyone was reassured, and the fealty-swearing occurred without incident.

Upon arriving in the city of Mexico, King Axayacatzin ordered that Prince Nezahualpiltzintli and [fol. 62r] the other four princes, his brothers, be seated as equals in an antechamber of the royal council and all the grandees and lords of the kingdom of Tezcuco be seated behind them. Once gathered in this room, two noblemen who were great orators entered to speak on behalf of the two kings of Mexico and Tlacopan. After welcoming them all, they conveyed their lords' great desire to elect the empire's third ruler and that this ruler should be the one with the most legitimate claim, so as to quell any doubts and ambitions. Then they made many other compelling arguments to this effect and withdrew. Subsequently, the two kings' captains general entered with other great lords of high station and preeminence bearing all the insignia and vestments that were customarily presented to kings at their coronations. They were followed by the two kings themselves. And taking the young Nezahualpiltzintli by his arms, the two captains general led him into the royal council chamber and seated him on a sumptuous throne. The two kings vested him with the royal clothing, crowned him, bestowed upon him the other insignia, and acknowledged him as king of Tezcuco, supreme lord of the Chichimecas, and one of the three rulers of the empire. Then, after congratulating him, everyone took their seats according to seniority and rank, and the celebrations and feasting began, to the great delight of the whole empire. On this occasion, however, they did not observe the idolatrous rites that typically marked such coronations because the new king was not yet old enough for them, but he did perform them in time.

The three princes, [fol. 62v] Nezahualpiltzintli's brothers Ichantlatoatzin, Xochiquetzaltzin, and Hecahuehuetzin, realized that they would not get away with their scheme, and as soon as they saw the two kings' intentions, they left for the city of Tezcuco, regretful and ashamed of their frivolous ambitions. Nezahualpiltzintli stayed in the city of Mexico for a few days before departing for the city of Tezcuco with his uncles—the two kings—and a great retinue, where once again he was celebrated with grand feasts. King Axayacatzin spent the greater part of each year in the city of Tezcuco with his entire court, for it was well suited to his health and pleasure. He did this especially at the beginning of the reign of Nezahualpiltzintli and during the life of his father, Nezahualcoyotzin.

🦚 CHAPTER [51]

Which deals with the war King Axayacatzin waged against
Moquihuitzin, lord of Tlatelolco, and his allies

Soon after Nezahualcoyotzin died, some lords of the empire—including Moquihuitzin of Tlatelolco, Xilomantzin of Colhuacan, and others of their house and
lineage—became restive and defiant toward King Axayacatzin, their lord. And
while it is true that they rendered neither tribute nor vassalage to him, they
were nonetheless subjects who fought alongside the Mexica. They found it easy
to be defiant because in those times they were very powerful within the empire.
Moreover, Nezahualcoyotzin had held them in great esteem, for according to the
songs that the natives today sing in their most important festivals and dances,
he had entrusted [fol. 63r] them with the most serious business of the empire;
they lacked only official titles. This rebelliousness and other issues moved King
Axayacatzin to send ambassadors to the two kings with whom he ruled the
empire to warn them of the disquiet and disobedience of these lords, which
would threaten the empire if allowed to continue. Once they were aware of this,
each king readied his people to go defend and support the Mexica king on the
day he had appointed.

Together, the armies of all three kings entered the city of Tlatelolco and
destroyed it in short order, killing the majority of its inhabitants. And although
Moquihuitzin barricaded himself in the main temple, he was defeated. He was
cast from the temple's highest tower and plummeted to his death. The order was
then given to punish all those who were found to be part of this rebellion, namely
Xilomantzin, lord of Colhuacan; Zoanenemitl, lord of Cuitlahuac; Tlatolatl; and
Quauhyacatl, lord of Huitzilopochco. By this deed and punishment, the grandees
of the empire henceforth became very compliant and maintained great respect
and reverence for its three kings and rulers. This occurred in 1473, which they
called *chicome calli*,[109] during the second year of the reign of Nezahualpiltzintli
and the sixth of King Axayacatzin.

---

109. Seven House.

[fol. 63v]

 CHAPTER [52]

Which deals with some things that Nezahualpiltzintli did
at the beginning of his rule that demonstrated the prudence
and common sense with which God had endowed him since
childhood, which the authors found very noteworthy

One of the concubines closest to King Nezahualcoyotzin was [. . .].[110] She had
continually sought to place her sons in the highest-ranking positions in the
empire, and were it up to her, she would have had any one of them inherit the
empire. To that end, she endeavored to take the lives of King Nezhualcoyotzin's
legitimate children, that is those he had with his queen, a Mexica noblewoman.
Indeed, she was primarily to blame for Prince Tetzauhpiltzintli's death. And so,
as soon as Nezahualpiltzintli became king, he granted to this woman's youngest
son—who held neither title nor position, though he was lord of some lands—the
town of Chiauhtla and other towns in the conquered territories, making him one
of the fourteen Aculhua grandees of the empire. This pleased the woman very
much and helped put an end to the schemes of the other three princes, since two
of them—Xochiquetzaltzin and Hecahuehuetzin—were her sons.

[fol. 64r] Prince Axoquentzin, who conquered the province of Chalco, saw that
his brother the king wished to honor and reward his siblings. So he approached
Nezahualpiltzintli and requested rewards for his services, because their father
the king had never granted him any, for he had been too young. The boy king
was very sympathetic to his brother's request, and before his counselor Prince
Acapipioltzin could utter a word, he summoned a painter along with an architect,
a mason, and a carpenter. He ordered them to go to Chalco and examine the
style and structure of the palace of Toteoçitecuhtli, king of that province, and
for each of them to report back on his area of expertise by a certain date. They
carried out their duty and reported back to the king, who then ordered a palace
built in the same style for his brother Axoquentzin in the best part of the city
of Tezcuco. He also bestowed other rewards, granting him certain towns and
lands in the province of Chalco and elsewhere, so that he would be their lord.

---

110. In the manuscript, a blank space was left for the name of this woman. She is the same
     unnamed concubine mentioned in chapter 44.

FIGURE 21. Nezahualpilli (Codex Ixtlilxochitl, fol. 108r). *Photo courtesy of the Bibliothèque nationale de France.*

Henceforth Nezahualpiltzintli began to govern on his own with great prudence and wisdom, leaving everyone confounded and amazed (fig. 21). No one could find a single flaw in him during the forty-four years that he reigned. And he always welcomed with great love the advice and good guidance [fol. 64v] of his brother Prince Acapipioltzin as well as that of the members of his council.

🌿 CHAPTER [53]

Which deals with some wars and conquests waged by the
three rulers of the empire—Axayacatzin, king of Mexico;
Nezahualpiltzintli of Tezcuco; and Chimalpopoca of Tlacopan—
and the death of Xihuitl Temoc, lord of Xochimilco

One of the lords who supported King Axayacatzin against the king of Tlatelolco
and his allies was Xihuitl Temoc, lord of the city of Xochimilco, a very courageous
captain and also a very skilled ball player. This was the cause of his downfall. After
the aforementioned war had ended, King Axayacatzin called for celebrations to
honor his supporters. One of the festivities that took place was a ballgame, a sport
of which the king was especially fond. Xihuitl Temoc, however, outmatched him,
and the king found himself losing many points. He flew into a rage, raised the
stakes, and bet his city's marketplace and the Lake of Mexico against a garden
that Xihuitl Temoc owned in Xochimilco. Blind to the king's ire and fury, Xihuitl
Temoc accepted the wager and swiftly defeated him. Outraged, Axayacatzin [fol.
65r] stewed over how he might give vent to his anger. After Xihuitl Temoc had
returned to his city, a number of soldiers from the king's guard arrived one day,
claiming they were there to visit him and deliver some of the revenues from the
lake and the market. Upon greeting him and presenting their gifts, they placed
around his neck a garland of flowers, within which some noblemen from that
city managed to conceal a cord. They garroted and killed him before he had a
chance to escape. This cruelty ensured that henceforth the rest of the lords took
care never to mock nor compete with the king in such contests.

Having marshaled their forces, the three kings marched against those of the
province of Matlaltzinco, defeated them, and settled the town of Xalatlauhco
with the captives. Then they marched against those of Tzinacantepec and against
the Ocuiltecas, Malacatepecas, and Coatepecas. They also marched against the
Chichimecas and Otomies in all the provinces that contain the three nations
of the Otomies, Mazahuas, and Matlatzincas, whose towns were Xiquipilco,
Xocotitlan, Xilotepec, Teuhtenanco, Tlacotepec, Caliymayan, Amatepec, Zimate-
pec, and Toloca. It was difficult to subjugate these three nations because they
were very warlike. [fol. 65v] In Xiquipilco, King Axayacatzin faced the greatest
challenge and the most danger; Tlilcuetzpalin, the lord of that province and a

very courageous captain, fell upon the king, and besides dealing him a blow to the thigh that left him badly injured, he inflicted many other wounds so that he overcame the king and was about to kill him. He would have prevailed with his audacity and brazenness were it not for Quetzalmamalitzin, captain general of Tezcuco and one of its fourteen grandees, who with great valor and daring, leaped in among the enemies and liberated the Mexica king. Tlilcuetzpalin was captured, along with many other captains who fought on his side. In all, more than twelve thousand enemy warriors were taken captive, while the empire suffered fewer than a thousand casualties in these battles. Although his wounds healed, King Axayacatzin was left with a lame leg.

After the conquered lands were divided among the three kings, they rewarded all the lords who fought on their side, giving them towns and villages in these provinces. Quetzalmamalitzin, lord of Teotihuacan and captain general and one of the grandees of the kingdom of Tezcuco, was among those who had most distinguished themselves. The three kings gave him a coat of arms [fol. 66r] that depicted a king's leg with tongues of flame emerging from the thigh, in recognition of his heroism in liberating the king of Mexico. Acapipioltzin, advisor to the king of Tezcuco, also distinguished himself; he received a coat of arms depicting three banners bearing three heads, all of gold and feathers. Another was Mozauhqui, who was made lord of Xalatlauhco. Many other lords were rewarded, and they were granted coats of arms according to their deeds and accomplishments.

Having established forts and garrisoned troops as needed in these provinces, the three kings returned to their lands. After they arrived in the city of Mexico, all the captives taken in these wars were sacrificed in the main temple. The king of Tezcuco received as his share the valley of Toloca, Maxtlocan, Zoquitzinco, and other places, which were to render him annual tributes of 880 bundles of cloth, finely made and interwoven with rabbit furs of various colors; another 360 bundles of blankets trimmed in the same material; and feather cloth amounting to 40 bundles plus an additional 7 pieces, which were used as bedcovers. Altogether this totaled 25,607 pieces of cloth, to say nothing of the many treasures of gold jewelry and fine feather ornaments. Furthermore, every year, each of these places was to deliver the harvest of one very productive field of maize. The steward and collector of [fol. 66v] all of this was called Yaotl. And according to the royal tribute rolls, the same amounts were allocated in the same manner to the king of Mexico; the king of Tlacopan received a portion that would be about a fifth of the total.

🌿 CHAPTER [54]

Which deals with the death of Axayacatzin and succession of
Tiçocicatzin, and children each had

The brave King Axayacatzin had governed for nearly fourteen years when death arrived and cut short his life with an ailment that was nearly identical to the one that killed Nezahualcoyotzin. He was deeply mourned by the entire empire, for he had been one of the most valorous princes of them all. According to the histories and songs that preserve the lives and deeds of these princes, he was hailed as the second greatest of all the Mexica, behind only the great Motecuhçoma, first of that name, and so they honored him with lavish funeral rites.

The two kings, Nezahualpiltzintli and Chimalpopoca, convened with the electors and selected by consensus Tiçocicatzin, brother of the deceased, as the seventh Mexica king and their partner in the tripartite empire. Both Tiçocicatzin and Axayacatzin were sons of Teçoçomoc and grandsons of Motecuhçoma. Motecuhçoma had no legitimate children except a single daughter, with whom Teçoçomoc had [fol. 67r] three sons, all of whom became kings one after the other: Axayaca, Tiçocicatzin—the subject at hand—and Ahuitzotzin, who inherited the realm after his brother's death. Tiçocicatzin was acknowledged and sworn fealty to, following the solemn ceremonies of their ancestors. His brother Ahuitzotl was given the title and position of governor and captain general of the Mexica kingdom.

These are the children they had. King Axayacatzin married Tiyacapantzin, daughter of Icelçoatzin—who was herself the daughter of King Nezahualcoyotzin—and Techotlalatzin, second lord of Iztapalapan and son of Cuitlahuatzin, first of that name. Their daughter was named Tiyacapantzin,[111] lady of the house of Xilonenco; she was one of King Nezahualpiltzintli's women and concubines and the mother of King Cacama. The second was Cuitlahuatzin, who became lord of Iztapalapan upon the death of his grandfather Techotlalatzin and later king of Mexico. The third was Motecuhçoma, likewise king of Mexico, during whose time the Spaniards arrived.

---

111. In the manuscript, identical syntactic constructions separated by a cross-out suggest the possibility that Alva Ixtlilxochitl made a copying error and unintentionally repeated the name Tiyacapantzin.

With another woman, who by common opinion was his legitimate wife and queen, Axayacatzin had another four children. They were Macuilmalinaltzin—who would succeed him—Tlacahuepantzin, Atlixcatzin, and the woman who was to be the legitimate wife of King Nezahualpiltzintli but who was punished for the treason and adultery she committed against him. Axayacatzin also had other children. They were Teçoçomoctzin, father of don Diego Huanitzin; Ixtlil-cuechahuac, who was lord of Tolan; Matlatzincatl; Iopihuehue; Coyoltzitzilin; Zecepatic; and Teiolpachoa.

King Tiçocicatzin's children were Tezcalpopocatzin, father of don Diego Tehuetzquititzin, likewise lord of Mexico; Yaotzin; Amaquemetzin; Imactlacua; and Mauhcaxochitl.

[fol. 67v]

 CHAPTER [55]

Which deals with the first campaign that King Nezahualpiltzintli
waged against those of Ahuilizapan, Tototlan, Oztoticpac, and
other provinces along the coast of the North Sea

King Nezahualpiltzintli suffered greatly because his tender age would not allow him to venture forth into battle and test his fate; each day seemed to him a thousand years. Every day, he practiced the art of fighting. He would also go to the rooms where the king, his father, had stored all the emblems, weapons, and raiment of war with which he had subjugated the greater part of the empire, but nothing fit him, which saddened and troubled him. Feeling unworthy, he refused to eat or dress like a king until he was forced to do so by his tutors and teachers. He would not even sleep on a comfortable bed, choosing instead to sleep on the floor like the lowest servant of his household. This was how he was found one morning by his older brothers and other lords who had come to visit and reprimand him. According to the histories, these lords entered the rooms where the king was sleeping and found him on the floor wrapped in the blanket of a poor and humble man. Believing him to be one of the servant boys, one of them approached and gave him a hard kick, scolding him for lying about so carelessly. Upon seeing the king's face, however, the lords felt very ashamed, [fol. 68r] begged his pardon for their error, and carried him to his throne. After discussing with him a number of issues pertaining to his kingdom, they began to chastise him, explaining that his vassals were ashamed and offended that he had not participated in a single battle, for when they went out to war, the Mexicas and Tepanecas insulted them, saying that the Aculhuas had an immature and effeminate king. These lords asked the king to look at the tassels they wore on their heads, ear plugs and lip plugs that adorned their faces, gems around their necks, armlets and bracelets on their arms, golden and jeweled greaves and sandals upon their feet, and fine cloth with which they covered themselves. All this finery they had won through their feats in war and battle, which proved they were worthy of any and all properties, lordships, and domains. These and their many other complaints, some excessive, pained the king.

The king responded with a stern and severe mien, thanking them for their concern for his honor and success. As for not having gone into battle, they could plainly see that he had not been old enough to go onto the battlefield and fight, but he expected that the creator of all things would grant him the will and strength to restore their honor. In fact, he intended to participate personally in the wars being fought in the east. And regarding their worthiness, he said that he would allow them to keep all they had gained during his father's time and even add to it, if they would now perform services to him as loyal vassals. [fol. 68v] And he warned all of them not to defy his will and reminded them of the last words and commands of the king his father.

Having received such a stern and scathing rebuke from the king, the lords lowered their heads and meekly departed to prepare for the journey. They mustered their warriors and departed, marching each day until they arrived in the province of Ahuilizapan, where they began their conquest. The king himself fought in the battle. He was so successful that he subjugated the entire province, along with those of Tototlan, Oztoticpac, and others along the North Sea to the east. The king personally captured many captains and soldiers, including one named Tetzahuitl, the most important of all the lords along that coast. After he established forts and distributed the land according to the conventions of the empire, he returned to the city of Tezcuco and entered in triumph. According to the annals, this conquest occurred in the year 1481, which they called *ome calli*.[112]

---

112. Two House.

🌿 CHAPTER [56]

Which deals with how King Nezahualpiltzintli enlarged the main temple built by his father and constructed living quarters for himself and the great expense and staff required to maintain them

King Nezahualpiltzintli concluded the aforementioned war with much glory and honor. And since, according to the priests, he had enjoyed the support and favor of the false god Huitzilopochtli, his first undertaking was to rebuild and enrich the temple. [fol. 69r] It thus became even more splendid than it had been under his father Nezahualcoyotzin and the largest and greatest temple ever built in this New Spain. For its inaugural festivities, he sacrificed all the captives taken during the wars described above. Afterward, he ordered the construction of a new palace alongside the large one that had belonged to his father, and although not as large, it was more finely and splendidly built than the other. There were exquisite labyrinths, gardens, baths, fountains, pools, ponds, and secret underground canals that flowed unseen to the big lake, by which they traveled when they wished to visit the gardens and retreats he maintained in Acatelco and Tepetzinco or the city of Mexico. And among the pools there was one, located in front of a great hall, which he named Ahuilizapan to commemorate the previously mentioned war. During his life, every single structure, garden, and labyrinth was erected in memory of one of his feats in this or other conquests, and their ruins, even today, testify to the greatness and majesty of their builder.

Because it is relevant, we will now address the great sums [fol. 69v] the king spent to support the people in his and his father's palaces—not only servants, but also lords, courtiers, judges, and other gentlemen and guests who ordinarily resided there. According to the royal accounts, each year they consumed 31,600 bushels of maize, 243 loads of cacao, 8,000 roosters, 5,000 bushels of large chiles, small chiles, and pumpkin seeds, and 2,000 measures of salt. To dress the king, lords and gentlemen, and rest of the people who attended at his house and court, 564,010 pieces of cloth—all of them very fine and extravagant—were used. All this came from the rents that the king collected from the provinces of his own royal estate, whereas the tributes from conquered provinces—having been divided in the manner described earlier—were stored in warehouses he maintained in the cities of Tezcuco and Mexico. The king used these tributes to reward his children and relatives and other worthy lords and captains for their accomplishments in war or in other righteous endeavors.

On the north side of Nezahualpilli's new palace, near the kitchens, were some granaries and storehouses of considerable size, where the king maintained a great quantity of maize and other seeds for use in years of famine. Each granary could hold between four and five thousand bushels. They were so well organized and managed that air [fol. 70r] flowed freely within them, thus preserving the seeds for many years. On the south side were the aforementioned gardens and labyrinths; the height and size of the palace itself shielded them from the north winds and the worst of the cold. On the east side, there was a pond with a variety of waterfowl.

✿ CHAPTER [57]

Which deals with the number of King Nezahualpiltzintli's
concubines; Queen Tenancacihuatzin, his legitimate wife; and
the children he had with her and the others

According to the histories, it appears that King Nezahualpiltzintli had more than two thousand concubines, although there were only forty, including the queen, with whom he was intimate and had children. He had 144 sons and daughters, of which 11 were his legitimate children born of the queen. The eldest, a son and the would-be successor to the kingdom, was named Huexotzincatzin. The second was named Tiyacapantzin; she married Prince Macuilmalinaltzin, heir-apparent to the kingdom of Mexico and legitimate son of King Axayacatzin. The third was a son, Quauhtliztactzin, and the fourth was Tetlahuehuetzquititzin, later named don Pedro.[113] The fifth was named [fol. 70v] Tlacoyehuatzin; she married the lord of Çoateotitlan in the province of Tepeyacac. The sixth was named Teicuhtzin; she married the lord of Coatlichan. The seventh was Xocotzin; she married the lord of Tepechpan. The eighth was Coanacochtzin, later named don Pedro, who actually succeeded to the kingdom. The ninth was Ixtlilxochitzin, who also succeeded to the kingdom; he opposed his brother and sided with the Spaniards. He was named don Hernando Cortés. The tenth, a son, was Nonoalcatzin, and the eleventh and youngest was Yoyontzin, later named don Jorge.

The queen was the legitimate daughter of Prince Xoxoccatzin, lord of the house of Atzacualco, one of the grandest houses subject to the kings of Mexico. Her mother was Teicuhtzin, daughter of Prince Temictzin and sister of Queen Azcalxochitl, the king's mother. This noblewoman, then, was Nezahualpiltzintli's first cousin, which is why he chose her as his legitimate wife. She was but one of the noble daughters of the Mexica kings who had come; they included the lady of the house of Xilonenco—mother of King Cacama and elder sister of the second Motecuhçoma and Cuitlahua, kings of Mexico.

Among the concubines, the king's favorite was called the lady of Tolan, not because of her lineage, but because she was the daughter of a merchant and so wise that she rivaled the king and the wisest men of the realm. She was also a

---

113. After the arrival of the Spaniards, native people who received baptism took a Christian name; in the case of nobles, it was often the name of their baptismal sponsor.

very accomplished poet. [fol. 71r] Owing to these talents and natural gifts, the king remained very devoted to her, and she got whatever she wanted from him. In this way she was able to live independently in great luxury and splendor in a palace that the king built for her.

✿ CHAPTER [58]

Which deals with the death of Tiçocicatzin, king of Mexico;
succession of Ahuitzotzin; and other things that occurred before
his death

According to the annals, in the entire five years and few days of Tiçocicatzin's
rule nothing of note occurred, except for a few lords' deaths and successions.
Techotlalatzin, the second lord of Iztapalapan, died in the year 1482, which they
called *yei tochtli*.[114] And in the next year of 1483, the people of Quauhnahuac
attacked the people of Huexotzinco at Atlixco and were utterly defeated. The
Huexotzincas thoroughly punished their audacity and killed most of them.
Quauhpopocatzin, lord of Coatlichan, died in the subsequent year of 1485 and
was succeeded by Xaquintzin. In the same year, Matlaquahuacatzin became
[fol. 71v] lord of Chimalhuacan. In the year 1486, which they called *chicome
tochtli*,[115] King Tiçocicatzin died. As to the cause of his death, the authors differ
in their views. Some say that his own followers killed him in secret, while others
say that his food was poisoned, but the history that I follow does not provide
information about this.

After he died, the electors met with the kings of Tezcuco and Tlacopan and
elected Ahuitzotzin—a very famous Mexica captain, high priest of the main
temple, and younger brother of Tiçocicatzin and Axayacatzin. As soon as he
became ruler, he fervently sought to enhance the graven images and temples of
their false gods. Therefore he began to build temples of greater splendor than
those of his forebears.

---

114. Three Rabbit.
115. Seven Rabbit.

🌿 CHAPTER [59]

*Which deals with the campaign that Nezahualpiltzintli
undertook on the coast of Nauhtlan and how he and the Kings
Ahuitzotzin and Chimalpopoca conquered certain provinces
to the south*

[fol. 72r] In this aforementioned year of 1486, King Nezahualpiltzintli mustered
his forces and marched on the coast of Nauhtlan, which today is called Almería.
And although the rugged and mountainous terrain of those provinces proved
difficult, he quickly subdued them and captured many of the greatest captains
and soldiers of the Totonaca nation of the Sierra Baja, including their lord. Thus
did that entire coastline, all the way to Panuco, become part of his domain.
And after establishing his forts and distributing the lands in the usual way, he
returned victorious to Tezcuco loaded with spoils.

There, in that same year, he and Kings Ahuitzotzin of Mexico and Chimalpopoca of Tlacopan mustered their forces and marched on the provinces of
Chinantla, Coyolapan, Hualtepec, Tlapan, Xoconochco, Xochitlan, Amaxtlan,
the Zapoteca, and the Mixteca Baja and Alta all the way to the province of
Chiapan. Although the kings brought their full might to bear, these conquests
proved extremely difficult. Nevertheless, they were successful in the end and
returned loaded with great and valuable spoils, as well as a great many captives,
numbering nearly a hundred thousand men. The empire, meanwhile, suffered
no more than seven thousand deaths [fol. 72v] during these conquests. Before
returning home, they stationed warriors in the most defensible parts of the cities
and capitals of those provinces and heavily fortified the borders adjacent to the
still-unconquered lands beyond. This was one of the greatest conquests that the
three rulers of the empire ever achieved in such a brief span of time.

King Nezahualpiltzintli also mounted an attack against those of the province
of Tzicuhcoac. They had rebelled against the empire and killed some merchants
from the cities of Tezcuco and Mexico who were buying and selling in their
territory. He subjugated them, punished the rebels, and left the forts and garrisons well manned before returning home with more than twenty-five thousand
captives in addition to the spoils. Also around this time, King Nezahualpiltzintli
marched against those of Atlixco, one of the three domains designated for the
practice of war and to provide captives to be regularly sacrificed to their false

gods. Quauhtliztactzin, lord and captain of that republic, entered the battlefield designated for these wars to face King Nezahualpiltzintli. He risked all of his best soldiers hoping to gain great honor and fame by becoming the one who was able to defeat such a powerful king in battle. But since Nezahualpiltzintli was astute, wise, and very well trained in warfare, he defeated and captured his opponent at their first encounter, along with many other renowned soldiers. Quauhtliztactzin was but one of the kings and lords that Nezahualpiltzintli himself defeated and captured. There were also many other captains and soldiers that he defeated and captured who are not mentioned here.

[fol. 73r]

 CHAPTER [60]

Which deals with how King Ahuitzotzin completed the
main temple of Mexico and the many sacrifices performed
at its inauguration; the deaths of Chimalpopocatzin, king of
Tlacopan, and other lords; and the ascension of Totoquihuatzin,
second of that name

In the third year of the reign of Ahuitzotzin—which was the year 1487, called
chicuei acatl[116]—the main temple of Huitzilopochtli, foremost idol of the Mexica
nation, was completed. It was the largest and grandest temple in the city of
Mexico. And he invited the Kings Nezahualpiltzintli of Tezcuco and Chimalpopocatzin of Tlacopan to its inauguration, along with all the other grandees and
lords of the empire. All of them, especially the two kings, arrived with great pomp,
bringing many captives to be sacrificed to this false god. For the inauguration
alone, they amassed 80,400 captives from among the four nations conquered
in the aforementioned wars, including those whom the king of Mexico brought
himself. Other authors give different figures, but there were sixteen thousand
captives from the Zapotec nation, twenty-four thousand Tlapanecas, sixteen
thousand Huexotzincas and Atlixcas, and twenty-four thousand Tziuhcoacas,
plus another four hundred, which adds up to the above total. All of them were
sacrificed in this temple of the devil during its inaugural festivities, and their
heads were set within niches carved out of the temple walls for that purpose.
These numbers do not include a smaller quantity of captives from other wars
who [fol. 73v] were sacrificed over the course of the year, which would bring the
total to more than one hundred thousand men. It is obvious that those authors
who overstate the number have conflated these two sets of captives. No other
king before or since Ahuitzotzin matched his butchery and cruelty, because in
addition to these, many others were sacrificed during his reign not only in the
city of Mexico, but also in Tezcuco and Tlacopan and in other large cities and
provincial capitals subject to the empire. Moreover, during this period, the devil
reaped no fewer souls in the provinces opposed to the empire.

---

116. Eight Reed.

Then, in the year 1489, God began to avenge the deaths of so many wretched souls by taking the lives of some of the rulers of the empire. For in this year, King Chimalpopocatzin of Tlacopan died and was succeeded by his son the crown prince, Totoquihuatzin, with the approval of the other two rulers, Nezahualpiltzintli and Ahuitzotzin. Several lords were installed in this year as well, including Teçoçomoc, who became the first lord of Azcapotzalco after its defeat and destruction, and Cuitlahuatzin in Iztapalapan. Both were descendants of the royal house of the kings of Mexico.

🌿 CHAPTER [61]

Which deals with the war that King Nezahualpiltzintli waged
against Huehuetzin of Huexotzinco and how he defeated and
captured him

The histories record that King Nezahualpiltzintli and the king of Huexotzinco, Huehuetzin, were born on the same day at the same hour. The astrologers and diviners drew both of their charts and found that Nezahualpiltzintli would be the one to be vanquished, and yet the songs of victory would be sung for him. These two princes, therefore, were always cautious of one another and anxious to make sense of this quandary. [fol. 74r] The older brothers of Nezahualpiltzintli remained consumed by jealousy, seeing him on the royal throne they had so desired, and therefore regularly corresponded with the Huexotzincatl[117] in secret, informing him not only of their brother's plans and activities but also of his inner thoughts. Thus, when they saw that their brother the king was preparing to attack the king of Huexotzinco, they warned him immediately, informing him of the size of Nezahualpiltzintli's army and describing the emblem he wore. They told Huehuetzin to deploy his most skilled troops and try to kill him at all costs, for his life and honor depended on it. The Huexotzincatl mustered his best people and showed the bravest soldiers and captains a drawing of the emblem that the king of Tezcuco would be wearing in the upcoming battle and ordered them to kill him at all costs so that he might be free and retain his honor. His men all promised to do as he said.

Nezahualpiltzintli arrived at the battlefield with his army. As the fighting was about to begin, he was warned of the treason that his brothers were plotting against him and of the secret pacts and agreements they had made with the Huexotzincatl. Thus, when he entered his tent to arm himself and don his emblem, he secretly summoned one of his most trusted captains and switched weapons and emblems with him. Nezahualpiltzintli told the captain that this service would benefit the royal crown, and he promised very generous rewards to him and, were he to die, to his wife and children and all those of his house and lineage. The captain thanked the king for the honor of choosing him above all others for this service, especially as there were others in the army more courageous

---

117. That is, the lord of Huexotzinco, Huehuetzin.

than he. [fol. 74v] After this, the captain went out from the tent accompanied by all the high-ranking officers of the army and took up the king's position to begin the battle. The king, meanwhile, donned the armor of the captain and secretly summoned seven of his most trusted soldiers, who were among the best in his army. He positioned himself with them in the most suitable location to confront his enemy.

As soon as the battle began, the Huexotzincas charged ferociously and fearlessly. After only a few clashes, they seized the unfortunate captain who wore the armor and emblem of the king. In an instant they had torn him into a thousand pieces, convinced that any soldier or captain who failed to seize a piece of his flesh or his armor and emblem was unlucky. With this they forced the Tezcucas to retreat more than two hundred paces. However, they were so blinded by their victory that King Nezahualpiltzintli was able to approach and confront the Huexotzincatl, pouncing like an angry lion. The two clashed, each landing many powerful blows, yet Nezahualpiltzintli subdued his foe and then seized him, intending to take him alive and lead him away as his prisoner. The Huexotzincas nearest to their lord rallied courageously to his defense, and they would have succeeded if not for the seven soldiers of the king's guard, who fought against seven captains that Nezahualpiltzintli had previously beaten. Shouting for everyone to stand back, that these were the kings, the seven soldiers valiantly held off the seven captains as they sought to aid their lord. [fol. 75r] The Tezcucas who were in retreat realized that their lord was missing and turned back upon the Huexotzincas like enraged tigers. So anxious were they to find their lord that in an instant they arrived to where he was embroiled with his enemy. Nezahualpiltzintli, finding himself lost and unaided amid his enemies as they rained blows and spear thrusts upon him, dropped to the ground and held his foe over him so that his opponents, fearing for their king, would not harm him. This trick did not fully protect him, however, as he was wounded in the leg and would remain lame for the rest of his life. Realizing that his men were pushing back against the Huexotzincas and coming to his rescue, he rolled over again and pinned Huehuetzin beneath him. Once he was captured, the Huexotzincas began to flee in dismay. The Tezcucas slaughtered those who resisted and took those who surrendered as captives.

Having accomplished this, Nezahualpiltzintli returned to his court victorious and entered the city in triumph. It was one of the most noteworthy and perilous battles that he or any of his forebears had fought and is emphasized by all the historians who chronicle these events. To commemorate the achievement, the king built an enclosure the same size and length as the distance there had been during the battle between him and his men while he was behind enemy lines. This enclosure contains the pond for waterfowl mentioned above; today it stands in front of his palaces. [fol. 75v] Thus, the historians say that in no way did the king's astrologers and diviners err in their predictions, as shown by this account of the battle.

🌿 CHAPTER [62]

Which deals with a curious and unusual deed performed by
Teuhchimaltzin, a noble descendant of the house of Tezcuco [118]

Among the famous and valiant lords and captains of those times was Teuhchi-maltzin of the house and lineage of the kings of Tezcuco, whose ancient origins can be traced back to the Chichimeca emperors. He was very familiar with the lands along the coast of the South Sea, having spent his entire life conquering and building defenses there. And since he understood the customs and language of its nations as if they were his own, he attempted a bold and daring feat.

In those days the fame of Yopicatl Atonal, the brave and powerful lord of Zacatula, was spreading. The armies of the empire—sometimes separately and sometimes all three together—had tried many times to enter his lands and conquer them, but they always returned in defeat having achieved very little. [fol. 76r] The Mexicas and Tepanecas had little interest in and little to gain from a campaign in this area. And because the Aculhuas of Tezcuco had started it, they would shout insults at the Tezcucas whenever they encountered them. Teuhchimaltzin, who felt responsible, was ashamed. He thus approached his lord the king and asked for permission to travel to the province of Zacatula with two Tezcuca merchants who traded there, offering to conquer those lands and bring the ruler back dead or alive. The king thought this plan was foolish and reckless; he believed it would fail and that Teuhchimaltzin would either die or be captured. But Teuhchimaltzin insisted, and the king reluctantly consented.

He immediately set out for the province of Zacatula in secret, together with the two merchants he had selected for his plan. When they reached its outskirts, he and the two merchants dressed as locals and went to trade in the markets, biding their time until they could carry out his scheme. Although Teuhchimaltzin believed he was safe, he could not disguise himself well enough to avoid discovery. He was seized and taken before the lord, who ordered that he be kept under heavy guard until the next festival, when he would be sacrificed to their false gods.

The time arrived. The day prior to the festival, the lord invited all the nobles and lords of his court to a grand banquet and celebration, which was customarily

---

118. In the margin of the manuscript: "Note: Check to see if this chapter takes place in the time of Nezahualcoyotzin."

held at night. As it began, all the noblemen made their entrance according to rank, [fol. 76v] greeting and toasting their lord. They drank so heavily—as the people of that nation were wont to do—that by midnight all the guests and hosts alike were drunk beyond care, and Teuhchimaltzin was able to safely leave the room where he was kept. He went to the banquet hall and joined the celebrations that were underway, but the revelers were too intoxicated to notice the enemy in their midst. Once they were senseless and sprawled out on the floor, he approached the king with a large knife, cut off his head, and took some of the insignia and jewels that he wore. Tossing everything into a sack that he had brought for that purpose, he left the palace and ran all the way to the boundaries of this province and crossed back into the empire.

When they returned to their senses and realized that they had been ruined by the fearless audacity of their captive, the nobles of Zacatula agreed to surrender and swear allegiance to Teuhchimaltzin's lord, Nezahualpiltzintli. They sent messengers after Teuhchimaltzin with a generous gift and when the messengers arrived at the outpost where he was, they begged him to return and take possession of that province in the name of his lord the king. Teuhchimaltzin responded by first demanding hostages [fol. 78r][119] to ensure his safety and the safety of the people he would bring with him. They summoned the children of their lord and other lords and noblemen, who were to remain in the outpost while Teuhchimaltzin went to take possession of the territory and place it under the control of the empire. Upon arriving, the first thing he did was assume command of the forces and fortifications of the Zacatultecas. He also took other measures in accordance with the laws and customs of the empire. He installed the heir to the lordship of that province as ruler and restored the other nobles to their prior status and rank. Then he returned victorious to his homeland and entered the city of Tezcuco triumphantly to great praise and fanfare. He presented the head and insignia of Yopi[catl] Atonal to the king along with a large quantity of riches, and the king rewarded him with great favors. Among other things, he named him lord of various places. He also had a palace built for him in the city of Tezcuco in the same style as the palace of the lord of Zacatula. This story served as a valuable lesson, which the kings of Tezcuco at times used to warn their subjects and vassals against the vice of drunkenness.

119. At this point in the manuscript several folios are out of place. Fol. 76v ends after "hostages" and the story continues on fol. 78r. Chapter 63 begins on fol. 77r, continues through fol. 77v, and then jumps to fol. 78v. The narrative progresses as follows: fols. 76r, 76v, 78r, 77r, 77v, 78v.

[fol. 77r]

🌿 CHAPTER [63]

Which deals with other wars of conquest that the empire waged
against the rebels of distant nations

In the year 1492, which they called *matlactli omei tecpatl*,[120] the conquest of the province of Zapotlan took place. In the following year of 1493, there was the conquest of Xaltepec, which had rebelled. In the year 1494, the people of Atlixco captured in battle Tlacahuepantzin, one of the legitimate sons of King Axayacatzin, and sacrificed him to their false gods. In the year 1495, the army of the Aculhuas marched against Tliltepec but did nothing remarkable; many people died in battle and they returned in defeat. In the following year of 1496, the armies of the three rulers of the empire marched on the province of Tehuantepec, but they were also defeated and lost much of their renown and reputation. There God unleashed his wrath against the empire and punished it for the many sacrifices they had made. It did not end there, however, for God inflicted more and greater punishments upon them, as will be seen. In the following year of 1497, [fol. 77v] they subjugated another two provinces: Amaxtlan and Xochitlan.[121]

They pursued these conquests, on the one hand, to recover all the kingdoms and provinces that had comprised the empire of the Toltecas, which they called Anahuac. The three rulers claimed dominion over them through direct descent and succession, especially the kings of Tezcuco, who were doubly entitled: first, they were descended directly from the Toltecas and second, their ancestor—the Great Chichimeca Xolotl, from whom they were descended by the direct male line—claimed and resettled these kingdoms after the fall of the Toltecas. Yet during the time of King Teçoçomoc's tyranny, these provinces rebelled against the Chichimeca emperor, to whom they had been subject. The other reason they pursued these conquests was because the Mexica kings wished to spread their religion and the worship of their false gods to all the lands of the empire. And since these provinces had rebelled, the three rulers united their armies to defeat them and punish them because their subjects and vassals complained of mistreatment when they went to trade in these lands. [fol. 78v] These were the reasons for the aforementioned wars, whether justified or not.

---

120. Thirteen Flint.
121. In the margin of the manuscript: "Note: this is written in the life of Nezahualcoyotzin, in the chapter about the laws."

🌿 CHAPTER [64]

Which deals with the exceptional severity with which King
Nezahualpiltzintli punished the Mexica queen for committing
adultery and treason against him

In the time of Axayacatzin, king of Mexico, he and other lords sent daughters
to King Nezahualpiltzintli so that he could choose one among them to become
his queen and legitimate wife. The rest became concubines, and if the queen
did not provide a successor, a son of the noblest and highest born among them
could enter the line of succession. Princess Chalchiuhnenetzin, Axayacatzin's
legitimate daughter, arrived with these Mexica noblewomen. Because she was
still a child at this time, Nezahualpiltzintli did not keep her with him. Instead,
he ordered that she be raised in great comfort attended by many servants in
another palace, as befitted the daughter of a lord as great as her father, the king.
More than two thousand people went with her in her service: governesses, maids,
pages, and other servants.

Although just a girl (which is why the king would not have her until she came
of age), Chalchiuhnenetzin was nonetheless very cunning and wicked. [fol. 79r]
Seeing that her servants were fearful and deferential due to her rank and status,
once she found herself alone in her quarters, she began to indulge in a thousand
vices. She would secretly send for any dashing and debonair young man who
struck her fancy to come have his way with her. After she had sated her desire,
she would have him killed. Then she would have a statue carved in his likeness,
adorn it with luxurious clothes and jewelry of gold and precious stones, and
place it in her hall. There were so many statues of those whom she killed that
they circled almost the entire room. When the king went to visit her and asked
about the statues, she responded that they were her gods. The king believed her,
because the Mexica nation was indeed very devoted to its false gods.

Yet no evil can remain hidden for long, and this is how she was found out.
For reasons of her own, she allowed three of her lovers to live. They were named
Chiauhcoatl, Huitzilihuitl, and Maxtla; one of them was the lord of Teçoiocan
and a grandee of the realm, while the other two gentlemen were very prominent
at court. The king saw that one of them was wearing a very precious jewel that
he had given to Chalchiuhnenetzin. [fol. 79v] And although he was certain she
had committed treason, he still wanted further proof. One night, when he went

to visit her, her servants told him that she was sleeping, believing that the king would leave, as he had before. But he was suspicious and entered the room where she slept. He reached out to wake her up, but it was not her. Instead, he found lying in her bed a mannequin, with a full head of hair, that was very lifelike and closely resembled Chalchiuhnenetzin. When he saw this replica of her and noticed how the servants were becoming nervous and flustered, the king summoned his guards and began to arrest everyone in the house. He demanded that Chalchiuhnenetzin be found. She was soon discovered carousing with her three lovers; all of them were arrested. The king referred the case to the palace judges, who were to investigate and interrogate all those accused. This they did at once with due diligence and care. Many people were implicated and found guilty of abetting this treasonous crime. Although most were her servants and maids, many others were merchants and craftsmen of all trades. Some had adorned [fol. 80r] and maintained the statues, while others had secreted into the palace the lovers represented by the statues, and still others had killed them and hid their bodies.

Once the case had been properly tried and the verdict rendered, Nezahualpilli sent his ambassadors to the kings of Mexico and Tlacopan to inform them of the situation and to indicate the date on which Chalchiuhnenetzin and the others complicit in this crime would be punished. He also sent a summons throughout the empire, calling upon all the lords to bring their wives and daughters, no matter how young, to witness and learn from the punishment that was to take place. He also declared truces with all the kings and lords who had been fighting against the empire, so that they or their representatives could likewise come freely to see the aforementioned punishment. When the time came, so many people from so many different nations arrived that they hardly fit, even in a city as large as Tezcuco. The punishment was carried out publicly in full view of everyone. Chalchiuhnenetzin and the three noblemen, her lovers, were garroted, and because they were of high rank, their bodies were burned along with the aforementioned statues. As for the rest of the condemned, who numbered more than two thousand, they were garroted one after the other and [fol. 80v] thrown into a great pit dug for that purpose in a ravine near a temple dedicated to the idol of adulterers.[122]

---

122. Here Alva Ixtlilxochitl added, but then crossed out, the following details: "and they buried their bodies by covering them with a large amount of lime and ash."

This punishment was so severe and made such an impression that everyone praised the king. The Mexica lords who were related to Chalchiuhnenetzin, however, were humiliated and outraged that the king had carried out such a public punishment. Giving no hint that the king's severity had filled them with indignation and anger, they planned to take their revenge at the first opportunity. If one considers carefully, it is no mystery that this treason and trouble befell the king's house. For it seems that he was made to pay the price for the unusual way by which his father, the king, obtained his mother, the queen—and a son—from the unfortunate Quaquauhtzin.

🌿 CHAPTER [65]

*Which deals with other conquests undertaken by the empire
during this time*

At this time, the armies of the empire were so eager to conquer lands and nations
that the soldiers considered it indolent and cowardly not to be at war. Going to
war promised great honor and fame, and they would return home laden with
spoils, in addition to the [fol. 81r] splendid gifts and rewards their kings would
grant them. Thus they remained at the ready, careful not to miss an opportunity.
Being so disposed, they seized the chance to march against Tehuantepec, where
they had been previously defeated; it was one of the richest and most powerful
provinces along the coast. They marched all the way to this province, advanced
into its territory, and laid siege to one of its largest and richest cities, which was
called Amextloapan. They attacked, defeated, and plundered it, capturing and
carrying off 27,400 people. Many thousands of Tehuantepecas died defending
it. These losses utterly defeated the people of this province, who had always
defended themselves well. Then, in the following year of 1500, which they called
chicuei tecpatl,[123] the armies of the empire attacked the people of the province
of Xaltepec, who had rebelled once again, and thoroughly defeated them. The
Xaltepecas were so completely subjugated that they never again considered
rebellion. As was law and custom whenever a people rose up against the empire,
their tribute obligations were doubled.

---

123. Eight Flint.

[fol. 81v]

 CHAPTER [66]

Which deals with a great flood in the city of Mexico that originated at a spring called Acuecuexatl

According to the histories, it would seem that even the forces of nature clamored for God to take his vengeance, and so they rose against King Ahuitzotzin, who was very dedicated to the worship of his false gods. For at this time the Mexicas sought to bring water from a spring called Acuecuexatl in the town of Huitzilopochco, near Coyohuacan, to the city of Mexico by way of a stone channel fixed with mortar. Yet when they tapped the spring for that purpose, a great gush of water sprung forth with such force that it threatened to rise above the walls of every house in the city. It was so violent that it quickly flooded the city and drowned many of its people. Moreover, enormous waves that seemed to reach the heavens rose from the lake, an extraordinary and astonishing sight that struck great terror and fear in all who saw it. Most of those who survived [fol. 82r] abandoned the city. The king, who was in a room in his garden, tried to escape as the waters poured in with great force, but he cracked his head open as he went through the doorway and was gravely wounded. He suffered terribly from this injury until it eventually killed him (as will be seen below). But he would have drowned then and there if his people had not arrived to rescue him.

Recognizing his plight, he sent ambassadors to King Nezahualpiltzintli, begging him as a very talented man to help him and use his skills to restore the city of Mexico. Nezahualpiltzintli was glad to have the opportunity to assist the Mexicas and their lord, for this would put to rest the scheming and the ill will that the Mexicas felt toward him for the way in which he had executed their princess. So he summoned all the architects of his realm and accompanied them to Huitzilopochco along with many laborers and canoes loaded with stakes, turf, lime, and other materials. When they arrived at the spring, he personally waded into it and skillfully staunched the flow of water and enclosed it in [fol. 82v] a strong cistern of stone and mortar. In this way he contained the spring and the floodwaters began to recede. Then he returned, passing through the city of Mexico, where he visited King Ahuitzotzin and comforted him in his suffering. The latter was very grateful and set about rebuilding his city.

 **CHAPTER [67]**

Which deals with how King Nezahualpiltzintli settled a
dispute that arose between his brothers Acapipioltzin and
Xochiquetzaltzin and some notable punishments that he
imposed on his sons

As mentioned in the above account of the life of Nezahualcoyotzin, the two princes Xochiquetzaltzin and Acapipioltzin participated in the conquest of the Huasteca; one was captain general of the army, while the other was sent later with reinforcements and was so skillful that he subjugated the entire region with his speed and sound strategies. The poets of those times, therefore, not only described the events of the conquest, but lauded Acapipioltzin's heroism in their songs. They also praised Xochiquetzaltzin, the brother who went as general and, although [fol. 83r] he arrived after Acapipioltzin, also performed some memorable feats. However, these were not enough to claim for himself the fame and glory of the conquest, and instead the credit and renown for it rightfully went to his brother Acapipioltzin. The matter remained unsettled between them, such that every time this conquest was commemorated with festivities, the musicians and minstrels of each brother would celebrate and sing of the victory separately, each in their own palace. Then they would go out into public, to the main plaza of the city, and perform their dances almost in competition with one another, and great tensions arose between the two brothers and their friends and allies. The rivalry became so heated that it nearly erupted in violence, which would have resulted in many deaths within the city.

Seeing the rivalry and lack of restraint between his two brothers, King Nezahualpiltzintli deliberated on the issue. He determined that credit for the accomplishment belonged to his brother Acapipioltzin, but he did not say a word. Instead, on the day that the brothers went to the plaza to perform their separate dances, the king also came out with all the grandees of his kingdom, and they began to dance. He went toward [fol. 83v] Acapipioltzin and, granting him the place of honor, danced with him and all the other grandees and lords who were there in the customary fashion. Seeing this, Xochiquetzaltzin and his supporters departed with their minstrels and musicians and never again dared to participate in this competition. The king declared that the song should be called *Teotlan Cuextecayotl*, which means "song of the conquest of the Huasteca by the house of Teotlan," in reference to the palace and ancestral estate of Prince Acapipioltzin. In this way, the king resolved this dispute and others that arose with great prudence and wisdom.

Whenever Nezahualpiltzintli determined that severe punishment was warranted, he applied the law scrupulously; not even his own children were exempt. This is what happened to Prince Huexotzincatzin, his first-born son and successor to the kingdom, who among other natural gifts and charms, was a very eminent philosopher and poet. He composed a satire for the lady of Tolan, the concubine who was closest to the king, his father. Since she was also a poet, they corresponded back and forth, which raised suspicions that he was trying to seduce her. [fol. 84r] Since the law held this to be treason against the king, carrying the death penalty, the matter came up for judgment. And although the king, his father, loved and adored him immensely, he felt compelled to carry out the sentence. He lamented the death of his son the prince so intensely that he ordered the palace the prince had lived in to be boarded up and that it be known henceforth as Ixayoc, which means "House of Tears."

He also punished his second legitimate son, named Iztacquauhtzin—who was the next oldest after Prince Huexotzincatzin—because on his own authority and without the king's permission he built a palace to live in without having performed any deeds to merit it. The law held that no one, not even the crown prince, should build a residence, dress or adorn himself with jewels or rich fabrics, or wear a feather tassel until he had fought in four pitched battles and captured at least four captains who were skilled and renowned as warriors. Or, if one was not given to military arts, he was to have attained all the knowledge necessary to [fol. 84v] become a scholar, philosopher, orator, and poet. Or, at the very least, he must be very skilled in the mechanical arts. Having fulfilled one of these requirements according to his inclination, he might enjoy the aforementioned privileges with the king's permission. To claim them otherwise carried the death penalty, which was the punishment imposed upon Iztacquauhtzin.

Also, Cequauhtzin, a judge who sat on one of Nezahualpiltzintli's tribunals, heard a case in his own home. Nezahualpiltzintli sent him to the gallows, because no judge was to hear a case or suit in his home, nor accept gifts or bribes, under penalty of death. Rather, all cases and suits were to be brought in the royal halls and council chambers, in the presence of all the pertinent judges, prosecutors, and other ministers of justice. They heard cases from morning until about midday, and then, after eating—and they all ate at the palace—they returned to their hearings until sundown. They were never to be absent except on feast days, when they were not required to attend, or due to illness or another unforeseen impediment, but for nothing else.

[fol. 85r] Nezahualpiltzintli also levied many other exemplary punishments. For example, he ordered another judge who was negligent and careless in deciding a case, to be taken to his house and the main door to be sealed, so that he could only go in and out through the backdoor and yard. He was also relieved of his duties and prohibited from entering the palace and communicating with the other judges and ministers of justice ever again. Nezahualpiltzintli also ordered the death of one of his daughters, a maiden, because she spoke with the son of a nobleman. He did the same with one of his concubines who drank some medicinal wine, because women who drank wine were sentenced to death. Nezahualpiltzintli ordered another judge to be hanged for favoring a nobleman over a commoner. Nezahualpiltzintli had the case retried and ruled in favor of the plebeian. Another two of his sons who participated in a conquest claimed for themselves captives that some of their soldiers had taken. When they returned from this war injured and wounded, he had them treated. But once they were well, he had them garroted, for that was the penalty for those who seized the captives of another.

🌿 CHAPTER [68]

Which deals with other notable cases that Nezahualpiltzintli
handled regarding laws and judges

In addition to the aforementioned judges and ministers, the kings of Tezcuco maintained secretaries and clerks who would carefully and faithfully paint the cases and suits brought before the tribunals. They would deliver precise reports of the cases to the kings and their judges, such that every case, especially the serious ones, was tried methodically until the final sentence was issued and approved by the king. Even serious cases were not to last more than eighty days; all others were concluded quickly and summarily.

Among the things that happened during Nezahualpiltzintli's time was that a secretary reported to him that the judges of the criminal court had sentenced to death two adulterers in the third degree: a musician and a soldier. [fol. 85v] The punishment was hanging. The chief magistrates of the four councils responsible for deciding serious cases had already approved this sentence, and the king's assent was all that remained. After hearing the secretary read the painted report, Nezahualpiltzintli took up a brush and painted a black line through the image of the musician but not the soldier. When the secretary showed the report to the chief magistrates, they believed the king to be disregarding and undermining the law, so they took the painting to him and demanded that he uphold the laws of his father and forefathers. The king responded that he was not contradicting the law and it was his prerogative to improve the laws, and therefore he decreed that henceforth any soldier or military man discovered to have committed adultery in the third degree should be sentenced to perpetual exile in one of the empire's frontier forts. He would thereby be punished sufficiently, and the republic would benefit, for it was soldiers who defended and protected it.

Similarly, he rescinded a law dealing with slavery that held that slaves would pass their status on to their children, who would often be sold as slaves. He ordered that law to be disregarded from then on and that all children should enjoy the natural liberty granted to them by God. He also punished severely the excesses of certain lords, which inspired fear and respect. For instance, Nezahualpiltzintli asked his brother Prince [. . .][124] to give him one of his daughters as one of his

---

124. In the manuscript, a blank space was left for the prince's name.

consorts and concubines. His brother brazenly refused, even though it was customary for kings and lords to ask for their nieces, cousins, and relatives beyond the second degree in marriage or to keep them as consorts and concubines. In this way they gained honor and protection, and in the event that there were no legitimate heirs, their children might inherit the kingdom or at least become lords of towns and estates. At a later time, the king made a second request of his brother. He asked for a musical instrument, called a *teponaztli*, that the prince possessed and had brought back as plunder from a conquest. It was the best of its kind in all the land. When it was played it could be heard from two or three leagues away, and its sound [fol. 86r] was very soothing and melodious. The king, who was very taken with it, promised in exchange certain lands and other gifts of much greater value to his brother than the instrument. It was almost as if the king did it to test his brother. The prince was so stubborn that he refused and did so without even a polite excuse. The king had the instrument seized anyway and ordered his brother's houses ransacked and razed to the ground for insubordination and contempt of royal authority. This was carried out at once, and the king had the instrument stored in the armory as a war trophy. It was never played, except during important royal festivals and celebrations. Later, the friars of St. Francis had it destroyed and burned because it inspired such esteem and veneration among the nobles. This punishment was so exemplary and impressive that his brothers respected and feared him greatly from that point forward. Whereas they had frequently disobeyed him before he imposed these punishments, afterward they never again dared go against his wishes, neither in public nor in private.

He levied another exemplary punishment on a noblewoman, the wife of a Tezcucan nobleman named Tzancitzin. During a feast and dance, this noblewoman fell so blindly in love with the king that she felt compelled to tell him of her feelings. The king sent her to his quarters. After he had lain with her, he learned that she was a married woman and so had her garroted and her body cast into the ravine where adulterers and adulteresses were thrown. And he sent her two children, whom she had brought with her, back to their father's house with great gifts, along with a number of nursemaids and servants to raise and tutor them.

After the messengers told the nobleman Tzancitzin what happened, he responded [fol. 86v] with great sadness because he had loved and cherished his wife, a beautiful and very graceful woman. Tzancitzin wondered why the king had killed her after enjoying her. It would have been better to have spared her life so that he would not have lost, as he had, the wife he so loved and cherished. The king learned of his reaction and ordered the nobleman imprisoned in the dungeons while he decided on an appropriate way to punish him for his response and his disregard for his own honor, because his was an unprecedented case. He was a prisoner in the dungeons for many days, where facing such a long and dark confinement, he composed a very elegant song that gave voice to his sorrows and travails. He asked the king's musicians, his friends and acquaintances, to sing it at one of the royal feasts and dances, which they managed to do. The song was composed with words so vivid and touching that they moved the king's soul to great compassion, and he ordered the nobleman's release from prison. The king summoned Tzancitzin and explained that he had compelling reasons to sentence his wife to death, for she had caused him to break and violate one of the laws of his kingdom. Her sweet and melodious words would have doubtlessly fooled him had he not noticed the children, who marked her as a married woman, to which she in fact confessed. The king offered other comforting and enlightening explanations and gave Tzancitzin a noble maiden for a wife, along with many other gifts and favors, which improved his situation. When they released him from the dungeons he looked like a wild man, as his hair had grown long and gray.

[fol. 87r]

 ## CHAPTER [69]

Which deals with the season and year in which the very valiant
Prince Ixtlilxochitl was born and things he did in his childhood
and youth

It is certainly worth acknowledging and contemplating the marvelous works of
our Lord God, the great order and mystery they embody, and to what end he
arranges and causes them to happen. For instance, the curious births of certain
princes are very noteworthy, such as Prince Ixtlilxochitl's, which occurred about
two months into the year 1500, around the same time as the birth, in the city
of Ghent, of the very fortunate and powerful Emperor don Carlos, our lord of
glorious memory; both were key instruments in the expansion and spread of the
holy Catholic faith. And no less noteworthy is the auspicious birth, fifteen years
earlier in 1485, of don Fernando Cortés, first Marquis of the Valley, at the same
time as that of the perverse Martin Luther; the latter was born to pollute and
dismantle our holy Catholic faith and sacred religion and the former to expand
it, as we will see over the course of this history.

Many signs and omens accompanied the birth of Prince Itlilxochitl that clearly
heralded what later came to pass. The astrologers and diviners of his father,
King Nezahualpiltzintli, foretold, among other things, that this prince would
eventually receive a new law and new customs, become a friend to foreigners
and an enemy to his own people and homeland, and [fol. 87v] oppose his own
flesh and blood. Others foretold that he would avenge the many captives whose
blood had recently been spilled and oppose completely their gods, their religion,
their rites, and their ceremonies. With this they beseeched the king, his father,
to kill him before it was too late. The king responded that it was futile to resist
that which the supreme God, creator of all things, had ordained, for it was not
without mystery or significance that he had given him such a son at the time
when the prophecies of his ancestors would soon come to pass: a new people
who were the children of Quetzalcoatl would come to take possession of the
land and would arrive from the east. The king thereby caused his counselors
and diviners great distress.

Ixtlilxochitl was so vivacious and sharp growing up, that the kind of man he
was to become was clear. For instance, he bewildered and amazed his nursemaids

when he was barely three years old by killing his wet nurse. He killed her because he saw a palace nobleman trying to seduce her. Ixtlilxochitl asked her for some water to drink, insisting that it be drawn from the well inside the palace. She wanted to please him and went to the well. As she leaned over to draw up the water with the rope, he shoved her. Caught off guard, she fell in. And although they rushed to save her, she drowned, for the well was very narrow and deep. Then the boy began to gather stones and throw them on top of his nurse, which astonished them. They brought him before the king, his father, who asked him why he had killed the nurse who had nurtured and raised him. He responded that in the chamber where the eighty [fol. 88r] laws were read, it was stated that no man should attempt to seduce the ladies and maids of the palace, nor should the women invite it, on penalty of death. Since his wet nurse had flirted with one of the palace noblemen, he killed her to comply with the law. The king, who could not deny the truth of this, was shocked to see such a small child commit such a deed.

When Ixtlilxochitl was seven years old he began to form squadrons and armies with the other boys. He ordered his tutors and teachers to make many balls out of reeds and grass and plenty of arrows and clubs of the same materials, and they used these as weapons when they fought. When these ran out, he would often attack the other boys with rocks and stones, injuring many of them. He kept the city in an uproar running around shouting with the other boys. The king, his father, was vexed by his son's reckless behavior and reprimanded his tutors and teachers for failing to control him. Two lords of his father's council advised Nezahualpiltzintli to take the life of this prince: he was far too bellicose for such a young boy and were he to reach manhood he would put the entire empire at great risk because he was too ambitious and proud, which would lead him to disinherit his brothers and other nobles. And while the king did not follow their advice, he was still concerned about his son's mischief and scolded his teachers harshly. Predictably, someone told Ixtlilxochitl all that the advisors had discussed with his father. His teachers [fol. 88v] begged him to behave so that he might avoid the fate the royal advisors recommended. Not only would it cost him his life, they would also pay with theirs, for as his teachers, they would be accused of negligence in his upbringing and education.

Having heard this, Ixtlilxochitl gathered three or four trusted military instructors from his guard and went with them one evening to the houses of these two advisors. He had them both hanged that very night, so that they were dead by dawn. They never stood a chance. He had called on them alone, as if he intended to discuss some important affairs with them privately. They had come alone and unsuspecting, and then, without warning, the men he brought with him clubbed them and hanged them as mentioned. The next morning, when the king found out what Ixtlilxochitl had done, he summoned the prince and asked how he could have committed a deed so wicked as to kill his advisors. Ixtlilxochitl responded:

> Sir, I never wronged your advisors such that they should wish me dead and anger Your Highness. If you were not so wise and prudent, they would have convinced you to order my death even though I had broken none of your laws or decrees. I am bellicose and drawn to the art of warfare, which is the most esteemed calling in your kingdom and part of my nature as ordained from above. It was, therefore, outrageous for them to oppose it, foolish to resist the forces of nature, and cruel for them to seek the death of an innocent. And so, mighty lord, I made the first move by taking your advisors' lives, since they wanted to take mine. No one in your court is to blame except me. For although I had help, my servants were only doing their duty to their lord.

The king could thus find no reason to punish him. Ixtlilxochitl's arguments were well founded and reasonable, and he had not done anything improper or criminal that deserved punishment; it was simply his ferocity of spirit, a harbinger of how high he would rise through warfare. The king told him to stop and that it was true that those noblemen had strongly urged him to have Ixtlilxochitl killed. Had that not been the case, he would have levied an exemplary punishment that would have certainly cost the prince his life. Ixtlilxochitl was about ten or twelve years old when he did this.

After he turned fourteen, he went to test himself on the battlefields of Tlaxcalan and Huexotzinco, where he performed wonders. And by the time he was sixteen, he already bore the tassels and insignia of a great captain. Around this time, his father died, and he opposed the ascension of his [fol. 89v] brother King Cacama, impeding his coronation and fealty-swearing.

☙ CHAPTER [70]

Which deals with the death of the valiant King Ahuitzotzin[125] *and the election of the famous Motecuhçoma, second of that name*

The affliction caused by King Ahuitzotzin's head injury progressed so far that the sickness overtook him, ending his life. Even though he was treated with care and diligence, and they even removed a few pieces of his skull, this was not enough to save him. His death was widely mourned, and everyone wept and honored him with solemn and elaborate funeral rites according to Mexica custom. The two kings, Nezahualpiltzintli and Totoquihuatzin, along with the electors of the Mexica kingdom, discussed the election of their counterpart, the king that the empire was missing. After some back and forth over the matter, the electors set their sights upon Prince Macuilmalinaltzin, the eldest legitimate son of Axayacatzin and the son-in-law of King Nezahualpiltzintli, married to Princess Tiyacapantzin, his legitimate daughter. Yet Nezahualpiltzintli was opposed, despite being his father-in-law, for he thought he was inadequate for a position as important as the one under discussion. He had such influence over the electors that debate began again. He then voted for Motecuhçoma, who at the time was the high priest of the main temple of Huitzilopochtli, for he possessed the qualities required of a king. But this came back to haunt him, and he lost his son-in-law, as will be shown in the course of [fol. 90r] this history.

After the customary coronation ceremonies, they held formal banquets and festivities. Motecuhçoma ascended to power on May 24 in the year 1503, which was the day *çe cipactli*,[126] the ninth day of the fourth month, called *toxcatl*,[127] in the year they called *matlactli once acatl*.[128] It was during the same season, on the very same day, that the great and valiant Motecuhçoma, first of that name, the great-grandfather of the one we deal with here, ascended to power.

King Ahuitzotzin had children with Tiyacapantzin, heiress of Tlatelolco. She was the daughter of Moquihuitzin—Tlatelolco's last lord and the one who lost the city—and his legitimate wife, the daughter of Nezahualcoyotzin. The very brave King Quauhtemoctzin, who after becoming Christian was named don Hernando,

---

125. The manuscript reads "Axayacatzin," but this is clearly an error.
126. One Alligator.
127. Drought.
128. Eleven Reed.

was the son of Ahuitzotzin and Tiyacapantzin; he was the last king of Mexico and the one who surrendered the city. Their other children were Tlacaelel, another Motecuhçoma, Citlalcoatl, Azcacoatl, Xoyetzin, Quauhtzitzimitzin, Xiconoc, Atlixcatzin, another Macuilmalina, Acamapich, Huitzilihuitl, Machimale, Yaotzin, and Tehuetzquititzin.

According to the true accounts and common opinion, the great Motecuhçoma had three daughters with Queen Teihuelcan, his legitimate wife and the daughter of King Totoquihuatzin of Tlacopan. The oldest was named Miahuaxochitzin, who was baptized with the name doña Isabel; the second was doña María, and the youngest doña Marina. He also had other children, including don Pedro Tlacahuepantzin [fol. 90v] and Xihuitl Temoctzin, Axayaca, Totopehualox, and Chimalpopoca. Doña Isabel married three times. Her first marriage, arranged by order of don Fernando Cortés, Marquis of the Valley, was to Alonso Grado, an hidalgo[129] from the village of Alcántara and one of the highest-ranking leaders of the conquest. Her second marriage was to Pedro Gallego, with whom she had a son named don Juan de Andrada Motecuhçoma; from whom are descended the Andradas. Her third marriage was to Juan Cano, from whom the Canos are descended.

Don Pedro Tlacahuepantzin did not have children with either of the two women whom he married within the Holy Mother Church, due to restrictions pointed out by his sister doña Isabel. She said that he could not be married to the first woman without a dispensation from His Holiness, for she was don Pedro's first cousin. To secure this dispensation and conduct other business, he left for Spain and remained there for some time. Meanwhile, his wife, believing him to be dead, married a conquistador. When don Pedro arrived back in Vera Cruz, he learned that his wife had already remarried. Rather than make use of the dispensation that His Holiness had given him, he came to the city of Tezcuco and married doña Francisca, the eldest legitimate daughter of don Pedro Tetlahuehuetzquititzin, lord of that city. Once doña Isabel found this out, she denounced her brother's marriages as contrary to church law. And so, from that time forward, don Pedro Tlacahuepantzin did not share a life with either the first or the second woman. All of his children were illegitimate. The oldest was don Martín Motecuhçoma, who inherited his estate. And although don Martín married his first cousin doña Magdalena Axayacatzin, lady of Itztapalapa, they had no children. So don Diego Luis Quayhuitzin, don Pedro Tlacahuepantzin's second son, inherited the estate. He went to Spain, and he has heirs and descendants there today.

---

129. A member of the Spanish lesser nobility.

[fol. 91r]

 CHAPTER [71]

Which deals with various events that occurred at this time
according to the annals

In 1504, the year after the ascension of King Motecuhçoma, Tehuehueltzin, lord of
the province of Quauhnahuac, died and was succeeded by Itzcoatzin. In the following years of 1505 and 1506, called *matlactli omei calli* and *çe tochtli*,[130] there were
famines. Nothing was harvested in the entire land except in the provinces and
mountains of Totonacapan, which provided some relief, so they called this famine
netotonacahuiloc, or as we would say, "the hunger remedied by Totonacapan."
The Kings Nezahualpiltzintli, Motecuhçoma, and Totoquihuatzin also opened
their storehouses to give aid to their subjects and vassals, and they suspended
their tribute obligations for one year. In the same year of 1506, the province of
Zoçolan was conquered. In 1507, the war with the province of Tochtepec took
place, wherein the Mexica lords Ixtlilcuechahuac and Huitzilihuitzin died.
And in the year 1508, Prince Macuilmalinaltzin, heir of Mexico, fought a battle
against the people of Atlixco. It is commonly believed that his brother King
Motecuhçoma made a secret pact with the people of Atlixco to defeat and kill
him in battle in order to avoid upheaval and eliminate a rival. Macuilmalinaltzin
died there along with Tzicquaquatzin, another of the Mexica lords, and 2,800
soldiers of their guard. King Nezahualpiltzintli's grief was boundless, and he
wrote the song [fol. 91v] called *nenahualizcuicatl*, which means "a song that
reveals treason and trickery."

At this point King Nezahualpiltzintli realized how misguided he had been,
and how his thoughts had tricked him into denying the kingdom to the one who
rightfully deserved it, only to give it instead to a man who was a bloodthirsty wolf
in sheep's clothing. Because, after Macuilmalinaltzin and the other Mexica lords
died in this and the other aforementioned wars, King Motecuhçoma began to
reveal the wrath and arrogance conveyed by his name.[131] The first thing he did was
to remove all the members of his councils who had served since the time of his
father and uncles and replace them with others of his choosing. He did likewise

---

130. Thirteen House and One Rabbit.
131. The name Motecuhçoma means "wrathful lord."

within the army and town councils of the kingdom. He did all of this to make himself absolute ruler. He was so proud and arrogant that he refused to allow any commoners to serve him, even if they had risen by their merits to become captains and valiant soldiers or gained other offices, dignities, and privileges. Instead, he found ways to kill them one by one or banish them from his court. This same year, Tliltemoctzin assumed the lordship of Huexotla after the death of Cuitlahuatzin. The next year, the province of Yopatepec was conquered.

Also around this time King Nezahualpiltzintli imposed an exemplary punishment on Teçoçomoc, lord of Azcapotzalco and King Motecuhçoma's brother-in-law, for committing adultery. The Mexica judges, to placate King Motecuhçoma, had sentenced him to exile and ordered his palace ransacked; the Tepanecas added that, as further punishment, the tip of his nose should be cut off; but the final ruling belonged to the king of Tezcuco. Despite everything the other judges had decided, he upheld the law of his father, ordering Teçoçomoc to be strangled and his body burned, as this was the punishment applicable to noblemen. Then he sent his agents to carry out the sentence, which they did. This left King Motecuhçoma upset, but King Nezahualpiltzintli had complied with what the laws of his ancestors demanded.

[fol. 92r]

 CHAPTER [72]

Which deals with the signs and omens that occurred before the
destruction and ruin of this empire

In the year 1510, which they called *macuili tochtli*,[132] a bright light shaped like a pyramid in flames[133] appeared high in the eastern sky on many nights. This struck fear and awe across the land, and confused even those well versed in astrology and the knowledge of divination and prophecy. This despite the fact that they had long known from their histories that the events foretold by Quetzalcoatl and other ancient philosophers and sages would soon come to pass. Kings Nezahual-piltzintli and Motecuhçoma were the most concerned because they would suffer the hardships of the empire's upheaval. The king of Tezcuco—who was highly accomplished in every branch of knowledge that their society had developed and mastered, especially astrology, which was confirmed by the prophecies of his ancestors—felt great sadness and all but gave up on his kingdom and lordship. He ordered the captains and generals of his armies to cease the wars they regularly fought against the Tlaxcaltecas, Huexotzincas, and Atlixcas for military training and for acquiring sacrificial victims for their false gods. They were only to defend the borders of the outer provinces where they had their forts and make no incursions. In this way, they might [fol. 92v] enjoy peace and tranquility during the little time that remained of his lordship and rule.

King Motecuhçoma, on the other hand, greatly desired to discuss with King Nezahualpiltzintli the meaning of these signs and his responses to them. But they were at odds and on bad terms. King Nezahualpiltzintli remained greatly saddened by the malicious death orchestrated against his son-in-law Prince Macuilmalinaltzin. Motecuhçomatzin, meanwhile, had his own grievances. The first was the harsh public justice dispensed against his sister Queen Chal-chiuhnenetzin. Additionally, King Nezahualpiltzintli had imposed two more punishments: one upon King Motecuhçoma's nephew Prince Huexotzincatzin and another upon Teçoçomoc, his brother-in-law and lord of Azcapotzalco. Yet the two kings met, and after they had settled their differences they discussed at length what the heavens foreboded.

---

132. Five Rabbit.

133. In Nahua pictorials, a burning building was the conventional sign for conquest.

The king of Tezcuco said that everything would come to pass and there was nothing to be done. And to show King Motecuhçoma what little regard he had for his own lordship, Nezahualpiltzintli wagered it on a ballgame. If King Motecuhçoma could score three times, King Nezahualpiltzintli would exchange his kingdom for three wild turkeys, and in fact, he wanted nothing more than their spurs. In this way, King Motecuhçoma would see clearly how little he valued all that he possessed. And so, the two kings played the ballgame, and Motecuhçoma scored twice in a row. Since he only needed one more to become king of the Aculhuas, he was overjoyed and began to celebrate. But the king of Tezcuco was losing on purpose. He told King Motecuhçoma that the pleasure he felt at imagining himself absolute lord of the entire empire would quickly fade once he understood how impermanent and [fol. 93r] ephemeral were the enjoyment and possession of worldly things. And as proof of the incontrovertible truth of his words, Motecuhçoma would see from the remainder of their game that, although he had scored twice, he would not win. They continued playing, and although Motecuhçoma did everything he could, he failed to score his final point. Nezahualpiltzintli scored three times and won. After celebrating his victory and discussing other business, the king of Tezcuco returned home to his court. And each day brought new signs and great omens and portents, which heralded the total ruin and destruction of the entire land and the transformation of the empire.

🌿 CHAPTER [73]

Which deals with a few uprisings and disturbances that occurred
in some provinces conquered and won by the empire and other
events

King Nezahualpiltzintli wanted to live in peace during the little time he had
left as lord. Nonetheless, it greatly pained him to see that the lack of activity on
the part of his soldiers and military men allowed many of the empire's most
important subject provinces to rise up and rebel, such as the cities and provinces
of the Mixteca, Zapoteca, Yopica, Tototepeca, and Tehuantepeca nations. These
nations saw that the soldiers in the border forts had given themselves over to
gaming, cavorting, and other harmful forms of recreation unrelated [fol. 93v]
to the art of war. This occurred not only in places where vigilance and care were
required to maintain conquered land but even within the very court of the king
of Tezcuco, where the people lived irresponsibly and with an excess of pleasure
and leisure. For this reason those who were subjugated and oppressed began
to look for ways to liberate themselves from the empire's domination. What
they found most helpful was that the soldiers of the army were careless and
given to self-indulgence and pleasures. They invited some of them to be their
guests and, after plying them with food and drink, they killed them. And others
they killed with weapons in hand and expelled the rest from their lands, as in
Coaixtlahuacan, Zoçolan, Tototepec, Tehuantepec, and Yopitzinco. This also
happened in the provinces of Huaxaca and Tlachquiauhco and in Malinaltepec,
Iztactlalocan, Izquixochitepec, and Tlacotepec.

Even though the king of Tezcuco had abandoned military pursuits, he was
compelled under these circumstances to muster his troops and send them to
join the armies of Kings Motecuhçoma and Totoquihuatzin, which maintained
greater discipline and vigilance. They marched on these provinces and subjugated
and brought them under the control of the empire. They returned weighed
down with plunder and leading many captives, who were sacrificed to their
false gods. Among the sacrificial victims were Zetecpatl, lord of the province
of Coaixtlahuacan; Nahuixochitl, lord of the province of Zoçolan; [fol. 94r]
Malinal, from Tlachquiauhco; and many other lords and captains taken captive
during these and other aforementioned campaigns. Thus, they subdued the
entire empire of this New Spain. They subjugated the territory from the borders

of the Chichimecas and the kingdom of Michhuacan to Huei Molan, Acalan, Verapaz, and Nicarahua, the furthest territories possessed by the ancient Tolteca kings, who ruled the whole of Anahuac. They also subjugated the territory from the region of the Cuextecas, which is the province of Panuco, to Huitlapalan, which is what they call the Red Sea or the Sea of Cortés, on the coast of the South Sea. These lands included great and splendid kingdoms and provinces such as those of the Cohuixcas, Yopicas, Cuitlatecas, Chochones, Mixtecas, Zapotecas, Quauhtemaltecas, Coatzaqualcas, Nonoalcas, Xicalancas, Totonacas, and many other nations. They all surrendered completely to the authority of the empire of the three rulers, which was more than four hundred leagues long and stretched from the North Sea to the South Sea. Other authors have written specifically about these lords' conquests, so I do not recount them extensively here. One may read about them in their histories, especially in the *Monarquía indiana*, written by the very diligent Father Torquemada. Following the paintings and annals that I have cited, I only include the conquests that I found relevant.

Finally, in the year 1514, the snows were so heavy that they destroyed the plants and trees, snapping off branches and breaking them into bits. And at this time, the army of the three rulers of the empire, which was marching on Amantlan, one of the aforementioned rebel provinces, was lost.

🌿 CHAPTER [74]

*Which deals with how King Motecuhçoma cunningly conspired
with the confederation of Tlaxcalan to assassinate the best
captains and soldiers in the kingdom of Tezcuco and thereby
came to rule all of the empire*

King Motecuhçoma's desire to be absolute ruler was insatiable. [fol. 94v] It seemed beneath him to have corulers and equals within the empire, and so he dedicated himself to plotting and devising means, strategies, and schemes to achieve his intent. In the final years of the reign of Nezahualpiltzintli, King Motecuhçoma did something diabolical. Seeing that the Aculhuas Tezcucas were so lax in their military discipline and busy with feasting and dancing, Motecuhçoma sent ambassadors to reprimand King Nezahualpiltzintli for the irresponsibility of his subjects. They said that the gods were angry with Nezahualpiltzintli because it had been four years since the empire had sacrificed captives from Tlaxcalan and the other two provinces that supplied the most suitable and pleasing captives to the false gods. Instead, they had only sacrificed captives taken by force from remote provinces in order to expand and preserve the empire; these were the least pleasing to the gods. Moreover, they thereby erased the memory of the heroic deeds of their elders and sullied the fame and glory of the Chichimecas and Aculhuas, their ancestors. It was therefore fitting to fight on the battlefields of Tlaxcalan in order to appease the gods, and King Motecuhçoma would be there personally. The ambassadors indicated the day the battle would take place.

King Nezahualpiltzintli said in response that his soldiers had not laid down their weapons due to cowardice or faintheartedness, rather their intent was to live peacefully for the short time they had left to enjoy, since the year *çe acatl*,[134] with all of the upheavals and calamities that had been foretold, was close at hand. Nonetheless, on the appointed day, the best men in his army would go to the battlefields of Tlaxcalan to prove their strength and valor.

After King Nezahualpiltzintli sent his response, he convened his war council [fol. 95r] and discussed what should be done. Then all the bravest captains and soldiers of the army came together and set out on the road to Tlaxcalan. The king chose not to go in person, as he did not want to have any confrontations with King Motecuhçoma, who would be there. Instead, he sent his sons Princes

---

134. One Reed.

Acatlemacoetzin and Tequanehuatzin, who had proven themselves in the afore-mentioned conquests of the remote provinces, as leaders of the Tezcuca army.

After learning of Nezahualpiltzintli's decision, Motecuhçoma secretly sent his ambassadors to the confederation of Tlaxcalan. They were to tell them that the king of Tezcuco had assembled the greatest and best of his army, but not for military exercises and sacrifices to their gods in accordance with the law and custom established and maintained by them and their elders. Rather, their intent was to destroy and raze the entire province and confederation and make Nezahualpiltzintli the ruler of that land. This would be a heinous act, and were Motecuhçoma not to have forewarned them, they would have held him account-able as an accomplice. Thus, they should gather the greatest and best of their soldiers and launch a preemptive strike so that the Aculhuas would not be able to achieve their goal. And even though Motecuhçoma would stand alongside the Aculhuas, he would do it only for the sake of appearance and not because he wanted to. He gave them his word that, instead of supporting the Aculhuas, he would help the Tlaxcaltecas by killing them from behind if necessary.

The ambassadors' message [fol. 95v] caused great agitation and distress to the confederation because of Nezahualpiltzintli's apparent disregard for his obliga-tions, both to preserve its lands and defend and support it. All that he possessed had been acquired with the help and support of their fathers and grandfathers, the Tlaxcalteca lords. Moreover, they all belonged to a single lineage. They sent their thanks to Motecuhçoma for the warning, then carefully and discreetly prepared themselves for the arrival of Nezahualpiltzintli's people.

Meanwhile, the Aculhuas came to the ravine called Tlaltepexic, near a hill named Quauhtepetl, where they typically spent the night prior to these battles. They were unaware of the betrayal and double-dealing planned against them. That afternoon and all night long they witnessed a thousand omens that foretold their total destruction and ruin. In one of them, they saw a large number of vultures (birds that seek nothing but dead flesh) swirling in the air around them. Flames also seemed to emerge from the earth, and even though it was the middle of the rainy season, great clouds of dust rose into the air. Tezcacoacatl, Temoctzin, Çitlaltecatl, and Ecatenan, the bravest captains in the army, all four at once dreamed that they were children running after their mothers crying for them to lift them up. These signs gave them much to think about, and in their hearts, they understood the fate that awaited them. That night, [fol. 96r] to dispel their bad dreams, they joked with each other. Very early the next morning, they sat down for a bite to eat in case they had no other chance that day. Suddenly, an unusually large cicada came flying through the air and landed on the round shield on which they were eating. It landed with great force and died, its head splitting from its body, which these captains took as a very bad omen. They decided not to wait any longer and began to wake their people to arm themselves and leave, in case their enemies were to ambush them in that ravine, where they could not make effective use of their weapons and skills. But this is exactly what happened; the Tlaxcaltecas fell upon the Aculhuas as soon as they saw them rise and instantly surrounded them with so much shouting and shrieking that they were unable to organize their defense. When they came to blows, the Tlaxcaltecas killed almost all of the Aculhuas, and only a few were able to escape and carry the news of the tragic events, betrayal, and deceit they had endured. The four captains mentioned above and many others performed feats of extraordinary bravery and exacted from the Tlaxcaltecas a high price for their lives.

The two princes Acatlemacoetzin and Tequanehuatzin were badly injured, and when they realized that they had been defeated by people of lesser rank, they asked their captors to finish them off, for they would not consent to enter their city as prisoners. But they brought them alive as prized trophies, and the princes resisted and defended themselves at every step, so their captors found it expedient to sacrifice them at the temple of their false gods nearest to the battlefield. There was so much blood from the dead and wounded flowing through the ravine that it seemed a raging river [fol. 96v]. King Motecuhçoma, looking on with his army from the base of a hill called Xocayoltepetl, did not move or go to their aid; rather, he stood there with his people reveling in the massacre and cruel death of the best of the Tezcuca nobility, making plain his betrayal.

A most famous captain called Chichinquatzin was among those who escaped and carried the sad news to King Nezahualpiltzintli. The king and all the members of his court greatly lamented the news, and the king's suspicions regarding Motecuhçoma's constant betrayals and schemes were confirmed. Besides this latest betrayal, Motecuhçoma had sought to do him ill through his sorcerers and necromancers. Nezahualpiltzintli, as a wise and astute man, had defended himself by means of his own court sorcerers who also exercised this diabolical power. As soon as he returned to his city, Motecuhçoma ordered the cities and towns of the *chinampa*,[135] which had customarily given a certain amount of tribute to the kings of Tezcuco, to cease doing so. He did other things that increasingly revealed his wickedness, as the songs that deal with this tragedy, called *yaocuicatl*, clearly demonstrate.

---

135. A chinampa is a raised agricultural bed constructed in lake waters. Chinampas were used in many places around the lakes in the central valley. Here Alva Ixtlilxochitl is referring specifically to the people of the chinampa agricultural zone in and around Xochimilco.

[fol. 97r]

🌿 CHAPTER [75]

Which deals with the death of Nezahualpiltzintli

King Nezahualpiltzintli found out that, among other contemptuous acts, King Motecuhçoma had forbidden the cities and towns of the lake to render the tribute and obeisance that they had always given to Nezahualpiltzintli and his father. So Nezahualpiltzintli sent his ambassadors to address this matter and demand that Motecuhçoma respect this longstanding custom of their forebears. Motecuhçoma, with great arrogance and presumption, told the ambassadors to tell their lord that times had changed, because whereas in the past the empire had been governed by three rulers, from now on it would be governed by only one, the supreme lord of all of heaven and earth. He said that Nezahualpiltzintli should never again demand anything of him nor bring matters before him because if he were to do so, Motecuhçoma would punish the affront. When Nezahualpiltzintli heard this shameless and arrogant response, he felt great sorrow, which was made worse by the realization that he did not have the strength to punish such madness and avenge Motecuhçoma's betrayal. Thus, he retreated to the most secluded chambers of his palace where, sad, anguished, and in despair, he died. This was in the year 1515, which they called *matlactli acatl*.[136] He had governed for forty-four years and was fifty-two years old.

When they learned of his death, his children and relatives sought to keep it secret. Nevertheless, they gathered together to perform his funeral rites, which were attended by [fol. 97v] all the grandees and lords of his kingdom, the ambassadors from Motecuhçoma and Totoquihuatzin, and other Mexica and Tepaneca lords. They performed the same rites as they had for his father. They burned his body, which was adorned with gold and silver jewelry with fine stones and a great variety of plumes and featherwork. They sacrificed two hundred slave men and one hundred slave women in his honor. His ashes were placed in a golden ark and carried to his tomb in the main temple in the city of Tezcuco, which was dedicated to the idol Huitzilopochtli. Nezahualpiltzintli had 145 sons and daughters, of whom 11 were legitimate, as has been mentioned.

This was the end of Nezahualpiltzintli, who was no less valorous or virtuous than his father. If one considers this carefully, it is clear that he followed closely

---

136. Ten Reed.

in his father's footsteps, for he was diligent in upholding the law and fortunate in battle. However, because he had not named any one of his children as his heir, his early death left his children at odds with one another and allowed his people to make false and baseless claims. Some say that he designated the youngest of his legitimate sons, Prince Yoyontzin. This cannot be believed because the heir was always the eldest legitimate son, unless that person did not merit the title for some compelling reason. For example, King Techotlalatzin was the youngest of his brothers and still inherited the empire because he always sided with Quinatzin, his father, while the rest of his brothers sided with the Chichimeca [fol. 98r] insurgents who rebelled against the empire, as seen in this history.

🌿 CHAPTER [76]

Which deals with the conflict that occurred among Nezahualpiltzintli's
sons over the succession to the kingdom

After they completed the funeral ceremonies for King Nezahualpiltzintli, they
asked King Motecuhçoma and Totoquihuatzin of Tlacopan what should be done
about the election of a new king because, as said above, Nezahualpiltzintli left
legitimate sons but had not declared which should be his successor. Tetlahuehuetzquititzin had the strongest claim based on lineage and birth order, but
he was not fit to rule a kingdom as great as Tezcuco, especially at a time when
great valor was required to withstand the tides of fate, which seemed to have
turned against them. On the other hand, Coanacochtzin and Ixtlilxochitl had
valor and strength, but some questioned their suitability because, even though
their brother Tetlahuehuetzquititzin was an excessively peaceful man and little
given to war, he was older than they were. This disagreement provided King
Motecuhçoma with an opening to orchestrate the ascension of his nephew Prince
Cacama, son of his older sister, the lady of the house of Xilonenco. To this end,
he dispatched his ambassadors to vote, along with the electors and grandees of
the kingdom, [fol. 98v] for his nephew. Motecuhçoma loved his nephew deeply,
and moreover, Cacama was old enough to govern and was a brave captain who
had proven his valor in war. Once a king had been chosen, all the grandees
and lords of Tezcuco were to go with his nephew to the city of Mexico, where
Motecuhçoma wanted the swearing ceremony to be held, as it had been for
Cacama's father and grandfather.

The grandees and lords of Tezcuco discussed King Motecuhçoma's plan.
Even though there were different opinions, it was agreed that the three princes
Cacama, Coanacochtzin, and Ixtlilxochitl, should gather together in the royal
council chamber to be informed of King Motecuhçoma's wishes and to explain
why it was best to crown Cacama. Coanacochtzin, who had grounds to contest
the election—since he and his brothers were Nezahualpiltzintli's legitimate
sons—nonetheless voted for Cacama. Whether out of the love and goodwill he felt
for his brother Cacama or because he had made a deal with King Motecuhçoma,
Coanacochtzin said that the election of Cacama was just and deserved because of
his bravery; although they had an older brother from among the legitimate sons
who was entitled to rule the kingdom, he was not suitable. Ixtlilxochitl, young

and bellicose, could not abide the tyranny and theft perpetrated against the legitimate branch of the family. He opposed the election and caused such turmoil among those in attendance that they were unable to reach an agreement. Prince Cacama was therefore forced to retreat to the city of Mexico and seek the support and assistance of his uncle King Motecuhçoma in order to be crowned king.

Ixtlilxochitl argued bitterly with his brother Coanacochtzin, who supported and defended Cacama's claim, and left the city. [fol. 99r] He set out for the mountains of Metztitlan, rallying anyone who would follow him in opposing his uncle King Motecuhçoma for the insults and injuries he had inflicted on the kingdom of Tezcuco and his two brothers. When he reached Metztitlan, the lords of that province, who were his tutors and teachers, pledged him their full allegiance and support and summoned all the people from the mountains of the Totonacas. And having gathered a large army, Ixtlilxochitl marched with great haste to the city of Tezcuco, defeating and subjugating all who opposed him along the way. Then, once he had gained the support of all the northern lands and provinces—some willingly and others by force of arms—Ixtlilxochitl encircled the cities of Tezcuco and Mexico, marking boundaries and building forts in the towns of Papalotlan, Acolman, Chiuhnauhtlan, Tecanman, Tzonpanco, and Huehuetocan. These were the places where it was possible for the Mexicas and the Tezcucas to make incursions and attack him, which would lead to a direct confrontation with his uncle Motecuhçoma and his brothers Cacama and Coanacochtzin.

In the meantime, the might of King Motecuhçoma was so great that, by choice or by force, his nephew Cacama was accepted as king, especially in the cities and provinces that Ixtlilxochitl had not occupied. Seeing Ixtlilxochitl's boldness and temerity, his uncle the king convened a war council to stop him in his tracks and thwart his plans. After the council had discussed at length what needed to be done, a nobleman from Iztapalapan named Xochitl, one of the bravest Mexica army captains, [fol. 99v] made an offer to King Motecuhçoma. He proposed to apprehend Ixtlilxochitl and bring him back bound and tied, which would put an end to all the uprisings and rebellions without risking the lives of any other men. King Motecuhçoma thought this was a good plan, and so it fell to Xochitl to restore order to the empire and allow for the peaceful ascension of King Cacama that King Motecuhçoma desired.

Ixtlilxochitl was ever vigilant and always well informed of all that was discussed at the court of his uncle the king. He took a squadron of soldiers into Mexica territory with the express purpose of confronting Captain Xochitl. The two came upon each other and ordered their men to stand aside because they wanted to fight each other alone, and their men complied. They clashed, and Prince Ixtlilxochitl quickly defeated the Mexica captain. He took him prisoner and decreed that Xochitl would be burned alive immediately, in the presence of the two armies, using reed grass he had brought for that purpose. After this deed, Ixtlilxochitl's enemies felt greater fear and respect for him. When his uncle the king learned of what happened, he ordered that Ixtlilxochitl be left alone for the time being, for he wanted to lull him into complacency in order to capture and punish him when a better opportunity arose.

But Ixtlilxochitl would not attack Tezcuco. Instead, he merely kept the city surrounded without harming any of its residents and, in fact, treated the nobles very well. As a result, the three brothers met together and [fol. 100r] discussed the terms of peace. However, Ixtlilxochitl absolutely refused to meet with his uncle. He harbored great hatred and hostility toward him, because Motecuhçoma caused the death of King Nezahualpiltzintli, his father, and Ixtlilxochitl yearned to avenge his death if he could. In the meantime, he would retain dominion and control of all the northern provinces and remain captain general of the kingdom of Tezcuco. As a result of Ixtlilxochitl's audacity and feud with his brothers and uncle, many provinces rose up and refused to obey Motecuhçoma, who rather than being merciful as his royal ancestors were, kept demanding ever more tribute of them with increasing cruelty and tyranny. The most defiant nations were those of the province of Totonacapan, which reaches as far as the coast of the North Sea. It appears that His Divine Majesty was arranging things as he saw fit in order to facilitate the arrival of the holy Catholic faith in this new world.

At this time, the armies of the three rulers of the empire waged war against the provinces of Mictlantzinco and Xaltianquizco, which they subjugated according to the same terms as the others, as described above. These were the empire's final wars and conquests. They occurred in the year 1516, which they call *matlactli once tecpatl*.[137]

---

137. Eleven Flint.

[fol. 100v]

 ## CHAPTER [77]

Which deals with the origins of the invincible don Hernando
Cortés, the first Marquis of the Valley, and begins to tell of his
heroic deeds

The Catholic monarchs don Fernando and doña Isabel reigned in Castile and Aragon when Hernando Cortés was born in the town of Medellín in Extremadura, and the year was 1485, as mentioned previously. His parents were Martín Cortés de Monroy and doña Catalina Pizarro Altamirano, both high born and of noble stock and very honorable, though they had little wealth. He learned grammar well with two years of study and began to study law, but later he changed his mind and turned to the military. He was boisterous and ambitious, and for this reason his parents gave him permission to go to the Indies in search of Nicolás de Ovando, Commander of Lares, who was the governor of Santo Domingo. He was nineteen years old when he reached this island, in the year 1504 around Easter. During the time he lived there, which was five or six years, he had mixed success working as a merchant before participating in the conquest of the island of Cuba, where he married doña Catalina Juárez. Francisco López de Gómara and Antonio de Herrera recount what happened to him in their histories, [fol. 101r] where all the details can be found (figs. 22 and 23). I shall include nothing more than what is relevant to the topic at hand.

As time went by and the exploration of the Indies progressed, Francisco Hernández de Córdoba made a voyage and discovered Yucatan on the mainland in the year 1517. But, since the Indians defended their territory and injured many Spaniards, he did nothing more than behold the land. They learned from this voyage that it was rich and fertile and in every way superior to the islands. This made Diego Velázquez[138] want to conquer it, and to that end he sent his nephew Juan de Grijalva with a substantial fleet in the year 1518. He took with him two hundred Spaniards and some merchandise which he traded for gold and other things of value from that land. Grijalva was absent for so long that Diego Velázquez suspected that he had gotten lost and wanted to know exactly what

---

138. The governor of Cuba.

FIGURE 22. López de Gómara, *Historia de las Indias y conquista de México*, 1552 (frontispiece). *Courtesy of the John Carter Brown Library at Brown University.*

FIGURE 23. Herrera, *Historia general de los hechos de los castellanos* (vol. 2, frontispiece). Courtesy of the John Carter Brown Library at Brown University.

had happened. He sent Cristóbal de Olid to either bring him back or, if the land was good, build a settlement and begin conquering. Before Olid could locate Grijalva, Pedro de Alvarado, who had gone with Grijalva, returned to Santo Domingo. Alvarado told Diego Velázquez about the great wealth of Yucatan and all that Grijalva had acquired through trade.

When he heard this news, Diego Velázquez was eager to begin the conquest and settlement of that land, first to spread our holy faith and second to gain honor and riches. To this end, he approached various individuals to help him assemble a company for this endeavor, but no one besides [fol. 101v] Hernando Cortés agreed to work with him. Cortés, who had two thousand ducats on deposit with the merchant Andrés de Duero, was prudent and possessed of self-control. Cortés was willing to make a deal and told Velázquez that he would be happy to work with him and that he would go in person to explore and conquer that land. They made their agreements and contracts, obtained a license from the Hieronymite friars—who governed the islands—and prepared the ships. Everything was ready when Juan de Grijalva returned to port on October 3, 1518, with great quantities of gold and silver and better knowledge of the land. This prompted Diego Velázquez to change his mind, and he sought to keep Cortés from leaving, which led to great hostility between them. Cortés, however, ignored Velázquez and embarked on his voyage anyway, borrowing four thousand ducats to buy ships and necessary supplies. Then his friends joined the expedition, and he covered all of their expenses and paid them money. Upon departing, he swore before a notary that he was paying all the costs himself and that Diego Velázquez did not have any part in the venture.

Cortés stopped in Macaca, where Alvarado and Olid and other allies of Velázquez tried to arrest him, but he found safety on the island of Guaniganigo. He landed there and reviewed his men. He counted 550 Spanish fighters and also some Indian servants. He formed them into eleven companies of fifty men each and took for himself the title of captain general. He had eleven ships and flagged each one with his coat of arms, which was of blue and white flames with a red cross in the middle with the Latin motto that said: "Friends, let us follow the cross because if we have faith, by this sign we shall triumph."[139] So [fol. 102r] equipped and with these few companions, Cortés conquered this new world and converted its natives to our holy Catholic faith and the law of the Gospel. This was the most difficult conquest the world had ever seen, unsurpassed even by Alexander the Great and Julius Caesar, as will be shown in the course of our history and as is described at great length by the authors whom I have cited.

---

139. Alva Ixtlilxochitl gives this motto not in Latin but in Spanish.

🌿 CHAPTER [78]

Which deals with how Cortés began the conquest of this New
Spain up to his arrival in Potonchan

Before Cortés left the island of Guaniganigo, he gave a long and eloquent speech to his men, reminding them of the great reward they would earn by their labor and the great service they would render to God our Lord if they committed to the conquest with Christian spirit and zeal. He sailed from that island on February 28, 1519, with the goal of converting souls, not to steal from those pagan and barbarous nations. He told his men to call upon the name of St. Peter the apostle, his patron saint, to protect them. The bad weather he encountered forced him to land on the island of Acozanil,[140] whose inhabitants fled to the mountains in fear, abandoning their homes and belongings.

Some of the Spaniards pursued them inland and brought back to Cortés four women with three children. One of the women communicated through signs that she was the [fol. 102v] wife of the lord of that place and the mother of the children. Because Cortés treated her well, her husband soon arrived. He gave our men many gifts and lodged them in his town. When Cortés saw that the natives were untroubled and at ease, he began to preach the Christian faith to them, entreating them to worship the cross and the image of our Lady. They accepted it joyfully and destroyed the idols in their temple, and Cortés replaced them with the cross and an image of our Lady. The Indians regarded these with great veneration and stopped sacrificing humans. They informed Cortés that in Yucatan there were bearded men like the Spaniards. Cortés sent men to find out if this was true, but they took so long that Cortés would not wait for them any longer. He landed on Yucatan at the place that they call Punta de las Mujeres. It appeared abandoned, and he went to Cotoche. But Pedro de Alvarado's ship took on water and in order to repair it they returned to the island of Acozanil.

It was there that one morning, on the first Sunday of Lent, they saw a canoe arrive with four naked men carrying bows and arrows. Some of the Spaniards charged at them with swords drawn, believing them to be hostile. When they were close, one of the four stepped forward and began to speak in Spanish, saying, "Gentlemen, are you Christians?" This stunned our men, and they responded,

---

140. Cozumel.

"Yes, and we are Spaniards." Then he knelt and, shedding tears of joy, said, "I give infinite gratitude to God, who has delivered me from infidels and barbarians. [fol. 103r] What day is today, gentlemen? I think it is Wednesday." They responded that it was not; it was Sunday. Andrés de Tapia helped him to his feet and they happily led him and the others to Cortés, who asked him who he was and how he had gotten there. He said he was named Jerónimo de Aguilar, from Écija, and that in the year 1511, he was on his way from Darién to Santo Domingo to collect funds for the war that Diego de Nicuesa was fighting against Vasco Núñez de Balboa at the time, when his caravel was shipwrecked near Jamaica. Twenty people took refuge on a small boat. Of them, seven died at sea and the thirteen who survived arrived in the province of the Maya, where they were taken prisoner by the Indians. They fell into the hands of a very cruel cacique,[141] who ate Valdivia after having him sacrificed and did the same to four others, holding a banquet for his friends and servants. And Aguilar and the rest were kept alive to be fattened and eaten on another occasion. They escaped from their prison and fell into the hands of another cacique, a great enemy of the first, who also imprisoned them. This one treated them very well while he was alive, and his heirs did the same. Then Aguilar said that all of his companions had died, and only he and Gonzalo Guerrero remained alive in that land. Guerrero was now married and very wealthy and did not want to come with Aguilar because he was ashamed to be seen with his nose pierced as was the local custom.

They were very happy to learn all of this, although [fol. 103v] they were frightened to hear that they were going to a land where people ate human flesh. Cortés recognized the importance of having found Aguilar, because Aguilar served as his interpreter whenever necessary, and without him everything would have been very difficult. They saw their delay as a miracle, because without the damage to Alvarado's ship they would not have found him. The next day, Cortés sent Jerónimo de Aguilar to preach the Christian faith to the Indians, since he knew their language. He did so well that through his admonitions they decided to convert. Previously, they had had a cross that they understood to be the god of rain.

After leaving Acozanil, they moored near the Tabasco River, also called the Grijalva River, since he discovered it first. Cortés went upriver and sighted a town surrounded by a wooden palisade with loopholes for shooting arrows. A large number of armed people came out in canoes to confront him, and he

---

141. An Arawak term for ruler. It was brought to New Spain from the Caribbean by the Spaniards.

fought them until he took the town, which was called Potonchan. That was the first town won on the mainland of the Indies. Cortés and all his companions slept peacefully that night inside its main temple, for the Indians had fled that place. The next day, he sent three groups in different directions to reconnoiter the land with the hope of finding someone from those parts who could tell them of its features and summon the cacique without further hostilities. They brought Cortés three or four natives, who were happy [fol. 104r] to go to their lord on his behalf. They begged him to go meet Cortés without fear, because he had not come to cause trouble but rather to reveal great secrets to him. And though they spent two days going back and forth, the cacique never consented to see them.

✿ CHAPTER [79]

Which deals with the things that happened to Cortés up to his arrival in Vera Cruz

Cortés again dispatched three of his captains to buy provisions and reconnoiter the land. While they were busy with this, armed Indians attacked them, injured many of the Spaniards, and killed some of the natives from Cuba. It would have been worse had Cortés not gone to their aid. The next day, he lined up five hundred men with thirteen horses and some pieces of artillery. As the army marched through some farmland, forty thousand men attacked, and he fought them. Though it was difficult and required great effort, he defeated them. According to those who were present at the battle, the glorious apostle St. James appeared there fighting on a white horse—the first time that he appeared on behalf of the Christians in this conquest. But Cortés maintained that it was the blessed St. Peter, prince of the apostles and his patron saint, to whom he always addressed his thoughts and desires and whom he called upon whenever he found himself in danger.

Sixty Spaniards were wounded. Later, our men and the natives made peace. Tabasco, who was the highest-ranking lord of that land, and the rest of the caciques and lords offered their friendship to Cortés and supplied [fol. 104v] him with many provisions. When they presented him with some gold, Cortés asked them where it had come from and whether they had a lot of it. They answered that they did not have mines nor did they want them, because their purpose was not to get rich but rather to live contentedly. But if they wanted gold they would find it in the direction of the setting sun. And among other things, they mentioned that out of those who had fought on horseback, the one in the lead had frightened them a great deal, which confirmed the miracle of the appearance of one of the twelve apostles. Cortés explained to them why he had come, which was to teach them the law of the Gospel and deliver them from the blindness in which they lived. This was why the king of Spain, his lord and the greatest in the world, had sent him. He then erected a cross in the main temple of the city of Potonchan, which delighted the natives. Then, during the celebrations of Palm Sunday, countless numbers of people swore fealty to the king of Spain, offering themselves as friends and vassals, the first that the royal crown of Castile acquired in those parts. Cortés set out from that city, which our people called Victoria.

Continuing along his journey, he arrived at a big river called Papaloapan and, since Pedro de Alvarado was the first to discover it, it was given his name. Going west along the coast, they arrived at San Juan de Culhua (which today is called Ulua) on Maundy Thursday. Before they made landfall, Teotlili—governor of the coast, appointed by the lords of the empire—sent his servants in two canoes to ask who the leader of the [fol. 105r] fleet was and where he was going. Cortés welcomed them, showed them hospitality, and sent them back to tell the governor that he should be neither afraid nor distressed, for Cortés had come only to bring him very good news that would make him happy. On Good Friday, they landed and set up camp on the beach where Vera Cruz is now. It has been known by that name ever since because they arrived on the Friday of the crucifixion. Many Indians came to see them and traded gold and very valuable featherwork for scissors, pins, glass beads, and other small trinkets of little value. But Cortés quickly ordered that no one should trade for gold, so that the Indians would not think that that was the only thing they came for. Two days later, on Easter Monday, the governor arrived accompanied by four thousand men carrying provisions that he gave to Cortés with valuable gifts and gold jewelry. Cortés embraced him and gave in return a velvet sash and other little trifles, which Teotlili greatly appreciated.

Since Aguilar did not understand their language, it pleased God to remedy this problem. Among the women given to Cortés by the lord of Potonchan, there was one who knew the language well because she was a native of the town of Huilotlan in the province of Xalatzinco. She was the daughter of nobles and the granddaughter of the lord of that province. As a girl, some merchants kidnapped her during a time of war and sold her at the market in Xicalanco, which is near the province [fol. 105v] of Coatzacoalco. She was passed from master to master until she came to belong to the lord of Potonchan, who, as has been mentioned, later gave her to Cortés. Cortés, with kind words and good treatment, converted her, and she became a Christian and took the name Marina. All of the other women with her also became Christians, the first converts in this New Spain. Later she served as interpreter together with Aguilar. First, Cortés would tell Aguilar what he wanted to say, then Aguilar would interpret it for Marina in the language of Potonchan and Tabasco, and Marina, who knew that language very well, interpreted it in the Mexica language. In just a few days, however, Marina learned Castilian, saving Cortés much trouble. This appears to have been a miracle and was very important for the conversion of the natives and establishing our holy Catholic faith. After some time, Marina married Aguilar.[142]

On the day that Governor Teotlili arrived, he ate with Cortés after having told him that he was in charge of all that land on behalf of the three rulers of the empire and that he was a servant of Emperor Motecuhçoma, the great lord of the city of Mexico Tenochtitlan. Teotlili asked Cortés to explain why he had come, so that he could inform the lords of the empire. Cortés told Marina to tell him that he was an ambassador from King don Carlos of Spain, lord of all the world; Cortés had come to visit Motecuhçoma on his lord's behalf to speak privately with him in order to deliver a written message that he had brought; Motecuhçoma would be very happy to hear it; and Teotlili should quickly ascertain from his lord where he wanted the message delivered. Teotlili responded that he was [fol. 106r] very happy to hear about another lord as great as Motecuhçoma, as he claimed the king of Spain to be, but he did not believe that any other in the world could be Motecuhçoma's equal, and he would inform his lord of Cortés's arrival and await his orders. Cortés asked him if Motecuhçoma had much gold, because it was good for heart ailments from which some of his men were suffering. Teotlili responded that he did indeed. He then had painted on cotton cloth a likeness of the Spaniards, their horses and ships, and everything else Cortés brought, along with the reasons he had come. He sent his messengers to go without delay to Mexico to inform Motecuhçoma, his lord, and Cacama, king of Tezcuco, and Totoquihuaztli of Tlacopan. They traveled so quickly that they arrived after only one day and one night. Teotlili returned to his home in Cuetlachtlan, leaving Cuitlalpitoc and other captains behind with our men, along with two thousand people to serve and care for the Spaniards.

---

142. This is inaccurate. Aguilar was a clergyman; doña Marina married the conquistador Juan Jaramillo.

❦ CHAPTER [80]

Which deals with the things that King Motecuhçoma did upon
hearing the news of the arrival of Cortés and his companions
and how Cortés learned of the factions in this land

When Teotlili's messengers arrived in the city of Mexico, their news caused King Motecuhçoma great confusion and fear, for he saw that the prophecies of his ancestors were about to be realized. He convened a council of all the lords of the empire to discuss what should be done. And, once assembled, he shared with them all that was weighing on his heart. He said that these men who had arrived from the east might be the god Quetzalcoatl and his sons, whom they had expected for so many centuries, and, if so, they would surely take their land away and make themselves lords of it all. It would, therefore, be prudent to impede their progress and keep them from entering the court. Or if, as they claimed, they were ambassadors of a great lord from another world in the east, it would be wise to receive them and hear their message.

All the kings and lords in attendance debated the matter for a long while. And when Motecuhçoma saw that there was no consensus, he asked his brother Cuitlahua for his opinion as a more experienced man, provided that his nephew King Cacama, [fol. 107r] who ought to have been the first to speak, would allow it. Cuitlahua told him: "My opinion, great lord, is that you should not allow into your house one who would expel you from it, and I shall say no more." King Cacama said:

My opinion is that it would be beneath the dignity of Your Highness, of us, and of the whole of the empire not to welcome the ambassadors from the lord of Spain, whom they claim is very great. For sovereigns have an obligation under the law to receive the ambassadors of others. And should they come under false pretenses, there are brave soldiers and captains to defend Your Highness and many relatives and friends to guard your honor and punish any treachery or disrespect. And if these newly arrived people come to bring disorder and tyranny, it would be better to have them come to court to deliver their message and state their intent as soon as possible. There is no good reason to hinder them. To do so would bring contempt and damage upon the greatness and majesty of the empire, because the ambassadors, seeing that you block the entry of a mere four foreigners, will believe Your Highness and everyone in the empire to be weak and lacking in courage, and this would only embolden them in their attempts to throw this land into upheaval. Moreover, with this delay, they will be able to identify the vulnerabilities within your court, who is your friend and who is your enemy. This weakness might even inspire many subjugated and oppressed provinces to rebel. Thus, come what may, it would be best not to delay the arrival of these ambassadors so much that they are able to discover and behold with their own eyes the secrets of the empire. This is my opinion.

The courageous lords among them agreed wholeheartedly with King Cacama—and in this I do not believe they were mistaken. But King Motecuhçoma and other lords of his court [fol. 107v] preferred the advice of Cuitlahua. Thus, Motecuhçoma sought to hinder the progress of Cortés and his men at every turn.

Teotlili's messengers returned with Motecuhçoma's reply. A week later, they reached Vera Cruz bearing, along with the response, magnificent gifts of gold and cotton cloth. They also brought greetings from Cacama, king of Tezcuco Aculhuacan, and Totoquihuaztli of Tlacopan, who expressed their happiness at having learned of such a great and powerful king as the king of Spain and the honor and joy they felt to be his allies and witness in their lifetimes the arrival of heretofore unknown people of such great valor. Therefore, the messengers also relayed instructions to the ambassador to attend to the Spaniards' needs, so that they might be well provided for. And as for meeting them and his uncle Motecuhçoma in person, it would be impossible because Motecuhçoma was unwell and ill-disposed to go to the coast; neither should Cortés go to the court because the journey was long and dangerous and many barbarous and cruel people, enemies of the Mexicas and the Aculhuas, lived along the way.

Having learned of King Motecuhçoma's wishes from the messengers, Cortés replied that nothing would stop him from going to see Motecuhçoma, nor from doing his duty and carrying out the orders from his king. Teotlili sent his messengers out again with this reply. In the meantime, there arrived ambassadors from Ixtlilxochitl, who was in dispute with his brother and his uncle King Motecuhçoma, to welcome Cortés and his men and extend his friendship to them. They explained the state of affairs in the empire to Cortés and relayed Ixtlilxochitl's desire to avenge the death of his beloved father King Nezahualpiltzintli [fol. 108r] and liberate the kingdom from tyranny; they also presented him with gifts of gold, cotton cloth, and featherwork. Cortés was delighted to hear of these rivalries and factions that had arisen because Motecuhçoma had aggrieved them and all but usurped their power. He saw a clear path to victory, which he would later achieve: He would join one of the factions and, once they had consumed one another, become lord of both.

Ten days later, the messengers returned with Motecuhçoma's definitive response, which was that Cortés should not persist in his efforts to see him or reach Mexico. That was the end of their exchange. When Cortés saw Motecuhçoma's resolve and that the governor had departed, he was determined to establish a settlement there and conquer the land right away. After securing food and other necessary items from places nearby, he began to build a town. After discussing what would facilitate the success of his endeavor with his men, he summoned the royal notary Francisco Hernández and, in front of everyone, he formally took possession of all the land in the name of King don Carlos, our lord of glorious memory. He named Alonso Fernández Portocarrero and Francisco de Montejo as magistrates. He also appointed, in the name of the king, a solicitor, constable, notary, councilmen, and all the other officers needed to establish a town council; he invested them with their staffs of office and installed them as the council of the Villa Rica de la Vera Cruz. Then he presented another declaration before the aforementioned notary and the new magistrates in which he ceded to them, in his capacity as the officer of royal and ordinary justice, the authority of captain and explorer granted to him by the [fol. 108v] Hieronymite friars on the island of Hispaniola in the name of His Majesty. It also stated that he renounced and divested himself of the authority given to him by Diego Velázquez, governor of Cuba. None of them had any jurisdiction over this land that Cortés and his men had just discovered and begun settling in the name of His Majesty as his loyal vassals. All of this was recorded by the notary. After the new officials assumed their posts, they held a council meeting and arranged for the good governance of their republic. And, in the name of His Majesty, they named Hernando Cortés governor and captain general, so that he would be in charge until the king should appoint someone else. They pleaded with Cortés until he accepted the position, which he wielded with such success and magnificence that neither Alexander the Great nor Julius Caesar nor any other famous captain in the history of the world surpassed him, as can be seen in detail in the histories by the authors I have cited and by many others who have written of the discovery, conquest, and pacification of this land.

🦋 CHAPTER [81]

Which deals with how Cortés met the lord of Cempoalan and
the lord of Quiahuiztlan and the alliance they offered to form
against Motecuhçoma

Cortés decided to go to Cempoalan and spent the first night near a river. The next day, one hundred men carrying food and gifts arrived on behalf of the lord of that province, who begged Cortés's pardon for being unable to come out to greet him personally because he was very fat and heavy. [fol. 109r] However, the lord wanted Cortés to feel very welcome and was expecting him at his home. They ate the food and then went to Cempoalan, where they were well received in the lord's house. The next day, he visited them and presented them gifts of gold, cloth, and featherwork. He did nothing more than greet Cortés and then left without further conversation. He later organized a very special feast for them with a variety of dishes and gifts. A few days after that, Cortés requested a meeting with the lord, if it pleased him. The cacique replied that he would be happy to receive him, and so Cortés and fifty of his men visited him and explained his endeavor and its purpose. And when Cortés was finished speaking, the lord responded through Marina with a long speech about the state of affairs in his realm and about how he and his ancestors had enjoyed enduring peace until recently, when Motecuhçoma had imposed his will upon them. Motecuhçoma and his people perpetrated a hundred thousand abuses against him and his men each day. To escape his tyranny, the lord and many others from nearby provinces would be happy to rebel against Mexico and join forces with the king of Castile. Even though Motecuhçoma was a great and powerful lord, he had many enemies, especially his nephew Ixtlilxochitl, who had rebelled against him. And those from Tlaxcalan, Huexotzinco, and other very powerful towns were perpetually at war with him, and if Cortés joined them, they could form an alliance against which Motecuhçoma could not defend himself.

This all seemed good to Cortés, and he offered all his support, saying that the main reason for his coming was none other than to right wrongs and punish tyranny. Among many other gifts, the cacique, or king, of that province gave Cortés [fol. 109v] eight young women, daughters of high-ranking men, one of whom was his own niece. Cortés returned to the sea by a different route and entered the capital of another province, the city of Quiahuiztlan, which was located on a hilltop. There he was also well received by the cacique and lord, and they discussed the same things as they had in Cempoalan. While Cortés was there, some of Motecuhçoma's tribute collectors arrived, and the lord became anxious, fearing that Motecuhçoma would be angry with him for having welcomed foreigners into his land. But Cortés, who noticed this, reassured him. And so that the lord could see how little regard he had for Motecuhçoma's anger and also to bring about the rebellion and the alliance, Cortés arrested the tribute collectors. That night, he had two of the four prisoners released and brought before him. He then sent them to Motecuhçoma to ask him earnestly, on Cortés's behalf, for his friendship. As his friend, Motecuhçoma would receive great benefits and learn secrets and mysteries never before seen or heard.

The next day, when the lord of Quiahuiztlan saw that two of the tribute collectors had left and would denounce him to Motecuhçoma, he saw no other option than to rebel openly. He sent messengers calling for the towns of his kith and kin to take up arms and not pay tribute to Mexico. They all rose up and begged Cortés to be their leader, promising to deploy one hundred thousand warriors to the field of battle. Cortés was greatly pleased by this because he saw that he had all the land in tumult. He had befriended both sides and could deceive them with double dealing. These ingenious achievements guaranteed his [fol. 110r] good fortune, because they cleared the way for him to attain all his goals leading to the subjugation of the empire. And with this he left Quiahuiztlan for Villa Rica, where the ships were, and they all began to build the town.

🌿 CHAPTER [82]

Which deals with what else happened to Cortés in Villa Rica and the burning of the ships

Hernando Cortés kept all the men in his army busy with the construction of Villa Rica. They were assisted by many native allies who had come to his side. They were fully occupied in this project when two nephews of Motecuhçoma arrived, accompanied by four elders who advised them. They came on behalf of Motecuhçoma and Cacama, bearing gifts of gold and very rich featherwork, to tell Cortés that the Mexica lords greatly appreciated his having released their servants and now begged him to release the other two who were still imprisoned. They said that they would pardon the crime and impudence of the one who had seized them,[143] but only for Cortés's sake. And since Cortés desired to meet with Motecuhçoma, the king would allow the Spaniards to see him, but Cortés should wait a little while, until the king sent for him. Cortés welcomed Motecuhçoma's two nephews and treated them lavishly. After sending them off, he told the lord of Quiahuiztlan what had happened with Motecuhçoma's ambassadors, and how, out of respect for Cortés, Motecuhçoma would not dare punish the lord's insolence. Thus, he and all his allies could be assured of their liberty and should cease paying tribute to the Mexica lords, for Cortés would defend them. With this trickery, Cortés kept [fol. 110v] Motecuhçoma and everyone else fooled for many days.

Wars broke out. Cempoalan attacked Tizapantzinco, where an imperial fort and garrison were located, to take control of that region. Then, Cortés and his people joined those from Cempoalan in their fight against the empire's army and forced them to retreat to Tizapantzinco, where they surrounded them. Although they defended themselves, the city was taken. So as not to anger Motecuhçoma, Cortés did not permit any of the inhabitants to be killed or the city to be sacked. With this, the whole region was liberated. They stopped paying tribute and were henceforth obliged to serve Cortés.

When Cortés returned to Vera Cruz, he found that sixty Spaniards had arrived, along with nine horses and mares, essential reinforcements given their

---

143. According to Francisco López de Gómara, whom Alva Ixtlilxochitl is following here, it was the lord of Quiahuiztlan who arrested the tribute collectors, at Cortés's urging.

present situation. He inspected his troops. He set aside a fifth of the spoils they had won and sent it to His Majesty with Alonso Hernández Portocarrero and Francisco Montejo. He wrote the king a long account of all he had done, asking him to recognize his service and promising to conquer and pacify all of this land and arrest or kill Motecuhçoma. The council also wrote to the king, requesting, if it pleased him, that he confirm their appointment of Cortés as captain and chief justice. Around this time, some of the men who were friends of Diego Velázquez began to grumble. They complained that Cortés had given himself those titles and repudiated the authority of Diego Velázquez, and they started a mutiny. Cortés seized the leaders of these men, had two of them hanged, and whipped the rest. This brought the mutiny to an end. Afterwards, he began [fol. 111r] to prepare for the expedition he wanted to make to Mexico. Everything they had done would have been in vain, if they did not meet with and defeat Motecuhçoma. If they did, they would gain eternal honor and fame.

Many resisted leaving on this expedition, because for five hundred men to go up against millions of enemy warriors seemed reckless rather than courageous. Cortés, seeing that most of them opposed his plan and that neither pleas nor reasoned arguments would convince them, undertook one of the greatest deeds the world has ever seen. Cortés bribed certain pilots with money and great promises to come tell him, while he was with the rest of the army, that the ships had been eaten by shipworm and were not seaworthy. He had also secretly arranged for certain sailors to bore holes in the bottom of the ships so that they would sink. They all did as he had instructed, and he showed such emotion and became so convincingly upset that at the time no one suspected his ruse. They told him that the ships were beyond repair, and he responded that they should at least salvage the wood and the rigging. Thus, they took apart four of their best ships. But before the other ships were dismantled, the men realized they had been deceived and began to whisper to one another about Cortés and sought to keep him from proceeding. Disregarding them, he tore apart the other ships anyway, leaving only one.

Cortés gathered together in the plaza all those who were displeased and upset and explained to them why he had taken apart the ships, which had not been in his own [fol. 111v] best interest, since they had cost him so much money and he now had nothing left. After offering these arguments to persuade them and inspire them to march on Mexico, he concluded by saying that they could not turn back now, since the ships were in pieces. Besides, no one would be so cowardly and so timid as to hold his life in greater esteem than Cortés held his own, nor so weak of heart as to hesitate to accompany him to Mexico, where there was so much to gain. If, by chance, anyone decided to abandon this journey, he could go with God's blessing back to Cuba in the ship that remained, but before long, he would tear out his beard in regret, seeing the great good fortune that Cortés expected. Everyone was so ashamed that there was no one who did not promise to follow him unto death and praise highly what had been done. Before leaving for Mexico, he readied his allies from the more than fifty cities and towns that had rebelled against Motecuhçoma, which brought another fifty thousand men to their side. Leaving one hundred fifty men in Villa Rica, he departed with the rest for Mexico, but not before dealing with the objections of Francisco de Garay, who had arrived from Cuba to stop him.

🌿 CHAPTER [83]

Which deals with Cortés's march to Mexico and what happened
to him along the way, until they reached Tlaxcalan

The first place that Cortés went with his army was to Cempoalan, which he called Sevilla. There he cast down their idols and placed Christian images and crosses in the temples. He left on August 16 of the same year of 1519 with one thousand Indian porters, thirteen hundred Indian warriors, and some hostages. In his company were four hundred Spaniards, fifteen horses, and seven [fol. 112r] small cannons. He walked for three days through friendly territory, where he was welcomed and feasted. Motecuhçoma's allies afforded him the same courtesies, because he was on good terms with everyone owing to his skill and cunning. After walking for three days through deserted land without food or water, he reached Tzacuhtlan, where Olintetl, the lord of that place, welcomed him with much rejoicing and celebration on behalf of Motecuhçoma. Through his interpreter Marina, he preached the Christian faith and told them about the king of Spain while at the same time gathering information about Motecuhçoma's power and wealth, the might and majesty of his empire and court, and the site and location of the city of Mexico. He spent five days in Tzacuhtlan, where he tore down all their idols and erected crosses, as he had done in other places.

While in Tzacuhtlan, he sent four Cempoalans to Tlaxcalan to tell the lords of that province of his endeavor and its purpose, believing that, since they were enemies of the empire, they would welcome him. The messengers took longer than expected, so Cortés left Tzacuhtlan without waiting for them. Passing a large wall, he came upon fifteen scouts armed with shields and macanas. When the scouts realized that they could not escape those on horseback, they took up their swords and fought fiercely and with such spirit that they killed two horses. One of these scouts severed the head of a horse with a single stroke, reins and all. Five thousand Tlaxcaltecas came out to defend the scouts, but then the confederation sent their messengers to Cortés. They apologized for what had happened and blamed some Otomies from the hills. They invited him to their city under false pretenses—according to the authors who describe these events—in order to seize and kill him.

The next day roughly a thousand Tlaxcaltecas came out to fight with great discipline and courage, and then they began to retreat with the goal of luring

Cortés and his men into an ambush of more than eighty thousand warriors. Cortés and his men found themselves in great danger and many were injured, though none died. They barricaded themselves in a village that night and, the next morning, received word that more than 150,000 men were coming to attack them. God performed great miracles in their defense. When these Tlaxcaltecas arrived within view, they began to ridicule and make fun of our men. Seeing how few of them there [fol. 112v] were, they sent them chickens, cherries, and cakes of maize to strengthen them for the fight so they could not say they were starving them. When it was time, they began to fight. Cortés and our men were very lucky that the Tlaxcaltecas never engaged them all at once, but rather in squadrons, coming out twenty thousand at a time. After each squadron was defeated, another came out, and over the two days of the battle, they killed countless Tlaxcaltecas. Seeing that they had not killed a single Spaniard, the Tlaxcaltecas believed them to be enchanted or that they were gods. On the third day, they refused to fight and instead sent Cortés some gifts as an offering. Cortés responded that he was not a god but rather a mortal man like them and that they were mistaken not to want his friendship, because they could see the harm that resulted from not welcoming him.

Nonetheless, the next day another twenty thousand men came out to fight him. On the following day, which was September 6, fifty men carrying food arrived in Cortés's camp. Cortés ordered their hands cut off, because a captain from Cempoalan named Teoc had informed him that they were spies. The Tlaxcaltecas were astonished that Cortés seemed to know their thoughts, since he had discovered their plan and that they were spies. Once they recognized the great valor of Cortés and his men, they ceased their spying and hostilities and earnestly sought his friendship. They justified what they had done as best they could, either by blaming the Otomies from the hills, or by saying that they thought Cortés was Motecuhçoma's ally. Even as this was taking place, Cortés received a valuable gift and message from Motecuhçoma in which he offered to be a friend and vassal of the king of Castile provided that Cortés turn back without continuing on to Mexico. Cortés entertained Motecuhçoma's envoys for a few days and had them witness some of the aforementioned battles with the Tlaxcaltecas, telling them that he was punishing the Tlaxcaltecas as a service to Motecuhçoma because they were his enemies. Later, they were camped in a field one night when they saw some fires in the distance. Cortés [fol. 113r] rode out with about two hundred of his men to see what it was. They got to Tzinpantzinco, a city of more than twenty thousand hearths. Since he caught them unawares, they did not resist and, instead, welcomed and feasted Cortés and his men and promised to reconcile him with the Tlaxcaltecas and make them his allies. When they got close to Mexico, many of Cortés's men showed weakness and fear and tried to abandon him and return to Vera Cruz without going any further. Cortés, however, spoke to them so effectively that the fainthearted gained courage and the valiant gained twice as much. All were determined to follow him and die with him on such a holy quest.

The confederation of Tlaxcalan saw Cortés's great valor and the futility of their efforts to defeat our men. They convened a council to discuss how it would be to their benefit to bring the Spaniards to their city quickly and ally themselves with Cortés. For if he were to go to Mexico and ally himself with Motecuhçoma, it would lead to their total ruin and destruction; they would lose their freedom and become slaves of the Mexica, who would take revenge on them for all the battles they had fought. The confederation, therefore, sent Tolinpanecatl Coztomatl, one of their highest-ranking noblemen, to meet with Ocelotzin Tlacatecuhtli, who had been tending to the needs of our men from the beginning of the peace negotiations and who was the younger brother of Xicotencatl, one of Tlaxcalan's four rulers. Together, they were to persuade Cortés to accompany them home.

When Tolinpanecatl arrived at Cortés's camp, Atempanecatl, the most senior of Motecuhçoma's ambassadors, said to him angrily, "Why do you come here? What business do you have? I want to know about it. And do you realize to whom you bring it? Do you believe yourself his equal and greet him with weapons, accustomed as you are to the profaneness of the military?" Before Tolinpanecatl had a chance to answer, Motecuhçoma's ambassador continued, saying, "Who is responsible for the shameless and continuous fighting that has taken place in Huitzilhuacan, Tepatlachco, Tetzmolocan, Teotlatzinco, Tepetzinco, Ocotepec, Tlamacazquicac, Atlmoyahuacan, Zecalacoayan, and all the land from here to Chololan? Let us see. What is it that you want to discuss with Cortés? I want to see and hear it."

Marina had been present for all of this. The ambassador from the confederation of Tlaxcalan turned to her and said, "In the presence [fol. 113v] of Captain Cortés, our father and lord, I want to respond to my cousin, the Mexica ambassador." Marina replied, "Continue your exchange." She then turned to the Mexica ambassador and said, "Do you have anything more to say?" He responded, "I have told you enough. I only want to hear what you want." Tolinpanecatl responded:

> Young cousin, you have no reason to speak ill of this land and the confederation of Tlaxcalan. Note that no one is pointing out to you the injustices

you have perpetrated by stealing the domains of others, from Cuitlahuac to the provinces of Chalco, Jantetelco, Quauhquecholan, Itzocan, Quauhtin-chan, Tecamachalco, Tepeyacac, and Cuetlachtlan, as far as the coast of Cempoalan. You committed a thousand misdeeds and offenses from one sea to the other, and no one said anything or tried to stop you. Because of you, because of your treachery and duplicity, the Huexotzincatl has forsaken our kinship. Your betrayals and tyranny have terrorized everyone, and you carry them out only to enjoy fine clothes and food. Shame on you. Do not attempt to have someone else fight your battles for you. If you want to fight, meet me on the field alone. I will risk my own life so you can take out your anger on me, for I do not fear death. And regarding what you say about my having greeted Captain Cortés with weapons, in fact, your friends who left Zacaxochitla, Teocalhueyacan, Quahuacan, and Maçahuacan fleeing from you, came into my lands, and it was they who made war against Captain Cortés. And now I shall carry him aloft and serve him.

After this argument, the Tlaxcalteca ambassador delivered the confederation's message to Cortés, begging him to leave with him at once for his city, providing a large quantity of sandals for the trip.

Cortés responded through Marina that the ambassador should tell the confederation that all their lords and nobles should come to that place in order to lead him to their city, so that he could gauge their intentions toward him. As Tolinpanecatl was leaving to deliver the response to his message, Marina spoke to Tolinpanecatl in secret, telling him that the Tlaxcaltecas should seize the Culhua[144] ambassador at the temple the next day and kill him, since he had greatly offended them. The Tlaxcaltecas were very pleased and told the confederation of Cortés's good will toward them.

The arrival of Xicotencatl's brother and Tolinpanecatl upset the [fol. 114r] Mexica ambassadors tremendously. They sought to prevent Cortés from befriending the Tlaxcaltecas, telling him not to believe them, that they were deceiving him, and that they wanted to take him into the city in order to kill him, for they were traitors and evildoers. One of the Mexica ambassadors had gone to tell Motecuhçoma all that was happening. He returned six days later with another elaborate gift from Motecuhçoma to Cortés and told him to be careful and not

144. That is, Mexica.

to trust the traitors from Tlaxcalan. At the same time, Cortés saw the actions of the Tlaxcaltecas, who said a thousand vile things about Motecuhçoma and his tyranny, and that they very much wanted to bring him to their city to join forces with him. All of this put Cortés in great doubt. But in the end, after weighing his options, he decided to move ahead, working in such a way that, by satisfying both sides, he would make himself lord of them all. And so, he gave orders for his departure.

When the confederation learned of Cortés's goodwill toward them, they all gathered together, and Xicotencatl, who was the eldest of the four rulers, said:

> Lords and noblemen, the time for debate has passed. I am of the opinion that each of the four capital cities of the confederation should appoint a number of nobleman to go bring the sun[145] to us, because asking all of the lords and rulers to go might be a trick to catch us unawares and kill us, since we have enemies in his army. Once he is here with us, however, he will see how well we treat him and how willingly we serve and support him, and he will come to love us and be certain of our loyalty. And for my part, I appoint two noblemen from my household, Apanyacatl and Tequachcaotli, to go on my behalf.

They all agreed wholeheartedly with Xicotencatl. And so Maxixcatzin appointed two noblemen from his household, Tlacatecuhtli and Chiquilitzin Xiuhtlatqui. And the lord of the capital city of Quiahuiztlan named two more, Chimalpiltzintli and Quanaltecatl. And the lord of Tepeticpac named two more, Tzopantzin Quauhatlapaltzin [fol. 114v] Ixconauhquitecuhtli and Hueytlapatipatzin Mixcoatzin.

After they were all selected, Ambassador Coztomatl Tolinpanecatl led them to Cortés. And when they came before him, they presented him with some jewelry of gold and precious stones and implored him on behalf of the confederation to agree to go to Tlaxcalan, where the rulers awaited him; they also explained that the rulers had not come in person to accompany him due to certain impediments. Cortés was pleased with this, and after this exchange, departed with his army for Tlaxcalan, where they welcomed him with a grand reception. Xicotencatl greeted him at the door of his palace, which was in the capital city of Tizatlan. He was so old that he had to be supported by other noblemen. All

---

145. *Traer al sol.* Reference unclear. Perhaps a conflation of Cortés and Pedro de Alvarado, whom the Nahuas often referred to as Tonatiuh, or "Sun," allegedly because of his blond hair.

the highest-ranking nobles of his court and household came out with him. They were Mocuetlazatzin, Tziuhcoacatl, Texinquitlacochcalcatl, Axayacatzin, Xiuhtecatl, Tonatiuhtzin, Tepoloatecuhtli, and Tenamazcuicuiltzin. The other three rulers were also present at this reception, accompanied by nobles from their courts and households. Maxixcatzin of Ocotelulco came with Tecpan-ecatl, Chiquilitzin, Chicoquauhtzin, Ixayopiltzin, Tlamaceuhcatzin, Tenancatl, Çeyecatecuhtli, Axayacatzin, and Calmecahua Ixayopiltzin. Citlalpopocatzin of Quiahuiztlan came with Tzicuhcoacatl, Çacancatzin, Quanaltecatl, Axoquentzin, Tequanitzin, Tenancacalitzin, Xochicacaloa, and Izquitecatl. Tlehuexolotzin of Tepeticpac came with Tequitlanotzin, Tzopantzin Calmecahua, Quauhatlapaltzin Ixconauhquitecuhtli, and Xipantecuhtli. With these men came many other lords and nobles from throughout the province of Tlaxcalan.

When they saw Cortés approach the place called Tizatlan, they went out to greet him. At the entrance to the palace, Xicotencatl was supported on one side by Maxixcatzin and on the other by Tequanitzin. When Cortés saw them, he dismounted from his horse, removed his hat, and greeted them with a grand and gracious gesture. He then embraced Xicotencatl and, through [fol. 115r] Marina, told them that he was very happy to be with all the lords and noblemen of the confederation and court of Tlaxcalan, he was delighted to see and meet them and serve them however he could, and everyone should be at ease and pleased by his arrival, for he had come for no reason other than their well-being and liberty. Maxixcatzin responded, "Sir, may you be very welcome here, for you have come home. Xicotencatl here is your father with all the rest of the lords and noblemen of the confederation of Tlaxcalan, who have been waiting for you and yearning to see and meet you. Come in and rest." Then Xicotencatl himself presented Cortés with a bouquet of flowers that Maxixcatzin had been holding. This made Cortés and all his men very happy. They began to play trumpets, drums, and flutes and to wave war banners as a sign of peace. Cortés took Xicotencatl by the arm, and they went together to the main hall of his palace. Xicotencatl gave his seat to Cortés and, after all his men were settled, entertained him lavishly, offering everyone a sumptuous feast on that day and every day that our men spent in Tlaxcalan.

In this chapter and those that follow, which deal with the confederation of Tlaxcalan, I do not follow the authors who have written of the history of the conquest, but rather I follow the history written by Tadeo de Niza de Santa María, native of the capital city of Tepeticpac, which was commissioned by the confederation when don Alonso Gómez was governor. This history was given to the friar Father Pedro de Osorio to be taken to His Majesty in Spain. It was written in the year 1548. His sources, who were present for all the events recorded in the history, were the eyewitnesses Miguel Tlachpanquizcatzin, permanent councilman and native of Quiahuiztlan; Toribio Tolimpanecatl; don Antonio Calmecahua; don Diego de Guzmán; don Martín de Valencia Coyolchichiuhqui; and others whose names are not noted here. It was written thirty-one years after Cortés arrived in this land and is the most accurate and true of all the histories written, since it was the product of consensus among those who were the most knowledgeable.

[fol. 115v]

🌿 CHAPTER [84]

Which deals with everything that happened to Cortés during
the time he was in Tlaxcalan

Cortés and his men stayed in Tlaxcalan for twenty days and were generously and hospitably treated. Cortés asked them to allow him and his men to visit the entire city, including the temples and palaces of the four lords of the confederation; he toured them and assessed their positions and defenses. He saw that the people were at ease with him and they lived in an orderly and civilized fashion under the rule of law and could, therefore, be trusted with any matter. So, he began to preach the faith of Jesus Christ our Lord and urge them to cease idolatry and human sacrifice. He explained to them that the idols they worshiped were a sort of demon, though he was unable to thoroughly convince them. Nonetheless, in the main hall of the palace, where Xicotencatl worshiped, Cortés placed a cross and an image of our Lady, and mass was regularly held there during his stay. The Spaniards erected another cross with great solemnity on the spot where the confederation had first received Cortés. The Tlaxcaltecas were astonished, believing the Christians to be worshiping the god they called Tonacaquahuitl, meaning "tree of life," which is what the ancients called him.

The confederation agreed to give their daughters to Cortés and his companions. Xicotencatl, whose idea it was, selected two of his daughters, Tecuiloatzin and Tolquequetzaltzin. Maxixcatzin selected Çicuetzin, daughter of Atlapaltzin. The lord of Quiahuiztlan selected Çaquancozcatl, daughter of Axoquentzin, and Huitznahuaçihuatzin, daughter of Tequanitzin. They also gathered many other young women and, along with these noblewomen, gave them to Cortés and his men. The women brought with them many gifts of gold, cloth, featherwork, and jewels. Maxixcatzin told Marina to tell the lord captain that these women were the daughters of Xicotencatl and the other noble lords and there for him and his companions to take as their wives. Cortés thanked them and distributed the women among his men so as not to appear ungrateful for the gift and the opportunity to establish bonds of kinship between our Spaniards and them. And to show his generosity and reciprocate the gift, he sent messengers to Cempoalan to bring back large quantities of cloth, [fol. 116r] underskirts, huipiles, loincloths, cacao, salt, shrimp, and fish. Once everything had been brought, he distributed it among the four rulers and all the other Tlaxcalteca lords. The gifts were a great boon for them because they lacked all these things.

One hundred twenty nobles and two hundred porters went to get the gifts, which were provided by a Spaniard who remained in Cempoalan and Chicomacatl, the local lord. They also went in order to secure a route between Tlaxcalan and Cempoalan. The highest-ranking nobles selected for this journey were Icueten, on behalf of Xicotencatl; Totatzin Chichatlapaltzin, on behalf of Maxixcatzin; Yaotzin, on behalf of Tlehuexolotzin; and others who shall not be named here to avoid verbosity. While Cortés was in Tlaxcalan, the people of Huexotzinco—a republic and capital city like Tlaxcalan—who were of the same lineage as the Tlaxcaltecas, came out to extend their friendship. The painting kept today in the town council building of the confederation of Tlaxcalan shows that its lords were baptized at that time by the priest Juan Díaz, and Captain Cortés was their godfather. The first to be baptized was Xicotencatl, who took the name don Bartolomé. Citlalpopocatzin followed him and took the name don Baltasar. Then came Tlehuexolotzin, who took the name don Gonzalo. The last was Maxixcatzin, who was still a young man and took the name don Juan. All the others were already old, and Xicotencatl was the oldest of them all.

During the time that Cortés was in Tlaxcalan, the ambassadors from Mexico beseeched him daily to leave that place and go to Mexico. When they saw that he finally wanted to depart, they advised him to go by way of Chololan, a very populous and wealthy city allied with Motecuhçoma. Even though the Tlaxcaltecas offered various arguments to stop him from going that way, in the end Cortés decided to go to Chololan anyway, taking with him six thousand Tlaxcalteca warriors, though they wanted to give him many more. The Tlaxcalteca captains were Tlepapalotzin, Tlacatecuhtli, Quanaltecatl, Tenamazcuicuiltzin, Miztli, Matzin, and Axayacatzin, though he later returned. More than ten thousand men from Chololan came out with great rejoicing to meet Cortés and his men on the road. They escorted them into the city, offered them very comfortable accommodations, and entertained our men with great hospitality. That night Motecuhçoma's ambassadors returned again to plead with Cortés not to travel to Mexico, offering him a thousand reasons, which made him suspicious of them and the Chololtecas. He commanded his allies, the Tlaxcaltecas, to place distinguishing marks on their heads so that they could be recognized, because he wanted to mete exemplary punishment upon the Chololtecas and Mexicas.

Cortés asked the rulers of Chololan to assemble all the highest-ranking nobles and lords in the council chamber, where they usually met, to discuss with them some important matters, because he wanted to leave their city. He also asked that most of the citizens be summoned to the patio of the council chamber so that he could select the required porters. So many arrived, both nobles and commoners, that the patio and the halls around it were overflowing with people. He gathered thirty of the highest-ranking nobles, [fol. 116v] arrested them, and had his men bar the doors so that no one could leave. Then he called for Motecuhçoma's ambassadors and told them that the detained men had confessed to having plotted to betray Cortés on Motecuhçoma's orders, but that he could not believe that their lord would try to kill him and his men. The Mexicas denied the accusation and asserted that they and their lord were innocent of any plotting or betrayal. Cortés had some of the thirty lords killed and a harquebus fired, which was the signal for the Spaniards to come out to the patio and kill the Chololtecas. In less than two hours, they killed more than six thousand people and sacked and burned the most important houses in the city and its temples, including the main temple, where many priests and noblemen had taken refuge and where the majority died.

This act provoked such terror and distress that news of it spread throughout the land. The city, which had been inhabited by merchants and was the richest city in the land, was abandoned in an instant; great quantities of gold, precious stones, cloth, and featherwork were taken as spoils. Cortés, having done this, freed the remaining prisoners with the understanding that they were to bring the people back to the city and restore peace and tranquility. They did this, and in one day the city was fully populated again, and they became allies of Cortés and the Tlaxcaltecas. The confederation saw that the violence and massacre in Chololan had left Cortés and his men with few provisions and so provided him with substantial support. Maxixcatzin and those from his city and Citlalpopo-catzin from the city of Quiahuiztlan along with Axoquentzin, Tlehuexolotzin, Tequitlanotzin, Tzopantzin, Axayacatzin, Mocuetlazatzin, and Tzicuhcoacatl went in person to see Cortés. They offered to aid Cortés in whatever way they could. He thanked them profusely and told them that for now they should go back home. He would let them know when he needed their support and courage, and they left.

During the two weeks that Cortés was in Tlaxcalan, he was always well treated and graciously hosted by the Tlaxcaltecas. While there, the ambassadors from [fol. 117r] Motecuhçoma returned to deliver another message from their lord, along with six bars of very fine gold, many bolts of cloth, and things to eat. They tried to convince him that what was being said about Motecuhçoma was a trick and a lie and that he could rest assured that Motecuhçoma would be a good friend. For confirmation, he had only to go to Mexico, where Motecuhçoma, who desired greatly to see and host him, would be waiting for him. Cortés then gave the order to leave for the city of Mexico.

🌿 CHAPTER [85]

*Which deals with Cortés's journey to the city of Mexico and what
happened to him there, up to Motecuhçoma's imprisonment*

After Cortés left the city of Chololan he spent the night in a place called
Quauhtechcac, which lies in the pass between the volcano and the Sierra Nevada.
The next morning, he saw the lake on which the city of Mexico was built and
many other beautiful towns. He marched with his army and spent the night in the
town of Amequemecan in the palace of the local lord, Cacamatzin, who received
Cortés very hospitably and complained bitterly of Motecuhçoma's excesses. He
set out and spent the night in Iztapalapan in the house of Cuitlahuatzin, brother
of Motecuhçoma and lord of that city. It was there that Cacama, king of Tezcuco
and Motecuhçoma's nephew, came out to greet him with all his court, who bore
him on a litter made of gold. Cacama welcomed Cortés with many gifts of gold
and precious stones and tried to persuade him to stay in Iztapalapan, from where
they would arrange a meeting with his uncle so Cortés could deliver his message.
Cortés did not want to delay his trip any further, so the following day he walked
toward the city of Mexico with a large entourage of lords and noblemen from the
courts of Mexico, Tezcuco, and Tlacopan. They arrived at a fort at the entrance
to the city, where the causeway met the city wall, and more than four thousand
high-ranking men came out to welcome him. They were all finely dressed and
bowed to Cortés as he passed, touching a hand to the ground and kissing it,
which is the way they greet great lords.

Cortés walked farther and, near a bridge, met [fol. 117v] Motecuhçoma, who
was coming on foot to greet him. His nephew King Cacama and his brother
Cuitlahua led him by the arm. The three men walked under a sort of canopy
made of green feathers and very fine gold and jewels, which was being carried
by two noblemen, the captains general of the armies of Mexico and Tezcuco.
Motecuhçoma, Cacama, and Cuitlahua were dressed alike, except that the two
kings wore diadems of gold and jewels on their heads and tassels hung from
the ribbons with which their hair was tied; their shoes were made of gold and
embellished with fine jewels and pearls. As they walked, carpets were laid down
for them to step on. They were followed by three thousand noblemen, their
guards and servants, who were all very finely dressed. When Cortés arrived,
he dismounted from his horse and, showing great respect, bowed deeply to the

kings. He attempted to embrace Motecuhçoma but was prevented from reaching the king. After exchanging elaborate courtesies, Cortés placed a necklace of glass beads that looked like pearls and diamonds around Motecuhçoma's neck. In return, King Motecuhçoma placed around Cortés's neck two chains of very fine gold, set with large red shrimp made of shell, which were very valuable.

After this, Motecuhçoma entrusted Cortés to his nephew Cacama, turned toward the city, and walked ahead with his brother Cuitlahua back to his palace. Cortés followed behind, hand in hand with Cacama. And with pomp and ceremony, they reached Motecuhçoma's magnificent palace, which had belonged to his father, King Axayaca. At the door, Motecuhçoma took Cortés by the hand and led him to a very large hall, where he seated him on an elegant dais and said to him, "Rest and eat, for this is your home. I shall return shortly." Cortés arrived in Mexico on November 8 in the same year of 1519.

Cortés and his men then sat down at the tables and ate while Motecuhçoma ate in his chambers. After he ate, Motecuhçoma went to see him with great ceremony. The king sat with Cortés [fol. 118r] on an elegant dais and spoke to him in earnest, saying that he was very happy to welcome such high-ranking and honorable people to his court and palace and that he was sad that they would think he could ever hurt them. He offered many apologies for insisting that Cortés not enter Mexico. Finally, he told him that his ancestors had prophesied that a great lord, one who had lived in this land in ancient times, would return with his people to give new laws and doctrine and take possession of the land as its ruler. Motecuhçoma said that he believed the king of Spain to be the great lord they had awaited. Then, he gave Cortés a very long account of his wealth and put himself at his service. He had great quantities of jewelry of gold and precious stones, cloth, and other treasures brought in, which he distributed among all the Spaniards, giving to each one what he thought they merited. Then, he bid them farewell.

Cortés spent the first six days studying and assessing the city's layout and features. He was visited and attended by all the great lords of the empire and he, his men, and the six thousand Tlaxcaltecas with him were generously provided for. At the end of those six days, after having considered carefully his precarious situation, he decided to seize Motecuhçoma. It was a very bold and risky move to do this with so few men to such a great and powerful king in his own palace amid more than five hundred thousand vassals—a frightening thing to consider, let alone carry out and get away with. To justify the arrest, he blamed Motecuhçoma for instigating what had happened in Chololan and other places in order to kill Cortés and his companions. Moreover, Quauhpopocatzin—lord of Coyohuacan and one of the grandees of the empire, who served in Nauhtlan as governor of the North Sea coast—had killed nine Spaniards who were with Captain Pedro Dircio on the road from Vera Cruz; Cortés would, if necessary, show Motecuhçoma letters to that effect.[146]

Cortés was walking around thus preoccupied when he passed by a hall and [fol. 118v] noticed that there was a small door that had recently been filled in and painted over. He became suspicious and had it opened up one night. When he went through it, he found other halls and rooms filled with large quantities of gold, featherwork, cloth, and other things of great value and worth. He was astonished by such a large quantity of treasure. He filled in the door again as best he could so that it would not be noticed. The next day, several Tlaxcaltecas and some Spaniards came to tell him that they had learned that Motecuhçoma wanted to kill them and planned to destroy the causeway bridges. However, I have in my possession an original letter signed by the three rulers of this New Spain written to His Majesty, our lord the emperor whom God has in his blessed kingdom, in which they absolve Motecuhçoma and the Mexicas of this and everything else they were accused of. The truth is that the Tlaxcaltecas and those Spaniards fabricated everything because they were fearful and anxious to leave the city and eager to carry off the mountain of riches that had come into their hands.

Be that as it may, given these allegations against Motecuhçoma and the plan Cortés had already devised, he decided not to delay the king's arrest any longer. To that end, he secretly positioned half of the Spaniards to guard the intersections and corners between his quarters and the palace. He sent some of his allies to stand two by two and three by three with their weapons concealed, as he usually carried his. Then he sent word to Motecuhçoma that he was on his way to visit. Motecuhçoma came out to greet him on the stairs with a pleasant demeanor. They entered the hall, along with about thirty Spaniards, and the two conversed for quite some time, as they were accustomed to do. Motecuhçoma gave Cortés some gold medallions to show Cortés how much he loved and valued him; he also showed his esteem during this conversation by urging Cortés to marry one of his daughters. Cortés responded that he was already married and, according to the law of the Gospel, could not have more than one wife. Then, he reached into his pocket and took out the letters from Captain Pedro Dircio. He complained to Motecuhçoma, accusing him of ordering Quauhpopoca to

---

146. Letters from Dircio, as seen later in the text.

kill the nine Spaniards and of plotting against him by having his men [destroy] [fol. 119r] the causeway bridges.

Accused of an evil deed that he never would have considered and that was so beneath his dignity, Motecuhçoma became extremely angry. Enraged and agitated, he said that both allegations were falsehoods and lies. To ascertain the truth, he summoned one of his servants, removed an armband set with a fine stone on which his face was engraved—which was the same as a royal seal—gave it to the servant, and ordered him to go with great speed to summon Quauhpopoca. After the servant was dispatched, Cortés turned to the king and said:

> Lord, it is best that Your Highness be arrested and accompany me to my lodgings, where you will be well treated and served, and I shall preserve your dignity until Quauhpopoca arrives. Forgive me, but there is nothing else I can do. My men would kill me if I were to ignore these things. Order your people to stay calm, because if any harm comes to us, Your Highness will pay for it with your life. Go quietly; your fate is in your own hands.

Motecuhçoma stood there listening to these absurd assertions. He remained silent for a while before saying very gravely, "I am not one to be taken prisoner. Even if I were to consent, my people would not allow it." Cortés responded that he could not avoid imprisonment. They spent more than four hours going back and forth. Motecuhçoma finally agreed to go with him, for he said he would continue to govern as if in his own palace. Motecuhçoma then called his servants and sent them to Cortés's quarters to ready a room for his stay.

All the Spaniards came to the palace, along with many of the noblemen and lords of the city who were the king's relatives and friends. The latter were all sad and tearful, studying his face for a sign that they should free him, but he ordered them to remain calm. They carried Motecuhçoma through the city on a litter embellished with gold and jewels. There was great commotion among his people, who wished to do something to free him. But he [fol. 119v] ordered them to be still, saying that he was not going as a prisoner, but rather as the guest of Cortés and his men. They believed him, because they saw him leave Cortés's house and take care of business as he had before and even go out of the city a league or two to hunt. The only difference they noticed was that Spaniards were always guarding him and, at night, he slept in Cortés's quarters. He joked and had fun with the Spaniards. His own men served him, and the Spaniards allowed him to speak in public and in private with whomever he wanted. He went out as he would normally to the temple to pray and offer sacrifices to his false gods.

He was guarded by eight Spaniards and three thousand Tlaxcaltecas. To test him, one day Cortés told him that his men had taken a quantity of gold jewelry that they found in his house. He responded that they could take whatever they wanted, but they should not touch the feathers, because they were the treasure of the gods. If they wanted more gold, he would give it to them.

✳ CHAPTER [86]

Which deals with other things that happened to Cortés in the
city of Mexico; how, after King Motecuhçoma was imprisoned,
Cacama, King of Tezcuco, became upset and sought to free his
uncle and expel the Spaniards from Mexico; and how his brother
Ixtlilxochitl cunningly captured him and delivered him to Cortés

As soon as Cortés took Motecuhçoma prisoner, he tried to prevent him from practicing human sacrifice to his false gods and began to destroy the idols. Motecuhçoma became very upset because his men were set on killing him for having allowed this to happen; they also wanted to kill Cortés for having ordered it. And so, on the advice of Motecuhçoma, Cortés stopped breaking the idols for the time being and contented himself with telling them of the [fol. 120r] blindness in which they lived, enlightening them, and setting them on the path of truth, virtue, and the law of the Gospel. He told them that this had been his main reason for coming. He had not come for riches, for they had not taken anything that had not been given to them. Nor had they laid a hand on their wives and daughters or committed other misdeeds. Their only objective had been the salvation of their souls. For there was no god but the one that the Christians worshiped, triune, eternal, without end, creator and sustainer of all things, ruler of heaven and earth. He presented many other arguments to persuade them of the truth of our holy Catholic faith, loathing their idolatry and the error of their ways. Cortés's good reasoning placated them somewhat. Motecuhçoma eventually promised that there would be no human sacrifice as long as Cortés was in the city. And he authorized a crucifix, an image of our Lady, and a cross to be placed between the two idols of Huitzilopochtli and Tlaloc in the chapel of the main temple, which had a rise of 114 steps.

Motecuhçoma had been held for twenty days, when Quauhpopoca arrived in Mexico with one of his sons and fifteen noblemen, who were blamed for the death of the nine Spaniards. After meeting with Motecuhçoma, he was turned over to Cortés. According to the letter mentioned above and the Mexica accounts, Quauhpopoca was not at fault. Rather, the nine Spaniards had committed certain aggressions and excesses and had been killed by natives from those parts. Cortés went with his men to Motecuhçoma's armory and took all the weapons he could find and did the same in the temples. He took the weapons to the main plaza, where he publicly burned them along with Quauhpopoca, his son, and the fifteen noblemen who had accompanied him. This act was no less bold than his previous ones. Prior to this, he put Motecuhçoma in [fol. 120v] shackles and threatened him in order to frighten him further. Even though Cortés then removed the shackles and offered to let him go, Motecuhçoma was so afraid that he did not want to return to his house. Meanwhile, Cortés looked for information to determine how large and wealthy the kingdoms of Motecuhçoma, his nephew Cacama, and Totoquihuatzin of Tlacopan were and learn about all the assets of these three rulers' empire—its gold and silver mines, the distance to the South Sea, and whether there was a better port than Vera Cruz for Spanish ships on the North Sea. Cortés asked Motecuhçoma about all of this, and Motecuhçoma gave him a complete response to every question, because he never hid anything from him.

Cortés sent people to reconnoiter the land and probe its secrets and assess the size and strength of the cities; they returned with samples of gold and news of allies that they found there. According to accounts from the city of Tezcuco, some Spaniards were dispatched to Tezcuco with Nezahualquentzin and Tetlahuehuetzquititzin, two of King Cacama's brothers, who were among the many natives of the city of Tezcuco who served Cortés and his men. They were to visit it and assess its size, power, and strength and also collect the gold stored in the king of Tezcuco's treasury. These two princes arrived at the palace that their grandfather King Nezahualcoyotzin had built in the city of Mexico in order to leave with the Spaniards in large canoes. While there, a messenger from Motecuhçoma arrived, took Nezahualquentzin aside, and told him that his uncle the king beseeched him to treat well the Spaniards going to Tezcuco and, in view of Motecuhçoma's plight, [fol. 121r] give them as much gold as they could as soon as possible.

The Spaniards thought that Motecuhçoma's messenger and Nezahualquentzin were conspiring, so one of them approached Nezahualquentzin, beat him, and took him prisoner to Captain Cortés, who had him hanged immediately. This greatly aggrieved Cacamatzin, who sent Icpacxochitzin, another of his brothers, in place of Nezahualquentzin, to go with Tetlahuehuetzquititzin and the Spaniards. They surveyed the city and communicated with Ixtlilxochitl. Then they gathered all the gold from Nezahualcoyotzin's treasury and filled to the brim a very large ark that was two fathoms long, one fathom wide, and one fathom deep. The Spaniards, who numbered about twenty, were not satisfied. They ordered Tetlahuehuetzquititzin and the rest of the city's noblemen to collect more gold, because what they had taken from the king's treasury was not enough. So, each of the noblemen took gold from his own coffers, which altogether was as much as the first amount. They took it to Cortés, and he was amazed to see such a large quantity of gold and unnerved when his men described the size and strength of the city of Tezcuco and the tremendous power it had. But he was glad to have Ixtlilxochitl as an ally because he was the most feared and respected person in the entire kingdom.

Cortés thought he should seize Cacama. But even though Cacama was there in the city of Mexico, Cortés did not dare arrest him because, first, Cacama was a very bellicose, spirited, and fearless man and, second, because it appeared to Cortés that Cacama abhorred and was offended by the imprisonment of his uncle Motecuhçoma. Seeing that the excess and impudence of Cortés and his men grew greater each day, Cacama bitterly scolded [fol. 121v] all the Mexica nobles for allowing a handful of foreigners to perpetrate such insults without killing them. They defended themselves by saying that the king, their lord, forbade them from taking up arms to free him and restoring the honor that the foreigners had taken from him. The Spaniards had disgraced him by imprisoning him; burning the blameless Quauhpopoca, his son, and relatives, along with the weapons and ammunition that they maintained for the city's defense and protection; stealing the treasures of the king and the gods; and the shameless acts and effronteries they committed every day. Even though the Mexica nobles witnessed all of this, they pretended not to see it so as not to anger their king, who remained such a devoted friend to the Spaniards. When Cacama saw the Mexicas' lack of bravery and resolve, he left the city and went to Tezcuco to gather his forces and liberate his uncle, the city, and the Mexica nobles from the servitude and dishonor in which they lived and also to avenge the unjust deaths of his brother Nezahualquentzin, Quauhpopoca, and the other noblemen who were his allies and relatives.

When Cacama arrived in the city of Tezcuco he was welcomed by his brothers Coanacochtzin and Ixtlilxochitl, who were in charge of governing the city and kingdom. They discussed his plans to raise an army to take to the city of Mexico. Ixtlilxochitl said they should discuss this further and convene a war council in the palace at the forest of Tetepetzinco, since it was on the lake. From there, they could scout the city of Mexico and decide where best to enter with the army without [fol. 122r] being noticed by the Spaniards. They gathered more than one hundred thousand men to carry out this plan. This army was to go from the palace compound of Oztoticpac to Tetepetzinco by land while King Cacama was to go with his brothers Ixtlilxochitl and Coanacochtzin in a large canoe. Cacama, who never suspected what was about to happen, put his trust in his brothers Ixtlilxochitl and Coanacochtzin. As soon as they boarded the canoe, Cacama was seized, taken to Mexico, and handed over to Cortés. This deed helped clear many obstacles from Cortés's path and facilitated the introduction of our holy Catholic faith. For King Cacama was strong, bold, and courageous; neither Cortés nor Cacama's uncle Motecuhçoma would have been able to prevent him from accomplishing his goals were it not for the friendship that Ixtlilxochitl always showed Cortés and the Spaniards.

🌿 CHAPTER [87]

Which deals with how King Motecuhçoma and the rest of the lords of the empire swore loyalty to the king of Castile and the rest that happened to Cortés up until he apprehended Pánfilo de Narváez, who was coming to challenge him

After Cortés had seized and imprisoned King Motecuhçoma and King Cacama, uncle and nephew, he told them to gather all the lords of the empire so he could explain his reasons for coming, begin the process of conversion, and establish our holy Catholic faith. Therefore, the kings issued a general summons to all the grandees and lords of the empire. When everyone arrived, they assembled in a large hall, arranged on seats and thrones according to rank. Motecuhçoma was in the middle, and at his sides sat his nephew King Cacama and his father-in-law, Totoquihuaztli, the king of Tlacopan. Cortés allowed them to discuss this business at length, [fol. 122v] though he had them under guard. Motecuhçoma took the floor and began a long speech. And, among the many things he mentioned in support of his position, he said that he thanked God for having granted him the opportunity to meet the Christians and learn of the great king whose arrival his ancestors had long awaited, and he was certain that it was none other than the one who had sent the Spaniards who were in his court. And if it had been determined from on high that the empire of the three rulers—Culhuas, Aculhuas, and Tepanecas—should fall, he would not resist the will of God. Rather, he would eagerly and willingly swear allegiance to the king of Castile and recognize him as his sovereign lord, under whose protection he hoped to live. He begged them on bended knee to do the same, for he believed it to be in their best interest. Motecuhçoma said all this with so many tears and sighs that his men, along with Cortés and the men with him, were greatly moved.

After they had cried and sat in silence for some time, Motecuhçoma made a solemn vow, pledging his loyalty to King don Carlos, our lord of glorious memory. His nephew Cacama and the king of Tlacopan, Totoquihuatzin, followed suit, and with them, all the grandees and lords of the empire who were present. They all promised to be King don Carlos's good and loyal vassals. Then, to guarantee their loyalty, they gave to Cortés as hostages some princes and princesses who were children and siblings of these three kings, along with many gifts and presents of gold, precious stones, featherwork, cloth, and riches for the king, their new lord. At their command, the rest of the grandees and lords did the same. According to the accounts and paintings from Tezcuco, Cacama and his two brothers Coanacochtzin and Ixtlilxochitl gave four of their brothers as hostages—the Princes Tecocoltzin, Tecpaxochitzin, Huitzcacamatzin, and Tenancacalitzin—along with four sisters. [fol. 123r] Cortés gave them many assurances, promising that they would always be well treated and remain the lords of all the empire and of all they possessed, just as before. Then, he began to orchestrate the conversion of the natives, telling them that, since they were now vassals of the king of Spain, they must become Christians just as he was. Some were baptized, but not many. And although Motecuhçoma asked to be baptized and knew some of the prayers such as the Ave Maria and the Credo, it was postponed until the next major feast day, which was Easter. Such was his misfortune, however, that he did not live to receive such a blessing. Our people, hindered and harried by events, neglected his baptism, and everyone lamented that Motecuhçoma died unbaptized.

Everything was going well for Cortés, and his plans were moving along swiftly, when Pánfilo de Narváez arrived at the port in Vera Cruz with ten ships, nine hundred Spaniards, many horses, artillery, and everything necessary to capture or kill Cortés. Narváez came on behalf of Diego Velázquez, the governor of Cuba, accusing Cortés of being insubordinate and usurping Velázquez's authority by making himself the leader on the mainland, assuming the title of captain general and chief justice, and establishing a settlement there. The Hieronymite friars and all the judges of the royal tribunal in Santo Domingo had sought to prevent Diego Velázquez from sending Narváez. Judge Figueroa was dispatched to Cuba on their and the king's behalf with the express purpose of prohibiting this expedition, threatening to denounce Velázquez to His Majesty, since this would greatly delay the conversion and conquest of these lands. Nonetheless, they were unable to stop him.

No sooner had Narváez's fleet arrived at Vera Cruz than Motecuhçoma learned of it, and he immediately informed Cortés, telling him that he should now prepare to leave. Motecuhçoma had already asked him to do so previously, but Cortés had given the excuse that he had no ships in which to go. Upon confirming that the news was true, Cortés became very upset. Intending to [fol. 123v] resolve this development peacefully, he wrote to Pánfilo de Narváez, pleading with him not to obstruct the conversion of these people but, instead, to join him, for with little effort the two of them could render a remarkable service to God and their king. Narváez paid no heed, for he believed that he could easily apprehend Cortés.

Narváez would spread news among the natives that he had only come to cut off Cortés's head and set Motecuhçoma free. Cortés was a fugitive, thief, and traitor to his lord the king, and the king was very angry about how Cortés had insulted Motecuhçoma. In this way, he would attempt to get in Motecuhçoma's good graces. This angered many of those who accompanied Narváez. Moreover, Judge Ayllón warned Narváez on behalf of the king, under penalty of death, not to be so heavy handed, because impeding the baptism and conversion of those people would greatly offend God and the king. At this, Narvaéz arrested Ayllón and sent him to Diego Velázquez, but he escaped and went to Santo Domingo. Narváez was so brazen that he tried Cortés in absentia, sentenced him to death, and publicly declared war against him. The people in Vera Cruz laughed at this, even those in Narváez's own company.

Cortés nonetheless tried to appeal to Narváez with reasoned arguments. He wrote many letters to him asking for peace but, when he saw that his efforts were in vain, decided to go see him in person. First, he told his men what he planned to do. Then he told Motecuhçoma that he only wanted to go to Vera Cruz to prohibit those who arrived with the fleet from doing any harm in territory belonging to the kingdom of Mexico and tell them not to leave without him, because he was almost ready to depart. He also begged Motecuhçoma to remain there with his Spaniards so that the Mexicas would not harm them. He assured him that he would return quickly and requested some people to accompany him. Motecuhçoma, along with Cacama and Totoquihuatzin, promised that they would and [fol. 124r] provided the people necessary for the trip. And they asked if he would mind if they celebrated a very important festival called Toxcatl, held every year, which would be done without human sacrifice, since Cortés had already forbidden that. Cortés told them to celebrate as they saw fit and that he would leave Captain Pedro de Alvarado in charge with 150 of his men. Accompanied by another 250 of his men and some of his native allies, Cortés left Mexico for Vera Cruz. On the way, he learned that Narváez was in Cempoalan. Cortés's cunning was such that he arrived swiftly and caught Narváez off guard. Losing only two of his men, Cortés seized Narváez and had him taken under heavy guard to Vera Cruz. Then all of those who had come with Narváez joined Cortés without much persuading, because most of them had been following Narváez reluctantly.

 **CHAPTER [88]**

Which deals with the unfortunate deaths of the Mexica lords
and nobles at the hands of Captain Pedro de Alvarado and his
men—which caused the Mexicas to rebel and endangered our
men, up until they were forced to flee the city of Mexico—and
the deaths of the great Motecuhçoma, Cacama, and other lords

While Cortés was in the port of Vera Cruz dealing with Narváez, as discussed above, the Mexicas celebrated the great festival called Toxcatl, which always falls around Easter. And as Cortés had prohibited human sacrifice, they simply planned a grand ceremonial dance in the patio of the main temple, where all the Mexica nobility gathered, lavishly adorned with all their jewelry of gold and precious stones and other finery. According to the histories of the city of Tezcuco that I follow and the letter that I have referred to previously, when the festivities were at their peak and the [fol. 124v] Mexicas were oblivious to the ambush that awaited them, certain Tlaxcaltecas seeking to take revenge on their enemies approached Captain Pedro de Alvarado, who was in charge while Cortés was away, with a false accusation. The Tlaxcaltecas were motivated, on the one hand, by bitterness, because they remembered how, in similar festivals, the Mexicas would regularly sacrifice a great number of Tlaxcalteca captives. On the other hand, they realized that this was the best opportunity to grab as much plunder as possible and satisfy their greed, which up until that time, they had not had a chance to do. Cortés would not have allowed these acts or believed their accusations, because he always acted sensibly and in a way that would advantage him. But it did not take much to convince Alvarado, for he was of the same mind as the Tlaxcaltecas. Moreover, Alvarado saw that all the lords and rulers of the empire were present at the festival and, if they were dead, it would be easy to subjugate their people.

Thus, Alvarado left some of his men to guard Motecuhçoma and his nephew Cacama and with utmost secrecy and stealth, he went to the plaza, or patio, of the main temple. Some of the Spaniards and the Tlaxcaltecas blocked the doors, while Alvarado and the rest of the Spaniards rushed in and slaughtered the unfortunate Mexicas in a great bloodbath. Since the Mexicas had never considered the possibility of such an attack, they were unprepared and unarmed. In a very brief span of time the Spaniards killed almost everyone there, and then they and the Tlaxcaltecas carried off great spoils and riches. Hearing the uproar and outcry, all the people of the city came to their lords' aid and drove Alvarado and the rest of his companions and allies back to their quarters, where Motecuhçoma and Cacama were. Seeing their lords so heinously betrayed, the Mexicas would have killed all of them and brought their houses down upon them, if it had not been for the kings, who ordered that they cease fighting, and because nightfall caused the crowd to disperse. In spite of all this, the Mexicas continued to supply the Spaniards with food, for they saw that their kings desired and ordered it.

Cortés was on his way back from Vera Cruz, victorious and well reinforced with one thousand soldiers and one hundred horses, when he learned that the Mexicas had risen up against those he had left [fol. 125r] behind and, if it had not been for Motecuhçoma, they would already be dead. Hearing this news, he hurried to the city of Tezcuco, where he regrouped and rested. He was given food and drink and informed of all that had happened by his close friend and ally Ixtlilxochitl, who gave him a full account and told him that even in the city of Tezcuco there were those, relatives and friends of those killed by Pedro de Alvarado and his companions in Mexico, who were angry. After planning how he would enter the city, Cortés left Tezcuco for Mexico on the feast of St. John, July 24, of the year 1520. He found the city at peace, though the residents did not come out to welcome him or celebrate his return. Motecuhçoma was very pleased with his arrival and his companions even more so, especially because he returned so well reinforced and victorious. They gave him an account of the travails each had suffered. The day after his return, Cortés harshly reprimanded the nobleman responsible for the city market, because it had not been held as usual. This rebuke reignited the rebellion through most of the city, because the residents were so fed up with the excesses and cruelties committed against them that it took little to provoke them.

Thus began a most cruel war between them. In the first battle, the Mexicas killed four Spaniards. The next day, they injured many. Every day, the Mexicas attacked them relentlessly and did not give them a moment's rest. On the seventh day, they attacked the lodgings of the Spaniards so ferociously that Cortés was forced to send King Motecuhçoma to the top of a high tower to command them to lay down their weapons. Motecuhçoma did it willingly and pleaded with his vassals to cease their fighting. But they were so infuriated, ashamed, and offended by their king's cowardice and how beholden he was to the Spaniards that they refused to hear him. They responded with angry insults, decrying his cowardice, and they threw arrows and stones, one of which hit him on the head. Within four days he died of his injury. Thus did this most powerful king meet his wretched end. No king in this new world, before or [fol. 125v] since, has equaled him in majesty or in arrogance, for he found himself to be the most prosperous, powerful, and wealthy in the world and all but demanded to be worshiped. Motecuhçoma was a man of medium stature, thin and very dark, with little beard. In matters of war and government, he was more cunning and crafty than valorous. He was a strict judge in matters related to preserving respect for his dignity and royal majesty. And he was a very severe man, though wise and gracious.

The death of this most powerful King Motecuhçoma brought severe consequences for Cortés and his men, because once the Mexicas realized that he was dead, they redoubled their efforts against our men. They felt little sadness at his death, because he had offended them by showing such favor to the Spaniards and such timidity when he allowed himself to be captured and mistreated by them. They then swore allegiance to his nephew Cacama, even though he was imprisoned, since he possessed all the qualities necessary for their defense, honor, and reputation. They intended to free him, but they were thwarted because the Spaniards, who were about to flee the city that night, stabbed Cacama forty-seven times before they left. Because Cacama was bellicose and had defended himself against them and acted bravely even as a prisoner, they felt it necessary to take his life in this way. After his death, which was greatly mourned by the Mexicas, they selected and swore allegiance to Cuitlahua, lord of Iztapalapan and Motecuhçoma's brother and captain general. Then Cuitlahua waged brutal war against our men and never allowed them any rest. There were great skirmishes and fights between our men and Cuitlahua, until Cortés lost hope of remaining in Mexico. He decided to leave the city, but he and his men faced such dangers and difficulties that Cortés was hardly able to take any of the wealth he had accumulated. Those of his men who tried to take riches with them were the only ones to die.

Cortés left Mexico on July 10 of the same year 1520. He left at night because he believed it to be safer, but [fol. 126r] the Mexicas noticed his escape and pursued him. They killed 450 Spaniards, 4,000 Indian allies, and 46 horses at the place which they now call the Leap of Alvarado and which the Mexicas call Tolteca Acalopan, which is the name of the canal in the neighborhood of Mazatzintamalco. Here and in other places where our men faced danger as they retreated, many nobles died, both Cortés's hostages and his allies. Among others, there were four Mexica lords named Çoacoatzin, Tzoacpopocatzin, Çepactzin, and Tencuecuenotzin, two of whom were sons of King Motecuhçoma. And three of the four daughters of King Nezahualpiltzintli who were given to Cortés as hostages died, though in a way one was set free, because she died having been baptized. She was named doña Juana; because Cortés loved her greatly and she was days away from giving birth, he made her a Christian. Another two sons of King Nezahualpiltzintli died. Xiuhtototzin, one of the grandees of the kingdom and lord of Teotihuacan, also died during this escape; he was Ixtlilxochitl's captain general and, on his behalf, had supported Cortés and his men.

🌿 CHAPTER [89]

Which deals with how Cortés with his men retreated to
Tlaxcalan, where he regrouped, and what happened during
this time

That night, having suffered such great losses, Cortés fled with his men through
the highlands of Tlacopan, toward the hill of Totoltepec, which today they call
our Lady of Good Remedy, where the queen of the angels miraculously helped
and aided them. According to the Tlaxcalteca account cited above, Captain
Cortés stopped there. He was sad, sorrowful, and weeping as he recalled, on
one hand, the many companions and allies left dead at the hands of his enemies
and, on the other, the clear miracle of his escape along with most of his followers
through the intercession of the queen of the angels, his protector the apostle St.
Peter, and the protector of the Spanish armies St. James.

He saw nearby Acxotecatl, Maxixcatzin's brother Quetzalpopocatzin, Chal-
chiuhtecatl Calmecahua, and other Tlaxcalteca noblemen and lords, as well
as hostage lords who were sons of Nezahualpiltzintli, the king of Tezcuco, and
Motecuhçoma, including Tecocoltzin and Tocpacxochitzin. He told them through
Marina that they should not interpret his grief and sadness as a lack of courage,
which it was not. Rather, it was because of the many friends and companions
that had died and also because of the great mercies that God had shown him
through the intercession of his blessed mother and his [fol. 126v] holy apostles.
He said that he did not fear the Culhuas, nor did he fear his own death, because
if they were to kill him and everyone with him, there would be no shortage of
other Christians to conquer them. The law of the Gospel would be established
in this land, regardless of any further obstacles and resistance. He gave his word
to all the lords who were loyal to him that if he conquered and pacified the land
and emerged victorious, he would not only preserve them in their titles and
dominions but also add to them in the name of the king of Spain, his lord, and
give them a share of all he conquered and subjugated.

These lords and noblemen all consoled and encouraged him. He spent the
night in Quauhximalpan, where he skirmished with the enemy. The next day,
he arrived in Teocalhueyacan, after fighting with the Mexicas all along the way.
He stopped there with his army for one day, and they ate nothing but grass.

Then he continued on his path and spent the night in Tepotzotlan, where he met with little resistance and rested for a day. The next day, he arrived in Aichqualco and spent the night. And the next day he arrived in Aztaquemecan, where he fought a bloody and perilous battle; a captain named Çinacatzin, famed native of Teotihuacan who fought on the side of the Mexicas, killed Martín de Gamboa's horse. And that night they stayed there and ate the horse.

The next day, after a great deal of effort, they came to the plains of the province of Otompan, where they were attacked by more than two hundred thousand men who had been pursuing them. They fought a very fierce battle, surrounding Cortés and his men so that there was no way for them to flee or retreat. Cortés was in the depths of despair but was not one to die without a fight. He spurred his horse, calling on God and St. Peter, his protector, and, fighting like a rabid lion, broke through the enemy line and reached the [fol. 127r] royal banner of Mexico, held by Zihuatcatzin, the captain general of their army. The banner was a net of gold they call *matlaxopilli*. Cortés speared Zihuatcatzin, who died at his feet, and he took the banner from him. This deed dismayed the Mexicas and they all began to flee, while our men regained their strength and courage and killed untold numbers of them. This was a miracle. Captain Cortés suffered a bad head injury and was missing a piece of his scalp; all our men and allies were stricken, injured, dying of hunger, and miserable; and they were surrounded by two hundred thousand men who were tearing them apart like rabid tigers. Cortés's valor and faith were such that, as soon as he called on God, on God's mother, and on his protector the apostle St. Peter, while his companions called on St. James, the tide turned in his favor, and according to popular opinion among the natives, these saints appeared to support and defend him. He kept the royal Mexica banner as a trophy from this perilous battle and carried it in triumph as he continued on his journey. This battle occurred at the place called Metepec.

When they arrived at the place called Teyocan, he fought another skirmish, in which innumerable enemy warriors died; this was the last he had during his retreat. He spent the night in Temalacayocan and the next day continued on to Hueyotlipan, where he spent the night. At a place they call Xaltelolco, which is at the foot of the hill called Quauhtepetl, he thanked his Tlaxcalteca allies and everyone else who had been present in these battles and retreat and promised, in the name of His Majesty, that besides preserving them in their titles and dominions, he would increase them and grant them new favors and rewards. He was welcomed in Xaltelolco by Citlalquiauhtzin, who had come in the name of the confederation of Tlaxcalan with a large amount of food and drink for him and all his men. He arrived in Hueyotlipan, where they also gave him provisions, and spent the night. The next day, Maxixcatzin came out to greet him in the name of the confederation. To repay Maxixcatzin's good will, generosity, and hospitality, Cortés gave him the royal Mexica banner, which he esteemed greatly and included in his coat of arms.

[fol. 127v]

 CHAPTER [90]

Which deals with the warm welcome that Cortés received in Tlaxcalan, all that he did in that city while he recuperated, and the death of King Cuitlahua and the elections of Quauhtemoc, Coanacochtzin, and Tetlepanquetzal

After Cortés and his men had rested in Hueyotlipan, Maxixcatzin, along with many other lords and more than fifty thousand of his Tlaxcalteca and Huexotzinca allies, urged him to go to Tlaxcalan. There, the four rulers and all the lords of the confederation came out to meet him and take him with great celebration into the city, where they treated his injuries and provided him with food, drink, and other forms of hospitality. Here I am following the aforementioned account from Tlaxcalan. The great majority of what I have written and shall continue to write is based on the accounts and paintings that were written by the native lords of this land just after its conquest, who were present for the events that occurred in those times. Matters related to our Spaniards and the most noteworthy events of those times are all described in great detail by Francisco López de Gómara in his *Historia de las Indias,* by Antonio de Herrera in his chronicle, by the Reverend Father friar Juan de Torquemada in his *Monarquía indiana,* and by an eyewitness, the invincible don Hernando Cortés, Marquis of the Valley, in the letters and accounts that he sent to His Majesty. Curious readers will find in these texts as much as they want to know. To return to the translation of the aforementioned accounts and paintings, the one from Tlaxcalan says that Cortés and his men stayed in the palace of Xicotencatl, as he had the first time. Among other things he told him regarding the successful conquest of the city of Mexico and the revenge for the wrongs described above, Xicotencatl said:

> Be welcome, lord, and rest. Consider this your home and country. I was told that you had considered regrouping in Hueyotlipan and then returning to Mexico to subjugate the Culhuas and punish them for their rebellion and the wrongs they committed against you, the Tlaxcaltecas, and your other allies. In my opinion, this would not have been a wise decision. Now that you are here, I beg you to rest with your men and recover. I believe that you should first subjugate Tepeyacac, which is a large and well-fortified

province where the Mexicas have [fol. 128r] positioned the bulk of their army to attack you from the rear and harm your allies. Thus, it would be better to subdue these people and the rest who surround us first, so that you may proceed more safely with your endeavor, which is important to all of us.

This all seemed very good to Cortés, and it was decided that they would follow Xicotencatl's advice.

While these events were taking place in Tlaxcalan, smallpox—which was transmitted by a black man who had come with Narváez—wrought such great and widespread damage that many thousands of natives died. King Cuitlahua, who had governed for only forty-seven days, was among those who died. To replace him, the Mexicas selected Quauhtemoctzin to be their king. He was eighteen years old and a very famous captain, which was advantageous given the challenge the Mexicas were facing at the time; he was also high priest of their false gods and lord of Tlatelolco. Totoquihuatzin, the king of Tlacopan, also died from smallpox. Those from Tlacopan selected as their king the crown prince, Tetlepanquetzaltzin. In the city of Tezcuco, after the death of King Cacama, they selected Coanacochtzin. All three were men of great valor and courage and fought on the side of the Mexicas. At their coronations, they held lavish feasts and sacrificed many captives to their false gods, including Spaniards, Tlaxcaltecas, Huexotzincas, Chololtecas, and other allies of Cortés who were captured in the battles and during the retreat.

Circumstances being what they were, the three kings debated what they should do: to either expel the Spaniards from the lands of the empire or kill the remaining few along with their leader, Cortés. They decided that the best way to do this would be to win over to their side all those who had protected the Spaniards and allowed them into their lands and territories. They would offer them great rewards, liberties, and lasting peace to ensure that no unknown foreigners would ever again use any of them as a means to conquer and rule over them all. They would also make peace with the kings and lords of the distant regions, with whom the armies of the empire had been continuously at war. They would establish peace with everyone on whatever terms necessary, even if it meant returning lands and regions that the empire had won. Then, they would ask them for their aid and support in crushing and annihilating our Spanish nation.

To this end, they sent out their ambassadors to negotiate [fol. 128v] aggressively in accordance with their plan, emphasizing the cruelty and tyranny allegedly perpetrated against them by the Christians, who stole their wealth and lands. They also fortified the city of Mexico as best they could. Six of the ambassadors they dispatched, individuals possessed of authority and respect, went to the confederation of Tlaxcalan. They delivered their message to the confederation with great eloquence, trying to persuade them to kill or expel Cortés and his men, as they were greedy foreigners who were eager to steal their domains. Among other arguments they presented to support their cause, they reminded them that they were all related and of the same lineage and, for this reason and leaving aside past fighting and disputes, they had an obligation to support their own nation over a few foreigners who had come to swindle them out of their land. They promised on behalf of their kings that, henceforth, they would forever keep the peace between them and they would share in the tribute from the empire's subject provinces. These ambassadors knew so well what to say to the confederation that almost all of the lords, after discussing and debating their proposal at length, were persuaded to join the Mexica side. They said to each other that the Culhuas and their partners were correct and if the kings of the empire did as they promised, it would be better to support the empire over the Spaniards, for they still did not know what would come of these foreigners' plans.

Of the four rulers, the most sympathetic to this position was Xicotencatl, the eldest of the four leaders of the confederation. He reminded them of earlier times when he was a young man and captain general, when they enjoyed great peace and accord with the kings of Tezcuco and Mexico, their close relatives. He said also that, during the first wars they had, when they brought down the king of Azcapotzalco, who was tyrannizing the empire, and conquered [fol. 129r] some of the distant provinces, he and the whole of the confederation had always been on the empire's side, shared in the best of the spoils, and received part of the tribute and land from the conquered territories. Then later, due to everyone's desire to conduct military training and obtain sacrificial victims for the gods, that friendship and accord was lost, and anger, enmity, and rancor arose between them. Thus, he argued that it would undoubtedly be highly beneficial to the confederation to accept the proposal of the Mexica lords as described by their ambassadors.

Maxixcatzin argued against everything that Xicotencatl said and very emphatically sided with Cortés and his men, offering many reasons and justifications. Miraculously, in the middle of this debate, which was taking place in the hall and oratory of Xicotencatl where they had placed the aforementioned cross, all of those present saw a cloud descend and cover the cross, and the hall became dark and gloomy. Witnessing this miracle intensified Maxixcatzin's passion and resolve to defend the Christians to the point that he came to blows with Xicotencatl the Younger, who fiercely supported his father's position. Maxixcatzin shoved him down the stairs at the entrance to the hall. After all the assembled councilmen witnessed such a great miracle, they changed their minds and sided with Maxixcatzin. Then they dismissed the ambassadors from Mexico, telling them that they would support and defend the Christians and were willing to give their lives for them, along with those of their wives and children. And, just as they dismissed them, the cloud cleared, the hall became bright and radiant, and the cross was resplendent. From that point on, they supported, served, and aided Cortés and his men with much greater conviction.

While these ambassadors failed, those who went to the province and kingdom of Michhuacan [fol. 129v] and other places brought back good news to the Mexica lords, saying that everyone offered aid and support to kill or expel Cortés and his men and punish those who were on their side. The Mexica lords were gladdened by this news and their allies encouraged. Meanwhile, Cortés's allies pledged to win or to die trying, so as to avoid falling into the hands of their enemies, who would treat any survivors worse than slaves. They thus threw in their lot with Cortés.

Cortés was recovering in the city of Tlaxcalan, and when he least expected it, all his men came to him very upset and determined to leave him. They demanded, in the name of His Majesty, that Cortés get them out of that land. This revolt distressed Cortés greatly, but he also knew how to bring them back around and reassure them. And everyone changed their mind and pledged to die with him wherever he might lead them. After twenty days, he decided to attack Tepeyacac, as Xicotencatl had advised. Thus, he gathered more than forty thousand Tlaxcaltecas, Huexotzincas, and Chololtecas. The Tlaxcalteca captain was Tianquiztlatoatzin, and he was accompanied by the sons of Xicotencatl and other lords from the four capital cities. He spent the first night in Tzonpantzinco and the next day organizing his forces. On the third day, he met enemy fighters at Zacatepec, where they had a bloody battle and many of the Mexicas and Tepeyacas died. On the fourth day, he camped in Acatzinco, where he captured those who had fled. On the sixth day, he entered the city of Tepeyacac without any resistance because the inhabitants and their Mexica defenders had abandoned it. After Cortés found and enslaved many of them, he remained there for twenty days to pacify that province and destroy their idols. He also founded a town he called Segura de la Frontera.

Cortés then turned toward Chololan and, after resting there, attacked Quauhquecholan, which quickly surrendered to him, and expelled the Mexicas.

After resting for a day here, he attacked Itzocan and defeated and subjugated it, though with difficulty, for they defended themselves with the help of the Mexicas, [fol. 130r] and many died. He spent twenty days here issuing orders for all that was necessary to carry out the conquest. He stayed at the palace of Ahuecatzin, lord of that province. From there, he returned to Tepeyacac, and the Tlaxcaltecas returned to their land. After staying in Tepeyacac for a few days, he returned to Tlaxcalan and found that many of its lords and noblemen had died from the smallpox sickness brought by the black man who came with Narváez, which had already spread through the land. Among those who died was Cortés's great friend and ally Maxixcatzin; Cortés lamented deeply his death and mourned him. Before leaving for the province of Tepeyacac, he sent forces to subjugate the provinces of Zacatlan and Xalatzinco and secure the strategic road to Vera Cruz. These provinces fought on the Mexica side and had killed some Spaniards. He dispatched twenty men on horse, two hundred foot soldiers, and many allies from Tlaxcalan and other places to go and conquer them.

🌿 CHAPTER [91]

Which deals with Cortés's strategy to march on the city of
Mexico and his progress until he reached the city of Tezcuco

At this time, the carpenters were very busy making the boards and beams necessary for the brigantines that Cortés ordered built to conquer the city of Mexico.
And, as he saw that the work was fairly advanced, he sent to Vera Cruz for all the
iron and nails they had, along with sails, rigging, and other things necessary for
the ships. On the second day of Christmas of the same year of 1520, he reviewed
his troops. He had 40 horsemen, whom he formed into four squadrons, and 550
foot soldiers, whom he divided into nine companies of 60 men each. And so as
to sustain the enthusiasm of his allies and companions, he spread the word that
he wanted to lay siege to the city of Mexico and not let up until it was destroyed.
The Tlaxcaltecas and other allies were very pleased because they greatly desired
to take revenge on the city that had so cruelly oppressed them. He gave a long
speech to his men, repeating what he had said on other occasions. He implored
them, since they had already begun to spread the faith in Christ our Lord [fol.
130v] among the pagan idolaters, not to falter until they had rid these most
bountiful lands of the idolatries and abominations that so offended God. Besides
their rewards in heaven, in this world they would gain great honor and untold
riches to provide comfort in old age. Everyone expressed their great commitment,
offering Cortés their lives and all they possessed. They pledged to hold inviolate
certain ordinances that he established befitting the service of God and his law,
which they followed. These were all righteous acts by a good and Christian
captain. Later he spoke again at length to the Tlaxcalan confederation, and all
the Tlaxcaltecas and his other allies present there offered their lives and wealth
to the cause of the war against Mexico.

Before Cortés left Tepeyacac, he wished to find out if the king of Tezcuco, who
at that point was Coanacochtzin, was his ally, because from Tezcuco Cortés could
easily lay siege to Mexico and his rear would be protected. He dispatched a nobleman named Huitzcacamatzin—a Tezcuco native and one of Coanacochtzin's
relatives who had accompanied Cortés when he retreated to Tlaxcalan—to tell
King Coanacochtzin that Cortés was determined to continue the war until the
Mexicas were subjugated. He wanted to inform him of his plans so that Coanacochtzin would not engage his forces and prevent him from entering his kingdom.

He reminded Coanacochtzin that he and his subjects had surrendered to our lord King don Carlos at the outset and made many other arguments which were meant to bring Coanacochtzin to his side. Huitzcacamatzin reached Coanacochtzin and delivered his message. But Coanacochtzin, who had sided with the Mexicas, would not hear of it and, instead, cut Huitzcacamatzin into little pieces. When Cortés saw that Huitzcacamatzin was delayed, he dispatched another messenger. He decided to send Tocpacxochitzin, known also as Cuicuitzcatzin and one of the four sons of King Nezahualpiltzintli who had been given as hostages to Cortés. He chose this high-ranking messenger because he would be believed and the matter would be quickly addressed. But when Tocpacxochitzin arrived in the city of Tezcuco and gave his message to his brother the king, Coanacochtzin [fol. 131r] did the same to him as he had done to the first messenger, Huitzcacamatzin.

Meanwhile, because the city and most of the kingdom of Tezcuco had been in great turmoil since the Mexicas had rebelled and Cortés had retreated, Ixtlilxochitl had gone to his farmlands on the outskirts of Tepepolco, one of the provinces subject to Tezcuco. When he learned that his brother Coanacochtzin had killed Cortés's two messengers and prevented Cortés's entry into the kingdom, he left for the city of Tezcuco with the sole purpose of opposing his brother the king and supporting Cortés. He arrived in Tezcuco just as Cortés was preparing to leave Tlaxcalan. In the name of God, Cortés departed from Tlaxcalan with twenty thousand allied warriors on the feast of the Holy Innocents of the year 1520. According to the Tlaxcalteca account that I have cited, he went by way of Tetzmolocan to Tlapechhuacan, reaching this side of the mountains swiftly and without incident. In Tlapechhuacan, Ixtlilxochitzin came out to greet him and gave him a gold banner as a token of peace and a sign of their old friendship. He welcomed him and invited him to the city of Tezcuco, for he would be shown hospitality there. He told Cortés that he was sorry for his troubles and regretted the infighting and rebellions caused by the Mexica lords—who were his uncles and relatives—and those who sided with them. If Cortés found that his brother the king and those from his court were also guilty, he should forgive them, because Ixtlilxochitl had come to apologize on their behalf and place himself at his service.

Cortés was very happy to see Ixtlilxochitl and be received with so much love on Coanacochtzin's behalf, which was what Cortés most wanted. They spent the night in Coatepec, which was subject to the city of Tezcuco. The next day, Monday, the last day of December, they continued on until they reached the city of Tezcuco, where Ixtlilxochitl housed Cortés and his men and provided them with all they required. But King Coanacochtzin knew that Cortés harbored grievances that, at the king's command, forty-five Spaniards and three hundred Tlaxcaltecas had been killed and their spoils from the city of Mexico confiscated. Fearing that [fol. 131v] these and other grievances might bring him to harm and because he had always sided with the Mexicas, Coanacochtzin embarked that very afternoon with all the lords and noblemen who shared his fears. Taking with them their wealth and women, they left for the city of Mexico and abandoned the city of Tezcuco. This dishonorable act threw the residents into chaos. Some of them followed the king over the lake, while others fled to the mountains; Ixtlilxochitl was left alone to try to keep them from leaving. He could not prevent Cortés and his men from seeing the chaos, however, and Cortés, suspecting a trap, wanted to sack the city and punish the instigators. Ixtlilxochitl stopped him and begged him to have pity on these wretched people, who were not at fault. Despite Ixtlilxochitl's efforts, the Tlaxcaltecas and other allies who had come with Cortés nonetheless plundered some of the most important houses of the city and burned most of King Nezahualpiltzintli's palace. The fire consumed everything within the royal archives for all of New Spain. This was one of the greatest losses that these lands ever suffered, because all the memories of their antiquity and other things that served as writings and records were destroyed at that time. Moreover, the craftsmanship of the palace was the best and finest anywhere in the land.

Once calm had been restored to the city, the Tlaxcaltecas, Huexotzincas, and other allies were sent home to their lands. However, the Mexica armies reached and killed many of them in Tlapechhuacan, which lies on the mountain slopes. They would have fared even worse were it not for the aid of Cortés. With his assistance, they managed to gain the slopes of Tetzmolocan, from where they proceeded safely to their homes. Cortés was very fond of Tecocoltzin, who was the last of the four sons of King Nezahualpiltzintli given to him as hostages, so he named him lord of Tezcuco. Ixtlilxochitl was very happy, and he made everyone acknowledge [fol. 132r] and obey Tecocoltzin. He did so because his brother King Coanacochtzin had abandoned the city, and it would not be fitting for someone of Ixtlilxochitl's standing to govern while his brother still lived, for he would be regarded as a usurper. Nevertheless, the kingdom always recognized Ixtlilxochitl as the foremost authority.

According to the accounts and paintings from the province of Chalco, it appears that Omacatzin, Itzcahuetzin, Nequametzin, Quetzalcoatzin, Zitlaltzin, Yaoceuhcatzin, and other lords and noblemen from there assembled and discussed what they should do and whether they should welcome Cortés and his men in peace or join forces with the Mexicas. They sent Zitlaltzin [and] Yaoceuhcatzin to the city of Tezcuco as their ambassadors to ask Ixtlilxochitzin what to do. Ixtlilxochitl, after hearing this message, told them to tell the lords of the province of Chalco that by no means should they take up arms against Cortés and his companions, for doing so would be detrimental to their province. Rather, they should seek to protect and curry favor with the Christians, set down their weapons, and receive the holy Catholic faith in peace. When the lords of Chalco saw Ixtlilxochitl's determination, they quickly sent messengers to Cortés, offering themselves as his allies. Similarly, the towns of Otompan, Huexotla, Coatlichan, Chimalhuacan, and Atenco, which had fought for King Coanacochtzin, joined them. This brought the entire kingdom of Tezcuco to the side of Ixtlilxochitl in support of Cortés and his men. They expelled from their lands the Mexica armies, and whenever necessary, some Spaniards went with them to support them. This was the case with Captain Gonzalo de Sandoval, who went to the province of Chalco and stayed until all the [fol. 132v] Mexicas had been expelled from those lands.

   In the city of Tezcuco, Cortés gathered all he needed to besiege and conquer the city of Mexico. He had them bring the boards and beams that they had been making for the brigantines in the city of Tlaxcalan. They also used some cut in Tezcuco from trees felled in one of their royal forests, which had been planted by the Tolantzincas in the time of Nezahualcoyotzin. Thus, there was more than enough wood, and they began to build and assemble the brigantines. In order to get them into the lake, following Cortés's plans and instructions, Ixtlilxochitl had a deep trench dug, more than half a league long and of sufficient depth, that ran from the great palace of King Nezahualcoyotzin, his grandfather, to the lake. This project lasted fifty days. Ixtlilxochitl ordered a *xiquipil* of workers, which is eight thousand, to labor each day and required that these men be warriors, in an attempt to assess the number of troops that could be deployed solely from the province of Tezcuco, which is called Aculhuacan. He was very happy to find that he had at his disposal two hundred thousand men who would be able to support the Christians in the upcoming campaign. He informed Cortés, who was no less happy to see the great power of the kingdom of Tezcuco, since the Aculhua nation alone could contribute two hundred thousand warriors. Likewise, Ixtlilxochitl gathered all the supplies necessary to sustain the army and garrisons that fought on Cortés's side. He had the maize and beans from the barns and granaries of Tezcuco's subject provinces brought into the city Tezcuco. He fortified the city, especially the great palace of his grandfather King Nezahualcoyotzin, where Cortés and his men were staying, so that if by chance the Mexicas defeated and routed them [fol. 131r] they could take refuge there. Meanwhile, King Quauhtemoc and his allies Coanacochtzin and Tetlepanquetzaltzin had diligently gathered into the city of Mexico people, provisions, and everything else necessary to defend themselves from their enemies and even to attack them if possible.

The empire's ambassadors went out to summon all the lords who had sided with them. As described above, the king of Michhuacan, who was very powerful and his people very bellicose, was one of these. And if God, in his infinite mercy, had not reached down to guide Cortés's endeavors, the king of Michhuacan would have undoubtedly ensured Cortés's defeat. God, however, worked a miracle. The first time the empire's ambassadors went to see Tangajuan, king of Michhuacan, they gave him an extensive account of what Cortés and his men had done in Chololan and what Pedro de Alvarado had done in Mexico, portraying them as cruel tyrants who steal titles and domains. The king's sister was present and heard the ambassadors describe the cruelties of Cortés and his men. She fully believed that this nation would take possession and become lords of this land, as her elders had foretold. In desperation, to escape having to see or hear them, she starved herself to death. It was customary in that land to place the bodies of kings and great lords in a crypt beneath the main temple and hold vigil for several days, after which they would burn the bodies and preserve the ashes. When she died, they did the same for her, as she was the king's sister. Four days after her death, she came back to life and ordered those who were keeping vigil to summon her brother the king, because she had a very important message for him concerning the welfare of the whole kingdom, his subjects and vassals. Everyone there was awestruck and shocked and went to summon the king. When he [fol. 133v] arrived, she told him to remain calm and composed and listen carefully to everything she would make known on behalf of the true God, Lord of heaven and earth. The king listened attentively, and she told him, on behalf of God, to lay down his arms and send away the men he had gathered on the plains of Aballos to go fight for the Mexicas, because they should not impede in any way the advance of these new people, who had come to establish the law of the true God. Rather, they should welcome and receive them peacefully into their kingdom, so that this law could also be established there and this God might be known and worshiped. As proof—besides the great miracle of raising her from the dead and giving her another fifteen years to live—on the day that the main market was held in the kingdom's capital city, a youth would appear in the eastern sky holding a light brighter than the sun in one hand and a sword like the ones wielded by the newcomers in the other. He would pass above the city and disappear in the west. She told him that he should in no way resist this nation, which brought as their defense and protection a cross, the sight of which caused all their enemies to surrender. She had seen the place where those who did not know the true God went; it was a place of intolerable and eternal suffering, and all her parents and grandparents were there. She had likewise seen the place of glory where all those who were saved through the faith and law that these new people brought were rejoicing in the presence of this God.

King Tangajuan was stunned to see her alive again and hear her message, including the vision she told him about. He laid down his weapons and refused to support the Mexicas, sending away the two hundred thousand men he had mustered for that purpose. One hundred thousand of them were Michhuaques, also called Tarascos; the other hundred thousand were Teochichimecas, the most bellicose people [fol. 134r] that ever lived in this New Spain. All that has been written here was taken from the accounts and paintings from the kingdom of Michhuacan, and I heard the story told many times by don Constantino Huitzimengari, a high-ranking nobleman from that province and grandson of King Tangajuan.

❧ CHAPTER [92]

Which deals with the battle of Iztapalapan, Cortés's reconnoitering of Mexico, and the war of Acapichtlan

The Mexicas had not entered the territory of Tezcuco for more than seven days, and neither had our men ventured out, for they were occupied with the fortifications and other preparations necessary to defend themselves and attack the enemy. Cortés left the city with two hundred Spaniards and more than four thousand natives of the city of Tezcuco, along with some from Tlaxcalan and other places allied with him. Ixtlilxochitl was the leader of the Tezcucas. They traveled along the shore of the lake until they reached Iztapalapan. They were spotted from the high outcropping at Tepepolco, and the Mexicas were alerted. Two leagues away from Iztapalapan, our men were attacked from both the water and the land, and the rest of the way they were entangled with the enemy, both those on land and those on the lake. But when they arrived at the city of Iztapalapan, all of the houses on dry land had been abandoned and the people had fled to the houses on the lake. And although they defended themselves and fought fiercely, our men eventually defeated them, driving them back to the water and plundering most of the houses on the lake. More than six thousand of them died. As night fell, Cortés withdrew his men and set fire to some of the houses in that city. He recalled having passed a place on the dike that divided the two lakes where he could be ambushed or attacked by the enemy, so he began marching quickly. When he reached that place, he found that the enemy had broken the dike and let the water through. He was forced to wade across it; some of his allies drowned, and all of the spoils were lost. When day broke, they saw countless canoes filled with warriors who had come to block their path. They continued on their way to Tezcuco, at times fighting warriors who attacked them from the lake. Only one Spaniard died in these skirmishes.

More than eight thousand Tlaxcalteca porters arrived with the boards and beams for the brigantines, along with more than twenty thousand warriors. They came with Captain and Chief Constable Gonzalo de Sandoval leading two hundred Spaniards on foot and sixteen on horseback. During the construction, Cortés decided to reconnoiter the city of Mexico from the surrounding area. He told no one of his intentions because he did not entirely trust the loyalty of the Tezcucas, and he feared that they might warn the Mexicas of his plans. This fear was understandable, given that his enemies were close relatives of the Tezcucas. He was disabused of this notion later, however, when he saw the great loyalty of Ixtlilxochitl and the rest of them. Cortés left with 25 horsemen, 350 footmen, 6 small field cannon, and 32,000 Tlaxcalteca and Tezcuca allies. The Tlaxcalteca captain was Chichimecatl Tecuhtli, and Ixtlilxochitl led the Tezcuca Aculhuas. They spent the night on the plains between Chiuhnauhtlan and Xaltocan, where they clashed with an enemy squadron, which they quickly defeated. The next day, they attacked Xaltocan, a well-fortified settlement in the middle of the lake. Though it belonged to Tezcuco, it had sided with Coanacochtzin and the Mexicas. The inhabitants defended themselves, but they were nonetheless expelled, and a large portion of the town was set ablaze. They spent that night a league away from Xaltocan.

The next day, they left very early in the morning. The enemy met them on the road screaming and shouting. They engaged them until they reached Quauh-titlan, which was abandoned, and they spent the night there. The next day, they continued until they reached Tenaiocan, where they did not meet any resistance. From there, they went to Azcapotzalco and from there to Tlacopan, which was the place Cortés wanted [fol. 135r] to reach in order to survey the city of Mexico. Even though the enemy put up fierce resistance, they expelled them from the city and took control of it. And because it was already late, all they did was take up lodgings in the palace of the king of Tlacopan, which was large enough to accommodate easily Cortés's entire army. The next day, their allies began to sack and burn the whole city. They were there for six days and fought the enemy each day. Cortés finally reached the outskirts of the city of Mexico. He wanted to find out if he could speak to Quauhtemoc and discuss terms for peace, but it proved impossible. Instead, he surveyed the area and determined how best to lay siege to the city of Mexico. He decided to return to Tezcuco to speed the building of the brigantines, so that he might blockade Mexico by water and by land. They camped in Quauhtitlan that night, then in Acolman the next night. And all along the way, they fought skirmishes with the enemy, who, when they saw them going back to Tezcuco, believed them to be retreating in fear. But instead, our men killed many enemy fighters, and the horsemen speared untold numbers of them. The next day at noon, they entered Tezcuco, where they were well received and feasted, and the Tlaxcaltecas left for home the following day laden with spoils.

During this time, the Mexicas had been harassing those in the province of Chalco, because they were allies of our men, so Cortés, at the request of the Chalcas, sent Gonzalo de Sandoval with twenty horsemen and three hundred footmen. When Sandoval arrived, he found the people ready and waiting for him, along with the Huexotzincas and Quauhquecholtecas, who had joined them. They settled on a strategy and left for Huaxtepec, where the Mexica forces were garrisoned and which served as the base for their attacks. The Chalcas fought the Mexicas until they had taken that town and others nearby, such as Yacapichtlan, which was well fortified and difficult to take. They killed and threw many enemy fighters off a cliff, so that for more than two hours they were [un]able[147] to drink from the river that [flowed] nearby, [fol. 135v] because it ran red with blood. Once this campaign ended, the enemy had been thoroughly punished, and peace restored to those towns, Sandoval returned to the city of Tezcuco with all his troops. But the Mexica lords sought to punish the Chalcas and sent a sizable army against them. The Chalcas met them in battle and fought so valiantly that they defeated the Mexicas. They killed many of them, took captive more than forty high-ranking warriors from the Mexica army, and expelled the rest from their territory. And although they had asked Cortés for help, by the time Sandoval arrived to offer assistance, the Chalcas had already defended themselves, as described. Sandoval spent a few days there on the border with Chalco and, seeing that the Mexicas had ceased their attacks, returned to Tezcuco.

Around this time, news came from Vera Cruz that three ships had arrived at port with many people, horses, and arms; they were all quickly sent to Cortés. This aid was miraculous, given how badly Cortés needed all of these things. They reached the city of Tezcuco without difficulty, because the entire route had been cleared of enemies. On March 27 of the year 1521, Holy Wednesday, Cortés sent two Mexica noblemen from among the forty captured by the Chalcas in the previous campaign to the city of Mexico. These two volunteered, while the rest were afraid that they would be sacrificed there. The messengers were to tell the Mexica rulers, on behalf of Cortés, to surrender and lay down their arms and that he would forgive all that had happened. The messengers asked for a signed letter so that the Kings Quauhtemoc, Coanacochtzin, and Tetlepanquetzaltzin would believe that he had sent them. Cortés did as they asked. But they did not return with a reply, because they [suffered] the very fate that the other captives

---

147. The final few folios of the manuscript are damaged and some passages have been lost. Whenever possible, we have reconstructed the missing text. Most minor reconstructions have been added without comment, while more substantial reconstructions appear within brackets. When the words cannot be confidently determined from fragments or context, we have inserted ellipses within brackets.

had feared. According to their laws, any nobleman who was [captured] was not to return to his homeland, under penalty of [death] by sacrifice.

Ixtlilxochitl continually tried [fol. 136r] to encourage devotion to and friendship with the Christians not only among the Tezcucas, but also among those in the distant provinces. He sent word to them that they should all surrender to Captain Cortés, even if some of them were to blame for past violence, because Cortés was so forgiving and desired peace so greatly that he would immediately embrace them as friends. Among those whom Ixtlilxochitl managed to attract to Cortés's side were those from the provinces of Toçapan, Maxcaltzinco, Nauhtlan, and others in the surrounding area. The rulers of these three provinces met with Ixtlilxochitl and gave him a large quantity of cloth and other things. Ixtlilxochitl sent them to Captain Cortés to present themselves as allies. They swore loyalty to His Majesty and, as a token of their obedience, offered a large quantity of cotton cloth. Cortés thanked them profusely and gave them his word that he would always consider them friends. They returned home very happy.

❧ CHAPTER [93]

*Which deals with the second time Cortés reconnoitered the city
of Mexico from the lake on all sides, the fighting on the rocky
hills of Tlayacapa, and the war of Xochimilco*

On Holy Saturday, Cortés learned from the Chalcas that the Mexicas had gathered a large army from all the lakeside towns and the province of Tlalnahuac, intending to take revenge and destroy them. Assembling his forces, Cortés left the city of Tezcuco the following Friday, [April] 15 of the said year of 1521, with thirty horsemen [and] three hundred footmen, leaving another twenty [horsemen] [fol. 136v] and three hundred footmen under the field command of Chief Constable Gonzalo de Sandoval. Cortés was accompanied by Ixtlilxochitl, who brought twenty-four thousand of his Aculhua vassals. They had two objectives. The first was to secure the province of Chalco and expel the Mexicas who continually harassed them, for the Chalcas were allies and had sided with our men. The second was to go and subjugate the territory of the Tlalhuicas and that of the Chinampanecas,[148] the most important of the lakeside nations, and reconnoiter the city of Mexico for a second time to gain a better position from which to begin his endeavor. He very much wanted to take that city and thereby vanquish the whole empire, for the rulers were holed up in that city and from there governed and sent their armies against Cortés and his men and against those from the kingdom of Tezcuco and the province of Chalco who were allied with Cortés and our Spaniards. Moreover, once he had defeated those from Tepeyacac and other provinces and expelled the Mexica armies from their territories, the towns beyond the mountains and volcano would be peaceable and on our side.

Having organized the aforementioned army, Cortés left the city of Tezcuco. He reached the city of Tlalmanalco, capital of the entire province of Chalco, where they were well received by its two rulers. He issued orders as to how to proceed. And after another forty thousand warriors from this province had gathered there along with other allies from Tlaxcalan, Huexotzinco, Quauhquecholan, and other places, they headed toward the province of Totolapan, which borders Chalco to the south. That is where the largest enemy force was gathered, concentrated mainly in the town of Tlayacapan, a well-fortified place surrounded by unassailable towering [peaks], where the enemy would be protected.

---

148. I.e., the Xochimilcas.

[After] passing through some rugged mountains, they reached the town of Tlayacapan one [fol. 137r] afternoon and saw, at the top of a high crag, all the women, children, and other defenseless inhabitants of those parts. Its slopes were covered with warriors who, as soon as they saw our men, began slinging rocks, shooting arrows, and throwing spears. Cortés decided to climb the peak, so he sent Cristóbal Corral, lieutenant in charge of sixty footmen, to attack and ascend with his men by the steepest route, with some gunmen and crossbowmen following behind. Meanwhile, Captains Francisco Verdugo and Juan Rodríguez de Villafuerte were to ascend by a different route with their men and other crossbowmen and gunmen. He also ordered Captains Pedro Dircio and Andrés Monjaraz to attack from a different side with other crossbowmen and gunmen. A harquebus was fired, which was the signal, and they all began their ascent at the same time, with Ixtlilxochitl with his men and the Chalcas following behind them and on the sides. However, they were unable to advance further than the second turn up the side of the mountain. It was so steep that they could barely hold on with their hands and feet, and the enemy cast many boulders down on them from above and greatly harmed our men. They killed two Spaniards and injured more than twenty; a much greater number of allies were injured and killed. At the same time, many enemy fighters came to the aid of those on the crag. These reinforcements swarmed the fields below and surrounded our men, who were forced to come down and fight on the valley floor. There, they fought the enemy until they cleared them from the field of battle, spearing and killing them. The fighting [lasted] more than an hour and a half, after which time they reached another crag that was nearly a league away from the first, with many [people . . .] [fol. 137v] not as strong. They spent the night nearby, though in desperate need of water. At daybreak, Cortés and his men began to climb the big crag by way of two smaller adjacent ones. There were a lot of warriors defending them, but when they saw our men climb, they abandoned the slopes in fear and went up to aid those on top. Our men pursued and killed many of them, while many others fell to their deaths as they fled. Finally, taking stock of their losses, the enemy surrendered. When Cortés saw this, he ordered that they should not be harmed further, welcomed them, and pardoned all they had done. Then they went and convinced those on the other crag to come surrender and ask for pardon as well.

Cortés and his men spent two days here, and the wounded were sent to Tezcuco. The following day, he left for Huaxtepec, where they were welcomed and given food and lodging at the country retreat that the kings of Mexico maintained there. The army spent one day there before leaving for Yauhtepec. Many enemy warriors had been waiting for them there, but once they saw them approaching, they fled, along with the townspeople, who abandoned their houses. They did not stop here, but pursued the enemy until they cornered them at Xicotepec, where they barricaded themselves in. Many of them were speared and killed; many women and children were taken prisoner. And the rest, seeing the losses they had suffered, abandoned the place, and our men stayed there for two days. On the second day, Cortés decided to set fire to the town, and those from Xicotepec and Yauhtepec surrendered.

He continued on his way and, around noon, reached the city of Quauhnahuac, the capital of the Tlalhuicas' province, which was well fortified. Within the city, there were many warriors defending it, and they had taken down the bridges so that it could not be entered from that side [. . .] that went for a league and a half from there to get around [. . .] they found a way across, though it was difficult, where [fol. 138r] a few of our men were able to enter. When the enemy saw them, they began to flee and the city was taken and sacked and many of its houses were burned. The lord of the city, called Yaotzin, retreated to the mountains. Ixtlilxochitl sent a reprimand to him for his rebellion and commanded him to come at once to surrender and beg forgiveness for all he had done. Yaotzin and his people arrived early the next morning to offer their services and support to the Christians, promising to help and be ever faithful to their cause, which, in fact, they were. Returning from Quauhnahuac, they attacked the city of Xochimilco, which was the best fortified and most populous of the cities on the freshwater lake. The inhabitants were well prepared for their arrival. They were ensconced behind many barricades and had, at all the entrances to the city, removed the bridges over the canals. They fought our men at the barricades but abandoned them when they saw the damage caused by the harquebuses. In less than half an hour, our men had taken most of the city; the fighting continued on water and land until nightfall.

The next day, the fighting resumed, and they killed two Spaniards. Cortés's horse collapsed from exhaustion, and he found himself in dire straits. When the enemy fighters saw him on foot, they surrounded him. He defended himself with a spear until Chichimeca Tecuhtli, captain of the Tlaxcaltecas, came to his aid along with one of Cortés's servants. Together with the forces that arrived soon thereafter, they routed the enemy. Our men went deeper into the city. That night, they had all the gaps in the canals where the bridges were missing filled in with earth and stone, so that the horsemen could come and go easily. By nightfall, all the gaps had been well filled. Our men spent the night on high alert, keeping guard with candles, because [. . .] day, the Mexicas arrived with a sizable [army by] water and land to defend the Xo[chimilcas] [fol. 138v] and trap our men inside the city. Cortés directed our men, who defended themselves valiantly, until they managed to take a fort located in the place called Tepepan. They divided themselves into squadrons and each one pursued the enemy independently. After our men defeated them, killing many, the enemy sought refuge at the base of the aforementioned hill. There our men fought a great battle and killed more than five hundred enemy fighters. The following day, they defeated another enemy squadron, which had come as further reinforcements from Mexico, and killed many of them.

When they returned to the city of Xochimilco, our men found that the ones who had stayed behind were in great need of assistance because they had been beset by the enemy and were exhausted from defending themselves and expelling the enemy from the city, killing many of them. They had had no time to rest when another Mexica squadron, larger than the last, arrived to aid and defend the city. Our men met them and quickly defeated them, forcing them to retreat to the water and the safety of their canoes. Our men returned to the city and set fire to all of it, except for their lodgings. They spent three days razing the city, after which time they left for Coyohuacan. When the Xochimilcas and their supporters saw them leave, they attacked them from behind, screaming and shouting. Cortés and the horsemen turned to face them and chased them back into the water. They continued on their way and, at midday, reached the city of Coyohuacan, which they found abandoned. They stayed in the palace of the local lord. The next day, they went to survey the city of Mexico, up to the point where the two causeways meet, the one that runs from Xochimilco to the city of Mexico and the one from Iztapalapan. At the point where they join, the enemy had erected a barricade, which was protected by countless numbers of them; there were also many canoes on the [lake] filled with [warriors]. Our men engaged them, and they [fol. 139r] defended themselves well, but ultimately, our men took the barricade and killed many Mexicas. [Cortés] decided that this would be [one] of the routes his forces would take to defeat the city of Mexico. [. . .] in Coyohuacan with the garrison, he returned, having only been able to burn a few of the most important houses and temples in this city of Coyohuacan.

The next day, they left for the city of Tlacopan, two leagues distant, fighting the entire way with the enemy coming from the lake. They did not stop at Tlacopan, but rather continued on to the city of Quauhtitlan, where they spent the night. During this march, they killed many enemy fighters, including some of the best among them. But it also cost them two Spaniards, servants of Cortés who were captured alive and sacrificed to their false gods, and some of our allies. The next day they camped in the town of Xilotzinco, which, like Quauhtitlan, had been abandoned. The next day at noon, they reached the town of Acolman, which belonged to the kingdom of Tezcuco, where they were well received and feasted. Later that same day, they arrived in Tezcuco to spend the night. There, Sandoval and those with him were very glad to see Cortés and his men after so many victories. Sandoval, too, had seen frequent combat against the Mexicas, who believed the city of Tezcuco to be defenseless while Cortés and Ixtlilxochitl were away.

Around this time, Cortés received news from Hernando de Barrientos and one of his companions, who had not been heard from in a year. They were in the province of Chinantlan, which borders the southern province of Tototepec. The lord of this province had joined Cortés's side and these two Spaniards had led them in many battles against the Mexicas' allies. For this reason and to defend the province were the enemy to return, the lord of Chinantlan had prevented them from leaving; he also wished to meet Cortés. [Cortés] was very pleased to hear this news and to learn that those Spaniards were still alive. He sent word for them to wait there until he could finish conquering Mexico.

[fol. 139v]

 **CHAPTER [94]**

*Which deals with how Cortés prepared to attack and lay siege
to the city of Mexico by land and water*

They finished building the brigantines and digging the trench to take them to the lake. They also made the final preparations necessary for the endeavor that Cortés had begun, to which Ixtlilxochitl and his brother Tecocoltzin had contributed greatly. Then they launched the brigantines into the trench. On April 28 of 1521, Cortés reviewed his troops and counted 86 horsemen, 118 crossbowmen and gunmen, more than 700 footmen with swords and shields, 3 large iron cannon, 15 small bronze cannon, and 10 hundredweights of gunpowder. When he finished his review, he gave a speech. He told them, in sum, to abide by the rules he had established for their conduct in the war. He also told them to steel themselves, for it was clear that God favored them at every turn and they would undoubtedly triumph over their enemies, who were so few in number that hardly any of them remained. The fact that His Divine Majesty had aided them and increased the number of their weapons, men, and horses in such a brief period of time clearly revealed that this was his fight, one meant to spread his holy Catholic faith and also to benefit greatly His Majesty the king by adding to the royal crown of Castile an empire as vast as this one, which had such large and splendid kingdoms and provinces and such grandeur and wealth. All this should inspire and embolden them to either conquer or die. They all responded that they would do so, and they expressed their eagerness for the war to end, for only then would there be peace and calm in this land.

The next day, Cortés dispatched messengers to the provinces of Tlaxcalan, Huexotzinco, and Chololan, asking their [rulers] [fol. 140r] to take all the people they had [mustered] according to his instructions and come quickly. In ten days' time, those [from] Tlaxcalan were to be in the city of Tezcuco and those from Huexotzinco and Chololan in the province of Chalco. Ixtlilxochitl and his brother Tecocoltzin issued the same orders, so that all the warriors and servants from the kingdom [of] Tezcuco Aculhuacan and its subject provinces would gather so as to attack the city of Mexico in support of Cortés and his men. First and foremost, they were to bring food and supplies needed by Cortés, his men, and the rest of his allies, because the provisions they gathered and prepared in the city of Tezcuco each day were insufficient and completely consumed due to the presence of our army and the daily assaults they carried out against the Mexicas.

The Tlaxcaltecas arrived in the city of Tezcuco five days before Pentecost, which was the appointed time. At the same time, those of Huexotzinco and Chololan arrived in Chalco. All of them were very well received. There were fifty thousand Tlaxcalteca warriors. Their leaders were Quauhxayacatzin, Miztliymatzin, Tenamazcuicuiltzin, Tequanitzin, Acxotecatl, Acamoyotzin, Tianquiztlatoatzin, Çeyecatecuhtli, Tepilçacatzin, Chahuatecolotzin, Cuitlizcatl, Cocomintzin, Tzicuhcoatl, Mixcoatecuhtli, Tlachpanquizcatzin, Tiçatemoctzin, Chiquaçen Maçatl, Ixconauhquitecuhtli, and Tlahuihuitztli, all of whom displayed emblems made of many different kinds of feathers and decorated with gold and jewels, according to the rank and status of their office. Ixtlilxochitl and his brothers welcomed them, lodged them in their palaces, and provided them with all the food they needed. For the few days they were there, they were treated very well. And the Huexotzincas, who numbered more than ten thousand, were led by Nelpilonitzin, Tozquencoyotzin, Xicotencatl, Mecacalcatl, Quauhxayacatzin, Huitzilihuitzin, Yecatlapitzqui, Tetepotzquanitzin, Quauhtonatiuhtzin, Tehuatecuhtli, Chichimecaltecuhtli, Tlacatecuhtli, [fol. 140v] and others, who displayed their coats of arms just as those from Tlaxcalan did. The Chololtecas, who also numbered almost [ten] thousand, did the [same]. They were all very well received [in] the province of Chalco.

On the second day of Pentecost, Cortés called all of his footmen and horsemen to the plaza of the [city] of Tezcuco in order to divide them among the captains, forming three companies that would be deployed to three cities around the city of Mexico. He named Captain Pedro de Alvarado general of one of the companies. Cortés gave him 30 horsemen, 18 crossbowmen and gunmen, 150 footmen with sword and shield, and 25,000 Tlaxcalteca warriors. This company was to set up camp in the city of Tlacopan, and his lieutenants would be his brother Jorge de Alvarado; Captain Pedro Dircio; Gutierre de Badajoz, who was his ensign; Juan Balante; the Basque Andrés de Monjaraz; Alonso Ortiz de Zúñiga, who commanded the crossbowmen; and Diego Valadez.

He made Cristóbal de Olid, who was from Baeza, general of the second company. He gave him 33 horsemen, 18 crossbowmen and gunmen, 160 footmen, and more than 20,000 warriors also from the Tlaxcalteca nation. They were to set up camp in the city of Coyohuacan. Cortés had reserved the naval battle for himself. But after some grumbled that he was choosing the least dangerous assignment, he gave it to Juan Rodríguez de Villafuerte. Cortés then joined this second company, making Cristóbal de Olid his second in command. This company's lieutenants were Captain Andrés de Tapia; the treasurer Julián de Alderete; the quartermaster Bernardino Vázquez de Tapia; the inspector Rodrigo Álvarez Chico; and Antonio Quiñones, who was captain of Cortés's guard—a post held after him by Francisco de Terrazas, who was his chief steward.

[fol. 142v][149] Cortés made [Gonzalo] de Sandoval, chief constable of [. . .], general of the third company. He gave him 24 horsemen, 4 gunmen, 13 crossbowmen, and [1]50 footmen, all good men that [. . .]. Cortés had brought them with him, along with [more than] 40,000 men from Tezcuco, [Huexo]tzinco, Chololan, and Chalco. This company was [to pass] through the city of Iztapalapan, destroy it, and proceed on the causeway over the lake with the brigantines protecting their rearguard. And while they waited for Cortés to arrive, they were to join and remain with the company that was in Coyohuacan. Once he arrived, this company advanced on the city's causeway and dike with the support of the brigantines until they reached Tepeaquilla, where the shrine to our Lady of Guadalupe is now located. The lieutenants of this company were the Galician Hernando de Lema, Captain Rodrigo Rangel, Luis Marín, and Vasco Porcallo. These were the captains that Cortés assigned at this point to the three companies into which he divided his army, not to mention many other captains appointed as needed, including Ruy González and Antonio de Arriaga.

For the thirteen brigantines that Cortés planned to use for the naval battle on the lake, he reserved 300 men, the majority of whom were seamen and very skilled in this type of warfare. Each brigantine carried 25 fighters, a captain, and 6 crossbowmen and gunmen. The captains of the brigantines were Juan Rodríguez de Villafuerte, captain of the flagship, who was said to be from Medellín; Juan Jaramillo, from Salvatierra; Francisco Verdugo, from Arévalo; Francisco Rodríguez Magariño, [fol. 142r] from Mérida; [. . .] de Don Juan; Pedro Barba, gentleman [from] the city of Seville; Antonio de Carv[ajal], from Zamora; Garciolguín [from] Cáceres; Jerónimo Ruiz de la M[. . .]; [. . .] de Briones, from Salamanca; Ro[. . .]jón de Lovera, from Medina del Campo; [. . .] from Portillo,[150] who had been a soldier [. . .] and was regarded as valiant; and Juan de Mancilla.

---

149. Though the foliation on the top right corner remains consecutive, fols. 141 and 142 were bound upside down. We have rearranged the text following the narrative, which progresses from fols. 140v to 142v, 142r, 141v, and 141r.

150. Alva Ixtlilxochitl appears to be drawing from the *Historia general de los hechos de los castellanos* (volume 3, book 1, chapter 12) by Antonio de Herrera y Tordesillas, who identifies the captains as: "Juan Rodríguez de Villafuerte de Medellín, Juan Xaramillo de Salvatierra en Estremadura, Francisco Berdugo de Arévalo, Francisco Rodríguez

The aforementioned order was given, and following their [instructions], the commanders of the two companies—Pedro de Alvarado, who was to go to his post in the city of Tlacopan, and Cristóbal de Olid, who was to go to Coyohuacan—set out from Tezcuco on May 10 of the year 1521. They stopped to sleep in Acolman, where they argued about how to set up camp that night, but Cortés quickly sent someone to reprimand and quiet them. They spent the next night in Quauhtitlan, which was within Mexica territory. They reached the city of Tlacopan early on the third day, where they took up quarters in the king's palace and set up defenses. The city had been abandoned during the last encounter, and the king and all his people remained in Mexico as allies of the Mexicas. As soon as they arrived, the Tlaxcaltecas caught sight of the enemy at the place where two causeways that lead to the city of Mexico begin and they fought against them for two or three hours. As night was beginning to fall, they returned to their post unharmed. They continued these sallies for the next five days. And the Spaniards destroyed two channels that brought fresh water to the city of Mexico from the forest of Chapoltepec; the enemy fiercely defended them on land and water because the city depended on them. They won some bridges and barricades and fixed the road so that the [horsemen] could cross easily from one side to the other. [fol. 141v] Although some Spaniards were wounded [. . .] some of the allies, countless enemy fighters [died].

On the sixth day after they arrived at this [place], in the aforementioned situation [. . .] entrance to the city of Mexico, Gar[ciolguín] and his company left for their post [at Coyohua]can, following the orders Cortés had given him [. . . with] him the Tlaxcalteca allies given to him by [Cortés]. They were from the two capital cities of Ocotelul[co and] Quiahuiztlan; those from the other two capital cities of Tizatlan and Tepeticpac remained in Tlacopan with Pedro de Alvarado. Meanwhile, before Cortés set out with the fleet, he had Axayacatzin,[151] one of the four rulers of Tlaxcalan, hanged for certain egregious acts. Those who had left for Coyohuacan took up quarters and set up defenses in the palace of the lord of that city, who was likewise in Mexico with all of his people; the city was abandoned.

---

de Magariño de Mérida, Christóval Flores de Valencia de Don Juan, García Olguín de Cáceres, Antonio de Caravajal de Zamora, Pedro Barba de Sevilla, Gerónimo Ruiz de la Mota de Burgos, Pedro de Briones de Salamanca, Rodrigo Morejón de Lovera de Medina del Campo, Antonio de Sotelo de Zamora, Juan de Portillo natural de Portillo." The remainder of the sentence does not come from Herrera.

151. Axayacatl was another of Xicotencatl's names.

Our men sallied out from here to skirmish on the causeway that runs from here to the city of Mexico. They met fierce resistance and found that the enemy had broken the causeway in many places and erected many fortifications, barricades, and other defenses on land and water. Those from both camps sallied out every day, joining together to kill and spear the enemy, raiding their stores of maize and anything else they found while attacking those in the city.

After learning that the camps were set up in the places where he had indicated, Cortés left with his fleet of brigantines on the Friday following the feast of Corpus Christi, despite the fact that the highest-ranking men of his army had demanded that he go with the aforementioned companies because they believed that going by land would be more difficult and going with the fleet less risky. In fact, however, his presence turned out to be necessary here, [fol. 141r] the most dangerous [. . .] of the battle. Before he embarked, he sent Gonzalo de Sandoval to Iztapalapan with his [company], which comprised twelve thousand Acul[huas . . .] the place they call Aztahuacan [. . .] to meet those from Chalco, [accompanied by] the Huexotzincas and Chololtecas, who together numbered thirty thousand warriors. The Chalcas were commanded by Quetzalcoatzin, Totomihuatzin, Chapolascatzin, Epcoacatl, Tecuhxolotl, Quetzaltlaçoltzin, Nequametzin, Ecatecolotl, Quetzalmaçatzin, Tetzauhquaquilli, Tlacatecpanecatl, Xochipoio, Caczole, Aquetzqui, Xocotecatl, and others with their coats of arms. The armies were financed and supplied by the lords Acacitzin and Omacatzin, who because of their tender age, did not go on this journey, but remained behind to dispatch reinforcements and supplies for the duration of the war.

They reached Iztapalapan a little after noon, set fire to the city, and began fighting the people there. Seeing the great might of Gonzalo de Sandoval's company of allies, who numbered more than forty thousand, the enemy retreated to their canoes and no longer offered any resistance. Thus, they took control of the city unopposed and took up quarters there while they awaited Cortés's orders. Ixtlilxochitl, Tecocoltzin, and their brothers remained in Tezcuco to gather as many reinforcements as they could and follow Cortés and provide his army with everything it needed, regularly sending food and necessary supplies by water and land. Twenty thousand porters and one thousand canoes went back and forth to carry out this task, while thirty-two thousand warriors defended them so that the enemy would not ambush them on the way and [take] what they [carried]. This [was] not the least of the services that Ixtlilxochitl [rendered] to [His] Majesty. He provided everything Cortés's army needed at his own [expense] and that of his brothers, relatives, and other [lords].

[fol. 143r]

🌿 CHAPTER [95]

Which deals with the triumph [. . .] brigantines on the lake [. . .]
by water and land, the first [skirmish . . .] in Mexico

While Sandoval was fighting [. . .] the city of Iztapalapan, Cortés arrived with his [. . .] within view of the craggy hill called Tepepolco, which [was] defended by many warriors, both from Mexico and from nearby towns, who sought to attack our men from behind and aid the people of Iztapalapan. Cortés was forced to stop there and invade this city. But when those in Tepepolco saw the fleet coming on the lake, they waited until they could ascertain where it was headed, and when they saw that it was heading to the craggy hill, they sent up smoke signals so that everyone in all the cities and towns of the lake would ready themselves for war. Cortés made landfall at the craggy hill with one hundred fifty men, and they climbed it and took the bulwark at the top, albeit with great difficulty and effort. They killed all those who were defending the hill. Soon, none were left alive except the women and children, who were spared out of pity. This was a significant victory, even though twenty-five Spaniards were wounded.

Since the warriors at Tepepolco and Iztapalapan had alerted the Mexica with smoke signals that Cortés's fleet was approaching on the lake, more than five hundred well-manned canoes came out to face it. But Cortés kept the fleet along the shore near the craggy hill, waiting to see what the enemy would do. Believing our men paralyzed with fear, the enemy advanced toward them, but once they got close, they stopped. And at this moment, God willed the wind to blow from the land toward the lake. Realizing that this greatly advantaged the brigantines, Cortés ordered the fleet to attack the enemy. They quickly engaged the canoes, splintering many of them and killing those on board. Other canoes collided as they fled, and many drowned. The brigantines then chased the few canoes that remained and bottled them in among the houses in the city of Mexico. This was a great feat, and with it, Cortés gained control of this lake. [fol. 143v] When the company at Coyohuacan [saw] Cortés coming [. . .] destroying the fleet of canoes, they were glad [. . .] wanted to see him and receive reinforcements, because [this position] and that of Tlacopan were the most dangerous. This was where the majority of the enemy forces [. . .] reinforcements arrived every day.

And so, [. . .] to go toward the city of Mexico, [fiercely] fighting until they won the barricades and bulwarks that the enemy had built and the gaps in the causeway where the bridges had been removed. They crossed the gaps using the brigantines, which had arrived by this time. They pursued the enemy, killing some of them while forcing others to throw themselves into the water on the side of the causeway opposite the brigantines. Our men advanced along the causeway for more than a league, until they took two towers along the approach to the city, which were in Acachinanco and Tocititlan, where Cortés moored the brigantines, for it was already late. Then he leaped ashore with thirty men and took the towers, despite great danger and difficulty. He scaled their walls, which were made of stone and mortar, and not even the throng of enemy fighters who defended them was enough to resist him. He brought ashore three heavy iron cannon from the brigantines and fired one of them up the causeway, causing great harm to the enemy. He wanted to continue firing the cannon, but the gunner accidentally burned all the gunpowder he had, so Cortés sent a brigantine to Iztapalapan that night for more.

Although Cortés had initially intended to leave for Colhuacan, he decided to make his camp here because he thought it advantageous to have the brigantines nearby. He sent for half the company of Coyohuacan and fifty of Gonzalo de Sandoval's footmen, who arrived the next day. Cortés spent the night on high alert and managed to defend himself from the Mexicas, who attacked at midnight. But seeing the precautions that Cortés had taken and the cannon and harquebus fire, the enemy did not dare advance farther. Once the reinforcements arrived, our men fought until they won a gap without a bridge and a barricade, backing the enemy into the houses on the edge of the city. Cortés saw [fol. 144r] that [the enemy] was causing great [damage] from the other side of the causeway, because the [brigantines] could not cross over [. . .] break part of the causeway near [. . .] that had been placed and pass [. . .] brigantines that clashed with the [. . .] trapped them among the houses and pursued [. . .] them. They had not dared do so before, because there were many poles and stakes hindering them. They fought against those in the canoes until some of them surrendered, and they burned many of the nearby houses.

The next day, Sandoval left for Coyohuacan with the people he had with him in Iztapalapan. Along the way, he fought with the people from Mexicatzinco, defeated them, killed many of them, and burned all the houses. And using two brigantines sent by Cortés, he was able to cross over the places where the enemy had broken the causeway. He left his forces there, took ten horsemen, and went along the causeway toward Cortés's camp. Before they reached it, they had to fight against those who were skirmishing with Cortés. There, Gonzalo de Sandoval's foot was pierced by a fire-hardened spear. But Cortés cut them down with cannon and harquebuses such that they no longer dared approach. Six days of fighting passed. And the brigantines continued burning the houses on the city's perimeter until they discovered a channel through which they could easily enter and navigate the edge of the city as well as further in. This was a very important development, because it forced the canoes to keep their distance, and they did not dare come closer than a quarter of the way to Cortés's camp.

Pedro de Alvarado informed Cortés that, on the other side of the city, near the Coyovasco causeway,[152] the enemy was coming and going freely, bringing provisions and reinforcements from the Mexica and Tepaneca towns on the mainland. Alvarado presumed the enemy, who was under much duress, would flee along that causeway. Cortés ordered Gonzalo de Sandoval, despite his injury, to make his camp in a small town called Tepeyacac, where the shrine to our Lady of Guadalupe is today. Sandoval left with twenty-three horsemen, one hundred footmen, and eighteen gunmen and crossbowmen. He left behind fifty footmen and sixteen thousand [. . .] [fol. 144v] designated from among the Aculhuas, Chalcas, [. . .] Huexotzincas, with which the city of Mexico was completely [. . .]

Seeing [. . .] company of more than 250 footmen, [. . .] crossbowmen and gunmen, and a very large number of allies, Cortés decided to follow the causeway into the center of the city. He placed the brigantines on either side of the causeway to protect his rearguard. He also sent word to the company at Coyohuacan ordering some of them to join him; the rest were to stay and guard the causeways and that whole side of the city to prevent those from the enemy cities of Xochi-milco, Coyohuacan, Iztapalapan, Huitzilopochco, Colhuacan, Cuitlahuac, and Mizquic, who fought alongside the Mexica, from attacking our men from behind. He ordered others to remain in Coyohuacan with another sixteen thousand Huexotzincas, Chalcas, and Tlaxcaltecas [. . .] mentioned. Cortés also sent orders to Pedro de Alvarado and Gonzalo de Sandoval to attack from their respective causeways at the same time as he did. Cortés advanced along the causeway on the appointed day and soon came upon the enemy who were defending a breach they had opened in the causeway, which was as wide and deep as a lance, from behind a strong barricade they had built. But eventually, our men won it and

---

152. Probably the northern causeway that ran from Tepeyacac to Tenochtitlan.

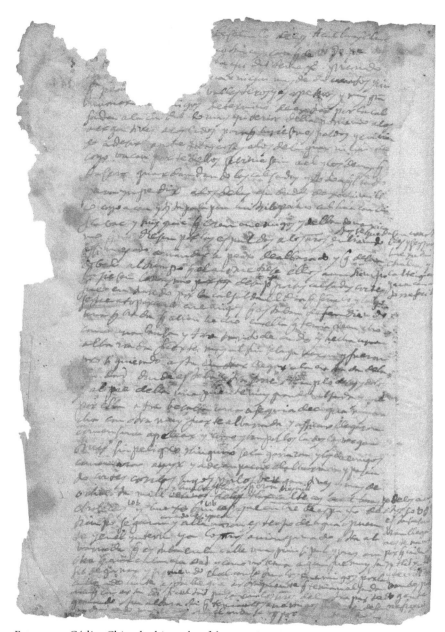

FIGURE 24. Códice Chimalpahin, vol. 2, fol. 144v. *Photo courtesy of the Instituto Nacional de Antropología e Historia.*

advanced up to the entrance of the city, where there was another tower or temple to their idols. They had removed a very large bridge from the gap at its base so that there was a wide channel running across the causeway as well as another strong barricade. They began fighting as soon as they arrived and, because the brigantines covered their flanks, they won it without coming to any harm. The enemy began to flee and abandon the barricade. Cortés and his men crossed over on the brigantines along with more than eighty thousand allies, including ten thousand Tlaxcaltecas, ten thousand Chalcas, ten thousand Huexotzincas, and no fewer than fifty thousand Aculhuas. There were so many Aculhuas by then because Ixtlilxochitl and Tecocoltzin had been sending reinforcements every day. They quickly filled in and smoothed this gap with earth and stone.

In the meantime, our men had won another barricade on the widest and most important avenue in the city. And since this section of the avenue was not broken by water, it was very easy to take. They chased the enemy up the street until they reached another gap without a bridge. Our men crossed it, though with great difficulty, and won another barricade that the enemy had built for their defense. The fighting lasted for two hours, and from the rooftops they [. . .] (fig. 24).

 WORKS CITED

Adorno, Rolena. 1989. "Arms, Letters and the Native Historian in Early Colonial Mexico." In *1492–1992: Re/Discovering Colonial Writing*, edited by René Jara and Nicholas Spadaccini, 201–24. Minneapolis: Prisma Institute.

———. 1994. "The Indigenous Ethnographer: The 'Indio Ladino' as Historian and Cultural Mediator." In *Implicit Understandings: Observing, Reporting, and Reflection on the Encounters between Europeans and Other Peoples in the Early Modern Era*, edited by Stewart Schwartz, 378–402. Cambridge: Cambridge University Press.

Alva Ixtlilxochitl, Fernando de. 1829. *Horribles crueldades de los conqusitadores de México, y de los indios que los auxiliaron para subyugarlo a la corona de Castilla, o sea, memoria escrita por D. Fernando de Alva Ixtlilxochitl*. Edited by Carlos María de Bustamante. Mexico City: Alejandro Valdés.

———. 1840. *Histoire des Chichimèques ou des anciens rois de Tezcuco par don Fernando d'Alva Ixtlilxochitl, traduite sur le manuscrit espagnol*. Vols. 12–13 of *Voyages, relations et mémoires originaux pour servir à l'histoire de la découverte de l'Amérique*, translated and edited by Henri Ternaux-Compans. Paris: Arthus Bertrand.

———. 1891. *Obras históricas*. 2 vols. Edited by Alfredo Chavero. Mexico City: Oficina Tipográfica de la Secretaría de Fomento.

———. 1969. *Ally of Cortés: Account 13, of the Coming of the Spaniards and the Beginning of the Evangelical Law*. Translated by Douglass Ballantine. El Paso: Texas Western Press.

———. 1975–77. *Obras históricas*. 2 vols. Edited by Edmundo O'Gorman. Mexico City: Universidad Nacional Autónoma de México, Instituto de Investigaciones Históricas.

———. 2015. *The Native Conquistador: Alva Ixtlilxochitl's Account of the Conquest of New Spain*. Translated by Amber Brian, Bradley Benton, and Pablo García Loaeza. University Park: Pennsylvania State University Press.

Aveni, Anthony. 1983. *Skywatchers of Ancient Mexico*. Austin: University of Texas Press.

Ayer, Edward E. 1950. "How I Bought My First Book," *Newberry Library Bulletin*, 2nd ser., no. 5 (December).

Bancroft, Hubert Howe. 1883. *The Native Races. Volume II: Civilized Nations*. San Francisco: A. L. Bancroft.

Bandelier, Adolph. 1881. *Notes on the Bibliography of Yucatan and Central America; Comprising Yucatan, Chiapas, Guatemala (the Ruins of Palenque, Ocosingo, and Copan), and Oaxaca (Ruins of Mitla)*. Worcester, MA: Press of Chas. Hamilton.

Barlow, R. H. 1945. "Some Remarks on the Term 'Aztec Empire'." *The Americas* 1, no. 3 (January): 345–49.

Benton, Bradley. 2014. "The Outsider: Alva Ixtlilxochitl's Tenuous Ties to the City of Tetzcoco." *Colonial Latin American Review* 23, no. 1 (January): 37–52.

———. 2017. *The Lords of Tetzcoco: The Transformation of Indigenous Rule in Postconquest Central Mexico*. New York: Cambridge University Press.

Berdan, Frances F. 1982. *The Aztecs of Central Mexico: An Imperial Society*. Fort Worth: Harcourt Brace.

Boone, Elizabeth Hill. 2000. *Stories in Red and Black: Pictorial Histories of the Aztecs and Mixtecs*. Austin: University of Texas Press.

Boturini Benaduci, Lorenzo. 2015. *Idea of a New General History of North America*. Translated and edited by Stafford Poole. Norman: University of Oklahoma Press.

Brading, D. A. 1991. *The First America: The Spanish Monarchy, Creole Patriots, and the Liberal State, 1492–1867*. Cambridge: Cambridge University Press.

Brian, Amber. 2014. "The Original Alva Ixtlilxochitl Manuscripts at Cambridge University." *Colonial Latin American Review* 23, no. 1 (January): 84–101.

———. 2016. *Alva Ixtlilxochitl's Native Archive and the Circulation of Knowledge in Colonial Mexico*. Nashville: Vanderbilt University Press.

———. 2017. "Shifting Identities: Mestizo Historiography and the Representation of Chichimecs." In *To Be Indio in Colonial Spanish America*, edited by Mónica Díaz, 143–66. Albuquerque: University of New Mexico Press.

Brundage, Burr Cartwright. 1972. *A Rain of Darts*. Austin: University of Texas Press.

Bustamante, Carlos María de. *See* Alva Ixtlilxochitl (1829).

Cañizares-Esguerra, Jorge. 2002. *How to Write the History of the New World: Histories, Epistemologies, and Identities in the Eighteenth-Century Atlantic World*. Stanford: Stanford University Press.

Carrasco, Pedro. 1996. *Estructura político-territorial del imperio tenochca: La triple alianza de Tenochtitlan, Tetzcoco y Tlacopan*. Mexico City: El Colegio de México.

———. 1999. *The Tenochca Empire of Ancient Mexico: The Triple Alliance of Tenochtitlan, Tetzcoco, and Tlacopan*. Norman: University of Oklahoma Press.

Charlton, Thomas H., Deborah L. Nichols, and Cynthia Otis Charlton. 1991. "Aztec Craft Production and Specialization: Archaeological Evidence from the City-State of Otumba, Mexico." *World Archaeology* 23, no. 1 (June): 98–114.

Chavero, Alfredo. *See* Alva Ixtlilxochitl (1891).

Clavijero, Francisco J. 1844. *Historia antigua de México y de su conquista*. Mexico City: Imprenta de Lara. First published 1780–81 as *Storia antica del Messico*.

Cline, Howard F. 1966. "The Oztoticpac Lands Map of Texcoco 1540." *Quarterly Journal of the Library of Congress* 23, no. 2 (April): 76–115.

Cortés, Rocío. 2008. "The Colegio Imperial de Santa Cruz de Tlatelolco and Its Aftermath: Nahua Intellectuals and the Spiritual Conquest of Mexico." In *The Blackwell Companion to Latin American Culture and Literature*, edited by Sara Castro Klaren, 86–105. Oxford: Blackwell.

Dibble, Charles E. 1951. *Códice Xolotl*. Mexico City: Universidad Nacional Autónoma de México, Instituto de Historia.

Diel, Lori Boornazian. 2008. *The Tira de Tepechpan: Negotiating Place Under Aztec and Spanish Rule.* Austin: University of Texas Press.

Douglas, Eduardo de J. 2010. *In the Palace of Nezahualcoyotl: Painting Manuscripts, Writing the Pre-Hispanic Past in Early Colonial Period Tetzcoco, Mexico.* Austin: University of Texas Press.

Echeverría y Veytia, Mariano Fernández de. 1836. *Historia antiqua de Méjico.* Mexico City: C. F. Ortega.

Fernández, Christian, and Sara Castro-Klarén. 2016. *Inca Garcilaso and Contemporary World-Making.* Pittsburgh: University of Pittsburgh Press.

Florescano, Enrique. 1985. "La reconstrucción histórica elaborada por la nobleza indígena y sus descendientes mestizos." In *La memoria y el olvido: Segundo simposio de historia de las mentalidades.* Mexico City: Instituto Nacional de Antropología e Historia.

Galarza, Joaquín, and María de Lourdes Bejarano Almada. n.d. "Catálogo de documentos del Fondo Mexicano de la Biblioteca Nacional de Francia." Amoxcalli: La Casa de los Libros online. Mexico City: Centro de Investigaciones y Estudios Superiores en Antropología Social and Consejo Nacional de Cultura y Tecnología. Accessed February 20, 2018. http://amoxcalli.org.mx/catalogo.pdf.

García Loaeza, Pablo. 2006. "Estrategias de familiarización: Fernando de Alva Ixtlilxóchitl y el Inca Garcilaso de la Vega." *Pegaso* 1 (Fall): 28–37.

———. 2009. "Saldos del criollismo: el *Teatro de virtudes políticas* de Carlos de Sigüenza y Góngora a la luz de la historiografía de Fernando de Alva Ixtlilxóchitl." *Colonial Latin American Review* 18, no. 2 (August): 219–35.

———. 2017. "A New Native Identity: Fernando de Alva Ixtlilxochitl." In *To Be Indio in Colonial Spanish America*, edited by Mónica Díaz, 243–65. Albuquerque: University of New Mexico Press.

Garcilaso de la Vega, El Inca. 1609. *Comentarios reales de los incas.* Lisbon: Pedro Crasbeeck.

———. 1617. *Historia general del Perú.* Córdoba: Viuda de Andrés de Barrera.

Garibay K., Ángel María. 1953–54. *Historia de la literatura náhuatl.* 2 vols. Mexico City: Porrúa.

———. 1964–68. *Poesía náhuatl.* 3 vols. Mexico City: Universidad Nacional Autónoma de México, Instituto de Historia.

Garza Martínez, Valentina. 2012. "Medidas y caminos en la época colonial: Expediciones, visitas y viajes al norte de la Nueva España (siglos XVI–XVIII)." *Fronteras de la Historia* 17, no. 2 (July–December): 191–219.

Gemelli Careri, Giovanni Francesco. 1700. *Giro del mondo.* Vol. 6, *Contenente le cosa più ragguardevoli vedute nella Nuova Spagna.* Naples: Stamperia di Giuseppe Roselli.

Gibson, Charles. 1952. *Tlaxcala in the Sixteenth Century.* New Haven: Yale University Press.

———. 1964. *The Aztecs Under Spanish Rule: A History of the Indians of the Valley of Mexico, 1519–1810.* Stanford: Stanford University Press.

Glass, John B. 1978. *The Boturini Collection and a Concordance of the Inventories, 1742–1918.* Lincoln, MA: Conemex Associates.

Goodwin, Gordon. 1892. "King, Edward, Viscount Kingsborough (1795–1837), antiquary." Oxford Dictionary of National Biography. Revised by Alan Bell, 2004. https://doi.org/10.1093/ref:odnb/15560. Accessed January 27, 2018.

Granados y Gálvez, José Joaquín de. 1987. *Tardes americanas.* Mexico City: Porrúa.

Hassig, Ross. 2001. *Time, History, and Belief in Aztec and Colonial Mexico.* Austin: University of Texas Press.

Herrera y Tordesillas, Antonio de. 1601–15. *Historia general de los hechos de los castellanos en las islas y tierra firme del mar océano.* 9 vols. Madrid.

Hicks, Frederic. 1982. "Tetzcoco in the Early 16th Century: The State, the City, and the 'Calpolli.'" *American Ethnologist* 9, no. 2 (May): 230–49.

———. 1994. "Texcoco 1515–1519: The Ixtlilxochitl Affair." In *Chipping Away on Earth: Studies in Preshipanic and Colonial Mexico in Honor of Arthur J. O. Anderson and Charles E. Dibble,* edited by Eloise Quiñones Keber, 235–39. Lancaster, CA: Labyrinthos.

Humboldt, Alexander von. 1811–14. *Political Essay on the Kingdom of New Spain.* 4 vols. Translated by John Black. London: Longman, Hurst, Rees, Orme, and Brown.

Karttunen, Frances. 1997. "Rethinking Malinche." In *Indian Women of Early Mexico,* edited by Susan Schroeder, Stephanie Wood, and Robert Haskett, 291–312. Norman: University of Oklahoma Press.

Kingsborough, Lord [Edward King]. 1829–48. *Antiquities of Mexico: Comprising Facsimiles of Ancient Mexican Paintings and Hieroglyphics . . . The Whole Illustrated by Many Valuable Inedited Manuscripts.* 9 vols. London: James Moynes and Colnagi.

Klein, Cecelia. 1993. "Teocuitlatl, 'Divine Excrement': The Significance of 'Holy Shit' in Ancient Mexico." *Art Journal* 52, no. 3 (September): 20–27.

———. 2001. "None of the Above: Gender Ambiguity in Nahua Ideology." In *Gender in Pre-Hispanic America,* edited by Cecelia Klein, 183–253. Washington, DC: Dumbarton Oaks Research Library and Collection.

Laird, Andrew. 2014. "Indigenous American Latinists." In *Brill's Encyclopaedia of the Neo-Latin World,* 2:993–94.

Lee, Jongsoo. 2008. *The Allure of Nezahualcoyotl: Pre-Hispanic History, Religion, and Nahua Poetics.* Albuquerque: University of New Mexico Press.

León-Portilla, Miguel. 1956. *La filosofía náhuatl estudiada en sus fuentes.* Mexico City: Instituto Indigenista Interamericano.

———. 1959. *Visión de los vencidos: Relaciones indígenas de la conquista.* Mexico City: Universidad Nacional Autónoma de México.

———. 1961. *Los antiguos mexicanos a través de sus crónicas y cantares.* Mexico City: Fondo de Cultura Económica.

Lesbre, Patrick. 1996. "Tezcoco-Aculhuacan face à Mexico-Tenochtitlan d'après les sources historiques, 1431–1521." PhD thesis, École des Hautes Études en Sciences Sociales, Paris.

———. 1997. "Historiographie acolhua du premier siecle de la colonisation genese d'une culture metises." PhD thesis, Université de Toulouse II–Le Mirail.

Lockhart, James. 1992. *The Nahuas After the Conquest: A Social and Cultural History of the Indians of Central Mexico, Sixteenth Through Eighteenth Centuries.* Stanford: Stanford University Press.

López de Gómara, Francisco. 1552. *Historia general de las Indias con todo el descubrimiento y cosas notables que han acaecido dende que se ganaron hasta el año de 1551.* Zaragoza: Agustín Millán.

Mann, Charles. 2006. *1491: New Revelations of the Americas before Columbus.* New York: Knopf.

Meyer, Michael, William L. Sherman, and Susan M. Deeds. 2011. *The Course of Mexican History.* 9th ed. New York: Oxford University Press.

Mignolo, Walter. 1995. *The Darker Side of the Renaissance: Literacy, Territoriality, and Colonization*. Ann Arbor: University of Michigan Press.

Mohar Betancourt, Luz María. 1994. "Acolhuacan in the Matrícula and Mendocino." In *Chipping Away on Earth: Studies in Preshipanic and Colonial Mexico in Honor of Arthur J. O. Anderson and Charles E. Dibble*, edited by Eloise Quiñones Keber, 225–34. Lancaster, CA: Labyrinthos.

———. 2004. *Códice Mapa Quinatzin: Justicia y derechos humanos en el México antiguo*. Mexico City: Comisión Nacional de los Derechos Humanos México and Miguel Ángel Porrúa.

More, Anna. 2013. *Baroque Sovereignty: Carlos de Sigüenza y Góngora and the Creole Archive of Colonial Mexico*. Philadelphia: University of Pennsylvania Press.

Motolinia [fray Toribio de Benavente]. 1858. *Historia de los indios de Nueva España*. Vol. 1 of *Colección de documentos para la historia de México*, edited by Joaquín García Icazbalceta. Mexico City: Librería de J. M. Andrade.

Munch G., Guido. 1976. *El cacicazgo de San Juan Teotihuacan durante la colonia*. Mexico City: Instituto Nacional de Antropología e Historia.

Mundy, Barbara E. 2015. *The Death of Aztec Tenochtitlan, the Life of Mexico City*. Austin: University of Texas Press.

Nicholson, H. B. 1957. "Topiltzin Quetzalcoatl of Tollan: A Problem in Mesoamerican Ethnohistory." PhD thesis, Harvard University.

———. 2001. *Topiltzin Quetzalcoatl: The Once and Future Lord of the Toltecs*. Boulder: University Press of Colorado.

Noguez, Xavier. 1978. *Tira de Tepechpan: Códice colonial procedente del Valle de México*. 2 vols. Mexico City: Biblioteca Enciclopédica del Estado de Mexico.

O'Gorman, Edmundo. 1975. "Estudio introductorio." In *Obras históricas*, by Fernando de Alva Ixtlilxochitl and edited by Edmundo O'Gorman, vol. 1, 1–257. Mexico City: Universidad Nacional Autónoma de México, Instituto de Investigaciones Históricas.

Offner, Jerome. 1980. *Law and Politics in Aztec Texcoco*. New York: Cambridge University Press.

Ortiz de Montellano, Bernard R. 1978. "Aztec Cannibalism: An Ecological Necessity?" *Science* 200, no. 4342 (May): 611–17.

Oviedo, Gonzalo Fernández de. 1526. *Sumario de la historia general y natural de las Indias*. Toledo: Ramón de Petras.

———. 1851–55. *Historia general y natural de las Indias*. 4 vols. Edited by José Amador de los Ríos. Madrid: Real Academia de la Historia.

Panes, Diego García. 1976. *La conquista: Selección de láminas y textos de los tomos V y VI del Teatro de Nueva España*. Mexico City: San Ángel Ediciones.

Parsons, Mary Hrones. 1975. "The Distribution of Late Postclassic Spindle Whorls in the Valley of Mexico." *American Antiquity* 40, no. 2 (April): 207–15.

Peñafiel, Antonio, ed. 1979. *Manuscritos de Texcoco*. Mexico City: Innovación.

Pomar, Juan Bautista. 1975. *Relación de Tezcoco*. Edited by Joaquín García Icazbalceta. Mexico City: Biblioteca Enciclopédica del Estado de México

Prescott, William H. 1843. *History of the Conquest of Mexico, with a Preliminary View of Ancient Mexican Civilization, and the Life of the Conqueror, Hernando Cortés*. 3 vols. New York: Harper and Brothers.

Ramos, Gabriela, and Yanna Yannakakis, eds. 2014. *Indigenous Intellectuals: Knowledge, Power, and Colonial Culture in Mexico and the Andes*. Durham: Duke University Press.

Robertson, Donald. 1959. *Mexican Manuscript Painting of the Early Colonial Period: The Metropolitan Schools*. New Haven: Yale University Press.

Schmidt Díaz de León, Ileana. 2012. *El colegio seminario de indios de San Gregorio y el desarrollo de la indianidad en el centro de México, 1586–1856*. Mexico City: Plaza y Valdés.

Schroeder, Susan. 1991. *Chimalpahin and the Kingdoms of Chalco*. Tucson: University of Arizona Press.

———. 1994. "Father José María Luis Mora, Liberalism, and the British and Foreign Bible Society in Nineteenth-Century Mexico." *The Americas* 50, no. 3 (January): 377–97.

———. 2010. "Introduction." In *The Conquest All Over Again: Nahuas and Zapotecs Thinking, Writing, and Painting Spanish Colonialism*, edited by Susan Schroeder, 1–14. Portland, OR: Sussex Academic Press.

Schroeder, Susan, Anne J. Cruz, Cristián Roa-de-la-Carrera, and David E. Tavárez. 2010. "Glossary." In *Chimalpahin's Conquest: A Nahua Historian's Rewriting of Francisco López de Gómara's* La conquista de Mexico, edited and translated by Susan Schroeder, Anne J. Cruz, Cristián Roa-de-la-Carrera, and David E. Tavárez, 471–77. Stanford: Stanford University Press.

Schwaller, John Frederick. 2014. "The Brothers Fernando de Alva Ixtlilxochitl and Bartolomé de Alva: Two 'Native' Intellectuals of Seventeenth-Century Mexico." In *Indigenous Intellectuals: Knowledge, Power, and Colonial Culture in Mexico and the Andes*, edited by Gabriela Ramos and Yanna Yannakakis, 39–59. Durham: Duke University Press.

Sigüenza y Góngora, Carlos de. 1680. *Theatro de virtudes políticas que constituyen a un príncipe*. Mexico City: Viuda de Bernardo Calderón.

Smith, Michael E. 2012. *The Aztecs*. 3rd ed. Malden, MA: Wiley-Blackwell.

Spitler, Susan. 1998. "The *Mapa Tlotzin*: Preconquest History in Colonial Texcoco." *Journal de la Société des Américanistes* 84, no. 2 (January): 71–81.

Tenorio Trillo, Mauricio. 1996. *Mexico at the World's Fairs: Crafting a Modern Nation*. Berkeley: University of California Press.

Ternaux-Compans, Henri. 1837–41. *Voyages, relations et mémoires originaux pour servir à l'histoire de la découverte de l'Amérique*. 20 vols. Paris: Arthus Bertrand.

Torales Pacheco, Cristina. 1998. "Don Fernando de Alva Ixtlilxóchitl, historiador texcocano." In *Historia general del estado de México*, Vol. 2, *Época prehispánica y siglo XVI*, edited by Rosaura Hernández Rodríguez, 79–108. Toluca: Gobierno del Estado de México, Colegio Mexiquense.

Torquemada, fray Juan de. 1615. *Veinte i un libros rituales i monarchía indiana con el orígen y guerras, de los indios occidentales de sus poblaciones, descubrimento, conquista, conversión y otras cosas maravillosas de la mesma tierra, distribuydos en tres tomos*. 3 vols. Seville: Mathias Clavijo.

Townsend, Camilla. 2017. *Annals of Native America: How the Nahuas of Colonial Mexico Kept Their History Alive*. New York: Oxford University Press.

Townsend, Richard. 1982. "Pyramid and sacred mountain." *Annals of the New York Academy of Sciences* 385, no. 1 (May): 37–62.

Umberger, Emily. 1996. "Aztec Presence and Material Remains in the Outer Provinces." In *Aztec Imperial Strategies*, edited by Frances F. Berdan, Richard E. Blanton, Elizabeth Hill Boone, Mary G. Hodge, Michael E. Smith, and Emily Umberger, 151–79. Washington, DC: Dumbarton Oaks Research Library and Collection.

Vaillant, George C. 1953. *Aztecs of Mexico: Origen, Rise and Fall of the Aztec Nation.* New York: Doubleday.

Velazco, Salvador. 2003. *Visiones de Anáhuac: Reconstrucciones historiográficas y etnicidades emergentes en el México colonial: Fernando de Alva Ixtlilxochitl, Diego Muñoz Camargo y Hernando Alvarado Tezozómoc.* Guadalajara: Universidad de Guadalajara.

Villella, Peter B. 2014. "The Last Acolhua: Alva Ixtlilxochitl and Elite Native Historiography in Early New Spain." *Colonial Latin American Review* 23, no. 1 (January): 18–36.

———. 2016. *Indigenous Elites and Creole Identity in Colonial Mexico, 1500–1800.* New York: Cambridge University Press.

 INDEX

Page numbers in italics refer to figures. In the text, noble names may receive the -tzin suffix. It is retained in the index only if all instances of the name have the suffix. If the suffix is not applied uniformly in the text, the root name is used in the entry (e.g., "Nezahualcoyotl" and "Nezahualcoyotzin" appear in the text; he is indexed under the former).

Acamapichtli, 46, 49, *43*, 58, 61, 65–66, 93

Acapipioltzin, 151, 167, 177, 181, 184, 185, 187, 212

Acatentehuatzin, 175

Acatlan, 61, 151

Acatlemacoetzin, 230–31

Acatlotzin, 64, 72

Acatomatl, 41, 47

Achitometzin, 49, 50, 65, 66

Acolhua, 51, 57, 58; death, 64; offspring, 46, 49, 53

Acolman, 73, 112–13, 235, 297, 304, 308; lords of, 66, 68, 81, 84, 129, 134; tribute from, 155

Acolmiztli (lord of Coatlichan), 52, 53, 57, 58, 64

Acolmiztli (son of Ixtlilxochitl). *See* Nezahualcoyotl

Acolnahuacatzin, 66, 173

Acozanil. *See* Cozumel

Aculhuacan, 48n34, 116, 121–22, 173, 248, 293

Aculhuas, 93, 101, 111, 143, 190, 204, 206, 229–31, 248, 309, 312, 314; arrival of, 44, 47; rulers of, 49, 125, 162, 226, 275, 297

Acxotecatl, 282, 306

Aguilar, Jerónimo de, 242, 245–46, 246n142

Ahuatepec, 64, 75, 76, 112, 130, 155

Ahuilizapan, 190, 191, 192

Ahuitzotl, 188, 196–97, 199–200, 211, 221–22

Alvarado, Pedro de, 259n145, 294, 306, 308, 312; flight from Tenochtitlan of, 277–81, 294; voyage to Yucatan of, 240, 241, 242, 245

Alvarado Tezozomoc, Fernando de, 7

Amaxtlan, 197, 206

Anahuac, 36, 43, 44, 55, 150, 206, 228

aqueducts, 120, 155, 157–58, 211

Atenco, 130, 155, 293

Atlixcas, 199, 225

Atlixco, 153, 196, 197, 206, 223

Atotonilco, 41, 58, 66

Atototzin, 49, 52, 66, 68

Aubin, Joseph Marius Alexis, 15

Axapochco, 64, 69, 130, 155

Axayacatzin (king of Tenochtitlan), 166, 170n99, 181–82, 196; ascension of, 169–70; death of, 188; offspring of, 188–89, 194, 206, 207, 221; wars of, 183, 186–87

Axayacatzin (lord of Tlaxcalan). *See* Xicotencatl
Axoquentzin, 166, 167–68, 184, 260, 262, 264
Ayer, Edward E., 22n34
Azcalxochitl, 159–62, 194
Azcapotzalco, 70, 71, 72, 87, 89, 91, 96, 119, 123, 127, 297; razing of, 86, 119; rulers of, 44, 46, 49, 51, 57, 58, 64, 65, 66, 69, 70, 121, 122, 125, 200, 224, 225, 287
Aztahuacan, 70, 309
Aztaquemecan, 155, 283
Aztatl, 57, 61

ballgame, 101, 101n72, 103, 136, 186, 226
Bancroft, Hubert Howe, 16
Bandelier, Adolph, 16
Barba, Pedro, 307, 307n150
Benavente, Toribio de, 30, 180
Boturini Benaduci, Lorenzo, 13, 14, 15, 22n34
Briones, Pedro de, 307, 307n149
burial, 52, 56, 67, 80, 87, 208n122
Bustamante, Carlos María de, 14

Cacama, 188, 246; ascension of, 220, 234–35; death of, 280, 286; interaction with Cortés of, 247–48, 252, 266–67, 271–80
cacao, 130, 145, 148, 170, 171, 192, 262
cacique, 242, 242n141, 243, 244, 250, 251
Çaiolan, 61, 62
Calcozametzin, 52, 60
Camaxtle, 111, 153
canals, 135, 155, 192, 280, 302
canoes, 97, 211, 241, 245, 272, 274; in battle, 43, 242, 296, 303, 309, 310, 311, 312
Capolapan, 109, 110, 112
Caravajal, Antonio de, 307, 307n150
Catholicism, 222, 237; clergy of, 7, 10, 11, 13, 20n5, 30n3, 32, 157, 180, 216, 240, 261, 263, 276, 285; converts to, 240, 241, 242, 245, 246, 263, 275, 276, 277;

spread of, 122, 154, 218, 236, 246, 271, 274, 275, 305
causeways, 161, 266, 303, 307; in battle, 268, 269, 308, 309, 311, 312, 314
Cempoalan, 48, 84, 110, 155, 250–51, 252, 255, 256, 258, 262, 263, 277
Çeyecatecuhtli, 260, 306
Chacha, 91, 96
Chalchiuhnenetzin, 207–9, 225
Chalchiuhtlatonac (lord of Colhuacan), 53, 66
Chalchiuhtlatonac (lord of the Tolteca), 36, 44, 47
Chalco, 54, 61, 79, 111, 117, 124, 129, 147, 166–68, 184, 258, 292, 297, 300, 309; lords of, 46, 46, 47, 61, 62, 111, 293; tribute from, 48, 155
Chapoltepec, 42, 57, 120, 308
Charles III (king of Spain), 14
Charles V (king of Spain), 218, 246, 249, 275, 291
Chavero, Alfredo, 16–17, 18
Chiauhtla, 51, 113, 134, 155, 180, 184
Chichimeca, 42, 43–44, 49, 54, 72, 186, 226–27, 229; arrival of, 20n1, 41–44, 57; civil wars of, 50, 51, 59–62, 74–77; distribution of provinces of, 44–48, 60, 61–63, 84, 151; rulers of, 57, 58, 64, 80, 81, 114, 121, 135, 143, 162, 182, 206
Chichimecatl Tecuhtli. *See* Great Chichimeca (title)
Chicoquauhiocan, 77, 78
chiles, 130, 130n85, 147, 192
Chimalhuacan, 73, 129, 134, 155, 196, 293
Chimalpahin Quauhtlehuanitzin, Domingo de San Antón Muñón, 7
Chimalpanecas, 61, 73
Chimalpopoca (king of Tlacopan), 181, 186, 188, 197, 199, 200, 222
Chimalpopoca (lord of the Tenochcas), 26, 66, 68, 81, 84, 89, 100, 103; ascension of, 67; death of, 96–98; imprisonment of, 90–95, *94*; offspring of, 67
chinampa, 232, 232n135
Chinantla, 197, 304

Chiquilitzin, 259, 260
Chiuhnauhtecatl, 41, 72
Chiuhnauhtlan, 59, 64, 65, 73, 129, 134, 155, 161, 235, 297
chocolate. *See* cacao
Chololan, 40, 42, 60, 110, 113, 152, 153, 181, 257, 305–06, 307; interaction of Cortés with, 263–64, 266–68, 288, 294, 305
Chololtecas, 60, 263, 264, 286, 288, 306, 309
Cholula, 34–35
Çilan, 100, 124, 155
Citlalpopocatzin, 260, 263, 264
Clavijero, Francisco Xavier, 13, 14
cloth, 49, 49n35, 135, 147n88, 171, 190, 246, 258, 264, 268; as gift, 109, 110, 299, 123, 126, 143, 145, 146, 160, 170, 248, 250, 262, 267, 275; as tribute, 127, 147, 187 148, 192
Çoacuecuenotzin, 70, 71, 74, 75, 77
Coaixtlahuacan, 147, 227
Coanacochtzin, Pedro, 194, 234, 235, 273–74, 276, 285, 293, 294, 297, 298; ascension of, 286; birth of, 194; interaction with Cortés of, 290–92
Coatepec, 73, 74, 99, 100, 124, 129, 130, 155, 186
Coatlichan, 44, 66, 73, 84, 110, 112, 129, 155, 293; lords of, 49, 53, 57–59, 61, 64, 67, 68, 69, 74, 84, 113, 123, 124, 134, 159, 194, 196
Coatzacualco, 35
Coaxochitzin, 52, 61
Codex Xolotl, 10, *11*, 19, 29n2, *43*, *48*, 61n45, *77*, *79*, *82*, *85*
Coiohua, 101, 103, 104, 109, 124
Colhuacan, 42, 43, 43n28, 53, 58, 63, 66, 119, 132, 140, 183, 311, 312
commoners, 74, 75, 91, 99, 107, 129, 131, 142, 214, 224, 264
Cortés, Hernando, 153–54, 222, 237; arrival in Tenochtitlan, 266–67; birth of, 237; burning ships by, 253; capture of Motecuhçoma by, 269–75; flight

from Tenochtitlan of, 280–84; march to Tenochtitlan of, 246–51, 255–267; recapture of Tenochtitlan by, 290–314; in Yucatan, 240–46
Coxcox, 58, 60, 63, 66
Coyohuacan, 119, 127, 211, 303, 306, 307, 308, 310, 311, 312; lords of, 53, 66, 87, 89, 268
Cozcaquauh, 41, 46, 47, 51
Cozumel, 241, 242
creation story, 33–35
crossbow, 301, 305, 306, 307, 312
cu. *See* temples
Cuba, 237, 244, 249, 254, 276
Cuetlachcihuatzin, 66, 67
Cuetlachtlan, 147, 246, 258
Cuetlaxxochitzin (daughter of Xolotl), 42, 46
Cuexteca, 47, 51, 52, 151, 181, 197, 212, 228
Cuitlahua, 188, 194, 200, 224, 247, 248, 266, 267; ascension of, 280; death of, 285, 286
Cuitlahuac, 61, 120, 183, 258, 312
Culhuas, 43–44, 43n28, 50, 54, 58, 60, 65–67, 166, 275, 285, 287; rulers of, 44, 39, 52, 53, 63, 65–66

Dibble, Charles E., 17
Dircio, Pedro, 268, 268n146, 301, 306
divination, 99, 201, 203, 225
domesticated animals, 38, 106, 130, 172, 192, 226. *See also* horses
Don Juan, Christóval Flores de Valencia de, 307, 307n150

Ecahue, 163–64
Echeverría y Veytia, Mariano Fernández de, 13
education, 7, 20n5, 21, 18, 31, 55, 137, 159, 216, 235; tutors, 54, 69, 99, 137, 163, 190, 219

famines, 146, 152–54, 163, 169, 178, 193, 223

feathers, 91, 137, 140, 213, 245, 264, 266, 268, 270; decorations of, 38, 54, 127, 133–34, 135, 144, 157, 174, 187, 213, 232, 306; gift of, 123, 126, 143, 145, 146, 160, 168, 248, 250, 252, 262, 275; tribute of, 146, 147, 148
firearms. *See* harquebuses
forest retreats, 47, 64, 72, 74, 155–58, 160, 161, 164, 165, 167, 273

Garcilaso de Vega, Inca, 7, 21n10
Garciolguín, 307, 308
gardens, 148, 155, 157, 158, 159, 186; in palaces, 96, 119, 132, 135, 139, 192–93, 211
Garibay K., Ángel María, 17
Gemelli Careri, Giovanni Francesco, 12
Gibson, Charles, 17
gold, 97, 135, 136 137, 140, 168, 175, 187, 264, 272306; decorations of, 54, 73, 91, 95, 133–34, 157, 166, 190, 207, 232, 266, 267, 269, 278, 283, 291; gift of, 95, 123, 126, 143, 145, 146, 160, 168, 244, 248, 250, 252, 259, 262, 266, 267, 268, 275; Spanish interest in, 137, 240. 244, 245, 246, 259, 266, 268, 270, 272–73; tribute of, 146, 273
Gómara, Francisco López de, 8, 11, 21n11, 29n3, 237, *238*, 252n143, 285
Granados y Gálvez, José Joaquín, 13
Great Chichimeca (title), 41–44, 47–51, 52, 121, 125–26, 143, 206
Grijalva, Juan de, 237, 240, 242
Gulf of California, 36, 44, 228
Gulf of Mexico, 36, 36n13, 38, 42, 52, 147, 190, 191, 228, 236, 268, 272

harquebuses, 264, 301, 311, 312
Hecahuehuetzin, 176, 182, 184
Hepcoatzin, 46, 53, 58, 61, 65–66; offspring of, 53
Hernández de Córdoba, Francisco, 237, 249
Herrera y Tordesillas, Antonio de, 11, 29n3, 237, *239*, 285, 307n150
Hieronymite Friars, 240, 249, 276

History of the Chichimeca Nation (original), 3–5, 7–20; modern scholars' use of, 18–19; previous editions and excerpts of, 13–18
horses, 246, 252, 260, 266, 276, 279, 290, 296, 297, 298, 300, 302, 306, 307; in battle, 244, 255, 283, 289, 297, 303, 305, 308, 312; death of, 255, 280, 283, 302
Hualtepec, 147, 197
Huasteca. *See* Cuexteca
Huaxtepec, 61, 147, 298, 301
Huecan Mecatl, 91, 93
Huehuetzin, 201–2, 258
Huemac. *See* Quetzalcoatl
Huetzin (lord of Coatlichan), 37, 38, 49–51, 52, 53, 59, 61, 129, 163; offspring of, 52
Huetzin (son of Nezahualcoyotl), 163–64
Huexotla, 50, 70, 73, 84, 106, 113, 155, 293; lords of, 51, 52, 53, 69, 74, 117, 119, 123, 124, 129, 134, 159, 224
Huexotzincas: army of, 113, 118, 196, 199, 202, 225, 285, 286, 288, 292, 298, 306, 309, 312, 314; lords of, 118. *See also* Huehuetzin
Huexotzincatl. *See* Huehuetzin
Huexotzincatzin, 194, 213, 225
Huexotzinco, 52–53, 60, 74, 83, 101, 108, 117, 119, 124, 129, 152, 153, 196, 220, 250, 263; armies of, 110, 153, 300, 305, 306; rulers of, 48, 109, 113, 158, 181, 201, 305
Hueyotlipan, 283, 284, 285
Huitlapalan. *See* Gulf of California
Huitzcacamatzin, 276, 290–91
Huitzilihuitl (lord of the Tenochcas), 33, 53, 66, 67, 93; death of, 67
Huitzilihuitzin (tutor of Nezahualcoyotzin), 69, 99, 101, 106, 111–12; offspring of, 66;
Huitzilopochco, 119, 183, 211, 312
Huitzilopochtli, 58, 64, 173, 192, 232, 271; temples to, 137, *138*, 139, 153, 168, 173, 199, 221
Humboldt, Alexander von, 14

Ichantlatoatzin, 167, 176, 182
idols, 47, 58, 61, 63, 64, 97, 167, 139,
   166–67, 180, 199, 207, 241, 255, 262,
   271, 288; worship of, 31, 40, 64, 66, 87,
   111, 152, 153, 180
Ilancueitl, 49, 53, 65
Inca Garcilaso. *See* Garcilaso de Vega, Inca
indigenous sources, 5–9, 29, 31–32, 136,
   180, 246, 292
Itlacauhtzin, 74, 117, 118, 119, 12, 124, 129
Itzcoatl, 33, 42, 93, 100, 116, 123, 125, 126,
   127, 146, 159, 180; ascension of, 97–98,
   99; assistance of Nezahualcoyotl by,
   118–22; death of, 150; offspring of, 170
Itzcoatzin (lord of Quauhnahuac), 223
Itzocan, 41,147, 258, 289
Itztapalocan, 70, 71, 73, 155
Ixconauhquitecuhtli, 259, 260, 306
Ixtlilcuechahuac, 189, 223
Ixtlilxochitl, Hernando Cortés (son of
   Nezahualpiltzintli), 14, 149, 194, 248,
   307; attempt to seize the throne by,
   234–36; birth of, 218; childhood of,
   218–20, interaction with Cortés of, 248,
   250, 271–74, 276, 279, 281, 291–93,
   296–302, 304–7, 309, 314
Ixtlilxochitl Ometochtli (emperor), 64, 66
   68–80, 81, 84, 100, 103, 114, 119, 176;
   ascendance of, 68–69; birth of, 64;
   death of, 78–80; offspring of, 68–69;
   ouster of, 72–77
Iztacquauhtli (lord of Maçahuacan), 41, 47
Iztapalapan, 200, 235, 266, 296, 303, 307,
   309, 310, 311, 312; lords of, 188, 196,
   280
Iztapalocan, 129, 130
Iztapalotzin, 167–68

Jaramillo, Juan, 246, 307
jewelry, 187, 190, 207, 232, 278; ear
   plugs, 190; gifts of, 245, 259, 267;
   headdresses, 91, 127, 134, 135, 144, 148,
   266; lip plugs, 95, 190; making of, 137,
   174; necklaces, 91, 166

King, Edward. *See* Kingsborough,
   Viscount (Edward King)
Kingsborough, Viscount (Edward King),
   15

La Campiña, 48, 129, 155
lady of the house of Xilonenco, 188, 194,
   234
lady of Tolan, 194, 213
Lake of Mexico. *See* Lake Tetzcoco
Lake Tetzcoco, 21n12, 41, 97, 120, 142, 127,
   157, 186, 211, 266, 273; battles on, 70,
   118, 292, 293, 296–97, 300, 303, 305,
   307, 310; infrastructure on, 123, 192,
   231n135
law, 18, 31, 32, 34, 83, 132, 150, 205,
   215–17, 247, 262, 267; of the Church,
   222, 240, 244, 268, 271, 282, 290,
   294; court description, 133–35, 140,
   213–14; infidelity and, 207–8, 224;
   Ixtlilxochitl's adherance to, 219–20;
   Nezahualcoyotl's establishment of and
   adherence to, 83, 134, 137, 140–45, 164,
   170, 177; Nezahualpilli's refinements
   to, 213, 215–17; Nezahualpiltzintli's
   adherance to, 224, 232–33; Nopaltzin's
   additions to, 52; punishments from, 83,
   140–45, 208, *141*, 164, 174, 213, 215–17,
   219, 224
León-Portilla, Miguel, 17
Lovera, Rodrigo Morejón de, 307, 307n150

Maçaapan, 65, 155
Maçahuacan, 47, 65, 148, 258
Macuilmalinaltzin, 189, 194, 221, 223, 225
maize, 50, 54, 130, 141, 145, 152, 170, 187,
   192, 193, 256, 293, 309; as tribute, 152,
   187
markets, 119, 133, 141, 142, 177, 186, 186,
   204, 245, 279, 294
Magariño, Francisco Rodríguez, 307,
   307n150
Malinalocan, 41
Matlalatzin, 66, 67
Matlalcihuatzin, 66, 68

Maxixcatzin, 259–60, 262–63, 264, 282, 284, 285, 287–88, 289

Maxtla, 66, 86, 99, 101, 116, 117; ascendance of, 87–95; death of, 119; defeat of, 114–115, 118–19

Medellín (Spain), 237, 307

Memexoltzin, 52, 61

merchants, 143, 194, 197, 204, 208, 237, 240, 245, 264

messengers,101, 109, 262; in diplomacy, 90, 99–100, 103, 106, 110, 112, 117, 123, 124, 160, 168, 205, 216, 246–48, 249, 255, 272, 291, 293, 298; in warfare, 143–44, 251, 305

Metztitlan, 41, 46, 54, 59, 65, 235

Mexica, 18, 20n3, 26, 74, 90, 91, 93, 100, 113, 114, 116–17, 204, 207; arrival of, 57–58; engineering of, 211; expansion of, 58; interaction with Cortés of, 248, 252, 257–58, 264, 268, 278–84, 288–314; lords of, 46, 58, 61, 65–67, 68, 72, 81, 87, 97, 99, 119, 123, 148, 196, 209, 223, 232, 273, 287; religion of, 153, 166, 180, 181, 199, 206, 207, 221, 278, 286; as Triple Alliance members, 121–22, 150, 176, 188; warfare of, 60, 61, 65, 118–20, 125–28, 143–45, 183, 187, 190, 235–36, 278–84, 296–314. *See also individual entries for lords*; Tenochtitlan; Triple Alliance

Mexico City. *See* Tenochtitlan

Mexitin, 57, 63

Michhuacan, 44, 57, 181, 228, 288, 294–95

Michhuaques, 44, 52, 295

Mitliztac, 41

Mixteca, 47, 48, 61, 197, 227, 228

Mizquic, 61, 312

Moçocomatzin, 58, 66

Mocuetlazatzin, 260, 264

Monjaraz, Andrés de, 301, 306

Montejo, Francisco de, 249, 253

Moquihuitzin, 132, 183, 221

Motecuhçoma (King of Tenochtitlan), 194, 250, 251, 252, 253, 254, 259, 278, 282; ascension of, 221–22; birth of, 188; capture by Cortés of, 269–76; dealings with Triple Alliance of, 225–26, 234–36; death of, 276, 279–80; interactions with Cortés of, 246–49, 255–58, 263–77; power consolidation of, 223–24, 227, 229–32

Motecuhçoma Ilhuicamina, 87, 90, 93, 116, 117, 118, 122, 159, 162, 175, 180; ascendance of, 150; birth of, 67; death of 169–70; offspring of, 188; role in the Triple Alliance of, 152, 164, 188

Motolinia. *See* Benavente, Toribio de

Motoliniatzin, 123, 124, 129

Muñoz, Juan Bautista, 14, 15, 16

Muñoz Camargo, Diego, 7

music, 135, 142, 212, 215, 217; instruments, 135, 168, 216, 260

Nahuatl language, 3, 17, 20n2, 25, 26, 27, 32n5, 43n28, 44n29, 63, 122, 245

Narváez, Pánfilo de, 275, 276–78, 286, 289

Nauhtlan, 197, 268, 299

Nenetzin, 53, 58

Nequametzin, 292, 309

Nezahualcoyotl, 8, 10, 12, 13, 16, 74, 75, 79–80, 84–86, 101, 129–31, 171–74, *178*; ascension of, 70–71; birth of, 68–69; death of, 176–80, 181, 183, 188; escapes from danger of, 78, 81–83, 87, 91–97, 99–107; laws of, 140–45; palaces and retreats of, 132–39, 155–58, 272, 293–94; marriage of, 159–62, 163; offspring of, 163–69, 176, 182, 184, 221; power consolidation of, 111–28; Triple Alliance under the rulership of, 146–49, 152–54, 169–70, 192; wars of, 146–51

Nezahualpiltzintli, 10, 13, 180, *185*, 212–14, 218; ascension of, 176–82; birth of 168–69; consolidation of power of, 184–85; death of, 232–33; laws of, 215–17; offspring of, 194–95, 207, 232, 234–36, 281, 282, 291, 292; palaces of, 192–93, 292; Triple Alliance under the rulership of, 183, 186–91, 197–203, 207–9, 211, 221–31; wars of, 190–91, 201–3, 227–28

Nezahualquentzin, 272, 273

Nicarahua, 42, 228

Nicholson, H. B., 17

nobles, 26, 31, 34, 54, 131, 194n113; laws regarding, 140–45, 299

Nonoalcatl, 62, 114, 124, 175

Nopaltzin (son of Xolotl), 42, 43–46, 47, 49–50, 52–53; death of, 53; offspring of, 46

Nopaltzin Cuetlachihui (son of Tlotzin), 48, 59, 60

North Sea. *See* Gulf of Mexico

Ocotelulco, 260, 308

Ocotoch, 50, 51, 59, 60

O'Gorman, Edmundo, 18

Olid, Cristóbal de, 240, 306, 308

ollamaliztli. *See* ballgame

Omacatzin, 292, 309

omens, 38, 112, 218, 225–26, 230–31, 287–88

Otomies, 65, 101, 105, 106, 107, 124, 186, 255, 256; rulers of, 44, 46, 50, 65

Otompan, 65, 69, 74, 75, 79, 84, 129, 134, 155, 283, 293

Otumba, 48n34, 99, 316

Our Lady of Guadalupe, 126, 307, 312

Oviedo, Gonzalo Fernández de, 8, 21n11

Oztoticpac, 50, 67, 155, 190, 191, 273

Pacific Ocean, 36, 40, 52 , 204, 228, 272

palaces, 89, 131–39, 175, 184, 192–93, 205, 207, 213; of Maxtla, 96–97; of Motecuhçoma, 267–69; of Nezahualcoyotl, 85, 100, 103, 120, 146–48, 155–58, 163, 169, 272; of Nezahualpiltzintli, 192–93, 292

Panes, Diego García, 14, 22n27, 16

Panuco. *See* Cuexteca

Papalotlan, 78, 129, 155, 235

Patlachiuhcan, 59, 107

Pochotl, 40, 42, 46, 47, 49, 56

Poiauhtlan, 41, 59, 60

Portocarrero, Alonso Fernández, 249, 253

Potonchan, 34, 241, 243, 244, 245, 246

Prescott, William Hickling, 16

priests: Catholic, 13, 20n5, 180, 263; indigenous, 31, 38, 58, 60, 87, 139, 150, 152–53, 166, 192, 196, 221, 264, 286

Quachquetzaloian, 41

Quacoz, 105–7

Quahuacan, 41, 50, 65, 258

Quanaltecatl, 259, 260, 263

Quaquauhpitzahuac, 53, 66, 67; death of, 67; offspring of, 67

Quaquauhtzin, 160–63, 209

Quateotzin, 106, 111, 117

Quauhatlapatl, 41, 47

Quauhchinanco, 41, 129, 134

Quauhiacac, 74, 82, 155

Quauhnahuac, 146, 157, 196, 223, 302

Quauhpopoca, 196, 268–69, 271–72, 273

Quauhquecholan, 42, 258, 288, 300

Quauhtemoc, Hernando 221, 285, 286, 294, 297, 298

Quauhtepec, 109, 153

Quauhtepetl, 118, 146, 230, 283

Quauhtitlan, 65, 71, 119, 127, 297, 303, 304, 308

Quauhtlatoatzin, 67, 98, 118

Quauhtlatzacuilotzin, 129, 180

Quauhtlatzinco, 64, 75, 130, 155

Quauhtlehuanitzin, 100–101, 107–8, 117, 159

Quauhtlizactzin (lord of Tzicuhcoac), 194, 198

Quauhtliztac. *See* Iztacquauhtli (lord of Maçahuacan)

Quetzalcoatl, 33, 34, 35, 139, 153, 218, 225, 247, 319

Quetzalcoatzin, 292, 309, 319

Quetzalmamalitzin, 129, 187

Quetzalmaquiztli, 84, 113

Quiahuiztlan, 38, 250–51, 252, 259, 260, 261, 262, 264, 308

Quinatzin Map, 5, *14*, *16*, *17*, *19*, 21n14, 21, 29n2
Quinatzin Tlaltecatzin, 48, 50–51, 52, 56, 57, 59–62, 63, 64, 233; death of, 62; offspring of, 52

Red Sea. *See* Gulf of California
Robertson, Donald, 17
royal courts, 41, 48, 56, 65, 69, 87, 96, 99, 204, 275; life at, 99, 134, 137, 181, 192–93, 199, 212, 275; of Motecuhçoma, 224, 235, 247–48, 255, 266, 267, 275, 291; of Nezahualcoyotl, 93, 99, 103, 123, 126, 128, 140, 144, 155, 160, 165, 176; of Nezahualpiltzintli, 202, 207, 226, 227, 231; of Quinatzin, 50, 52, 56; at Tezcuco, 57, 106, 130, 182, 227; in Tlaxcalan, 259–60; of Xolotl, 41, 42, 49, 51, 56

sacrifice, 47, 64, 89, 119, 139, 166–67, 180, 197, 199, 204–5, 227, 231, 271, 286; collection of humans for, 142–43, 144, 152–53, 197–98, 225, 287, 298–99; Cortés and Spanish restrictions against, 241, 262, 269–71, 278; of humans, 90, 111, 119, 139, 154, 180, 187, 192, 199, 206, 227, 229, 232, 242, 286, 304
Saint James, 244, 282, 283
Saint Peter, 241, 244, 282, 283
salt, 130, 140, 172, 192, 262
Sandoval, Gonzalo de, 293, 296, 297–98, 300, 304, 307, 309, 310, 311, 312
Santo Domingo, 237, 240, 242, 276, 277
Sea of Cortés. *See* Gulf of California
Sigüenza y Góngora, Carlos de, 12–14
slavery, 105, 142, 152, 153, 160, 180, 215, 219, 232, 288; markets, 119; as punishment, 140, 141, 144, 172, 257
smallpox, 286, 289
soldiers, 82, 96–97, 113, 144, 153, 191, 210, 223, 229–30, 290, 305; in battle, 79, 187, 191, 197–98, 201–2, 251, 255, 283, 296, 302, 303, 309, 310; discipline of, 142–43, 214, 215, 227; as king's guard,

97, 107, 135, 143, 167, 186, 202, 208, 219, 223, 235–36, 247; in police actions, 100, 101, 104–6, 109, 116; as sacrifices, 153–54, 197–98, 225, 287; supporting Cortés, 255, 263, 279, 289, 290, 291, 293, 297, 298, 300, 301, 305, 306, 307, 311, 312
sorcerers, 142, 231
South Sea. *See* Pacific Ocean
subsistence, 40, 50, 54–55, 59, 75, 106, 109, 141, 152, 187, 193, 244, 291, 293. *See also* cacao; chiles; chinampa; domesticated animals; famines; maize

Taiatzin, 66, 86, 87, 89, 90
Tangajuan, 294, 295
Tapia, Andrés de, 242, 307
Techotlalatzin (emperor), 52, 58, 63–65, 67–68, 129, 155, 188, 233; offspring of, 64, 170n99
Techotlalatzin (lord of Iztapalapan), 188, 196
Techotlalatzin (lord of Teçoiocan), 129
Tecocoltzin, 276, 282, 292, 305, 309, 314
Teçoçomoc (king of Azcapotzalco), 64, *85*, *88*, 100, 113, 116, 161, 170, 170n99, 188, 189, 200, 206, 224, 225; conflict with Ixtlilxochitl, 68–73, 75, 78; death of, 67, 87–89; offspring of, 66–67, 170; rulership of the Chichimeca empire of, 81–89; wars of, 65–67
Teçoçomoc (lord of Azcapotzalco), 46
Teçoçomoctzin (lord of Chiuhnauhtlan), 129
Teçoiocan, 64, 129, 134, 155, 207
Tecpatl, 41, 47, 66
Tecpaxochitzin, 66, 68
Tecuhxolotl, 106, 111–12
Tehuantepec, 181, 206, 210, 227
Tehuetzquititzin, Diego, 189, 222
Teiolcocoatzin, 68, 81, 84, 113, 129
Temalacatitlan, 41
Temictzin, 66, 159, 160, 194
temples, 31, 97, 141, 168, 173, 199, 208, 314; burials in, 88, 232, 294; Cortés

and interactions with, 241, 243, 244,
255, 258, 262, 264, 269, 271, 303;
destruction of, 113, 119, 126, 183,
241, 264, 303; to Quetzalcoatl, 35; of
Tenochtitlan, 196, 199–200, 271, 278;
sacrifices on, 90, 111, 166, 187, 231,
278; of Tetzcoco, 132, 137–39, *138*,
192–93, 232; of Toltecas, 63–64, 81; of
Xolotl, 47, 53. *See also* Huitzilopochtli:
temples to
Tenaiocan Oztopolco, 41, 42, 51, 53, 56, 57,
58, 119, 127, 158, 297
Tenamazcuicuiltzin, 260, 263, 306
Tenamitec, 41, 47
Tenancacalitzin, 46, 56, 58
Tenochcas 46, 53, 58, 65, 66, 93, 97
Tenochtitlan, 16, 20n3, 21n6, 21n12,
26–27, 70, 116, 117, 132, 140, 152,
175, 187, 192, 211, 312n152; Cortés's
conquest of, 10, 14, 16, 70, 247, 249,
253–57, 263, 265–76, 278–81, 288–314;
Nezahualcoyotl in, 85, 91, 97, 99,
118–20, 123, 125–28; rulers of, 33, 42,
65, 68, 127, 135, 136, 144, 147, 148,
158; settling of, 57–58, 58n43. *See
also individual entries for rulers of
Tenochtitlan*
Teocalhueyacan, 258, 282
Teochichimecas, 42, 295
Teotihuacan, 21n7, 40, 48, 50, 64, 129, 134,
155, 187, 281, 283
Teotlili, 245–48
Tepanecas, 58, 65, 69, 70, 74, 91, 101, 105,
109, 121, 146, 275; arrival of, 44; rulers
of, 49, 63, 81, 116; warfare of, 71, 80, 97,
106, 113, 118, 119, 190, 204, 224
Tepechpan, 19, 64, 129, 134, 155, 160, 161,
194
Tepepolco, 48, 39, 64, 69, 84, 109, 110, 291;
Cortés fighting in, 296, 310; tribute
from, 130, 155
Tepeticpac, 259, 260, 308
Tepetlaoztoc, 42, 49, 50, 64, 81, 112, 129,
134, 155
Tepetzinco, 155, 192, 257

Tepexoxoma, 42
Tepeyacac, 47, 126, 147, 194, 258, 285;
Cortés in, 288–89, 300, 312
Tepotzotlan, 51, 65, 71, 127, 283
Tequanehuatzin, 230–31
Tequanitzin, 260, 262, 306
Tequitlanotzin, 260, 264
Ternaux-Compans, Henri, 15
Tetepetzinco, 161, 273
Tetlahuehuetzquititzin, Pedro, 194, 222,
234, 272
Tetlepanquetzal, 285, 286, 294, 298
Tetzauhpiltzintli, 163–64, 184
Tetzcoco (city), 3, 5, 8, 10, 12, 13, 16, 17,
20, 20n3, 21n6, 21n12, 27, 29n2, 32,
32n5, 57n42, 192; Cortés in, 272, 279,
290–94, 296–98, 300–301, 304–6, 309;
districts of, 61, 84, 140; founding of,
50, 57; palaces of, 67, 85, 96, 132–39,
184, 205, 294; rulers of, 50, 99; temples
of, 64, 137–39, *138*, 173, 232; warfare
involving, 59, 65, 70–71, 74, 100,
110–13, 119, 236. *See also individual
entries for rulers*
Tetzcoco (kingdom), 65, 81–82, 114–15,
132, 134, 135, 148, 181, 181, 235, 291,
293; wars of, 70, 113, 119, 123, 146, 147,
187
Tetzcotzinco, 62, 106, 111, 155, 157, 164,
167, 174
Tetzmolocan, 129, 257, 291, 292
Teuhchimaltzin, 204–205
Tezcatlipoca, 153
Tezcucas, 27, 74, 204, 216, 229–31, 299;
warfare of, 72, 168, 202, 235, 296–97
Tezcuco. *See* Tetzcoco (kingdom)
Tianquiztlatoatzin, 288, 306
Tiçaiocan, 64, 155
Tiçocicatzin, 188–89, 196
Tira de Tepechpan, 20
Tiyacapan (wife of Axayacatzin), 188, 194,
221–22
Tizatlan, 259, 260, 308
Tlacahuepan, 189, 206
Tlacahuepan, Pedro, 222

Tlacatecuhtli, 257, 259, 263, 306
Tlacateotzin, 66, 67, 70, 81, 84, 90, 93, 96, 97; offspring of, 67
Tlachpanquizcatzin, 261, 306
Tlacopan, 127, 165, 200, 282, 297; as part of Triple Alliance, 21n6, 121–22, 125, 127–28, 132, 135, 144, 147, 150, 158, 164, 176, 181, 196, 199, 208, 234, 246; Cortés's interaction with, 248, 266, 272, 275; rulers of, 66, 119, 136, 286, 297; warfare involving, 148, 187, 197, 303, 306, 308, 310. *See also* Chimalpopoca (king of Tlacopan); Totoquihuatzin (first king of Tlacopan); Totoquihuatzin (third king of Tlacopan)
Tlacotepec, 186, 227
Tlailotlacan, 61, 80, 140
Tlailotlac Tecuhtzintli, 91, 93, 140
Tlalanapan, 64, 155
Tlalhuicas, 146, 300, 302
Tlalmanalco, 106, 111, 117, 300
Tlalnahuac, 48, 74, 300
Tlaloc, 64, 137, 153, 227, 271
Tlalolin, 129, 146
Tlapechhuacan, 130, 291, 292
Tlatelolcas, 46, 53, 58, 58n44, 98
Tlatelolco, 58n44, 66, 67, 70, 81, 84, 96, 97, 118, 183, 186, 221, 286, 316
Tlatzalan, 42, 48, 50
Tlaxcalan, 53, 60, 119, 124, 129, 282, 291, 293; assistance to Nezahualcoyotl from, 82, 83, 84, 101, 109–10, 113, 117, 118, 146, 151; confederation of, 109, 109n76, 110, 146, 151, 152, 153, 160, 230, 284; interaction with Cortés of, 250, 255–65, 267–70, 278–79, 282–84, 285–293; relationship with Triple Alliance of, 152–53, 181, 229–31; rulers of, 48; settling of, 74; warfare involving, 118, 153, 160, 161, 225, 229–31, 296–97, 300, 305, 306, 308, 312, 314
Tlehuexolotzin, 260, 263, 264
Tlilcuetzpalin, 186, 187
Tlotzin Map, 19, 29n2

Tlotzin Pochotl, 46, 48, 49, 53, 54–56, 57, 59; death of, 56; offspring of, 49
Toçapan, 42, 299
Tochintecuhtli, 46, 48, 50–51, 52, 53, 59–60; offspring of, 53
Tochpan, 42, 147
Tochtepec, 36, 147, 223
Tocpacxochitzin, 282, 291
Tocuiltecatl, 72–73
Tolan, 36, 40, 41, 157, 189, 194, 213
Tolantzinco, 36, 40, 48, 84, 129, 146, 148, 155
Tolinpanecatl, 257–59
Toloca, 186, 187
Tolquauhiocan, 48, 69
Toltecas, 9, 16, 51, 57, 63, 64, 80, 81, 143, 157, 206; early history of, 38–43; mythic origin of, 36–37; practices learned from, 50, 54, 56, 59; rulers of, 38–40, 44, 46, 47, 61, 228
Toltitlan, 119, 127
Tonacaquahuitl, 34, 262
Torquemada, Juan de, 7, 10–11, *179*, 180, 180nn107–8, 228, 285
Toteoçitecuhtli, 83, 106, 111, 112, 117, 166, 184
Totolan, 190, 191
Totolapan, 40, 42, 61, 300
Totomihua, 74, 124, 309
Totonaca, 197, 228, 235
Totonacapan, 146, 152, 223, 236
Totoquihuatzin (first king of Tlacopan): ascension of, 121–23; assistance to Nezahualcoyotl from, 127, 146, 162; role in Triple Alliance of, 150, 152, 164
Totoquihuatzin (third king of Tlacopan): ascension of, 199–200; death of, 286; role in Triple Alliance of, 221–22, 223, 227, 232, 234, 246, 248, 272, 275, 277
Tototepec, 41, 54, 59, 59, 101, 110, 113, 123, 227, 304
Toxcatl, 277, 278
Tozquentzin (wife of Nonoalcatl), 114, 124, 161, 161, 175

Tozquentzin (wife of Techotlalatzin), 58, 64
tribute, 43–44, 47, 82, 131, 132, 136, 183,
    231, 232, 251, 252, 287; as inducement,
    143–45; lists of, 127–28, 130, 146–49,
    187, 223, 236; onerous amounts of, 49,
    65, 114, 116, 210, 236; redistribution
    of, 152, 172, 178, 192–93, 223. *See also*
    cacao; chiles; cloth; maize
Triple Alliance, 18, 21n6, 131, 225–26;
    expansion of, 143–51, 186–87, 190–91,
    197–98, 204–6, 210, 227–28; founding
    of 121–22, 132, 144–45; interaction
    with Cortés of, 245–314; internal
    conflict of, 125–28, 181, 227–28, 229–
    32; laws of, 132, 140, 207–9, 212–14;
    mutual aid of members of, 146, 176,
    183, 211; relationship with Tlaxcalan
    of, 152–54; ruler succession within,
    121–22, 150–51, 169–70, 181–82,
    188–89, 200, 221–22, 234–36
Tzancitzin, 216–17
Tzicuhcoac, 42, 147, 197, 199
Tzicuhcoacatl, 260, 264
Tzihuacxochitzin, 42, 46, 66
Tzihuinquilocan, 149, 155
Tzinacanoztoc, 64, 74
Tzonpantecuhtli, 46, 65
Tzontecochatzin, 87, 91, 93, 95, 100, 101,
    107, 108
Tzontecomatl, 44–46, 49, 75; offspring of,
    46, 49
Tzopantzin, 259, 260, 264

Ulmecas, 34, 36

Vaillant, George C. 17
Velázquez, Diego, 237, 240, 249, 253, 276
Vera Cruz, 222, 257, 272, 298; Cortés in,
    244–46, 248–49, 251–54, 276–79, 290
Verdugo, Fraincisco, 301, 307
Villafuerte, Juan Rodríguez de, 301, 302,
    307
Villa Rica. *See* Vera Cruz

warfare: laws regarding, 142–45; ships
    used during, 290, 293, 305, 307,
    309–11, 312, 314. *See also* canoes: in
    battle; Cortés, Hernando; messengers:
    in warfare; soldiers; weapons; *and*
    individual entries for cities, kingdoms,
    rulers, and wars
weapons, 73, 73n58, 139, 143, 164, 172,
    190, 219, 231, 271; European types of,
    305; indigenous types of, 106, 139, 143,
    144, 255, 301, 312. *See also* crossbow;
    harquebuses; horses

Xaiacamachan, 101, 103, 109, 118
Xalatlauhco, 186, 187
Xalatzinco, 245, 289
Xalixco, 36, 57
Xaltepec, 69, 206, 210
Xaltocan, 44, 46, 50, 65, 119, 129, 155, 297
Xicalancas, 34, 36, 228, 245
Xiconocatzin, 96–97, 117
Xicotencatl, 151, 153, 306, 308n151;
    interaction with Cortés of, 257–60,
    262–64, 285–89, 308
Xicotepec, 42, 129, 134, 146, 155, 302
Xihuitl Temoc, 186
Xilomantzin, 66, 132, 183
Xilonenco, 188, 194, 234
Xilotepec, 71, 186
Xiuhcozcatl, 33, 42, 180
Xiuhtecuhtitlan, 41
Xochimilco, 120, 123, 127, 186, 231, 300,
    302, 303
Xochipoio, 75, 309
Xochiquetzaltzin, 151, 167, 176, 182, 184,
    212
Xochitl, 235–36
Xochitlan, 197, 206
Xocotitlan, 41, 186
Xolotl, 41–51, 52, 53, 54, 55, 68, 143, 206;
    death of, 51; offspring of, 42

Yacanex, 54, 59, 60; war of, 49–51
Yahualiuhcan, 65, 109, 155

Yancuiltzin, 91, 99, 111, 114
Yaoceuhcatzin, 292–93
Yaotl, 130, 147, 187
Yauhtepec, 301–2
Yopica, 227, 228
Yopicatl Atonal, 204, 205
Yoyontzin, Jorge, 194, 233
Yucatan, 237, 240, 241

Zacatitechcochi, 42, 59
Zacatlan, 41, 47, 101, 110, 113, 289
Zacatula, 204–5
Zacaxochitla, 106, 258
Zapoteca, 197, 227, 228
Zitlaltzin, 292–93
Zoçolan, 223, 227
Zoltepec, 59, 112